THE PUBLIC REALM

parochial space

- not really about space here - or arch/people
interaction - (yps - later ch4+5)

- gardens made by god
city = cain
pleasure gardens, men? -

The Public Realm

Exploring the City's Quintessential Social Territory

LYN H. LOFLAND

ALDINE DE GRUYTER
New York

About the Author

Lyn H. Lofland is Professor and current Chair of Sociology at the University of California, Davis. She is the author of, among numerous other works, *A World of Strangers* (1973), *The Craft of Dying* (1978), and *Analyzing Social Settings* (with John Lofland, 1983, 1995), and the co-editor (with Spencer Cahill) of *The Community of the Streets* (1994). In 1995 she was awarded the Robert and Helen Lynd Award for lifetime contributions by the Community and Urban Sociology Section of the American Sociological Association.

Copyright ©1998 by Walter de Gruyter, Inc., New York

ALDINE DE GRUYTER
A division of Walter de Gruyter, Inc.
200 Saw Mill River Road
Hawthorne, New York 10532

This publication is printed on acid free paper ∞

Library of Congress Cataloging-in-Publication Data
Lofland, Lyn H.
    The public realm : quintessential city life / Lyn H. Lofland.
      p. cm. — (Communication and social order)
    Includes bibliographical references and index.
    ISBN 0-202-30607-0 (cloth : alk. paper). — ISBN 0-202-30608-9
(pbk. : alk. paper)
    1. Cities and towns. 2. Public spaces. 3. Open spaces. 4. Human territoriality. 5. Social perception. 6. Geographical perception.
I. Title. II. Series.
HT 151.L6 1998
307.76—dc21   97-42290
                                        CIP

Manufactured in the United States of America

10 9 8 7 6 5 4

For

Gregory Stone
Jane Jacobs
Erving Goffman
William H. Whyte

Pioneers in the Study of the Public Realm

Contents

Preface

This book continues, develops, and—I hope—improves upon an intellectual interest first expressed in 1973 with the publication of my *A World of Strangers: Order and Action in Urban Public Space*. Then, as now, much work in urban and community sociology treated the city as either the locus of all popular social ills (for example, depending on era, gangs, skid row alcoholics, homelessness, poverty, racial conflict, juvenile delinquency, immigrants) or as a dependent variable that is patterned by national and, increasingly, international economic, political, technological, and cultural forces. Similarly, then as now, many contemporary scholars identified with the field argued (sometimes implicitly, sometimes explicitly) that these two concerns constitute the *only* legitimate subject matter of community and urban sociology. I took then and I take now a very different view. In my judgment, there are at least three additional research areas very much deserving of acknowledgment and inclusion: the study of urban social organization, the study of communal sentiments in the urban milieu, and—most critically then and now—the study of the city as a social-psychological environment.

The first area deserves attention because while many organizational forms located in urban settlements may be found elsewhere—friendship cliques, personal networks, bureaucracies, and so on—there also exist forms that seem peculiar to cities, the "salon," the "promenade," and certain variants of the "social world" for example. The second area, which involves questions about the fate of "community" in the urban setting, about whether communal sentiments can survive large-scale urbanization, is as salient today as when such questions were first raised by the founders of the discipline in the nineteenth century. But it is the third research area that is, as noted, critical. In my view, *the city, quite uniquely, provides a kind of social-psychological environment that is not duplicated elsewhere*. I am not here referring to the sheer scale and physical complexity of the urban form, although those are important aspects of urbanness. Rather, what I want particularly to emphasize is that *the city provides, on a permanent basis, an environment composed importantly of persons who are personally unknown to one another—composed importantly of strangers*. No matter how great the impact of "world systems" on local events, no matter

xi

how far the tendrils of political and economic machinations reach into the everyday experiences of women and men, no matter how effective the modern technologies of information collection and dispersal may be in manufacturing the "global village," no matter how hegemonic the corporately produced cultural streams, the fact of the matter is that a person standing on the streets of Chicago or Hong Kong or Moscow or Buenos Aires is in a very different social and psychological environment than a person standing in the middle of a village in North Dakota or Morocco or Nicaragua or Tibet. That difference was the central concern of *A World of Strangers* and is the central concern here.

In this current exploration of the unique social and psychological environment provided by urban settlements—I refer to that environment as the *public realm*—I will be using an extraordinary array (perhaps *hodge-podge* is a better word) of data sources: my own direct observations and interviews; contemporary photographs; historic etchings, prints, and photographs; historic maps; and a goodly smattering of popular writings, newspaper stories, cartoons, and columns. I will also be using a great deal of data from the scholarly literatures of environmental psychology, geography, history, anthropology, architecture, and urban planning and design, as well as sociology. Of course, collected as most of these data were, for purposes far removed from my concerns, I have necessarily subjected them to extensive recoding and reinterpretation, and in some instances, I must admit, the recoding and reinterpretation move beyond "extensive" to become "radical."

My exploration will be shaped by these diverse data, but it will also be shaped by the personal sympathy I bring to the subject matter. I like urban settlements and I especially like the portions of these settlements which compose their public realms. Word of warning, then: In the pages ahead I have certainly struggled to maintain the analyst's dispassionate gaze. But where I have failed to hold an expressionless countenance, I have at least transformed it into a look of fondness and affection for the city, or into grimace and a glare for the city's opponents, rather than—as has been the case with so many of the authors who have written about urban matters during the past two hundred years—the reverse.

You will find the book heavily referenced—too heavily referenced, in the eyes of some reviewers. And perhaps they are correct. But given, as I try to make clear in the Prologue, that one of my goals in writing this is to encourage others to join me in the *explicit* study of the public realm, it seems reasonable to provide anyone so encouraged with the "paper trail" I followed as I sought potentially relevant data in both likely and unlikely places. One consequence of this heavy referencing is that footnotes cannot always be reserved, as I would prefer, for commentary. Throughout, I have had to make use of them to avoid cluttering the text with long strings of citations. But lest this fact discourage readers from looking at the notes, let me assure you that there is still plenty of commentary to be found in them.

This work has been a long time "aborning" and over the years I have benefited enormously from the generosity of colleagues, students, and friends who, subjected to bits and pieces of what would eventually become a book, have responded by providing guidance, encouragement, helpful criticism, newspaper clippings, references, cartoons, corrections, and—perhaps most importantly of all—the bolstering knowledge that there were folks out there who actually found what I had to say "interesting." I want here publicly to thank Patricia Adler, Peter Adler, Mitch Allen, Robert Beauregard, Mattias Duyves, Michael Brill, Lodewijk Brunt, Spencer Cahill, Francesca Cancian, Kathy Charmaz, Mark Francis, Judith Friedman, Gary Alan Fine, Gary Hamilton, Milmon Harrison, Ruth Horowitz, David Hummon, Carole Joffe, Roderick Lawrence, Clark McPhail, Leon Mayhew, Barbara Metcalf, Thaddeus Muller, Jeffrey Nash, Jan Oosterman, Judith Stacey, Ralph Turner, and the many students in the many offerings of my "City Life" and "Social Interaction" courses. I am also deeply appreciative of the work of Susan Gerard, who undertook the herculean task of trying to bring congruence between those bits and pieces that constitute the internal citations and those bits and pieces that constitute the bibliography. Thanks also to Jennifer Cross for her help in tracking down missing, incomplete, and incorrect references.

Of course, not everyone who helped was inflicted with only "bits and pieces." A small, brave, and stalwart group not only read but provided extensive comments on the entire manuscript: an act that is the nearest equivalent academic life has to martyrdom among the religiously inclined. They know how much I owe them. They also, regrettably, will soon know not only which elements of their good advice I wisely chose to heed, but which elements I rashly chose to ignore. Luckily for them, with the appearance of any book reviews, each will undoubtedly be afforded the opportunity to say, "I told you so!" Blessings to Leon Anderson, Mark Hutter, David Maines, John Lofland, Melinda Milligan, and David Snow.

As always, John Lofland's contributions go far beyond collegial into the realm of the personal. Mostly, the personal contribution took the form of "nagging"—not incessant nagging, but nagging that was frequent enough to become "expected." It got to the point that when he didn't ask the questions of me, I was asking them of myself: Was I ever going to finish the book? How much had I written so far? What was I doing with my time if my progress was so slow? Wasn't it getting embarrassing for me that this damned manuscript had been "in progress" forever? What was the possibility that by the time I actually got the thing finished, there would already be sixteen books on the exact same topic? In the end, of course, the nagging worked and it is with love and gratitude that I thank John for recognizing

really open in her preface/blunt

a chronic procrastinator when he sees one, for giving me all those symbolic "kicks in the rear," and for encouraging me to believe not only that I could but that, in fact, I would complete the task I had set for myself.

Finally, I want to give special acknowledgment to four of the people who, at the production end, turned a manuscript into a book. I am enormously grateful to Mike Sola for his meticulous copy-editing of the original manuscript; to Gabriel Unda of UCD's Creative Communications Services for transforming my wrinkled magazine pages, badly printed cartoons, imperfect reproductions, and fuzzy photographs into text-ready illustrations; and to Richard Koffler and Arlene Perazzini of Aldine for their support, their faith, and—perhaps most especially—their patience.

Lyn Lofland
Davis, California

Prologue
A *Regio Incognita*

This is a book about a particular form of social space or territory: the public realm.[1] In Chapter 1, I will attempt a fairly precise definition, but for now it is sufficient to think of "public realm" as being an equivalent term for "urban public space." And it will help to orient you to what is to come if you can begin to think of urban public space or the public realm as a kind of kingdom, one that is inhabited importantly, though not entirely, by persons who are unacquainted with one another: a "world of strangers" as it were (Lofland [1973] 1985). Like "real" kingdoms, the public realm not only has a geography, it has a history, a culture (behavioral norms, esthetic values, preferred pleasures), and a complex web of internal relationships. Again, similar to "real" kingdoms, it is the object not only of perceptions, but of conceptions as well. While there are certainly persons who are unaware or only vaguely aware that the public realm even exists, it also has its partisans and defenders and enemies and attackers, as well as "neutrals" who, while bearing no active animus, "wouldn't want to live there" and are even uncertain about the advisability of a visit.

My goal in the pages ahead is to describe as carefully and completely as I can what I have been able to discover about these various aspects of the public realm: its history and geography and interrealm relations, its culture, about the images of it—positive and negative—that people carry in their heads, and the very real consequences of those images. However, I need to emphasize from the outset that what we know about the public realm is greatly overshadowed by what we do not know. Vast areas of the "map" are marked: "unexplored," or, in the more evocative phrasing of the sixteenth-century mapmaker, *regiones incognitae*. Now while a full answer to the question of why so much of the public realm has remained so long a *regio incognita* is itself an unknown, this seems like a good place for me to at least offer a few of the possible reasons (since they may help you to interpret both the commissions and omissions ahead) for this state of affairs.

A first, and I think most crucial, reason is that until fairly recently, scholars, especially social scientists, have tended to view the public realm as barren and uninhabited; it did not require exploration because it contained nothing worth finding. For example, when I entered graduate school in sociology in the mid-1960s, most textbooks and many professors were still echoing the 1926 views of Nicholas J. Spykman:

> On the street, in the subway, on the bus, [the city dweller] comes in contact with hundreds of people. But these brief incidental associations are based neither on a sharing of common values nor on a co-operation for a common purpose. *They are formal in the most complete sense of the term in that they are empty of content.* (Spykman 1926:58, emphasis added)

That is, the conventional wisdom held that much or all public realm activity was thoroughly asocial and, thus, from the point of view of social scientists, thoroughly irrelevant and uninteresting. Exactly why this should have been the case is also not clear, but I can point to a couple of strands of thought that may have contributed to this point of view.

One strand emerges from the work of the Pragmatic philosopher George Herbert Mead, especially as it was interpreted by the sociologist Herbert Blumer. As he worked to construct the influential perspective within sociology known as symbolic interactionism, Blumer followed Mead in distinguishing between "symbolic" and "nonsymbolic" interaction. In his summarizing statement of "The Methodological Position of Symbolic Interactionism," he reiterated that classic distinction in these terms:

> Non-symbolic interaction takes place when one responds directly to the action of another without interpreting that action; symbolic interaction involves interpretation of the action. Non-symbolic interaction is most readily apparent in reflex responses, as in the case of a boxer who automatically raises his arm to parry a blow. . . . In their association human beings engage plentifully in non-symbolic interaction as they respond immediately and unreflectively to each other's bodily movements, expressions, and tones of voice, but their characteristic mode of interaction is on the symbolic level, as they seek to understand the meaning of each other's action. (1969:8–9, emphasis added)

Now, as will become clear in Chapter 2, a goodly portion of urban public space activity consists of humans responding "immediately" and *apparently* "unreflectively" to others' bodily movements and expressions (for example, when crossing through a busy intersection or standing in a crowded subway car). That is, a goodly portion of urban public space activity consists of what the Mead-Blumer perspective identified as nonsymbolic interaction. And while their schema did not actually banish such interaction to the nether regions of asocial behavior, it did suggest that responses that are "immediate and unreflective" are simply not as sociologically relevant as those mediated by the interpretive process.

The other strand of thought had its sociological genesis in Georg Simmel's essay, "The Metropolis and Mental Life" ([1902–1903] 1950), was developed further in Louis Wirth's classic "Urbanism as a Way of Life" (1938), and reached maturity in the work of the psychologist Stanley Milgram, especially in his 1970 essay, "The Experience of Living in Cities." The essential argument in this strand is that the public areas of the city are so densely packed with sights and sounds that they engender "stimulus overload." Humans cope with this by "shutting down" or "turning off." Thus, much human activity in these settings is asocial because, as a defense against stimulus overload, persons are simply ignoring one another. David Karp, in an article that argues against it, has nicely summarized this point of view:

> The quality of urban life is seen largely as a manifestation of the thorough anonymity of the city. . . . Urbanites are seen as interacting "almost subliminally, demanding nothing of each other, making no contacts with each other, merely passing near each other" (Strauss 1961:63–64). The city, in short, supports a degree of noninvolvement, impersonality, and aloofness not to be found elsewhere. (Karp 1973:431.)

A second reason for the *regiones incognitae* character of so much of the public realm is that so many of the explorers who *have* entered it have done so not because they were interested in the realm per se but because they have had to cross it, as it were, on their way to another destination. That is, scholars have told us about the public realm importantly as a by-product of telling us about something else: for example, the role of women in the nineteenth and early twentieth centuries (Peiss 1986; Ryan 1990), the history of outdoor illumination in Europe (Schivelbusch 1988), or the characteristics of the "interaction order" (Goffman 1959, 1963a, 1963b, 1971, 1983). The result is a knowledge-situation similar to what would be the case if one's picture of California, say, were built up mostly from the fragments of observations made by travelers who just happened to be "passing through." For example:

> Before we entered Oregon, we spent a day and night in California. The residents seem peculiar, to say the least, especially with regard to speech styles and political views. The next morning, rejoicing that California was not our final destination, we entered Oregon. What a beautiful place! I will begin my detailed portrait of Oregon with a description of its wonderful flora and fauna . . .

> En route from New York to Tokyo, we had a two-hour layover in Los Angeles. Maude and I used the time to explore the area around the airport. The day seemed very warm for early spring and the visibility was poor—smog,

I guess. Mostly all we could see were many-laned streets, freeways, and hotels. The flight to Tokyo was smooth and pleasant and . . .

The problem is not that any single fragment of information is wrong (although it may be). The problem is that, most obviously, fragmented knowledge is, by definition, incomplete knowledge, and, less obviously, fragmented knowledge—because it lacks a surrounding context—is difficult to evaluate. Not only is there much that we do not know, then, but it is also hard to judge how important or generalizable what we do know may be.

A third possible reason for so much of the public realm being a *regio incognita* will be dealt with in some detail in Chapters 5, 6, and 7, so I will only mention it here. I refer to the tendency of many scholars and intellectuals, especially in the social sciences, to grant the social character of public realm activity but to dismiss that activity as unimportant, irrelevant, and/or immoral and to dismiss students of that activity as tarred with the same brush. Spencer Cahill has succinctly captured the situation.

> To many students of social life and probably most who live it, those of us who study . . . the "social life of the public realm" are engaged in a frivolous pursuit. This assessment of our efforts is seldom expressed in print or public forums but subtly conveyed by benign neglect and through the patronizing grins with which our work is often received. Our readers and audiences may sometimes find what we have to report and say mildly entertaining, but only as a temporary diversion from more serious matters. (1994:3–4)

Thus, much of the public realm remains "unknown territory" because the reward system of social science discourages explorers both from entering it in the first place, and, if once entered, from remaining within it too long.[2]

                                *   *   *

Given what I have been saying about the *regio incognita* character of the public realm, it should come as no surprise that this is a book more about beginnings than endings, more about questions than answers, more about possibilities than accomplishments. And I frankly intend it to serve as invitation, as allurement, as enticement, as temptation, as bait, as tantalization. That is, I hope to persuade you that the public realm is not only an interesting social territory, but that it is a *significant* one as well and, as such, it deserves its own phalanx of eager explorers. It deserves, just as much as any other arena of social life, to be transformed from a *regio incognita* to a "known quantity."

NOTES

1. Earlier versions of some of the sentences, paragraphs, or whole sections contained in this book may be found in Lofland (1983, 1984, 1989, 1991, 1994, 1995).

2. This tendency for sociologists to denigrate the study of certain areas of social life that they define as not "big" enough, not "important" enough, and not sufficiently amenable to "hard" techniques is part of a syndrome that I have elsewhere (Lofland 1990) labeled "exaggerated manliness."

1

Toward a Geography and History of the Public Realm

Humans invented the city some five to ten thousand years ago,[1] but up until the past two and a half centuries, most especially until the past century, only a miniscule proportion of the human population had ever had the experience of urban living. While some preindustrial cities may, even by modern standards, have been quite large in population, the majority were modestly sized.[2] Morever, at any given historical moment, extant cities were few in number, with most of the earth's population living out their lives in less complex physical and social environments: small bands, nomadic tribes, villages. As late as 1800 "only 3% of the human population lived in cities of 100,000 or more" (Sadalla and Stea 1978:140). In marked contrast:

> The number of metropolises with over a million inhabitants has tripled during the past 35 years. . . . U.N. projections indicate that there will be 511 metropolises exceeding a million inhabitants by 2010. Thereafter, more than 40 such metropolises will be added every five years, so that in the year 2025, there will be 639 metropolises exceeding one million residents. *Before the children born in 1985 become adults, half of the world's population will be urban, and half of this half will be located in metropolises with over a million inhabitants.* (Dogan and Kasarda 1988:13, emphasis added.)

In other words, in a phenomenally brief period of time, humans have managed to transform themselves from a predominantly rural people to a significantly urban people.

Given the lightening-fast character of this transformation, perhaps we should not be surprised at how little they know about their new environment, how negatively some of them view it (what a source of dis-ease it is to them), or even how resistant some of them are to granting it more than temporary status. But the brevity of the human encounter with the city may not tell the whole story. The antiurban feelings themselves, combined with the belief that the city is an "unnatural" and therefore impermanent human habitat, may contribute to the lack of knowledge. In the words of Jane Jacobs's mildly sarcastic query, "How could anything so bad be worth the attempt to understand it?" (1961:21). And such willful ignorance may, in turn, help to create urban conditions that generate and/or reinforce anticity sentiments.[3] In sum, among the many other "pickles" the human species has gotten itself into of late, add this one: a near majority of us are now or will soon be living in a social-psychological environment that we do not understand, that many of us despise, and that, because we act toward and on it out of ignorance and prejudice, we may be making unlivable.[4]

This book is written in the naively optimistic belief that having gotten ourselves into this particular pickle, we can get ourselves out again. I hope it will make a contribution to a body of literature that, beginning in the late 1950s and early 1960s and developing over the past several decades, has sought to understand the urban settlement rather than condemn it, to study it rather than dismiss it, and to look upon city as human habitat rather than to shun it as alien territory.

The city in its entirety is not, of course, what we shall be exploring here. We shall, as specified earlier, be looking at only one component—but a quintessential one—of the urban settlement form: the public realm. The major burden of this chapter is to sketch the outlines of a geography and history of that realm, as well as to provide a brief overview of subsequent chapters. First, however, two preliminary matters demand our attention.

PRELIMINARIES

Before getting on to the central business of this chapter we need (1) to look briefly at the work of four people who were crucial in challenging social science's conventional wisdom about the asocial character of the public realm and (2) to spend a little time pinning down some working definitions for words that have the unsettling habit of taking on a whole variety of meanings.

Pioneering the Study of the Public Realm

For a social scientist to proclaim in the 1990s that life in the public realm is thoroughly social is merely to proclaim the commonplace, to enunciate the obvious. But, as we have seen in earlier pages, such was not always the case, and the transformation in the perception of public realm activity from "obviously" asocial to "obviously" social was a hard-won victory. There were numerous contributors to this victory and different scholars would undoubtedly single out different clusters of individuals for special mention. I lay no claim, then, that my cluster—composed of Gregory Stone, Jane Jacobs, Erving Goffman, and William H. Whyte—is everyone's quartet of choice, but I think there is no question but that most social scientists would identify all four *as* contributors and that one or more of my nominees would appear on many lists. None of these scholars, of course, think or thought of themselves as being concerned with the public realm per se: that phrase appears nowhere in their work. And three of them, like most public realm explorers, were simply "passing through" on their way to someplace else. But the observations they made en route and, in one instance, in situ were especially crucial in helping me to see the public realm as a *social* territory and to see it as one worthy of detailed exploration.

Gregory Stone stepped into the public realm because he was interested in the question of the social integration of urban populations.[5] His "City Shoppers and Urban Identification," published in 1954, reported the surprising fact that, for some persons, a degree of integration with the local community appeared to be achieved through an identification with purely economic institutions. Specifically, he found that a portion of retail establishment customers, rather than viewing clerks as either utilitarian instruments or asocial physical objects (as received truth on these matters would have it), infused customer-clerk interactions with meaning and feeling. Or to phrase it in the more technical language of the sociologist, these customers injected elements of primary group relationships into what were "supposed" to be purely secondary relationships. In the obviously anonymous and impersonal world of the city, personalism had been espied.[6]

Jane Jacobs's concern in *The Death and Life of Great American Cities* (1961) was with understanding how a city, which she conceived of as a problem in "organized complexity," actually operated. But in pursuing the question of how the various building blocks of the city—its households, streets, local neighborhoods, districts—affected one another and the whole, she devoted over eighty pages (ibid.:29–111) to a close and textured analysis of the city's streets and parks, or, in other words, to a close and textured analysis of portions of the public realm. Where she "should" have found a social vacuum, she found rich and complex acts, actions, and interactions; what should have been an empty stage turned out to be the setting for an "intricate ballet in which the individual dancers and ensembles all have distinctive parts which miraculously reinforce each other and compose an orderly whole" (ibid.:50). In the obviously anonymous and impersonal world of the city, webs of social linkages had been discerned.

While the aforementioned writings of Stone and Jacobs are landmarks in the study of the public realm, each made only a single contribution to that study, each struck only a single blow, as it were, to conventional beliefs about the realm's asocial character. In contrast, *Erving Goffman* struck multiple blows. Goffman, like Stone and Jacobs, meandered into the public realm on his way to somewhere else; in his case, on his way to an elucidation of what he later came to think of as "the interaction order"

(1983). But because a fair amount of his interaction order data dealt with people who were "out in public," Goffman almost inadvertently focused his enormous talent for microanalysis on numerous instances of public realm interaction. In much of his work, but especially in *The Presentation of Self in Everyday Life* (1959), *Behavior in Public Places (1963a), and Relations in Public* (1971),[7] Goffman demonstrated eloquently and persuasively that what occurs between two strangers passing on the street is as thoroughly social as what occurs in a conversation between two lovers, that the same concerns for the fragility of selves that is operating among participants in a family gathering is also operating among strangers on an urban beach. In the obviously anonymous and impersonal world of the city, evidence of ritually sacred interchanges had been unearthed.

Of the four pioneers, only *William H. Whyte* entered the public realm because that is where he intended to go. While the term *public realm* is not one he himself has used, since at least the mid-1960s he has been unabashedly interested in the public spaces of cities.[8] That interest found some very preliminary expression in the 1968 book *The Last Landscape*, but it came to full flower in two more recent volumes: *The Social Life of Small Urban Spaces* (1980) and *City: Rediscovering the Center* (1988). In these widely read works, Whyte not only confirmed Stone's, Jacobs's, and Goffman's observations of a flourishing public realm social life, he also, and most crucially, began the task of constructing a political argument for the indispensability of public space to the life of the city. Referring especially to that portion of the public realm located in the city's center, Whyte has written:

> [T]he center is the place for news and gossip, for the creation of ideas, for marketing them and swiping them, for hatching deals, for starting parades. This is the stuff of the public life of the city—by no means wholly admirable, often abrasive, noisy, contentious, without apparent purpose. But this human congress is the genius of the place, its reason for being, its great marginal edge. This is the engine, the city's true export. Whatever makes this congress easier, more spontaneous, more enjoyable is not at all a frill. It is the heart of the center of the city. (1988:341)

In the obviously anonymous and impersonal world of the city, someone had located not only social life but a socially important life.

Defining Some Terms

As a second and last preliminary matter, it is necessary to spend a little time making clear exactly what I mean by four crucial terms: *city* or urban settlement, *stranger*, *public* (as opposed to private) *space*, and *public realm*.

City. There have been times when and there still are places where "city" creates a quite distinct pattern on the landscape. The "large, dense and heterogeneous" settlement—to use Louis Wirth's time-tested definition (1938)—is, precisely because of these characteristics, easily distinguishable from the lightly populated, low density, and homogeneous villages that might be near it. It is distinguishable also because it is *geographically bounded*—clearly separated from other cities and other settlement forms by a visual demarcation—often a wall combined with open space in the premodern period (see Illustrations 1.1 and 1.2); simply expanses of open space in more recent times. For example, in the United States, despite long experience with "suburbanization" (see Fishman 1987; Jackson 1985), up until the late 1930s and early 1940s the political boundaries of most cities were largely coterminous with their visual boundaries.[9] In the post–World War II period, however, that initially *distinct* pattern becomes both less and less distinct and less and less a pattern. With the emergence of the settlement form known as "undifferentiated urban mass" (sprawl, for short), the physical referent for the word *city* is nothing if not elusive, and, as a not-very-surprising consequence, the everyday language we Americans use to talk about varying settlement forms is nothing if not confusing. Students in my urban courses who were born and raised in the densely populated suburban landscape of California, for example, tell me that they have never "lived in a city." Persons who grow up in metropolitan area settlements of twenty thousand, fifty thousand, or even seventy-five thousand or more, as another example, tell of going off

Illustration 1.1. Fifteenth-century Florence. From Toynbee (ed.), 1967.

Illustration 1.2.   Delhi in 1858. From Toynbee (ed.), 1967.

to the "city" and then, exhausted by the pace of city life, happily returning
to the "small town" whence they came:[10]

> Many of those who do return [to the suburbs] are like Clay Fry, who
> moved back to Lafayette [a Bay Area community of about 23,000] after liv-
> ing in Oakland and working in an architectural office in San Francisco. His
> life in the *urban environment* lasted "365 days—almost to the hour," he said.
> "It was really stimulating, but after a while, the rat race got to me," said Fry,
> 30, who now works in Walnut Creek [another Bay Area community, popula-
> tion: 58,650]. "I'm used to trees. When I was working *in the city*, I found
> myself longing for those days with the trees in the 'burbs." (Congbalay 1990,
> emphasis added)

The definitional efforts of people like my students and this young man
have their own logic: they are attempts to make sense of the diversity of
the built environment within sprawling urban regions or metropolitan
areas. For these speakers, the word *city* is reserved for the largest, oldest,
and (usually) the densest of the many named and unnamed settlements
within those areas. Similar efforts to use language to "capture" the physical and social heterogeneity of urban areas can also be found in the scholarly literature—the distinctions between and among the terms *central city,*

suburbia, exurbia, and *arcadia* being a prime example (see, for example, Vance 1972).

The problem with such distinctions, useful as they are for some purposes, is that they obscure the fact of the *cityness* of the entire area. A settlement of fifty thousand next to one of five hundred thousand is unarguably smaller than the latter, but that doesn't make it a "small town." A municipal entity with a population of two thousand may be defined by its residents as a village, but if it is bordered on all sides by other municipal entities, "village" can be no more than a courtesy title. Under conditions of "metropolitanization," the urban (or rural) character of a settlement can be determined neither by comparing its size to that of its larger or smaller neighbors nor even by its official population. Thus, in tracking the urban experience of the United States, the U.S. Census Bureau speaks not of cities and their nearby towns and villages, but of "metropolitan statistical areas."[11]

My definition of the term *city* is both simpler and more inclusive than those employed either in everyday speech or in scholarly discourse. For my purposes, a city is "a permanently populous place or settlement."[12] The simplicity of the definition is self-evident; its inclusiveness perhaps a little less so. This latter quality comes from using "place" loosely and imprecisely enough that it is allowed to cover *both* those large, dense, and heterogeneous settlements—past and present—that are visually distinct from their surroundings *and* those jumbles of variously sized settlements that are woven together into the urban blankets the U.S. Census Bureau calls "metropolitan statistical areas."

Stranger. The above definition stresses the populous character of urban settlements because, as we have seen, I am interested in the presence of strangers within them. The larger the number of people within some bounded space, the smaller the proportion of people within that space who can be personally known to any one of them.[13] That is, as the population of a "place" increases, so does the number of strangers.[14]

As should be obvious from what I have just said, I am here using *stranger* in the quite straightforward, everyday, and dictionary sense of "a person with whom one has had no personal acquaintance" (Random House 1987) or "a person or thing that is unknown or with whom one is unacquainted" (Merriam 1971). I must warn my readers, however, that this usage, despite its common currency, is neither recommended (nor approved) by many scholars who claim a sociological interest in the "stranger." As David Karp and William Yoels remind us (1986:97–98), beginning with Georg Simmel's six-page discussion (1908), the word *strangers* has been reserved almost exclusively to mean "cultural strangers . . . those who occupy symbolic worlds different from our own" rather than "biographical strangers . . .

those we have never met before" (Karp and Yoels 1986:98). That is, the dominating concern for most students of strangerhood has been in the relationship between a newcomer/outsider and the members of some established collectivity, [15] rather than that between persons or groups who are "newcomers" as it were, to one another.

In the pages ahead, we shall mostly be concerned with social and psychological spaces containing biographical strangers, but we shall not be ignoring the Simmelian tradition altogether. As will become apparent, a crucial dynamic of the public realm emerges from the fact that not only do many of its inhabitants not "know" one another in the biographical sense, they often also do not "know" one another in the cultural sense. The public realm is populated not only by persons who have not met but often, as well, by persons who do not share "symbolic worlds."

Public Space.   A central assumption permeating this book is that it is meaningful to distinguish between different types of physical space and that the "private-public" axis constitutes one sort of meaningful distinction. Unfortunately for any claims I might want to make about universality, not every group subscribes to this "reality." As Gloria Levitas, writing about an "anthropology and sociology of the street," tells us,

> the street with boundaries that separate interior from exterior, private from public space does not exist in hunting and gathering societies. The compound of encampment or village itself, which seems to function as "a field of interaction," is not defined as a series of destinations in a linear system. . . . The absence of the street in circular villages appears to reflect no strongly felt need for boundaries between public and private behavior. (Levitas 1978: 228)

Adding to the complexity, even among groups that do make the distinction, exactly where the line is drawn and what is understood by each term are matters of enormous historical and cultural variation.[16] However, at least at this early juncture, we may safely ignore such definitional vertigo. For the peoples and the periods with which we will mainly be concerned (see Commissions and Omissions below), space *is* routinely divided into public and private and there appears to be a rough consensus—at least theoretically—about which is which. Public spaces (whatever their ownership) are generally understood to be more *accessible* (physically and visually) than private spaces (see, e.g., Benn and Gaus 1983a,b,c; Franck and Paxson 1989:123). Dictionary definitions capture this quality with great clarity and for our purposes, for now, these definitions will suffice. A public place, according to *Webster's Third New International Dictionary of the English Language* (Merriam 1971) is "accessible or visible to all members of the community." The *Random House Dictionary of the English Language* (Random House 1987) concurs. Such a location is "open to all persons . . . open to the view of all" and stands in sharp contrast to private space, which is "not open or accessible to the general public."

Public Realm. To this point, I have used "urban public space" and "public realm" as synonyms. They are not, and exactly how and why they are not will become clearer in the next section. Here, I want only to offer a preliminary—and unnuanced—definition. The public realm is constituted of *those areas of urban settlements in which individuals in copresence tend to be personally unknown or only categorically known to one another.* [17] Put differently, the public realm is made up of those spaces in a city which tend to be inhabited by persons who are strangers to one another or who "know" one another only in terms of occupational or other nonpersonal identity categories (for example, bus driver–customer).

It may help to clarify what I mean to think about settlement forms in which the public realm does not exist. For example, using the dichotomous contrast between the private and the public (or communal) space, one can note that in pre- or nonurban settlements (bands, tribes, villages, small towns) these conjoin. The characteristic form of social organization in such settings is the community (defined as overlapping geographical, cultural, and acquaintance space, see, for example, Gusfield 1975). That is, pre- or nonurban settlements are primary groups containing other primary groups. In them, when one leaves one's immediate personal or private space (if the group even makes such a distinction), one moves into a world of acquaintances, kin, friends, enemies, and so forth, with whom one shares a culture and a history. All relationships are primary and what is defined as appropriate behavior among various categories of primary group members is as appropriate in private as in public space. In contrast, in the city, this conjoining disappears. As the city emerges, so does the separate and quite discrete public realm. In the city, when one leaves private space, one moves into a world of many unknown or only categorically known others (biographical strangers), many of whom may not share one's values, history, or perspective (cultural strangers). In short, the public realm is a form of social space distinct from the private realm and its full-blown existence is what makes the city different from other settlement types. The public realm, as my subtitle indicates, is the city's quintessential social territory.[18]

*   *   *

Having completed the preliminaries, it is time to turn to the topics with which this chapter is centrally concerned: the public realm's geography and its history. That accomplished, I will conclude with an overview of both what is and what is not to be found in the pages ahead.

MAPPING THE PUBLIC REALM: A
RUDIMENTARY GEOGRAPHY

In the prologue, I labeled the public realm a *regio incognita*, an "unknown territory." It is certainly that, but it is not totally that. Enough is known to sketch a crude map, to initiate movement toward a rudimentary geography—and that is what we shall do in this section. We will begin by contrasting the public realm to its adjacent territories; go on to ponder the less than "rooted" character of social, as distinct from physical, space; and conclude by facing the protean nature of realm boundaries.

The Three Realms of City Life

A goal in all mapmaking is to render the visual image in such a way that different phenomena are distinguishable from one another: oceans from land masses, for example, or one nation-state from another. I began to do this above by distinguishing between the public realm and the private realm, and for preliminary definitional purposes that simple dichotomy was quite serviceable. But as we move into mapmaking, the very simplicity of the dichotomy makes it less useful; exactly because it is simple, it distorts the messier empirical reality it is supposed to illuminate. A trichotomous distinction, though still a long way from matching the complexity of the real world, can provide a significantly greater degree of precision. Thus, in what follows, we shall be concerned not only with private and public realms, but with *parochial realms* as well. Following Albert Hunter (1985), I will define the private realm (order, in his terms) as *characterized by ties of intimacy among primary groups members who are located within households and personal networks*, and the parochial realm (or order) as *characterized by a sense of commonality among acquaintances and neighbors who are involved in interpersonal networks that are located within "communities."*[19] To oversimplify a bit, the private realm is the world of the household and friend and kin networks; the parochial realm is the world of the neighborhood, workplace, or acquaintance networks; and the public realm is the world of strangers and the "street." Through the lens of this trichotomy, we can see that tribes, villages, and small towns are composed simply of the private and parochial realms (or, if the group has no conception of private space, simply of the parochial realm). Again as we saw above, not until the invention of the city does the public realm come into existence. But what Hunter's triadic distinctions allow us to see in addition is that cities are the most complex of settlement forms because *they are the only settlement form that routinely and persistently contains all three realms.*

Hunter's distinctions do even more. By means of them it becomes possible—though granted in only a very rough sort of way—to sort among cities, or within cities, among areas, in terms of the patterns formed by the relations among the three realms. For example, one might note that a crucial difference between, say, San Francisco and Tucson is that the former has a robust public realm, the latter a less well developed one. Similarly, one could argue that in many parts of many American cities, while the private realm flourishes, the world of the parochial realm, the world of "commonality among acquaintances and neighbors who are involved in interpersonal networks located within communities," is truncated. Manifested as neighborhood community, the parochial realm is radically anemic. As another example, the argument by the historian Donald Olsen (in *The City as a Work of Art*, 1986) that nineteenth-century London was far more "domestic" than were Vienna and Paris in the same period can be translated as saying that in these latter cities, for whatever reason, the private realm took up a smaller portion of the "life space" of its inhabitants than it did in London. Or, as yet another example, one can contrast the worlds of varying segments of the populace of, say, eighteenth-century London, by noting that elite females were heavily restricted to the private realm, while working- and lower-class men and women, and middle- and upper-class males (like Samuel Johnson) spent a great deal of time in the parochial and public realms.

Realms As Social, Not Physical Territories

Except under conditions of cataclysmic geological or political change, maps of physical territories possess the satisfying quality of rootedness. The Pacific Ocean, for example, has a certain position on the map, a certain relationship to the land masses that border it. Over millennia, that position and relationship may change a bit, but for all practical purposes, I can presume that the Pacific Ocean will, next week, be in the same "place" it is in today. Unfortunately for my attempt at mapmaking, *realms are not geographically or physically rooted pieces of space*. They are social, not physical territories. Whether any actual physical space contains a realm at all and, if it does, whether that realm is private, is parochial, or is public is *not* the consequence of some immutable culturally or legally given designation (claiming, for example, this street *is* public space, this yard *is* private space). It *is*, rather, the consequence of *the proportions and densities of relationship types present and these proportions and densities are themselves fluid*. For example, a personal residence, if it is empty of human beings, contains no realm. And while a populated residence is usually a private realm space, it is quite possible for it to be transformed into a public realm space, as when its rooms are inundated with strangers who have paid for a "house tour." Similarly, an empty public park has no realm, and one in which a portion has been "reserved" for a wedding or family reunion contains a private realm "bubble" within it. Or, as a last example, in a small city with a stable population and a very high "density of acquaintance-ship" (Freudenburg 1986), what the outside observer might quite reason-ably take to be public space (streets, parks, and so forth) may, in fact, be almost totally within the parochial realm.

What I am saying here is certainly not new, though the language I am using to say it may be unfamiliar. More than thirty years ago, for example, Anselm Strauss (1961) observed that many public areas are not, in fact, very public (or, in my terms, space that is legally and culturally designated as public, may—sociologically speaking—be parochial) and this led him to distinguish between what he called "locations" and what he called "locales." By location, Strauss meant a street (or other "public area) in which the physical segregation of "life-styles" is maximized—that is, where only persons of similar values and identities are likely to be found. In contrast, a locale is a street (or other public area) that draws to itself dif-ferent sorts of populations.

Now the value of Strauss's distinction is not limited to the insight that legally public space may be parochial. Perhaps more importantly, it opens up the possibility that *social territories or realms may, in general, be "out of place.* That is, if we extend his definitions just a bit and define locations as "bounded" or identifiable portions of nonprivate space dominated by communal relationships (a neighborhood bar is an example) and locales as "bounded" or identifiable portions of nonprivate space dominated by stranger or categorical relations (an airport terminal, for example), then we can note that while locations may be said to be naturally "at home" when surrounded by parochial space, and locales when surrounded by public space, both are quite capable of taking up residence in alien space, as seen in Table 1.1, which depicts the independent relationship between realms and their spaces.

Similarly, as I indicated just above, small pieces of the private realm—"bubbles"—may intrude into public or parochial space. Just as they do when they reserve portions of public parks for weddings or family reunions, persons who are linked by ties of family and/or friendship may, if they are sufficient in number, create little bubbles of private space in a sea of public or parochial territory. Of course, even the lone individual or the dyad may do this to some degree. When we speak of norms like "civil inattention" (see Chapter 2) we are speaking about a mutual willingness to concede that there is a thin layer of private space around the bodies of the people with whom we are sharing nonprivate space. [20] But if a group

Table 1.1   Spaces and Realms as Independent of One Another

	(Physical) Public Space	*(Physical) Parochial Space*
Locale (Public realm territory)	(1) City center plaza	(2) Newly trendy ethnic restaurant in a cohesive neighborhood
Location (Parochial realm territory)	(3) Exclusive home territory bar in city center	(4) Neighborhood bar

Locales (small public realm territories) are naturally "at home" amidst public realm space; locations (small parochial realm territories) are naturally "at home" amidst parochial realm space (cells 1 and 4) but both can be found in alien space (cells 2 and 3).

is large enough, it can do more than accept this almost universally granted concession. It can, in addition, transform the character of a *substantial portion* of the space within which it is located. A "home territory" (see Chapter 2) is a widely recognized form of bubble (Cavan 1963, 1966; Lofland, [1973] 1985; Lyman and Scott 1967). Less well known is the "traveling pack":

> [I]n any particular public place when a group is sufficiently large, there is created for the individuals who make it up an area of private space. That is, a sufficiently large group provides for its members a kind of mobile "home territory" which they may move about with them from setting to setting. This is possible because a group is (by definition) made up of persons who know one another well and who identify with one another and who thus reciprocally ensure mutual protection and self-confirmation. Any need for concern with establishing one's identity to strangers or with ascertaining the identity of strangers is eliminated. . . . The group itself provides all the reassurance and support necessary. What constitutes "sufficiently large," however, will vary depending upon a number of other factors such as the size of other groups also present, the dimensions of the space itself, or the amount of leeway allowed by the setting in what is considered acceptable behavior. . . . Whatever the requisites for sufficient size, when a group reaches the necessary numbers, its members begin to act in a way that is in stark contrast to the actions of those others in the same locale who are alone or with one or two others. . . . They use public space with abandon, in such a way that, for example, a group of adolescents can choose to play running games in an air terminal. They feel free to indulge in backstage behavior, calling each other by name, yelling at one another across the expanse of the setting, using obscene language and laughing loudly at private jokes. And they express proprietary attitudes. If their numbers are plentiful enough, they may even force others to depart, as when the overflow from a convention invades a city's nightspots. (Lofland [1973] 1985:138–139)

The unrooted character of these social territories goes yet further. Humans may disagree over whether a particular piece of physical space belongs to group A or group B or whether it should be designated Fredonia or Altoona, but they generally agree about *where* that space is located. The social territories that are realms breed no such consensus. Whether a specific piece of space is considered private, parochial, or public is often a matter of conflict and/or negotiation. And spaces have histories. Even those that are consensually defined at one time may be redefined or subject to warring definitions at another time.

Mercurial Boundaries

As a last point in this rudimentary geography, we need to face the discomforting fact that not only are realms unrooted, but their boundaries are protean, mercurial. This is true in two senses. First, in the above discussion, although I have treated the various distinctions as though they were discrete categories, in reality they are better conceived as variables. Concrete places often exist on a continuum between private and public, between private and parochial, between parochial and public. Even if we limit our consideration to nonprivate spaces, we must recognize that any given piece of these exists on a continuum between locations and locales and the locations and locales are situated amidst surrounding space that is itself on a continuum between the parochial and the public. Second, just as definitions of what kind of space this is may be subject to conflict, so may be understandings of just where the boundaries between different kinds of spaces are located.

In sum, realms as social territories come into being only in actual physical space—in physical territories. However, whether any actual physical space contains a realm, and if so what type, is always a matter to be discovered empirically. The realm type (private, parochial, or public) is not defined by the physical space in which it is located but by the relational form that dominates within it:

- A private realm exists when the dominating relational form found in some physical space is intimate.
- A parochial realm exists when the dominating relational form found in some physical space is communal.
- A public realm exists when the dominating relational form found in some physical space is stranger or categorical.

*   *   *

That cities are homes to three sorts of social territories or "realms" that bear varying relationships to one another, that these realms are mobile, that their boundaries are fluid—these geographical matters will prove to be of some import as we try to understand both what goes on in the public realm and the animus this social territory evokes. Of equal import is some grasp of its history.

NOTES ON THE HISTORY OF THE PUBLIC REALM

Just as a reasonably complete map of the public realm has yet to be constructed, so a reasonably complete history has yet to be written. Still, we know bits and pieces, and many of those bits and pieces will find their way into the pages ahead. At this point, I want only to draw attention to one particular plot-line in the larger historical narrative. To wit, in the late eighteenth and early nineteenth centuries in Britain and northern Europe (and later throughout the rest of the world), the Industrial Revolution wrought a critical shift in the relationships between private, parochial, and public realms.

As students of urban history well know, a cardinal characteristic of cities prior to late eighteenth century—wherever they were located—was that a significant portion of their social life occurred in the public realm. That is, social life and public life overlapped in the preindustrial city to a remarkable degree—remarkable, at least, by standards of late nineteenth- and twentieth-century urban forms. This was not necessarily, in fact not even probably, a matter of choice. Like their tribal and village counterparts who lived in "communities" whether they wanted to or not, preindustrial city dwellers, given the technology available to them, lived in the public realm out of necessity. Let me review a few of the reasons this was so.

Since the preindustrial city had a largely illiterate population and lacked a technology for the broadcasting of pictorial messages, news had to circulate by moving among copresent human beings via the spoken word. A single person communicating to many others simultaneously proved, of course, more efficient than one-to-one communication: thus the very widespread institution of the town crier. To find an audience, the town crier went into the city's public realm; to hear the news, announcements, and pronouncements, the city's populace did likewise. Similarly, without telephones or telegraphs and, again, with a largely illiterate population, most personal messages, like public messages, had to be delivered personally. To communicate to anyone outside one's own household, one had to leave the household and walk through the public realm until one reached the home or workplace of the message's recipient. And note that I

Illustration 1.3.   London in 1560.

said *walk*. Elites, who by the way represented a very small portion of the total population, could afford litters or horse-drawn conveyances that allowed them to encase themselves in cocoons of privacy and thus to insulate themselves from the public realm—just as modern affluent Westerners are able to do by means of their private automobiles. But most people, in moving from one place to another in the city, had to walk and they had to be both in and of the public realm when they did so. Not only the movement of messages required one's presence in the public realm; for everyone but elites (all of whom had servants and some of whom had quite advanced plumbing systems), the securing of water and the disposal of garbage and body wastes did so as well. The same necessity to be in public was true for a myriad of other activities: shopping, political action, entertainment, religious devotion, and so forth. Add to this the fact that, again excepting some elites in some places, for most of the city's populace, their private space was crowded and uncomfortable even by the standards of their time. For many people, to be in the public realm was to be warm instead of cold, cool instead of hot. It was to breath air—however bad— less fetid than the air of one's private quarters. It was to move into space— however teeming with people—less cramped than home. In sum, the preindustrial city was overwhelmingly a city characterized by the domi-

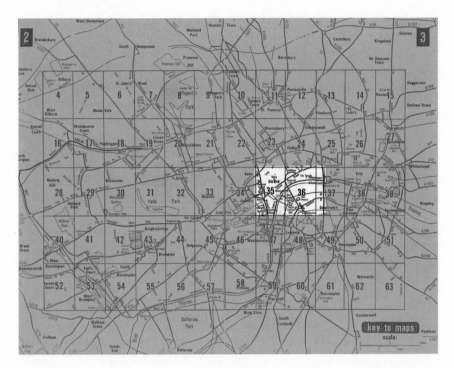

Illustration 1.4. Late twentieth-century London. The enormous growth in the size of London can be seen most clearly by comparing the relation of the city's expanse to the bend in the River Thames (highlighted portion of schematic map) here with that shown in Illustration 1.3. And this schematic is of "inner London" only! Crown Copyright MC/98/22. Reproduced by permission of Geographer's A–Z Map Company Ltd.

nance of public life. (This portrait is drawn from Lofland [1973] 1985 and the references contained therein.)

However, as that complex of events and conditions and phenomena and actions and choices we choose to encapsulate by the term "Industrial Revolution" began to unfold, new possibilities for enlarging and strengthening the city's private and parochial realms emerged. Two characteristics of the late eighteenth-, nineteenth-, and twentieth-century city are especially relevant: (1) innovations in forms of transport allowed this city to be much larger in area than its preindustrial ancestor (see, for example, Illustrations 1.3 and 1.4), and (2) innovations in construction and communication allowed this city to enclose many more activities than had cities of the past. To put it briefly, these two characteristics—enlargement and enclosure—together made possible the separation of workplace from place of residence, made possible the development of highly specialized and large workplaces (e.g., factory districts), made possible the development of homogeneous and large areas of residence (e.g., working-class neighborhoods), made possible the siting of much round-of-life activity within the place of residence or neighborhood, and eventually, with the introduction and widespread personal ownership of the automobile, made it possible for an individual to connect pieces of widely dispersed space without the necessity of actually being, in any socially meaningful sense, in the intervening spaces. That is, it truly became *possible* for large numbers of late eighteenth-, nineteenth-, and twentieth-century city people, as it had not been possible for preindustrial city people, to spend significant portions of their lives entirely in the private and/or parochial realms.

Why I have labeled this shift a "critical" one will become clear as we proceed. For now, I ask only that the reader keep in mind my assertion that such a shift did occur.

COMMISSIONS AND OMISSIONS: AN OVERVIEW AND SOME CAVEATS

In Part I of this book, we shall explore three aspects of the public realm. Chapter 2 deals with the realm's normative principles (or, straining at the kingdom metaphor, its legal system), confronting questions like the following: What "rules" or interactional principles do people seem to be following when they are out in public? How do they conduct themselves and negotiate their way through space when they are surrounded not by intimates or colleagues but by strangers? Does everyone agree on "how to act" and what happens if they disagree? If we move about in space (culture) and time (history), do the rules stay the same? Chapter 3 looks at the relational forms or types that are characteristically found in the public realm. It investigates such issues as whether strangers can form relationships with one another and still remain strangers; whether emotional bonds are possible between and among people who do not "know" one another; how private and parochial realm ties can intrude into the world of strangers; and how one relational type can be transformed into another. In Chapter 4, the last chapter of Part I, we focus on the many pleasures uniquely available to denizens of the public realm and on the unique esthetic principles that seem to guide their judgments of environmental attractiveness.

Part I, then, provides a partial "portrait" of the public realm. Part II focuses on its opponents and some of their variously configured assaults: the negative image of the realm found commonly in Anglo-American art, literature, and political discourse (Chapter 5); the widespread personal fear of strangers and an apparent retreat into private space (Chapter 6); and the work that architects and developers have done and are doing in either destroying the public realm or taming it (Chapter 7).

Finally, in Chapter 8 and in an Epilogue, I will hazard, first, some observations about "functions" the public realm seems to serve and thus about what we might lose if its enemies are successful and, second, some guesses about its future.

This, then, is the promised overview of what lies ahead. But what of the caveats? They have to do with very serious limitations regarding space and time. Not the space available for my words, nor the time it will take me to write them, but the cultural areas and the historical eras that will be dealt with. Most of the data available to me—both what I have collected myself and what I can glean from the work of others—has to do only with Europe (especially northern Europe and, most especially Britain) and North America and is focused on the nineteenth and twentieth centuries. Where the data allow me to speak of other periods and places, I will do so; in the main, however, this is a book about the public realm as it exists only in a certain period and only in a certain place. But, remember, at the very outset, I did warn you that we would be exploring a *regio incognita.*

NOTES

1.   These quite disparate estimates are a consequence less of individual readings of the archaeological record, per se, than of differing assumptions about the necessary prerequisites to city life, the defining characteristics of a city, and the physical nature of the "urban form." See, for example, Arensberg (1980), Jacobs (1969:Chapter 1), Lofland ([1973] 1985:182, note 8), Price and Brown (1985), and Sjoberg (1960:Chapter 2).

2.   Some scholars estimate that the population of Rome at the end of the first century A.D., for example, was a million or more (Carcopino 1940, 1952). Others suggest that two hundred thousand is a more likely number (Russell 1958; Sjoberg 1960). In contrast, there seems general agreement that by the early decades of the fifteenth century, the Chinese city of Nanking had a population of about a million (Mote 1977; see also Skinner 1977).

3.   I think a strong case could be made that the fate of the urban settlement in the United States provides a textbook demonstration of the validity of these propositions. Chapters 5, 6, and 7 contain materials relevant to this assertion.

4.   Having written this sentence, I now wonder why I find this situation remarkable. After all, the exact same situation exists in our relation to the natural environment: a species prepared to poison the air and water it needs to survive is hardly likely to be "house proud" vis-à-vis its built environment.

5.   This interest eventually led Stone to a concern with the sociology of sports. See, for example, Stone (1968).

6. It is not clear that Stone appreciated the implications of this finding. In describing the "personalizing consumer," he wrote:

> Without access to either formal or informal channels of social participation, because of her lower social status, her very few or very many children, and the fact that she had spent the early years of her married life outside the local area, this type of consumer established quasi-primary relationships with the personnel of local independent retail institutions. (1954:42)

In other words (as I will discuss in more detail in Chapter 3), Stone appeared to view such public place attachments as rather pathetic (though functional) substitutes for more "authentic" relationships with friends and neighbors. As we will see in Chapter 5, the assumption of the moral superiority of the worlds of home and neighborhood over the "world of strangers" is a recurring feature of both scholarly and popular writing about the city.

7. Goffman never let book titles get in the way of analytic development, and neither of his two books with "public" in the title is exclusively or even particularly concerned with genuinely public space. In *Behavior in Public Places*, for example, he defines "public places" in the traditional manner: "regions . . . freely accessible to members of [the] community," but the focus of the work is on the analytic unit, gatherings: "occasions when two or more persons are present to one another" (1963a:9).

8. For example, the research project that eventually resulted in the publication of *The Social Life of Small Urban Spaces* (1980) and *City: Rediscovering the Center* (1988) was entitled "The Street Life Project." As another example, Whyte is a founder of the New York–based "Project for Public Spaces, Inc."

9. The bounded character of the city is, for one who has lived through the suburbanization and metropolitanization of the United States after 1950, particularly striking in pre– and immediate post–World War II Hollywood films. One can see this especially clearly in the films of the 1920s and 1930s, but even as late as 1947, in *Dark Passage*, Lauren Bacall—leaving her San Francisco flat and driving across the Golden Gate Bridge—is immediately surrounded by bucolic countryside and, in very short order, is on a little-traveled narrow road in the vicinity of San Quentin Prison. And in 1948 when *Mr. Blandings Builds His Dreamhouse*, he does so in a deeply rural part of Connecticut, which is only a short commute from his Manhattan office.

10. David Hummon reports similar confusions among persons he interviewed about their settlement imagery and preferences:

> Some residents of Hillcrest [an upper-middle-class suburb in the San Francisco metropolitan area] and Bayside [a working-class suburb in the same metropolitan area] are best characterized as *Suburban Villagers*. When questioned about their community preferences, they say that they prefer to live in a small town or the countryside. *But more significantly, they also think of their community as a small town* rather than a suburb [or city], and they typically enjoy living in "their town." (1990:110)

The confusions in everyday speech are replicated in scholarly discourse. The term *city*, in particular, has generated a kaleidoscope of definitions. In 1921, Max Weber, for example, suggested that

> all settlements should be classified as cities in which "the resident population satisfies an economically important part of its daily needs in the local market, and to a large

extent with products which have been produced or otherwise obtained for sale in the market by the residents and by the residents of the nearby countryside." (discussed in Bahrdt 1966:78)

More recently, George Hillery defined cities as "localized systems integrated by contracts and families" (1963:782), and Harold Proshansky offered the suggestion that the city should be understood as a "differentiated but unified physical system" (1978:162). In fact, the range and self-contradictory character of extant definitions is so confusing that most recent urban sociology textbooks have simply eschewed all effort to be precise about the "thing" they are analyzing. In part, these competing definitions arise out of the varied research interests of their authors, but they seem also to be a consequence of the social and physical complexity and diversity of the phenomenon they seek to capture. Gulick (1989:1–5) provides a convincing argument for the futility of any attempt to develop *a single* definition.

11. As early as 1910, the bureau introduced the concept of the "metropolitan district," but by 1950 this was no longer adequate and the "Standard Metropolitan Statistical Area" (SMSA) entered the bureau's conceptual cupboard. In 1983, the SMSA concept—in its turn perceived as lacking the refinement necessary to capture increasingly complex urban patterns—was discarded and eventually a quintet composed of "metropolitan area" (MA), "metropolitan statistical area" (MSA), "New England county metropolitan area" (NECMA), "primary metropolitan statistical area" (PSMA) and "consolidated metropolitan statistical area" (CMSA) came into use. For discussions of the Census Bureau's ongoing struggle to develop an adequate "urban" language, see Choldin (1985:1354–5), Federal Committee on Standard Metropolitan Statistical Areas (1979, 1980), Gottdiener (1994:7–8), Scott (1968:192–97), Shyrock (1957), and Starr (1987). As of 1993 in the United States, there were 328 MAs comprised of 241 MSAs, 17 CMSAs, 58 PMSAs, and 12 NECMAs (Slater and Hall 1995:A-1).

12. I am not being entirely arbitrary here. *Webster's Third New International Dictionary of the English Language, Unabridged* (Merriam 1971) defines city as (among other definitions) "a populous place."

13. For a discussion of the boundaries and of the melting of the boundaries between personally known others and strangers, see Lofland ([1973] 1985:16–19).

14. For a discussion of just why this should be the case, see Lofland ([1973] 1985:9–11). Depending on the criteria they use to judge "urbanness," scholars may categorize differing settlements very differently. Writing of the history of Houston, Texas, for example, Anthony Orum and Joe Feagin note that up until about 1930, the city's maximum size was "only a little over 50,000 people, *clearly a small town by any standard* "(1991:126, emphasis added). Fifty thousand may be "small" by Orum's and Feagin's standard; it is certainly not by mine (see Lofland [1973] 1985:11). Among other problems, such a high population threshold for granting city status eliminates from that category most of the world's historic "urban" settlements.

15. See, for example, Berger and Kellner (1964), Greifer (1945), Harman (1988), Levine (1979, 1985), Meyer (1951), Park (1928), Schutz (1944), Tiryakian (1973), and the numerous works cited therein. Some of these scholars feel quite proprietary about the topic of strangerhood and are apparently made uneasy by any use of the term that differs from their own. Donald Levine has made the case for this position succinctly:

Finally, it should be noted that the sociology of strangerhood articulated by this paradigm is limited by its adherence to one essential feature of Simmel's conception: the depiction of strangerhood as a "figure-ground" phenomenon, in which the stranger status is always defined *in relation to a host*. Other kinds of phenomena, however, have been linked with this concept, namely, those in which *both* parties to a relationship are labeled strangers. In this usage, strangerhood is defined simply as a function of the degree of unfamiliarity existing between the parties. In Lofland's elaboration of this notion ([1973] 1985), individuals are strangers to one another simply when they lack personal and biographical information about one another.... Applying a similar model at the collective level, relations between ethnic groups have been conceived in terms in terms of attitudes and transactions between stranger communities. (Williams 1964)

Important though such topics are, there is a danger that in characterizing the content of strangerhood so broadly that what has always been most fascinating about this subject may become obscured. (Levine 1985:87, emphasis in original; see also Levine 1979:35)

16. For a small sampling of the literature describing this variation, see Fei (1992) and Pellow (1993) on the Chinese; Krygier (1983) on preliterate or "stateless" peoples; Saxonhouse (1983) on the ancient Greeks; Pitkin (1993) on contemporary Italians; Al-Kodmany (1996) on traditional Arabs; and Vera (1989) on the contemporary Dutch. On the public-private distinction more generally, see Altman (1975), Benn and Gaus (1983a), Bensman and Lilienfield (1979), Madge (1950), Meyrowitz (1985:Chapter 6), Sennett (1977a), and Shapira and Navon (1991). Pateman (1983) reviews feminist critiques of the public-private dichotomy; see also Imray and Middleton (1983).

17. The term "public realm" (and the related terms "public order," "public sphere," "public world," and "public life") are sometimes used in the restrictive sense I am employing here, but more frequently their usage carries implications of political and economic activities that I do *not* intend (see, for example, Arendt 1958; Fischer 1981; Habermas [1964] 1974; Hohendahl [1964] 1974; Ketcham 1987). In contrast, Charles Goodsell's (1988) term "civic space" and Richard's Sennett's (1977a) "public domain" are near synonyms for "public realm." See also Chermayeff and Alexander (1963) on the "six domains of urbanity."

18. Among nonurban peoples, the public realm experience may well have been *intermittently* available, as in the markets and fairs of an agrarian economy (see, e.g., Davis 1966; Harrison 1975; Moore 1985). What is unique about the city is that it transforms intermittent availability into permanence.

19. Interestingly enough, most classic ethnographies of city life—older and modern—are studies of the parochial realm. From Whyte ([1943] 1993) to Gans (1962, 1967) to Suttles (1968) and Liebow (1967), to Horowitz (1983) and Rieder (1985), it is the world of neighborhood of friend and kin networks, and of acquaintances that has been lovingly documented by urban sociologists and anthropologists [Anderson (1990) is a rare and wonderful exception]. Presumably, problems of access account for the absence of a comparable numbers of works on the private realm [but see Handel (1986) for a somewhat different view]. And disattention to the public realm is quite reasonable, given the long tenure of the belief that nothing social or nothing socially important occurs there.

20. See, for example, Goffman (1971:28–61) on "the territories of the self."

I
CHARACTERISTICS OF THE PUBLIC REALM:
Aspects of a Social Territory

What is the public realm like? That is, what kind of social territory is it? How do its inhabitants behave? Do they form relationships with one another and, if so, what sorts of relationships? How do they relate to the territory itself? And what pleasures, if any, do they find in it? In short, what is the "culture" of the public realm? Or, put more simply, what are some of its important characteristics?

The research I have used to address these questions is, almost without exception, unconcerned with the public realm per se. The people who produced it were interested instead in such wildly diverse topics as (among many others) customer relations in supermarkets, cross-cultural misunderstandings, the management of shame and embarrassment, the social life of the homeless, sexual and racial harassment, the behavior of bureaucrats, human altruism and callousness, anonymity and alienation in modern life, sexual mores, historical shifts in manners and morals, friendship patterns, collective behavior episodes, urban renewal in the United States, the sociology and psychology of emotion, "livable" built environments, and the patterning of social interaction. As I hope will become apparent, gleanings from this rich hodgepodge of information do not transform a *regio incognita* into a known territory, but they do make a good start.

are there benefits to unknown territory?
I think there might be —
heterotopias of difference

2

The Normative or "Legal" System
Patterns and Principles

What do we mean when we say that someone has "street smarts"? Why do certain public behaviors elicit embarrassment[1] or anger? And how is it that cosmopolitans—people we think of as "urbane"—seem to move so easily across the city spaces of differing cultural groups? The answer to these questions is to be found in one of the characteristics of the public realm: its possession of a normative or (speaking metaphorically) a "legal" system.[2] And it is this characteristic that we shall be exploring here. However, before beginning that exploration, it will be useful to pause long enough to appreciate one of the characteristic's more remarkable outcomes: the *patterning* of public realm interaction.

INTRODUCTION: THE PATTERNING OF
PUBLIC REALM INTERACTION

Literary and filmic images of the "chaotic streets of the city" notwithstanding, what has struck those researchers with the discipline and patience necessary for careful observation of public behavior is the *orderliness*, the *patternedness* with which city denizens seem to conduct even their most fleeting and ostensibly "trivial" encounters. For example, Michael Wolff, in his 1973 study of pedestrian behavior, reported that

> among the most outstanding characteristics of pedestrians that have emerged from this study are the *amount and degree of cooperative behavior* on the streets of the city. While at the immediate and superficial level, encounters on the street are hardly noticeable and devoid of pleasantry and warmth, pedestrians do, in fact, communicate and do take into account the qualities and predicaments of others in regulating their behavior. (1973:48, emphasis added)

Wolff also found it useful to describe some of what he observed by using a language that hints of the dance—of choreography:

25

[A]t higher densities a common behavior, especially between members of the same sex, was not total detour and avoidance of contact, but a slight angling of the body, a turning of the shoulder and an almost imperceptible side-step—a sort of *step-and-slide*. (ibid.:39, emphasis in the original)

What is a mere hint in Wolff's report becomes much more explicit in later work. In 1979, the geographer David Seamon introduced the term "place ballet" to convey—via a very overt linkage to choreography—what he observed to be the thoroughly patterned, almost "directed" character of human movement over time in a particular public space.[3] And by the late 1980s when William H. Whyte published *City: Rediscovering the Center*, he could speak unambiguously of "the great dance":

> If there is a proper place for it, there will be [during the evening pedestrian rush hour] a great dance. The best of the old railroad stations provided such places, and where these remain the movement is splendid. Stand on the balcony overlooking the main floor of Grand Central. At left, with three of the four escalators heading down, there is a mass of people going the same way. But only for a moment. They split into an infinity of directions. Some swirl around the information kiosk clockwise, some counterclockwise. Hundreds of people will be moving this way and that, weaving, dodging, feinting. Here and there someone will break into a run. Almost everyone is on a collision course with someone else, but with a multitude of retards, accelerations, and side steps, they go their way untouched. It is indeed a great dance. (1988:67; see also 1980)

Patterning in human activity implies both some shared expectations (norms or rules) and cooperation, shared expectations and cooperation imply genuine interaction. But as we have seen, the idea that the public realm could be the setting for genuine interaction, the idea that individuals who have no personal relationship with one another—who are strangers to one another—the idea that such persons could, in any sociologically meaningful sense, *interact* emerged in the discipline neither early nor easily. To reiterate what I said in the Prologue, as late as the mid-1960s, views such as those expressed by Nicholas J. Spykman were still being taken very seriously:

> On the street, in the subway, on the bus [the city dweller] comes into contact with hundreds of people. But these brief incidental associations *are based neither on sharing of common values nor on cooperation for a common purpose. They are formal in the most complete sense of the term in that they are empty of content* (1926:58, emphasis added; see also Davis and Levine 1967; Doob 1952).

This is one version of the "stimulus overload" argument, which, as we saw, originated in the work of Georg Simmel ([1902–1903] 1950), was accepted and developed further by Louis Wirth (1938), and as late as 1970 found an especially influential spokesperson in Stanley Milgram:

> This term [overload], drawn from system analysis, refers to a system's inability to process inputs from the environment because there are too many inputs for the system to cope with, or because successive inputs come so fast that input *A* cannot be processed when input *B* is presented. When overload is present, adaptations occur. The system must set priorities and make choices. *A* may be processed first while *B* is kept in abeyance or one input may be sacrificed altogether. City life, as we experience it, constitutes a continuous set of encounters with overload, and of resultant adaptations. Overload characteristically deforms daily life on several levels, impinging on role performance, the evolution of social norms, cognitive functioning, and use of facilities. ([1970] 1973:2; see also Deutsch 1961; Newman and McCauley 1977)

What the pioneers and current practitioners of public realm research like Gregory Stone, Jane Jacobs, Erving Goffman, and William Whyte (as well as other researchers pursuing other agendas) have accomplished, then, is a thorough demolishment of this particular strand of social science "conventional wisdom." Through their descriptions and analyses of the extraordinarily rich interactional life occurring "on the street, in the subway, on the bus," they have demonstrated that in the "incidental associations" Spykman referred to there is, in fact, a good deal of "sharing of common values" and "cooperation for a common purpose." That is, public realm interaction is patterned because, far from "shutting down," persons in urban space appear to be paying careful attention to what I shall here conceive of as "principles of stranger interaction."

The goals of this chapter are twofold: (1) to describe five overarching principles that research has unearthed and detail a number of the uses to which they are put and (2) to explore some of the complexities that an appreciation of historical and cultural variation brings to our understanding of these principles. A concluding section will address misunderstandings about the normative system that ensue when researchers confuse public realm spaces with parochial realm spaces and misread their own data.

PRINCIPLES OF STRANGER INTERACTION

If we use the term *rule* in a very broad and general sense, it seems fair to say that the public realm is no more rule-bound than other areas of social life but it is also no less. While we cannot hope to understand what goes on there simply by invoking a set of normative principles or behavioral patterns or customs, neither can we get much of a handle on its "doings" without appreciating that the participants are—symbolically speaking—carrying and consulting multiple guidebooks to help them define the situation and direct their own conduct. At the risk of belaboring the analogy, let me suggest a few titles for these books. One might be called *Grammars of Motility* and recommend specific rules of social and physical movement in the public realm:[4] making one's way through crowded streets and intersections, choosing a seat in a bar, restaurant, or bus, escaping unwanted attention, joining or participating in a queue, achieving social invisibility, driving on relatively modern road systems or through the narrow streets of a third-world city, going to the assistance of a stranger in minor or major trouble, or avoiding what appears to be a dangerous scene. [Goffman's *Behavior in Public Places* (1963a) and, more particularly, his *Relations in Public* (1971) may be read as legal textbooks in the microinteraction of public motility.] Another possible title might be *Urban Visual Aids: Rules for Coding Space, Appearance, and Behavior*, a book devoted to detailing the "interpretation principles" by which urbanites "make sense of" the raw data emanating from their physical and social environment and thus define the situations in which they find themselves. Some of my own earlier work on urban public space (Lofland [1973] 1985) is concerned importantly with this topic (see also Jackson and Johnston 1972). Inhabitants of the city's public places probably also carry *Verbal Sociability Customs*, a volume that assists them in determining when, with whom, and how they may or may not try to engage their fellow urbanites in direct conversation.[5] A close inspection of these (and other) interrelated normative areas will certainly tell us much about interaction in the public realm and we shall be looking at some of these "regulatory minutiae" in more detail shortly when we get to the discussion of "employment." At this point, however, I want to suggest that what we know of the normative system of the public realm is probably more easily grasped—at least initially—if we conceive of it in terms of "overarching principles" rather than in terms of a plethora of narrowly focused rules.

Overarching Principles

Based on the relevant research to date, it is possible to identify five principles that appear to guide—to provide the normative context for—the intricacies of public face-to-face interaction: (1) cooperative motility, (2) civil inattention, (3) audience-role prominence, (4) restrained helpfulness, and (5) civility toward diversity.

Cooperative Motility. To introduce the idea that stranger interaction is patterned, I highlighted the dancelike, almost choreographed character of pedestrian behavior; and in so doing I provided an early glimpse of the cooperative motility principle in operation.[6] If one grants that stranger interaction is, in fact, patterned, then the leap to the idea of cooperative motility, to the idea that strangers work together to traverse space without incident, is a simple one. In their movements in and about the public realm, humans are making their way through an often fairly daunting environment composed of inanimate objects, animate objects, and inanimate objects propelled and/or inhabited by animate ones (e.g., doors, buses, automobiles, elevators).[7] Inanimate objects alone pose minimal challenge (at least for most people—we all know the exceptions). However, animate objects and animately propelled inanimate ones—involving, as they do, movement that is guided by *intention*, are harder to read, their paths are harder to predict. Will the people inside keep the elevator door open long enough for me to reach it? Will that bus begin to move through the intersection before I'm across the street? Just where is that woman I see approaching me on the sidewalk headed and wherever it is, what route is she going to use to get there? Is that person just ahead holding the door open for me or only for herself? Nonetheless, most of us get through doors without incident, most pedestrians don't collide with other pedestrians, most buses and cars do not flatten human beings, and most people do not get body parts crushed by closing elevator doors. Most of the time our movement through the public realm is simply *uneventful*, and it is so because humans are *cooperating* with one another to make it so.

Civil Inattention. In *Behavior in Public Places*, Erving Goffman introduced the concept of civil inattention as follows:

> When persons are mutually present and not involved together in conversation or other focused interaction, it is possible for one person to stare openly and fixedly at others, gleaning what he can about them while frankly expressing on his face his response to what he sees—for example, the "hate stare" that a Southern white sometimes gratuitously gives to Negroes walking past him. It is also possible for one person to treat others as if they were not there at all, as objects not worthy of a glance, let alone close scrutiny. Moreover, it is possible for the individual by his staring or "not seeing," to alter his own appearance hardly at all in consequence of the presence of the others. Here we have "nonperson" treatment, it may be seen in our society in the way we sometimes treat children, servants, Negroes and mental patients. Currently in our society, this kind of treatment is to be contrasted with the kind generally felt to be more proper in most situations, which will here be called "civil inattention." What seems to be involved is that one gives

to another enough visual notice to demonstrate that one appreciates that the other is present (and that one admits openly to having seen him), while at the next moment withdrawing one's attention from him so as to express that he does not constitute a target of special curiosity or design. (1963a:83–84)

Whether or not the principle of civil inattention is exactly as Goffman describes it here,[8] there can be no question of its existence and power—and its omnipresent operation. It is practiced on buses, in restaurants, on park benches, in airplanes, in hotel lobbies, even on that stereotyped symbol of urban alienation, the subway:

When seated [in subway cars], people usually assume inconspicuous behavior—sitting squarely, at first turning neither left nor right, and maintaining expressionless faces. . . . People without books or papers . . . may begin to stare at fellow passengers, alternating fleeting or blank stares with an innocent staring off into space. These stares and glances at fellows are quite restricted and concealed and are made so because they are not to be interpreted as invitations to others to begin an encounter; they are the behavioral components of what Goffman . . . has termed "civil inattention." (Levine, Vinson, and Wood 1973:210)[9]

Civil inattention makes possible copresence without commingling, awareness without engrossment, courtesy without conversation. We may speak of it, perhaps, as the sine qua non of city life. It is important here to note the stark contrast between this principle and the Simmel-Spykman-Wirth-Milgram vision of "stimulus overload" and "psychological shutdown" leading to the presumed "typical" urban attitudes of emotional coldness and unconcern. Civil inattention suggests that when humans in the public realm appear to ignore one another, they do so *not* out of psychological distress but out of a ritual regard, and their response is *not* the asocial one of "shut down" but the fully social one of politeness.

Like most broad social principles, civil inattention is surrounded by exceptions and variations. In the quotation above, Goffman himself makes note of "nonperson treatment" and the "hate stare" as exceptions that prove the rule, and his further discussion of the topic provides additional qualifications and elaborations. And to get ahead of the story just a bit, we must note that there are also cultural, subcultural, and situational variations in the applicability and appropriateness of the general principle. In the mid-1980s, for example, Russian youth were not at all shy about approaching total strangers whom they identified as Westerners, fingering their clothing and making offers to purchase one or another garment. And persons who have staked out "home territories" (see Chapter 3) in public places appear to feel little reticence about intruding upon the privacy of anyone who enters their space (Cavan 1963; Gmelch and Gmelch 1978; Hong and Dearman 1977; Lofland [1973] 1985).

Audience Role Prominence.   As Goffman made clear in his initial statement, civil inattention is not disattention. The principle of civil inattention may require that one not be obviously interested in the affairs of the other, but it does not require that one not be interested at all. As such, it is fully compatible with the third principle: inhabitants of the public realm act primarily as audience to the activities that surround them.

Given this pattern, it is not surprising that descriptions of public space are often clothed in the language of the theater, as in this passage from Suzanne Lennard and Henry Lennard's, *Public Life in Urban Spaces*:

> [I]t has long been assumed that public life, just like a theatrical production, requires actors and audience, a stage and a theater. . . . Public life may take place on center stage where the actors are clearly visible to most of the audience, or in more secluded areas visible only to a few. A public space, however, is at once both stage and theater, for in public the spectators may at any moment choose to become actors themselves. . . . Successful public places accentuate the dramatic qualities of personal and family life. They make visible certain tragic, comic and tender aspects of relationships among friends, neighbors, relatives or lovers. They also provide settings for a gamut of human activities (Lennard and Lennard 1984:21–22)[10]

Just *how much* will be available for the voyeuristic pleasures of the audience is quite variable. Certainly, as we have seen in Chapter 1, contemporary cities are outclassed by their preindustrial predecessors in the amount of public realm activity (Lofland [1973] 1985:Chapter 2) and automobile-oriented settlements like Brasilia, Houston, and Phoenix are no match for older, denser, more walkable places like London, New York, or San Francisco. Similarly, *what* will be available—the range or diversity of the theatrical performances presented—also varies across time and space. For the average urbanite in twentieth-century North America the dramaturgic menu would appear to include intentional performances by street musicians, mimes, jugglers, magicians, and others (Harrison 1984); commercial and sexual exchanges—legal and illegal;[11] presumptively private acts (Feigelman 1974); love scenes and fight scenes among dyads (McPhail 1987); the mundane ballet created when aggregates of people walk, sit, converse, sleep, read, and watch their watchers (Love 1973; Whyte 1980); and the dramatic tragedy inherent in accidents and other health emergencies (Palmer 1983).

This last fact—that humans often quite enthusiastically assume the audience role in the face of what are very seriously problems, even catastrophes, for those most intimately involved—has provided repeated occasions for moralistic hair-tearing and teeth-gnashing, as we will see in discussing the work of John Latané and Bibb Darley. Yet also as we will see, such behavior is best understood not as evidence of human perfidy, but as normal and natural within the "legal" system of the public realm.

Restrained Helpfulness. Just as the principle of civil inattention does not preclude the principle of audience role prominence, so the latter does not preclude the principle of restrained helpfulness. Specifically targeted and clearly limited requests for mundane assistance and a response of restrained helpfulness—what the sociologist Carol Brooks Gardner has called "public aid" (1986b)—are a constant feature of life in the public realm.[12] "Could you tell me the time?" is answered by "It's 5:12." "Am I on the right street to get to the city hall?" receives, at minimum, a "Yes" or "No," more frequently, a set of detailed instructions. "May I borrow your newspaper for just a minute?" or "If you're not going to use the sugar, would you mind if we moved the bowl to our table?" elicits a murmured, "Of course," the murmur, often accompanied by a "restrained" smile.

As with the other principles, restrained helpfulness may not always be granted gracefully, may sometimes even be denied altogether—or, at least, so a correspondent to "Miss Manners" suggests:

Dear Miss Manners:

Please . . . offer some put-down for people who seek instant information from complete strangers who are going about their business and not bothering anyone. I seem to be the born victim of such people, who stop me on the street wanting to know the time . . . or when the shops open or, in the case of tourists . . . , where one can get a good breakfast. . . . What's the best way to squash such people? They usually ask for directions when your arms are full of bundles so a blunt instrument isn't too practical. (Martin 1991:108–9)

Such complaints aside, requests for mundane assistance and positive responses to those requests are the mundane "stuff" of everyday stranger encounters[13]—so unremarkable that in many studies they are not even mentioned or mentioned only in passing.

Civility toward Diversity. The fifth and final major principle, civility toward diversity, specifies that in face-to-face exchanges, confronted with what may be personally offensive visible variations in physical abilities, beauty, skin color and hair texture, dress style, demeanor, income, sexual preference, and so forth, the urbanite will act in a civil manner, that is, will act "decently" vis-à-vis diversity. As with the other principles, there are, of course, innumerable variations and exceptions. But the sense of freedom from judgment that many people report (personal interviews) as a major pleasure of being "out in public" testifies to the principle's operation.

Let me be clear. To be civil toward diversity is not necessarily to act in a manner that will be defined as nice or pleasant. The fabled rudeness of New York City service personnel can be as expressive of civility as the pseudo-*gemeinschaftlich* smiles and the entreaties to "have a nice day" emanating from their California counterparts. The crux of this principle is evenhandedness and universality of treatment, not demonstrations of friendliness or fellow-feeling. Civility probably emerges more from indifference to diversity than from any appreciation of it.

One of the more interesting aspects of this principle is that it seems to excite remark only in its breach. As an example, I have spent many hundreds of hours making observations in public spaces and have observed thousands of instances of civility toward diversity. Yet almost without exception (instances of civility in the face of quite extreme behavioral "eccentricities;" Lofland [1973] 1985:Chapter 8), these have gone unrecorded. Only the very few instances of observed *incivility* made it into my notes. Similarly, the social science literature dealing with the topic tends to assume the normality or unremarkability of the principle's operation and to focus either on general conditions that support it, or create it in the first place or on instances of its breakdown.[14]

The topic of breakdown, of breach in the operation of the principle of civility toward diversity, brings us back to a distinction made in Chapter 1 (in the discussion of geography) and takes us toward a generalization that applies to public realm rules more generally. The applicability and appropriateness of all the principles being outlined here does not extend into the territories of the parochial or of the private. Where the boundaries between the three realms are unclear or disputed or, even more simply, at border points between them, ruptures in the moral order are not only possible but are, under some conditions, probable. One of the excitements, but also one of the dangers, of the urban environment is the uncertainty of knowing exactly where one is and, thus, of knowing exactly what rules apply.

Although I have described each principle as if it were a separate thing, standing on its own, in fact, the five principles are profoundly interwoven, intertwined. *Civil inattention,* for example, ensures that people will not become so thoroughly engrossed in the doings of the strangers who surround them that they are unable to maintain the level of alertness necessary for *cooperative motility* and will also be available to respond to requests for *restrained helpfulness. Audience role prominence* is fueled by the environmental scanning and alertness involved in cooperative motility and itself fuels the mind-set required for both restrained helpfulness and *civility toward diversity.* And the latter two principles buttress the more general commitment to politeness required for civil inattention. Interweaving gives each single principle strength; it can also increase the vulnerability of the package. When there is a violation of one of the principles, we are likely to see (as we will shortly), a simultaneous violation of one or more of the others.

Principle Employment

In referring to these principles as overarching and characterizing them as providing the normative context for stranger and other public realm interactions, I am emphasizing the thoroughly nonformulaic character of those interactions. Humans are not simply following rules; their actions are neither ritualized nor fully predictable. Rather, the principles contribute to individuals' overall "definitions of the situation" and those definitions, in turn, help people to construct their actions, to guide their conduct. Stated most generally, what appears to be going on is that persons draw upon—employ—their knowledge of these principles, as well as their presumptively shared understandings about the meanings of body language, appearances, and space-specific appropriate behaviors and identities to produce—among other possible outcomes—(1) privacy, disattention, and avoidance; (2) territorial defense; (3) the possibility or impossibility of rescue; (4) sociability; and (5) equality or inequality.

Ensuring Privacy, Disattention, and Avoidance. As we have seen, according to the Simmel-Spykman-Wirth-Milgram view of the urban world, unacquainted persons are socially irrelevant to one another. They may be copresent in the physical sense of occupying adjacent space at the same time, but they are not copresent in any sociological sense. It follows then that the absence of verbal and/or visual exchanges among them requires no explanation. It is simply a "given" of the setting, of urban public space. But what researchers have demonstrated is the exact opposite. Far from being a given, the absence of verbal or visual exchanges must be *achieved*. In fact and paradoxically, privacy, disattention, and avoidance *can only be accomplished by means of principles-guided social interaction*. Thus, by utilizing their knowledge of the principles plus their understandings more generally about "how things work," strangers are able to communicate to one another messages such as the following:

"I want my privacy and am not available to be spoken to or encountered in any way."

An individual makes private a public place by making interaction with others impossible or at least highly inconvenient. . . . In the [bus] depot, this end seemed to be effected through two major categories of means: involvement with some activity, and body position. . . . The most notable use of body positioning occurred when all four seats of a set were occupied. If an individual was seated next to someone, he would noticeably adjust his position by turning himself away from his neighbor. (Henderson 1975:49–50)[15]

"I know you are present and you know I am present but we are, of course, each invisible to the other."

Protecting oneself via shielding does not stop once an individual goes into the [pornographic] bookstore. . . . Under no circumstances in these stores do customers make physical or verbal contact with one another. The normative structure appears to demand silence and careful avoidance of either eye or physical contact. (Karp 1973:439–49)[16]

"I am not intruding and will not intrude into your personal space; in fact, I am going out of my way to avoid doing so"

A variation on the canonical form of civil inattention is also commonly performed in the open region of public bathrooms, most often by men using adjacent urinals. . . . [Males] must . . . partially expose their external genitalia in order to [urinate]. . . . What men typically give one another when using adjacent urinals is not, therefore, [canonical] civil inattention but "nonperson treatment" . . . , that is, they treat one another as if they were part of the setting's physical equipment. . . . When circumstances allow, of course, unacquainted males typically avoid occupying adjacent urinals and, thereby, this ritually delicate situation. (Cahill 1985:41–42)[17]

In sum, what we see in these examples are communications that assume the principle of civility toward diversity but then go on to heighten or intensify the civil inattention and cooperative motility principles so as to reduce both requests for help and audience focus. That is, a knowledge of all the principles is being employed in an attempt to "privilege" a select number.

Defending Territory. Something similar seems to happen when the goal is territorial defense—not surprising, perhaps, since the line between the production of privacy, disattention, and avoidance and the production of defense is neither solid nor stable. In numerous studies, descriptions of communications designed to forestall encounters may gradually shade into descriptions of quite direct defensive maneuvers. In Margaret Henderson's study of "acquiring privacy in public," for example, a detailed discussion of varying body postures that merely "give off" privacy signals is interrupted by an example of a clearly targeted communication:

A young girl and her boyfriend were seated side by side. The boyfriend left
to make a phone call. During the interim, an elderly male approached the
apparently vacant seat. At this, the girl *slapped her hand on the seat with a glar-
ing look*—and the old man simply shuffled away. (Henderson 1975:451,
emphasis added)

Similarly, in Robert Edgerton's study of Southland Beach, the lack of
encounters among users is emphasized, as are the body postures and
props that communicate a desire to be left alone. Nonetheless, the book is
peppered with brief descriptions of defensive encounters:

[M]ost invasions of private space are by small children or dogs. These intru-
sions almost always take the form of running through another person's territory. The observed reaction to such occurrence is usually slight, *although it
may involve a dirty look or a yell to be more careful.* (Edgerton 1979:151, emphasis added)

In both examples, civil inattention is mildly violated so as to emphasize
the exact character of the individual's claim to cooperative motility.

Many of the studies of defensive encounters focus exclusively on the
use of body language and "props" to signal displeasure or hostility over
spatial invasion,[18] but this is not to gainsay the importance of verbal defensive encounters. As we saw above, Edgerton's beach-users sometimes
resorted to "yelling." And Snow, Robinson, and McCall (1991) have
detailed a series of linguistic strategies used by women to "cool out" men
in singles bars and nightclubs (see also Gardner 1988). Nonetheless, verbal
defensive encounters violate the principles of civil inattention and audience role prominence much more severely than do "mimed" communications and they also run a greater risk of being misinterpreted as incivility
toward diversity. As such, we should not be surprised if, as the current
research record would seem to suggest, their employment is both less frequent and more selective.

Inhibiting or Facilitating Rescue. All of the principles, but particularly those of civil inattention, audience role prominence, and restrained
helpfulness, provide a strong disincentive to *active, open-ended* involvements in other people's business. Not unexpectedly then, when the public
realm generates instances of quite *serious* needs for (in fact, "emergencies"
calling for) quite *serious* help (in fact, "rescue"), they may well be met—as
newspapers seem daily to remind us—with a *failure* on the part of
bystander-strangers to intervene. The multiple field experiments of the
psychologists John Darley and Bibb Latané are probably the best known
explorations of this situation, a situation that has been dubbed. "bystander

apathy."[19] Their interest was sparked, as they report, by the infamous Kitty Genovese case:

> On a March night in 1964, Kitty Genovese was set upon by a maniac as she came home from work at 3 A.M. Thirty-eight of her Kew Gardens neighbors came to their windows when she cried out in terror—none came to her assistance. Even though her assailant took over half an hour to murder her, no one even so much as called the police.
> This story became the journalistic sensation of the decade. "Apathy," cried the newspapers. "Indifference," said the columnists and commentators. "Moral callousness," "dehumanization," "loss of concern for our fellow man," added preachers, professors, and other sermonizers. (Latané and Darley 1973:62–63)

In response to such conventional and moralistic views, Latané and Darley demonstrated that a bystander's decision to intervene or not was a highly complex and thoroughly social matter:

> Intervention . . . requires choosing a single course of action through a rather complex matrix of possible actions. The failure to intervene may result from failing to notice an event, failing to realize that the event is an emergency, failing to feel personally responsible for dealing with the emergency, or failing to have sufficient skill to intervene. (ibid.:67)

However, even those who are fully aware that they are witnessing an emergency and who are able to help may not do so *if other bystanders are present*—a rather remarkable and counterintuitive finding, which the researchers explained as follows:

> We have suggested four different reasons why people, once having noticed an emergency, are less likely to go to the aid of the victim when others are present: (1) Others serve as an audience to one's actions, inhibiting him from doing foolish things. (2) Others serve as guides to behavior, and if they are inactive, they will lead the observer to be inactive also. (3) The interactive effect of these two processes will be much greater than either alone; if each bystander sees other bystanders momentarily frozen by audience inhibition, each may be misled into thinking the situation must not be serious. (4) The presence of other people dilutes the responsibility felt by any single bystander, making him feel that it is less necessary for himself to act. (Latané and Darley 1970:125; see also Darley and Latané 1968; Latané and Darley 1968)

Latané and Darley, of course, do not clothe their findings in the language of "principles," but it requires little imagination to interpret those findings in that language. As I suggested above, the principles of civil inattention, audience role prominence, and restrained helpfulness *in particular* go a long way toward helping us understand why both the presence and the inaction of personally unknown others would inhibit interference. After all, the inaction of others puts them in conformity with the principles; for an individual to act in such a situation is to be in violation of the principles, to be deviant.

If intervention is ever to occur—if it is to be facilitated—what seems to be required (in addition to recognition, acceptance of responsibility, and requisite skills) is the presence of conditions that nullify or override the principles—as, for example, when there is only a single bystander present (unwitnessed deviance), or when a group of friends or acquaintances are among the bystanders (group-supported deviance), or when a bystander has special qualifications (for example, a special responsibility for the physical space or medical or police training) that support, if not compel, intervention (acceptable deviance).

Generating Sociability.   In addition to the "employments" thus discussed, strangers may also use their understanding of the public realm's normative system to provide themselves with the simple pleasures of sociability—that is, to engage in fully focused visual and/or verbal encounters simply because it is "fun" or "interesting" or "informative" to do so. We will encounter this topic again in some detail in Chapters 3 and 4. Thus, at this juncture and in this context, a relatively brief treatment will suffice.

The exact sociability-pleasure sought in these encounters may occasionally be sensual, as when total strangers manage to initiate and conclude a sexual exchange in what is commonsensically understood to be a public place. Usually such encounters are managed with the cooperation and support of like-minded others who guard entries or provide cover (e.g., Corzine and Kirby 1977; Humphreys 1970), but sometimes they occur even without the help of others but still without surrounding strangers being aware that "something unusual is happening." This seems to be possible exactly because those surrounding strangers are "doing their duty" and abiding by the principles of civil inattention and cooperative motility but doing so in a context (e.g., dim visibility, crowding) where participation as audience is limited:

> The utilitarian purposes of public spaces aid in the reduction of visibility
> during sexual activity and curb the chances of apprehension. . . . Shoulder to
> shoulder, side by side, and looking "past" the clandestine activities of the
> other, different categories of the urban mass assume that his [sic] neighbor
> will honor the commonly shared and morally defined definitions of public

demeanor and behavior. . . . In effect, multiple social realities can be manip-
ulated in the same time and space zone as long as the knowledge of one can
somehow be safeguarded from the other. (Delph 1978:39; see also Davis
1983:20–26)

More frequently, however, the pleasures sought are mundane ones: passing the time with a "chat," sharing an unexpected experience, getting
some information on a topic of interest, basking in the momentary glow of
"fellow feeling," even commencing a possibly intimate relationship.

Yet there is a mystery here. We have seen above that the principles of
stranger interaction provide a strong disincentive for direct and active
involvement in other people's business; similarly, they also provide a
strong disincentive for fully focused visual and/or verbal encounters.
How then can such encounters be not only possible but relatively frequent? The answer appears to be that certain conditions either nullify the
principles or provide legitimate exceptions to them. For example, one condition is the presence in the public realm of *open persons*: individuals who
because of subordinate (child, disabled) or occupational (policeman) status or because of situationally specific identities (fellow American in
China) are seen as more available for an encounter than others. Another
condition involves *open regions*: locales (for example, drinking establishments, residence lounges of hotels, city streets during carnival, some cafes)
in which all the inhabitants are mutually accessible to one another.[20] Yet a
third condition has to do with the possibilities for *triangulation*: a term
introduced by William H. Whyte and defined by him as a "process by
which some external stimulus provides a linkage between people and
prompts strangers to talk to each other as though they were not
[strangers]" (1980:94; 1988:154–55). Triangulation stimuli may be as mundane as children (Gardner 1986a) or dogs (Robins, Sanders, and Cahill
1991), as esoteric as public place art (Whyte 1980), or as infrequent as
shared emergencies (Goffman 1963a:Chapter 8).

Perpetuating Equalities and Inequalities.   Finally, the public realm's
governing principles may be employed to express, to create, to re-create,
to fabricate, or to refashion societal or regional or local systems of equality
and inequality. To understand how this is possible we need to understand
that *the principles themselves are instruments for communicating equality.* To
use them is to proffer to surrounding strangers the gift of what Goffman
called "ritual deference." As Spencer Cahill has explained the situation:

In those regions of the community that "are freely accessible to members of
the community" (Goffman 1963a:9) . . . , Goffman located a domain of social
life where we . . . routinely express collective ideas and sentiments. As we

now know, what he found there were "brief rituals one individual performs for and to another, attesting to civility and good will on the performer's part and to the recipient's possession of a small patrimony of sacredness" (Goffman 1971:63). (Cahill 1994:6–7)

In sum, to give others ritual deference via the principles implies that one understands them to possess a basic level of humanness, that one admits them into the human family, that one accepts their claims to the rights of citizenship; and that one understands, admits, and accepts these matters even if these surrounding strangers are *unlike oneself and are persons who might be actively disliked—possibly even despised—if known personally.*

Now it is exactly because the employment of the principles is such an effective tool for perpetuating systems of equality that their *violations or misapplications are effective in perpetuating systems of inequality.* Strangers may use their understandings of the "legal" system of the public realm, then, not only to deal deferentially with one another, they may also use those understandings to deal disrespectfully. Thus if equality is communicated by means of civil inattention, inequality may be communicated by its absence[21]—recall Goffman's identification of both the "hate stare" and "nonperson" treatment. Witness also the following:

In a Santa Fe supermarket, a young woman waits in line with her cart, two young men behind her watching her posterior with appreciation. It is Halloween time. "Bought your punkins yet?" one young man booms to the other, and the young woman shifts uncomfortably. (Gardner 1989:50; see also 1980, 1995)

I [an African-American university professor] was driving. . . . It was about 9:30 at night, and as I've said, my car is old and very ugly, and I have been told by people shouting at intersections that it's the kind of car that people think of as a low-rider car, so they associate it with Mexican Americans, especially poor Mexican Americans. Well, we were sitting at an intersection waiting to make a turn and group of middle-class looking white boys drives up in a nice car. And they start shouting things at us in a real fake-sounding Mexican American accent, and I realized that they thought we were Mexican Americans. And I turned to look at them, and they started making obscene gestures and laughing at the car. And then one of them realized that I was black, and said, "Oh, it's just a nigger." And [they] drove away. (quoted in Feagin 1991:110).

It was late afternoon [in Austin, Texas] and the homeless were congregating in front of the Sally [Salvation Army] for dinner. A school bus approached that was packed with Anglo junior high students being bused from an eastside Barrio school to their upper-middle and upper-class homes in the city's northwest neighborhoods. As the bus rolled by, a fusillade of coins came flying out the windows along with a few obscene gestures and injunctions to "get a job." (Snow and Anderson 1993:198)

Similarly, if civility toward diversity admits the "full humanness" of the strange other, incivility can express ambivalence or hostility toward such an admission, as poignantly illustrated by Elijah Anderson's depiction of "face work" between groups separated by both class and race:

> [W]hites of the Village [a gentrifying neighborhood] often scowl to keep young blacks at a social and physical distance. As they venture out on the streets of the Village . . . they may plant this look on their faces to ward off others who might mean them harm. Scowling by whites may be compared to gritting by blacks as a coping strategy. At times members of either group make such faces with little regard for circumstances, as if they were dressing for inclement weather. (1990:220–21)

Or, as final examples, anyone who has ever been deliberately "bumped" or "rubbed up against" by strangers understands full well that these violations of cooperative motility do not signal respect (see, e.g., Gardner 1995; Henley 1977), any more than do the exaggerated helpfulness[22] and intrusive questioning with which the physically disabled are so often besieged (Cahill and Eggleston 1994; Goffman 1963b).[23]

A few pages ago, I suggested that the public realm's overarching principles tended to form a "package" such that if one were violated, there was likely to be a simultaneous violation of one or more of the others. We have just seen some examples of this. When young white males yell "nigger" at and make obscene gestures toward an automobile containing African-Americans, they are breaching not only the principle of civil inattention, but the principles of audience role prominence and civility toward diversity as well. Or, when the physically disabled are offered unwanted help or subjected to unwanted questions, their tormentors are guilty of ignoring the principles of civility toward diversity and civil inattention in addition to those of audience role prominence and restrained helpfulness.

*   *   *

I have been speaking of the patterning of interaction in the public realm and I have described some of the principles (and some of the employments to which those principles can be put) that shape that patterning. What we need to confront now is the fact that these normative regularities are not timeless; rather, they are located in a specific historic period and in specific cultural spaces. When we move out of that period or away from those spaces, the "legal system" of the public realm changes accordingly.

COMPLEX "LEGAL" PATTERNING: SOME LESSONS FROM
HISTORY AND CULTURE

In subsequent chapters, we shall have many occasions to confront the variations that history and culture bring to the public realm—not only to its normative system, but to its characteristic relationships, its pleasure and esthetics, its physical context, and so on, as well. For now, a small sampling of some lessons from history and culture will suffice.

Let us begin with Norbert Elias's work detailing the transformation of "manners" in Europe from the Middle Ages to the present. Elias uses the equivalent of our etiquette books to document both usual behaviors and attempts by various writers (the "Miss Manners" of their time) to "civilize" those behaviors. The portrait of the interactional milieu of earlier Europeans that emerges from this approach is one few of their descendants can view with equanimity. For example:

> One should not, like rustics who have not been to court or lived among refined and honorable people, relieve oneself without shame or reserve in front of ladies, or before the doors or windows of court chambers or other room. (quoted in Elias [1939] 1978:131)
>
> A number of people gnaw a bone and then put it back in the [common] dish—this is a serious offense. (quoted in ibid.:85)
>
> A man who clears his throat when he eats and one who blows his nose in the tablecloth are both ill-bred, I assure you. (quoted in ibid.:96)
>
> It is not decent to poke your fingers into your ears or eyes, as some people do, or to pick your nose while eating. These three habits are bad. (quoted in ibid.:88)
>
> It is very impolite to keep poking your finger into your nostrils, and still more insupportable to put what you have pulled from your nose into your mouth. (quoted in ibid.:147; see also Elias [1939] 1982, especially Part Two; Coser 1978; on the modern requirement for a highly controlled "body idiom," see Goffman 1963a:Chapter 3)

More recent variations are equally telling. Brian Harrison (1971, 1973) has charted the substantial decline of both a tolerance for and—presumably—the occurrence of public drunkenness in England between 1815 and 1872 and a similar story could be constructed for the United States (see, for example, Monkkonen 1981).[24] Bertram Wyatt-Brown's work *Southern Honor* details the unspoken and arcane rules of "gentlemanly" behavior regarding drinking and gambling between and among strangers and acquaintances (violation of which easily eventuated in "duels") in the ante- and postbellum American South (1982:Chapter 13). Carol Zisowitz Stearns and Peter N. Stearns (1986) argue persuasively that the "feeling rules" for the expression of anger in all spheres of life have become increasingly repressive over the course of American history and that, especially after about 1920, anger in the workplace—including public realm workplaces—was not only proscribed but quite successfully controlled. And John Kasson's description of the 1829 public reception following Andrew Jackson's inauguration leaves little doubt that the interactional proprieties of modern Americans stand in considerable contrast to the rough egalitarian manners of their forebears:

> According to one horrified account, "a rabble, a mob of boys, negroes, women, children, scrambling, fighting, romping," swept into the White House, elbowed dignitaries aside, and almost trampled the President himself. In its wake the "mob" left fainting ladies and men with bloody noses, carpets and chairs smeared with muddy footprints, and several thousands dollars' worth of broken glassware and china. The insolence of an egalitarian order, if unchecked, apparently knew no bounds. (Kasson 1990:58–59)

But we do not have to move backward through time to encounter unfamiliar normative arrangements; we can hold time constant and simply move through space. For example, in discussing the principle of restrained helpfulness, I wrote as if what constitutes "help" is unproblematic, something that "everybody" knows. But, in fact, "help" appears very much to reside in the cultural eye of the beholder, as Raymonde Carroll, writing about "cultural misunderstandings" between Americans and the French, details:

> When I (a French person) go to the post office in the United States to find out how to send my packages, I am informed of every possibility, even those I am not considering; I am given all sorts of information about special rates, the fastest means, the least expensive, the useless ("you'd be better off not sending it this way"). Of course, it is not because I am French that I receive such a response, but it is because I am French that I am struck (and sometimes overwhelmed) by the veritable flood of information, this labyrinth through which I am supposed to find my way. And this dizzying feeling hits me almost everywhere, whether I seek information about car rentals, train departures, different types of carpeting, tires, computers or screwdrivers, or about different flavors of ice cream. (Carroll 1988:112)

Similarly, hidden within my assertions about how systems of equality and inequality may be perpetuated is the assumption that "we" can all identify civility or incivility when we see it. Well, maybe "we" can—as long as we stay put. But if we move about in space, as both the impressions (for example, Glazer 1984b; Oldenburg and Brisset 1994) and the systematic observations (for example, Rafaeli 1989) of social scientific travelers suggest, we will encounter very different civility milieux:

> A[n Israeli supermarket] customer said, "In America, all the cashiers smile."
> [The] cashier replied: "So go to America. What do you want from me?"
> (ibid.:263)

And as a final example, we can note that while the principle of cooperative motility implies a universality in the meaning of physical distances between humans, Edward Hall (1959, also 1966, 1974) taught us more than thirty years ago that there are great cultural variations in the meaning and use of space. Stanford Gregory's discussion of contemporary Egyptian spacing rules provides a case in point:

> The notion of "queue discipline," or waiting for one's turn in line, for example at the airport, for bread, etc. is one of the most difficult experiences for Westerners in Egypt. The "rules" are not obeyed in the Western sense because Egyptians "butt in" as they are advocates of the interference rule. To keep your place in line, you must physically impose yourself upon the intruder into your space; if you allow him to take it, he assumes you did not want it in the first place. (Gregory 1985:344, note 7)

The complexities that history and culture[25] bring to our understanding of the public realm's normative regulations are most easily seen when we focus on great distances—whether temporal or spatial. The danger in such a focus is that the blatant will blind us to the subtle. Small distances—from subculture to subculture or from age group to age group, for example—can also invalidate our knowledge about "how you're supposed to behave around here."[26] As we proceed, it will be important to bear this in mind.

CONCLUSION: MISREADINGS AND MISUNDERSTANDINGS

I earlier suggested that the applicability and appropriateness of the public realm's overarching principles does not extend into the territories of the parochial or the private and that when the boundaries between the three realms were unclear or disputed or—even more simply—at border points between them, ruptures in the moral order were not only possible, but were under some conditions probable. Before leaving the topic of the "legal" system, I want to expand on these ideas just a bit.

For actors located in such confusing or conflictual settings, the potential consequences include disorientation, embarrassment, and occasionally even physical danger. But actors who are also researchers, while risking the same consequences, add one more: they may return from the field with data about the rules of one realm, which—in all good faith—they believe to be about another. More specifically, of particular interest to us here, they may claim to be reporting on the normative structure of the public realm when their data are actually drawn from a quite different social territory.

For example, suppose the observer thinks she is standing foursquare within the public realm but, in fact, she is located on a border where the public and the parochial realms come together. Border areas are often especially difficult to identify. Once well inside the boundaries of a highly cohesive and densely acquainted neighborhood—what Herbert Gans (1962) called an "urban village"—it may become quite obvious to a researcher that she is in a place where, quite literally, almost everyone knows everyone else and the stranger, rather than being the norm, is a readily identifiable "spatial anachronism." She may be able to see very clearly that although she is standing in ostensibly public space, she has actually entered another kind of social territory altogether. But if this same researcher is located not well inside such a village, but at a point where it abuts an area of public realm space, her appreciation of just where she "is" may be considerably less keen. Adding to her confusion, the participants in the scene may themselves be confused or conflictual about where *they* "are." Some may be attempting the niceties of civil inattention while others are aggressively defending their turf. A portion of the conflict that Elijah Anderson reports between the residents of a newly gentrifying area of Philadelphia and the residents of an adjoining ghetto ("Norton") may have to do with such boundary confusion and conflict. The middle- and upper-middle-class residents of the "Village" appear to define the streets, stores, and trolleys they share with black ghetto dwellers as public space; the latter seem not to concur:

> For residents of the Village, proximity to the ghetto brings a variety of social complications and opportunities that may require new learning and cultural adaptation. Perhaps the most important adjustment is sharing public institutions. . . . This social situation . . . means being exposed to occasional crime and harassment in the streets and in other public places. . . . Where the Village meets Norton, black males exercise a peculiar hegemony over the public spaces, particularly at night or when two or more are together. . . . The residents of [Norton], including black men themselves, are likely to defer to unknown black males, who move convincingly through the area as though they "run it," exuding a sense of ownership. They are easily perceived as symbolically inserting themselves into any available social space, pressing against those who might challenge them. The young black males, the "big winners" of these little competitions, seem to feel very comfortable as they swagger confidently along. Their looks, their easy smiles, and their sponta-

neous laughter, signing, cursing, and talk about the intimate details of their
lives, which can be followed from across the street, all convey the impression
of little concern for other pedestrians. The other pedestrians, however, are
very concerned about them. (Anderson 1990:138, 164)

Anderson understands that he is talking about behavior at neighborhood
boundaries but he also clearly believes that he observed, and in this passage and throughout is reporting happenings in, the public realm. I am suggesting instead that when he made many of his observations, he may actually have been located on a boundary between the public and parochial
realms and that that border area was itself subject to diverse definitions.

Let us take a second example. The researcher may be well within the
boundaries of the parochial realm but simply not recognize this fact. This
is possible because while some parochial realm territories may be easy to
identify (a close-knit ethnic enclave using a language different from that of
the host society, for example, or an especially insular and hostile-to-out-
siders neighborhood bar), other territories may appear, on the surface, to
be fully public. And the problem this poses for researchers is that many of
us never think to look below the surface. This is, in part, because of our
unfamiliarity with the very idea of "parochial realm." We are members of
a cultural group in which a conceptual distinction between private-public
is an unquestioned given, but as Albert Hunter notes, "[b]ecause it moves
out of the household, the parochial social order is often defined as but
another variant of the public order over and against the private social
order." Such definitions are, in Hunter's view, simply wrong because the
"parochial order is qualitatively distinct from the public order" (1985:235).

But what difference does it make if the researcher "misreads" where
she's been? Particularly if the mix-up attributes parochial realm data to the
public realm, the difference—if Albert Hunter is correct—may be a quite
profound misunderstanding of the latter. Hunter argues that the parochial
realm (again, "order," in his terms) may in contemporary American cities
be *the* most problematic territory in terms of effective social control. Effective social control in parochial space depends upon the operation of local
institutions and the labor of "volunteers"—both of which may be

> difficult to elicit and maintain in the face of increasing expectations that the
> state should provide many of these services. Rising social disorder in urban
> communities would therefore appear to be more the result of a disarticula-
> tion [of state control] with the parochial [realm] than a failure of the state to
> provide social control in the public [realm]. (ibid.:238-239)

In other words, much of the "menace" that we identify with the public
realm (see Chapters 5 and 6) may actually have to do with problems of

<u>social control in the parochial realm</u>. And contributing to *that* confusion may be the reports of researchers who are unclear about the nature of the social territory they are inhabiting.

*   *   *

We turn now to the topic of relationships. How do persons in the public realm relate to one another and how do they relate to the social territory whose "legal" system provides the context for those relationships?

NOTES

1.   See, for example, Cahill (1991), Edelmann (1985), and Gross and Stone (1964).

2.   Those who eschew or are highly critical of normative language often argue that since we "infer the codes and rules from the behavior to be explained" (McPhail 1991:3), such language is essentially tautological. Others object on the grounds that conceiving of behavior as "rule governed" implies a view of social life that is incompatible both with what we know to be the negotiated and emergent character of interaction and with what we know about the constructional and strategic capacities of human beings. Relative to the latter objection, my own view is that unless we postulate rules or principles as being rigidly controlling and constraining, there is nothing about normative language that does violence to the idea of human agency. For example, *Webster's Seventh New Collegiate Dictionary* (Merriam 1971) provides many definitions of the word *rule*, one of which seems especially appropriate in this context: a rule is "a prescribed *guide* for conduct or action; an accepted *procedure, custom,* or *habit*" (emphasis added). On the "rule perspective" in social science, see Edgerton (1985).

3.   See also Seamon (1980) and Seamon and Nordin (1980).

4.   Many nineteenth- and early twentieth-century American etiquette books were, in fact, very much concerned with bodily movement and control in public.

5.   The literature that could be used actually to produce such guidebooks is substantial. Sample studies include Kleinke and Singer (1979), Mazur, Rosa, Faupel, Heller, Leen, and Thurman (1980), Newman and McCauley (1977) on eye contact; Alexander and Federhar (1978), Ryave and Schenkein (1974), Wolff (1973), Wolfinger (1995) on pedestrian behavior; Becker (1973), Cavan (1966), Davis, Seibert, and Breed (1966), Lofland ([1973] 1985) on seating patterns; Cahill (1985), Snow et al. (1991) on avoidance; Levin et al. (1973) on subway behavior; Hraba and Siemienska-Zochowska (1983), Mann (1969, 1973), Schwartz (1975) on queuing; Henderson (1975), Karp (1973), Lilly and Ball (1981), Sundholm (1973) on achieving social invisibility; Gregory (1985), Richman (1972), Shor (1964), Turnbaugh and Turnbaugh(1987), Wallace (1973) on driving interaction; Amato (1981), Latané and Darley (1970, 1973), Messer (1982), Pearce (1980) on helping strangers; Gillis and Hagan (1983), Latané and Darley (1970, 1973), Milgram (1977), Solomon et al. (1981) on avoiding danger; and Britton (1983), Cloyd (1976), Corzine and Kirby

(1977), Gardner (1980, 1986b, 1994), Gmelch and Gmelch (1978), Kenen (1982), Khuri (1968), Whyte (1980), Wiseman (1979) on sociability among strangers.

6. Additional studies of pedestrian behavior include Cary (1978), Collett and Marsh (1974), Lofland ([1973] 1985), McPhail and Wohlstein (1982, 1986), Nasar and Yurdakul (1990), and Sobel and Lilleth (1975). As Clark McPhail has recently reminded us, "Goffman gave detailed attention [1963a, 1971, 1983] to the single pedestrian as a unit of analysis in the study of purposive human behavior and to the pedestrian 'with' as a particularly important unit in the study of purposive social behavior" (1991:1) and most students of pedestrian behavior build upon his published or (in some cases) personally communicated observations. On the size of pedestrian "withs," see Bakeman and Beck (1974) and McPhail (1994).

7. To reduce the complexity somewhat, at this point I will ignore the presence in the public realm of nonhuman animate objects, for example, dogs, cats, horses, pigs, oxen. As we will see later, strangers often interact with one another, at least initially, *through* these "critters." More importantly, perhaps, humans interact *with* these critters, independent of other human beings. On human-nonhuman animate interaction more generally, see Sanders (1993).

8. Goffman may have made an error in defining aspects of the civil inattention principle too specifically, as in his assertion that when passing another on the street "civil inattention may take a special form of eyeing the other up to approximately eight feet, during which times the sides of the street are apportioned by gesture, and then casting the eyes down as the other passes—a kind of dimming of the lights" (1963a:84). For a while, such specificity generated a virtual cottage industry devoted to proving that "it ain't exactly so." See, for example, Cary (1978), Collett and Marsh (1974), Hall (1974), Scheflen (1972), and Wolff (1973).

9. Additional studies of civil inattention include Argyle and Cook (1976), Edgerton (1979:Chapter 8); Karp, Stone, and Yoels (1977, 1991:Chapter 4), Karp and Yoels (1986:Chapter 4), Lofland ([1973] 1985, 1989), Scheflen (1972), Schwartz (1968), and Shapira and Navon (1991).

10. In Chapter 4, we will see that this principle connects with a major type of public realm pleasure: people watching. But as we will also see in Chapter 7, awareness of both the principle and the pleasure by architects, designers, developers, and others has made possible one of the most serious and far-reaching assaults on the public realm, its destruction via its replacement by "imagineered" environments. Additional data testifying to the existence of the principle may be found in Cahill (1985), Gross (1986), Hannerz (1980:Chapter 6), MacCannell (1973), Seamon and Nordin (1980), Silverman (1982), Snow, Zurcher, and Peters (1981), and Tilly (1984:130–31).

11. See, for example, Cloyd (1976), Delph (1978), Fields (1984), Kornblum and the West 42nd Street Study Team (1978), Maisel (1974), and Wiedman and Page (1982).

12. See, for example, Amato (1990), Amato and Saunders (1985), Lofland ([1973] 1985:170, 1989), House and Wolf (1978), Pearce (1980), and Shapiro (1980). There is some evidence that persons target their requests to strangers whom they perceive to be sufficiently "like me" to be unthreatening (Gardner 1980; Goffman 1963a:Chapter 8). For more general discussions of trust and social obligations, see Gouldner (1960), Henslin (1973), Muir and Weinstein (1962), and Shapiro (1987).

13.   It is perhaps the very ordinariness of requests for help that accounts for their being so routinely used as "opening ploys" by persons who actually have a much larger and very different agenda in mind: a "pick-up" for sexual purposes, for example.

14.   On supportive conditions, see, for example, Becker and Horowitz (1972), De Puymege (1983), Fischer (1971), Gold (1982), Issel (1986), and Lofland (1972). On breakdown, see, Gold (1982) and Karp et al. (1977, 1991).

15.   See also Edgerton (1979:Chapter 8), Lofland (1972, [1973] 1985), Martin (1991:106–18), Schwartz (1968).

16.   See also, Lilly and Ball (1980, 1981), Stein (1990). Sundholm (1973).

17.   See also, Barefoot, Hoople, and McClay (1972), Karp et al. (1991:Chapter 4), Linder (1974), Lofland (1972, [1973] 1985, 1989), Martin (1991:106–18).

18.   On signaling displeasure over spatial invasion, see Ashcraft and Scheflen (1976), Becker (1973), Brower (1980), Felipe and Sommer (1966), Fine, Stitt, and Finch (1984), Firestone and Altman (1978), Harris, Luginbuhl, and Fishbein (1978), and Ruback, Pape, and Doriot (1989). On human territoriality more generally, see Friedmann (1989), Jason, Reichler, and Rucker (1981), Lyman and Scott (1967), and Ruback and Snow (1993).

19.   Darley and Latané (1968) has been designated one of the "citation classics" and Latané and Darley (1968) was the winner of the 1968 Socio-Psychological Prize of the American Association for the Advancement of Science as well as the Century Psychology Prize for 1968. For a sampling of the extensive research on bystander intervention and nonintervention, see Crader and Wentworth (1984), Davis (1991), Edgerton (1979:155–61), Gillis and Hagan (1983), Kammann, Thomson, and Irwin (1979), Lau and Blake (1976), Messer (1982), and Solomon et al. (1981). On "professional" interveners, see Palmer (1983).

20.   On "open persons," see, for example, Cahill (1990), Gardner (1980, 1992, 1994), and Goffman (1963a:Chapter 8). Studies of "open regions" include Cavan (1966), Cloyd (1976), Goffman (1963a:Chapter 8), Nathe (1976), and Shapira and Navon (1991). For a not very successful attempt to formulate precise conditions for the initiation of such encounters, see Lofland ([1973] 1985:168–73).

21.   The inferior status of children, for example, receives daily expression in their exemption from civil inattention (see Cahill 1987, 1990).

22.   During the early days of the mid-twentieth century women's movement in the United States, the issue of who was to open the door for whom generated a good deal of conflict and hostility. In the language in use here, we might say that— at least in dealings with those they did not know personally—women defined the exaggerated helpfulness of male door-openers as conveying not courtesy and politeness but the women's inferior status. For an insightful analysis of the conflict, see Walum [Richardson] (1974).

23.   Phillip Davis (1991) provides a sensitive analysis of the tensions generated when expectations about civil inattention, audience role prominence, restrained helpfulness, and so forth collide with emergent proscriptions on methods of physical punishment for children.

24.   If William Hogarth's visual representations bear any relation to reality [and many historians believe they do; for example, Jarrett (1974)], public drunkenness in eighteenth-century London was truly commonplace. For reproductions

and discussions of Hogarth's work, see Gowing (with Paulson) (1971), Paulson (1975), and Wheatley (1909). On changing standards of public drunkenness in nineteenth- and twentieth-century France, see Haine (1997).

25.   A third source of variation—the weather—has been suggested by Jeffrey Nash. See his "Relations in Frozen Places: Observations on Winter Public Order" (1981).

26.   See also Suzuki (1976) on tensions between Germans and Turks generated by differing rules for walking and loitering. Informal observations suggest that in the United States there may even be regional variations in the "rules" of coopera- tive motility. William H. Whyte, for example, has asserted, "People in big cities walk faster than people in small cities" (1988:65) and that "of all pedestrians, New York's are the best. They walk fast and they walk adroitly. They give and they take, at once aggressive and accommodating. With the subtlest of motions they signal their intentions to one another—a shift of the eyes, a degree or so off axis, a slight move of the hand, a wave of a folded newspaper" (ibid.:60). Similarly, colleagues have described noticeable regional variation in driving styles and etiquette (Har- vey Choldin, Debora Paterniti, personal communications).

3

The Relational Web
Persons, Places, Connections

As a *social* territory, the public realm is not merely the locus of rule-guided interactions, it is also the locus of a complex web[1] of relationships. Some of these, of course, are created and have their anchorage in the private or parochial realms, as when lovers attend the theater or neighbors sit in the park. To understand what goes on in public realm space requires that we be sensitive to the presence, frequency, and spatial magnitude of such nonpublic relational forms. This is because, as we saw in Chapter 1 and again at the end of Chapter 2, realms are social rather than physical environments; that is, they are not geographically rooted. What brings one or another of the three types of realms into being are the proportions and densities of relationship types present. A space—even a legally public space—dominated by private or intimate relationships constitutes a private realm; a space—even a legally public space—in which neighborly or work connections are in the majority is a parochial realm; only in spaces—legally public or otherwise—where strangers and/or categorically known others have the relational edge does the public realm exist.

While remaining alert to the presence of exogenous or "alien" forms then, it is exactly the relationships between and among strangers and between and among categorically known others (the realm's "indigenous" connections, as it were) that are of particular interest to us in the first part of this chapter. But while the dominant type of linkage between people defines a realm, it does not fully constitute the realm's relational web. We will want to look also at person-to-place connections, and an exploration of these makes up the chapter's second major section. In a third and final section, we will briefly consider what consequences space and time (that is, culture and history) may have for the presence and patterning of both person-to-person and person-to-place connections.

PERSON-TO-PERSON CONNECTIONS

While, by definition, public realm relationships are those between and among strangers and categorically known others, not all stranger and cat-

egoric linkages are identical. What we want to investigate now are variations within the public realm's indigenous connections.

Relational Types: New Vocabularies

To appreciate the range of indigenous connections found in the public
realm, one begins by jettisoning sociology's traditional dyadic conception
of human relationships. The classic distinction between primary relationships (Cooley [1909] 1962) and secondary relationships (Park 1925; Spykman 1926) works well for many purposes, but too much allegiance to it
can blind us to the existence of more complex realities. For many years
now, scholars who studied social life in pubs, taverns, bars, and other
drinking settings have been struggling with the problems generated by
that dichotomy. If the setting under study were mostly populated by kin
or friendship groups with an independent existence, the researcher could,
without further ado, simply code the relationships as "primary." But what
were they to make of relationships that had limited or no existence outside the setting? What of relationships in which persons who seemed
"close" did not even know one another's surnames, had never been to
one another's homes, were not part of one another's "intimate networks"?[2] In reading some of the older "tavern" studies (e.g., Mass Observation 1943), one is appreciative of the honesty and detail with which the
complicating data are described but one cannot help but notice that their
authors seem unable to get beyond description. They describe complex
linkages but they do not conceptualize them. It was not until the mid- and
late 1950s that new vocabularies for talking about presumptively "secondary" relationships began to appear, and two of the first scholars to
proffer new terms were Fred Davis and, as discussed in Chapter 1, Gregory Stone. In his study "The Cabdriver and His Fare" (1959), Davis identified what he called the *fleeting relationship* as being characteristic of the
tie between these two roles. Similarly, Stone offered us the "personalizing
consumer" who "established *quasi-primary relationships* with the personnel of local independent retail institutions" (1954:42). Over the years, the
referents for the fleeting and the quasi-primary relationship have shifted;
the terms no longer apply to the kinds of linkages Davis and Stone were
talking about.[3] But the terms themselves have not only lasted, they have
spawned numerous offspring. I am not here going to attempt a complete
inventory of the dichotomy-transcending relationships that have been
identified. Some, such as those involving parochial linkages, are not
directly relevant to our concerns. Others overlap with one another and
seem to confuse more than they illuminate. Still others direct our attention
to highly specialized and infrequently observed connections. What I want

to do instead is to look at four subtypes of stranger and categorical relationships that seem especially important to an understanding of the social life of the public realm: the fleeting, the routinized, the quasi-primary, and the intimate-secondary.

Fleeting Relationships. In terms of sheer volume, fleeting relationships are the most representative of public realm associational forms. Occurring between or among persons who are personally unknown to one another, they have, as the name implies, a very brief duration: from seconds to minutes. Characteristically, although not necessarily, fleeting relationships involve no spoken exchanges and when such exchanges do occur, they are, by definition, brief and likely to be in the form of inquiry/reply—in fact, exactly the sorts of interactions we discussed in Chapter 2 relative to the principle of restrained helpfulness: "Can you tell me the time?"/"It's just noon." "Is this where you catch the bus to Stone Park?"/"Yes." "Are you finished with that newspaper?"/"Help yourself." "Is this seat taken?"/"Sorry, it's saved."

The fleeting character of so much public realm social life may, in part, be a function of who is to be found there. Having reviewed the empirical research on the character of that population, Clark McPhail describes the findings from some representative studies:

> John James (1951, 1953) recorded the distribution of individuals and "withs" among 22,625 persons in a variety of public places in Portland, Oregon. He reported that approximately 45% of the members of those gatherings were alone and 55% were "withs," ranging in size from two to six. James Coleman (1962) recorded the distribution of singles and "withs" among 2,897 pedestrians in Seoul, Korea and reported that approximately 59% were alone and 41% were "withs," ranging in size from two to five. William Berkowitz (1971) recorded the distribution of 21,163 pedestrians in 17 cities around the world and reported that 43% were individuals and 57% were "withs." William H. Whyte's (1980) study of persons in New York City plazas and parks established that approximately 61% of the occupants were alone, 39% were "with others." (McPhail 1987:4; see also Bakeman and Beck 1974; Edgerton 1979)

Typically then, in the public realm large numbers of persons, alone or in small groups, find themselves in copresence with large numbers of other persons, also alone or in small groups and have, somehow, to manage that situation. If they are to get about their business, few if any of these loners, dyads, etc. have the time for much more than the briefest of interactions with surrounding others. Thus, a good deal of what we discussed in Chapter 2 regarding principles and their employment—getting through an intersection, choosing a seat, queuing, communicating civil inattention or

territorial defense, and so forth—constitute the interactional nitty gritty of
fleeting relationships.

Routinized Relationships. Just as fleeting relationships are especially
likely among strangers, routinized relationships are especially likely
among categorically known others. Relationships of this sort are what
sociologists are often referring to when they reiterate the classic distinction
between primary and secondary relationships mentioned above. Primary
relationships are presumed to involve the sharing of personal, biographical, idiosyncratic, often emotional aspects of self; in secondary relationships, only very limited categories of self (most usually, an occupational-
instrumental role or identity) are brought in to participate in the
interaction. I am here using the term *routinized* rather than secondary
because I want to emphasize the relatively standardized character of the
interaction in such relationships—the interaction-as-learned-routine. In
some instances the relational routine is so well known to both parties that
they can go through the motions without giving much thought or psychic
energy to the exchange. Robin Leidner's description of the corporately
managed interaction between McDonald's customers and window clerks
is a case in point:

> Workers were not the only ones constrained by McDonald's routines, of
> course. The cooperation of service-recipients was crucial to the smooth func-
> tioning of the operation. . . . [A]lmost all customers were familiar enough
> with McDonald's routines to know how they were expected to behave. . . .
> They sorted themselves into lines and gazed up at the menu boards while
> waiting to be served. They usually gave their orders in the conventional
> sequence: burgers or other entrees, french fries or other side orders, drinks,
> and desserts. (1993:74–75)[4]

In other instances, one of the parties may have a less comprehensive understanding of the role he or she is expected to play, leading the relational part-
ner to do some coaching. John Slosar's analysis of the "problems and adap-
tation of the metropolitan bus driver" provides a case in point:

> Bus drivers have . . . developed special mechanisms for controlling passen-
> gers. . . . Somewhat more sophisticated in terms of controlling passengers is
> the device of strategically positioning the bus at bus stops. Rather than stop-
> ping right in front of a waiting crowd, the driver will stop about twenty feet
> before the crowd so that as people walk over to the bus they become strung
> out in a line rather than all wedged together in the doorway. (Slosar
> 1973:357–58)

Similarly, Fred Davis's classic study "The Cabdriver and His Fare" (mentioned just above) details various strategies that drivers use (with limited success) to coach their customers in the dos and don'ts of tipping behavior (1959:161–64; on cab driver decisions about entering into the routinized relationship in the first place, see Henslin 1973). In yet other instances, both parties may know the general outline of the encounter but be shaky on the details, and here we are at the outer edge of what may be considered "routinized" relationships. Robert Lejeune's studies of the management of the mugging act (1977) and of the experience of being mugged (Lejeune and Alex 1973), for example, describe a dangerous relationship made even more dangerous by the uncertainty-generated fear experienced by both criminal and victim.

While routinized relationships are by no means limited to the public realm (they are ubiquitous in parochial realm work settings, for example[5]), it is also the case that the public realm teems with them: as we have seen, the bus or taxi driver and the fare; the fast-food clerk and the hamburger eater; the mugger and the muggee. Add to those couples the waitress and the customer, the street prostitute and the "john", the beat patrolman and the citizen, the bartender and drinker, the beggar and the potential donor, the street con and the mark, the checkout clerk and the grocery buyer, the vendor and the purchaser, the paramedic and the accident victim, the "squeegee" man and the automobile driver, and so on through a myriad of dyadic pairings.[6]

Both fleeting and routinized relationships are probably most fruitfully analyzed in terms of the *interactions* that they produce. Viewed *as relationships*, they are too brief and/or too standardized to be of any sustained sociological interest. But both are also capable of transformation into quasi-primary or intimate-secondary connections—and these latter are, for the relational analyst, very rewarding subjects indeed.

Quasi-Primary Relationships. As we have seen above, the term "quasi-primary relationship" was invented by Gregory Stone. But it is Jacqueline Wiseman, in 1979 in her discussion of the ubiquitous friendlike linkages that are to be found in secondhand clothing stores, who defined it: an emotionally colored relationship of "transitory sociability," which takes place in public space. If we substitute the word *sociality* for *sociability* so as to eliminate Wiseman's intended connotation of pleasure and enjoyment, what she meant by the term is also what I mean by it. Quasi-primary relationships are created by relatively brief encounters (a few minutes to several hours) between strangers or between those who are categorically known to one another. They are produced when some of the interactional principles we discussed in Chapter 2 are put into use for purposes of, for example, defending territory, generating sociability, or perpetuating inequalities. They certainly *may be* pleasant—as Wiseman suggested—but they need not be and often are not; their essential characteristics are relative brevity (they are "transitory") and emotional infusion.

Among quasi-primary relationships of the emotionally positive sort are those created when actors "generate sociability": the friendly chat between dog owners during encounters on the street or in the park (Robins et al. 1991; Wolch and Rowe 1992a); the exchange of criticisms among pedestrians who have stopped to inspect a large street sculpture (Whyte 1980) or to watch a street performance (Harrison 1984; Harrison-Pepper 1987)[7]; the more extended conversations between seat mates on buses and airplanes (Greenblat and Gagnon 1983), users of laundromats (Kenen 1982),[8] or travelers "killing time" in an airport bar; the enactment of "kinship claims" when gay men "recognize" other gays who are otherwise strangers to them (Gardner 1994); and, of course, the helpful interactions between and among customers of secondhand clothing stores.[9]

As I suggested above, quasi-primary relationships may be pleasant to all concerned, but they need not be and often they are not. Recall the situations described in Chapter 2 when one or more parties to a stranger-interaction were busy "perpetuating inequality": for example, offering sexually loaded commentary on a woman's body, jeering a cluster of homeless men, or verbalizing racial or ethnic slurs. The emotions permeating these brief relationships of structural inequality—hatred, disgust, fear, shame, anger, embarrassment—are hardly associated with pleasantry, as perhaps, given their context, we would not expect them to be. It is important to understand, however, that a quasi-primary relationship can be unpleasant—at least for one of the interactants, if not for both—even when no issues of structural inequality appear to be involved. Singles dances and "body bars," for example, may be the settings for multiple instances of sexual rejection, with the consequent experiences of shame and embarrassment (Beck 1977; Schwartz and Lever 1976). More seriously, minor violations of cooperative motility may escalate into violent exchanges and, in rare (though usually well-publicized) cases, may even result in one or more deaths.[10]

Intimate-Secondary Relationships.   Like quasi-primary relationships, intimate-secondary linkages in the public realm are defined by being emotionally infused. However, unlike quasi-primary relationships, they are relatively long-lasting: running the gamut from a duration of weeks or months to one of many years. Anyone who has done observations in public spaces or who has read the published reports of such observations has most certainly encountered relationships of this sort, for example, among elderly persons who congregate in and enjoy encounters with the other customers of "downtown" restaurants (Pratt 1986); among riders of a commuter bus who develop a "community on wheels" (Milich 1987; Nash 1975); among "racetrack buddies" (Rosecrance 1986); among habitues of nonparochial drinking establishments;[11] among cafe friends (Haine 1997) or coffeehouse patrons (Nathe 1976; Sommer and Sommer 1989); or among gay, lesbian, and straight users of a predominantly gay park (Canavan [1984] 1988); or among elderly women who create support systems in the restroom lounges of department stores (Brent 1981).

The concept "intimate-secondary relationship" is actually the creation of Peggy Wireman, who conceived it as a way to capture the parochial realm-based connections she was observing "among members of the Oakland Mills Village Board, part of the community association in Columbia, Maryland":

> The term . . . at first appears to contradict itself. This seeming contradiction was a deliberate choice; the concept describes relationships that have the dimensions of warmth, rapport, and intimacy normally connected with primary relationships yet occur within a secondary setting and have some aspects of secondary relationships. The dimensions are: intense involvement, warmth, intimacy, sense of belonging, and rapport; mutual knowledge of character; minimal sharing of personal information; minimal socializing; involvement of the individual rather than the family; a commitment that is limited in time and scope and with a relatively low cost of withdrawal; a focus on specific rather than diffuse purposes; consideration of public rather than private matters; and a preference for public meeting places. [Wireman (1984:2–3); see also Kleinman (1981) on "personalized structural relationships"]

Public realm-based intimate-secondary relationships may involve more sharing of personal information, more socializing, and more diffusion of purpose than Wireman's definition allows, but with those minor exceptions, the public realm relational form is a clone of its parochial realm sibling.

The routinized relationships of people who "know" one another only categorically seem especially capable of being transformed into connections of an intimate-secondary sort. The "personalized link" that sometimes develops between retail grocery clerks and their customers (which is, of course, exactly what Gregory Stone was describing) is a case in point (Groncki 1989; Tolich 1993), as is the similar link between bartenders and their regulars (Katovich and Reese 1987), hairdressers and their patrons, deliverymen and shopkeepers (Robertson 1987),[12] employees from adjoining mall stores (Ortiz 1994), or vendors and hustlers who share a street or area (Boggs and Kornblum 1985; Kornblum 1988; Kornblum and the West 42nd Street Study Team 1978). In some instances, the severing of such a relationship—especially if it has been of long duration—may engender both private grief and its public expression, as in the following story of the pharmacist and his elderly customers:

> It was a day to remember at the Arrow Pharmacy on Bernal Heights, and not just because cod liver oil was 25 percent off. I've never seen anything like this, said pharmacist Mike Callagy, who would have dabbed his eyes with a Kleenex if they hadn't all been sold in his going-out of business sale. Inside his small store stood two dozen senior citizens, many leaning on canes and walkers, there to wish Callagy well on his last day before retirement. They had marched en masse from the senior center a block away, slowly, carrying balloons and signs. Two of the women were dressed as giant antacid pills. On a count of three, they proceeded to lift their voices and do, a cappella, what few drugstore customers have done in the history of drugstores: *You are my pharmacist, my only pharmacist, you make me healthy, and happy too, you'll never know, Mike, how much we love you, please don't take my pharmacy away . . .*
>
> *You were a good friend, and oh so helpful, you made us feel better, every day, you'll never know, Mike, how much we'll miss you, that's why we sing this song today . . .*
>
> For 32 years, Callagy ran the pharmacy on Cortland Avenue. He made free deliveries, even on a $2 bottle of aspirin, and he made them when he said he was going to. "He was always on time," said Olga Pellegrini, 86. "And he told you about the side effects," said Josephine Campagna, 92. "They're all supposed to tell you about the side effects, but not all of them do." (Rubenstein 1996)

But grief is not limited to categorical relationships turned intimate-secondary; the links between ostensible strangers may also be deeply—and often, to the person affected, surprisingly—meaningful, as in this relationship between the street person and the businessman:

> [Describing a story by Dena Kleinman in the March 27, 1987, issue of the *New York Times*]: In this story, Ms. Kleinman offers information concerning what she calls "an ordinary paid newspaper notice": "One of NYC's homeless died March 24, 1987, on 40th St. and Madison Ave. He was a cleanup person on the block for over 15 years; may he have a better life." It was signed "E.F. Markham & Company." For some 15 years, on his way to his office on Fortieth Street, Mr. Markham would acknowledge a friendly, but rumpled man who became part of his life. On March 24, 1987, when Mr. Markham took his usual route to work, he saw an ambulance, and the homeless man that he had befriended was sprawled unconscious on the ground with an apparent heart attack. Having continued to his office, Mr. Markham found it impossible to go on with the day. He told his colleagues that he wanted, and needed, to do something. Delores Castro, a junior tax accountant in the office who also knew the homeless man, suggested taking out a notice in the *New York Times*. The two of them did so; they are quoted as saying, "We thought it

would be a nice gesture. We figured he's lived and died and no one would remember he was even here. He was a human being; we figured he should pass out of this life with some dignity." What intrigued Mr. Markham was that this man, whose name he didn't know, seemed to care about the neighborhood; and many people in the neighborhood had an affection for him. A manager of Lamston's, where the homeless man spent his afternoons, said, "Customers bought him socks, coffee, shirts." "Everyone liked him," said a waitress in the Lantern Coffee Shop on Madison Avenue between Forty First and Forty Second Street. "He saw all of us for so many years. My friend Alice is really going to be upset." (Zigun 1990:5–6)

Unlike quasi-primary relationships, intimate-secondary linkages seem to be uniformly positive in emotional ambience. Presumably, the "relatively low cost of withdrawal" that Wireman identifies is the most obvious reason for this situation: why, after all, maintain a highly delimited and fully voluntary connection that is also unpleasant? But—harking back to our Prologue discussion of the "regio incognita" character of so much of the public realm—we must also allow for the possibility that such connections actually do exist but have simply not yet found their way into the research record. As this possibility suggests, there is much about person-to-person connections that we do not know. We know even less about person-to-place connections, the topic we will turn to next. But before we do, two further points relative to the relationships we have just been discussing need to be addressed. The first has to do with the less-than-solid character of these relational forms, the second with the less-than-major status they have been accorded in the social science literature.

Relational Fluidity

While it is, I believe, highly fruitful to view the public realm from the perspective of the indigenous (as well as the exogenous) relational forms that are to be found there, it is also important to bear in mind that the forms themselves are not static, they have the potential for and are often to be found in the process of transformation. That is, they are characterized by *fluidity*. As we have seen, quasi-primary and intimate-secondary relationships are often the end products of what began as mere fleeting or routinized connections; what we have not seen is that the two end products are also capable of reversion to their original forms and that all four types of relationships may be metamorphosized into forms that are indigenous not to the public but to the parochial or private realms. Today's brief encounter—friendly or hostile—that transformed a fleeting relationship into a quasi-primary one may, tomorrow, simply be a fleeting relationship

again. Or, today's fleeting relationship may—in the twinkling of an eye—
become an incipient friendship or romance, as when the daughter of one
my colleagues began dating a young man she met on a subway in New
York. The fact of fluidity adds yet another complication. As relationships
metamorphosize from one to another form, there are points in the process
in which they are neither one form nor the other, but something partaking
of both—and a relationship may "freeze," at least for a time, at one of those
points. The link between the mugger and his victim discussed above, for
example, might better be conceived, not as I have done, as a routinized
relationship, but as some kind of routinized-quasi-primary hybrid. Similarly, Stanley Milgram's (1977) concept of the "familiar stranger"—the person who is not "personally known" but, because of a shared daily path or
round (see below), is recognizable—may signal a connection that exists
somewhere on a continuum between fleeting and intimate-secondary.[13]

This characteristic of fluidity takes on special import when we recall
again that the proportions and densities of the relational types present in
them is what give specific pieces of space their identities *as realms*. A public setting in which the once dominant intimate-secondary relationships
have all been transformed into friendships that both exist in but transcend
that setting may still—legally and commonsensically speaking—be a public setting. But it is no longer part of the public realm. It is also the case that
even settings securely "stuck" in the public realm may have very different
"feels" to them, depending on the proportions and densities of the indigenous relational types. A locale dominated by fleeting relationships has
quite a different ambience from one dominated by intimate-secondary
ones, or dominated by some mixture of intimate-secondary, quasi-primary, routinized and fleeting, or dominated by that quartet with a smattering of parochial and private realm linkages thrown in as well. My guess
is that mixed locales are more "comfortable" places for a newcomer—
especially a lone newcomer—to be than are monorelational locales, but
that is only a guess. Like so much about the public realm, the part that the
relational web plays in creating pleasure or discomfort for the realm's
inhabitants is well beyond the boundaries of what we know.

Challenging the Primacy of the Primary Relationship

Earlier in this chapter, I suggested that an appreciation for the relational
web requires that we jettison sociology's traditional distinction between
primary and secondary relationships. I want now to suggest that a jettisoning of sociology's traditional granting of primacy to primary relationships is also required. I refer here to the fact that, within the sociological
tradition (and in Western thought more generally), there has been more to

the primary/secondary dichotomy than simply a dichotomy. There has been moral evaluation as well. Primary relationships and the social organizational forms they create (families, friendship groups, neighborhoods, tribes, communities) have been judged to be the *best* relationships and organizational patterns—the sine qua non, as it were, for the creation of "healthy" children and "healthy" adults. Witness Michael Hammond's assertion that "there is an innate preference for strong personal affective ties in mating, family and friendship, and that this represents an emotional "wiring" of human emotional life" (1987:2). Conversely, secondary relationships are seen, not as different and equally valuable, but as lesser and inferior (though certainly utilitarian) relational forms. As recently as 1990, for example, Arthur Stinchcombe noted with approval the characterization of Goffman's work as being about "superficial interaction" in public places.[14] The primacy tradition is of long standing and is not easily assaulted, even by those willing to challenge the tradition of dichotomy. At the same time that Gregory Stone was depicting the "personalizing consumer" and her "quasi-primary relationships," for example, he was also gently bemoaning her "need" to find such a poor substitute for more meaningful connection:

> *Without access to either formal or informal channels of social participation* . . . this type of consumer established quasi-primary relationships with the personnel of local independent retail institutions. . . . The quasi-primary relationships she was *forced* to develop on the market compensated for her *larger social losses*. (1954:42, emphasis added)

Nonetheless challenge has occurred; the primacy tradition has been critiqued and that critique has taken two forms. Most commonly, the challenger simply argues that nonintimate relations are worthwhile—that they have value in and of themselves: much of the literature depicting quasi-primary and intimate-secondary linkages represents this form of critique, as does Harvey Farberman and Eugene Weinstein's 1970 discussion of "personalization in lower class consumer interaction." The "regretful" tone of the Stone article has been replaced by a suggestion of appreciation:

> In any event, the general paucity of personalized relationships in consumer contexts increases the importance of those contexts that do support such interaction. For these, as rare as they are, might provide additional enclaves of primacy [i.e., primary-type relationships] which contribute to integration and legitimation. (Farberman and Weinstein 1970:456; see also Prus 1986/87)

Appreciation is more than "suggested" by Mark Granovetter (1973, 1982) when he argues for the "strength of weak ties":

[W]eak ties, often denounced as generative of alienation (Wirth 1938) are here seen as indispensable to individuals' opportunities and to their integration into communities; strong ties, breeding local cohesion, lead to overall fragmentation. (1973:1378)[15]

Many renditions of the positive argument are to be found in works that detail the beneficial functions of settings in which nonintimate relationships abound. What Ray Oldenburg has called "the third place"[16] is "a generic designation for a great variety of public places that host the regular, voluntary, informal, and happily anticipated gatherings of individuals beyond the realms of home and work" (1989:16):

What modern society is losing in its failure to proliferate third places is that *easier* version of friendship and congeniality that results from casual and informal affiliation. As a complement to friendships with strain built into them [read, intimate relationships], there ought to be those in which people meet only to enjoy one another, with an immunity from the costs and impositions that other kinds of friendships entail. What is needed is that optimal staging of selves and sociability that the third place offers and that guarantees that the price of friendship will be rock bottom even while those assembled are in a most enjoyable state. Those who discount this kind of affiliation and this "lesser" form of friendship in favor of more demanding relationships do us no service. Some of the joys and blessings of being alive ought to be as easily achieved as a stroll down to the place on the corner—but there does have to be a place on the corner! (ibid.:1989:65; see also Oldenburg and Brissett 1982)

As I have suggested, most of the critiques of the primacy tradition are of the "positive argument" sort. But there is also a small body of work that makes the challenge by addressing the issue of "negatives" embodied in primary relationships. One can see a hint of this in the passage from Granovetter quoted above. It can be seen also in the work of the political scientist Glenn Tinder, who has written about community as a "tragic ideal" (1980). And David Maines participates in this version of the critique when he reminds us that while "we are more likely to be mugged by a stranger than a friend . . . our friends are more likely than strangers to rape or murder or assault us" (Maines 1989:194). However, it is Richard Sennett, more than any other social scientist, who has taken direct aim at the high value that modern Western thought ascribes to intimate and "authentic" relationships. Beginning with *The Uses of Disorder* in 1970, Sennett put forth the argument that in the modern search for homogeneous community, in our avoidance of the painful confrontations of the city's disorder, we, as a people, were condemning ourselves to retarded psyches—to less than mature psychological lives. Our demands for serenity and authenticity and our locating of them in suburban privatism and intimacy were cause and consequence of our transformation into a nation of psychological adolescents. In the brief essay, "Destructive *Gemeinschaft* " the attack is even more direct:

> What I want to show is that this celebration of intersubjectivity is in fact interpersonally destructive: that is, gemeinschaft relations under the conditions of advanced industrial society are mutually destructive to those who want to be open to each other. (1977a:172)

And in *The Fall of Public Man* (1977b), Sennett's thesis reaches maturation. The contemporary search for "community," our dismissal of urban impersonality as "cold" and "meaningless," our demand for continuous intimacy, are all simultaneously indicators, causes, and consequences of widespread and disabling psychological narcissism and political false consciousness:

> [T]he notion of a civilized existence [is one] in which people are comfortable with a diversity of experience and indeed find nourishment in it. . . . In this sense, the absorption in intimate affairs is the mark of an uncivilized society. (ibid.:340)

We will see more of Oldenburg's arguments regarding the value of the "third place" in the next chapter and again in Chapter 8, where we will also once again encounter the work of Richard Sennett. In the interim—in Chapters 5, 6, and 7—we will get a better sense of just what it is that people like Oldenburg and Sennett are arguing against. For now it is sufficient simply to recognize that, despite tradition and conventional wisdom, not all analysts dismiss the public realm's person-to-person connections as being either superficial or unimportant.

PERSON-TO-PLACE CONNECTIONS

The second major component of the public realm's relational web is person-to-place connections[17] In this section, we will be looking at three "ways" that public realm places matter to people, three forms of connection. But before identifying these forms, let me spend a little time outlining the argument embedded in this discussion. The argument, in a nutshell, is that not only do places matter, but *public places matter.*

From Space to Place: Locales and Emotional Attachment

The idea of "place" is an increasingly important, if somewhat mystical addition to the conceptual cupboard of geographers, especially existential or humanist geographers. As formulated by Edward Relph,

> The essence of place lies in the largely unselfconscious intentionality that defines places as profound centres of human existence. There is for virtually everyone a deep association with and consciousness of the places where we were born and grew up, where we live now, or where we have had particular moving experiences. The association seems to constitute a vital source of both individual and cultural identity and security, a point of departure from which we orient ourselves in the world. (1976:43)

Yi-Fu Tuan offers further clues to the term's meaning:

> "Space" is more abstract than "place." What begins as undifferentiated space becomes place as we get to know it better and endow it with value. . . . The ideas "space" and "place" require each other for definition. From the security and stability of place we are aware of the openness, freedom, and threat of space, and vice versa. Furthermore, if we think of space as that which allows movement, then place is pause; each pause in movement makes it possible for location to be transformed into place. (1977:6)

Put less mysteriously, by "place" geographers appear to be referring to pieces of space that are, individually or collectively, well known or known about. Places are *especially meaningful spaces*,[18] rich in associations and steeped in sentiment.[19]

The element of sentiment brings the geographer's interests into line with those of the urban sociologist's. At least since the 1945 publication of Walter Firey's "Sentiment and Symbolism as Ecological Variables," urban sociologists have acknowledged that pieces of space (more particularly, in terms of urban sociologists' particular interests, pieces of the built environment) can matter to people. But over the years, they have mostly assumed that the spaces that were places, that is, the spaces that mattered in the built environment[20] were largely constituted by home and neighborhood—thus the poignancy associated with Herbert Gans's study of an "urban village" that was about to be "redeveloped" out of existence (1962) and our appreciation for Marc Fried's (1963) account of the displaced who were "grieving for a lost home."[21] The idea that private and parochial realm spaces matter has even become enshrined in regulations governing environmental impact reports: in some localities, at least, proposed developments must be evaluated not only for what they might do to the natural environment, but for what they might do to "communities" (read, neighborhoods) as well.

Nonetheless, this is a rather limited grasp of the idea that space may be emotionally meaningful. Fortunately, it is exactly the work that geographers have been doing of late with the concept of place that seems to me to allow for an expansion of the sociological understanding of these matters. If you will look back at the definitions of place proffered by Edward Relph and Yi-Fu Tuan, you will note that there is nothing in those definitions that restricts "place" to private or parochial spaces. If places are understood to be especially meaningful spaces, rich in associations and steeped in sentiment, then locales—those smaller pieces of the public realm—are unquestionably as eligible for that status as are homes and neighborhoods. The sociological literature does not as yet contain any articles about "grieving for a lost barbershop" nor any ethnographies detailing the destruction by redevelopment of well-beloved bars (journalists, as we have seen and will see, have filled in some of the void). But the relatively scant literature that does exist on the links between people and particular pieces of public space contains strong suggestions of their emotionally meaningful nature. Thus, borrowing from the geographers, I speak here of person-to-*place* rather than person-to-*space* connections.

Relational Types: Toward a Language of Public Realm Place

There is no question but that the connections that humans forge between themselves and places are somehow coupled to the connections they forge between themselves and other humans in those places. For example, hangouts and home territories, as we will see below, are often densely populated by intimate-secondary relationships. But I want to emphasize the modifier *somehow* in the phrase "somehow coupled." We really don't know either the how or the extent or even the necessity of that coupling, so in the absence of such knowledge, it makes sense to try to understand the person-to-place connection in its own right and not simply to subsume it as a by-product of human-to-human involvements. In that spirit, let me offer the following provisional formulation of person-to-place connections: (1) memorialized locales, (2) paths/rounds/ranges, and (3) hangouts and home territories.

Memorialized Locales. By "memorialized locales," I refer to small pieces of the public realm that, because of events that happened and/or because of some object (e.g., a statue) that resides within them, take on, for some set of persons, the aura of "sacred places" (e.g., Swearingen 1997). Of course, not all sacred places are in the public realm (in fact, my guess is that the majority are to be found in parochial realm space). But when they are—precisely because of their "publicness"—they can become lightening rods for feelings of "community" and for expressions of conflict. The "gay monument" in Amsterdam, for example, is an important symbol to the city's homosexual men of political recognition and, thus, of legitimized identity (Mattias Duyves, personal communication). As such, it becomes, at least potentially, an especially appropriate focus of attention for persons wishing to express antigay sentiments. I have no knowledge that this familiar Amsterdam icon has been so abused but there is no question but that memorialized locales in general—war memorials, certain cemeteries or sections of cemeteries, and so forth—are often the scenes of antagonistic demonstrations and are often the targets of anything-but-random vandalism.[22]

Familiarized Locales: Paths/Rounds/Ranges. The concept-cluster composed of paths, rounds, and ranges refers to locales that persons encounter or move through on a daily or nearly daily basis and with which they establish a familiar relationship. The fact that particular actors can be said to have paths, rounds, and ranges both makes possible the repeated fleeting relationships that transform strangers into "familiar strangers" and is often the enabling condition for the establishment of quasi-primary or intimate-secondary linkages (witness the case of the businessman and the homeless person). But even in the absence of these human links, the physical objects that compose and are visible from paths, rounds, and ranges can come, with repeated exposure, to seem like old friends.

Roger Barker (1968; see also Barker 1963, and Barker and Associates 1978) was probably one of the (if not *the*) first scholars to suggest that the paths that people trod daily, their geographical "rounds" of life, and their home ranges are phenomena worth knowing about, but his actual empirical work was done in a small town—a parochial realm setting in my terms. Later researchers certainly recognized the applicability of Barker's ideas for understanding even urban behavior patterns [see, for example McCall and Simmons (1982) on "home ranges" and Goffman (1983) on "daily rounds"] but that recognition has not resulted in any significant effort actually to observe people as they move through public space [Chapin (1974) is an important exception; see also Giddens (1984)].

But we do not really require a fully developed research record to know that familiarized locales exist, to know that people get attached to the spaces that are part of their daily routines. We know these things from our own experiences or from the experiences of our friends or neighbors. Recently in my small city, for example, a locally owned grocery store permanently closed its doors for reasons that were never made entirely clear. The Letters to the Editor section of the local newspaper was flooded with letters—both before and after the closure—testifying to the important place the market had had in the writer's "round of life." The following letter, though from someone who no longer lives in the city, is nonetheless typical in both its "plot line" and emotional ambience:

> I wept. It was weird. A friend of mine sent me a copy of [local columnist's] column (January 14, 1996) about the closing of State Market, and when I started to read it aloud to my wife, Dawni, I just choked up and wept. It may be strange for a grown man to cry over the closing of a store, but during the nine years while I completed my studies at the university, we lived next door to State Market. Those people were close friends. The market was an extension of our kitchen: someone in our family of four shopped there just about every day. They fed my children, as it were. . . . [Local columnist] expressed it perfectly when he described this closure as a "death in the family." (*Davis Enterprise*, January 30, 1996).

The responses of people on the street to the newspaper's roving reporter question—"What do you think about the announcement that State Market is closing?"—elicited briefer but emotionally similar responses:

> I was devastated. I live two blocks away. These people are family. It's horrible. I am very depressed. I think it's ridiculous. It's a great little market. I'm really sad. I was really shocked to see it. I always come here for fruits and vegetables. (*Davis Enterprise*, January 7, 1996)

In this instance, the removal of a locale occasioned for many people the necessity for a change of pathways, an alteration of home ranges. We know from Peter Marris (1974) that all changes, even those that may appear to outsiders as trivial, can be experienced as loss. So it is not surprising that citizen response to the market's departure frequently resonated, as in the examples above, with a sense of grief.[23] But I suspect that even lesser alterations may often be met with feelings of sorrow. For example, again in my city, a small, locally owned and highly rated restaurant also recently went out of business. I did not actually patronize this restaurant with any great frequency; on average I probably went there no more than once or twice a year. But the restaurant was, for me, an important element in the fabric of my city's "downtown"—an area that is very much a part of my "home range." It gave me pleasure to know the restaurant was where it was, I liked glancing in its windows and smelling the aromas that came out its door. I feel sad, and a bit angry, that it is gone. A small loss, perhaps. Nothing earthshaking. Nothing tragic. But a loss nonetheless.

When we do turn to what we know from the research record, we find that the people and their familiarized locales we know most about are—

perhaps unsurprisingly—the homeless. David Snow and Leon Anderson, for example, detail the morning segment of some typical daily rounds of Austin's homeless men:

> The men stack their mats at the back of the room and amble outside to the breakfast line under the red-and-white Salvation Army sign. . . . It will be dark for another hour, an hour most of the men will spend waiting on the sidewalk. Groggy and withdrawn, they stand quietly in the breakfast line or walk around to the side of the building to relieve themselves. . . . By a quarter past five the first group of men are let into the dining room and seated shoulder to shoulder in front of already dished-up plates. . . . At a quarter to six a few weathered old men, barely able to stand at this time of day, stumble off into the darkness to find a business doorway, a vacated building, or some other sheltered spot in which to go back to sleep. The younger men, especially the recently dislocated and the straddlers, head out to look for work. By half past six they have deserted the Sally for the day. . . . By 8:30 or 9:00 A.M., most of the homeless who will find wage labor for the day are out on jobs. The rest—the unlucky job seekers and those who are too discouraged to look for work—have turned their attention to other ways of making do. Some have hiked three miles north to the city's two plasma centers, a few have wandered over to the main branch of the city's public library—more to escape the elements than to read in peace—others have drifted to the park along Town Lake, some are just hanging out on selected corners killing time, and still others have begun to make their way to a local charity that hands out sandwiches on weekday mornings. (1993:74–76)[24]

As this example suggests, the mapping by researchers of the paths and rounds and ranges of the homeless is proceeding apace. But physical mapping is not being matched by emotional mapping. Just what array of sentiments attach to these familiarized locales is not clear. Certainly fear, unease, distrust seem likely sentiments, as Michael Stein and George McCall tell us:

> For whatever reason a person may stay in the streets, a sense of distrust prevails. The streets are much less under the control and supervision which characterizes shelters. Although in some regards this may be viewed as a benefit, it also exposes one to greater potential danger, which in turn can create an aura of distrust. A former veteran of the street with whom we have talked and "toured" told us he would abandon any place if others began to hang around the vicinity. . . . In another case, a man who had established himself on a loading bay of an abandoned warehouse—a place where he slept on a nightly basis for several weeks—suddenly moved on when a couple occupied the inside of the building. (1994:88; see also Anderson, Snow, and Cress 1994)

Whether these feelings are sometimes or even usually mixed with more positive ones, we do not know. Certainly Stein and McCall's description of one welcoming setting suggests at least the possibility of warmer sentiments:

> [A] branch of the public library is frequented by many of the homeless, due to management's "open door policy," a reflection of the open, public nature of the place. So typical was the presence of homeless persons in this locale that, for a time, the library sent representatives to monthly staff meetings of shelters. (ibid.:83)

One wonders, then, if, despite the overall harshness and danger of their environment, the removal (whether via redevelopment or social control) of "spots" (Stein and McCall 1994) in their home ranges—such as downtown benches or sections of parks where they had congregated—might not engender in the homeless some of the same sense of loss, the same feelings of grief experienced by the domiciled when some of *their* favorite "spots" are no more.

Hangouts and Home Territories. The one person-to-place connection that *has* been the recipient of much social science attention is that between people and their hangouts—or, to use more scholarly language, their "home territories." The original articulation of the concept (borrowed, admittedly, from animal studies) is to be found in Stanford Lyman's and Marvin Scott's 1967 piece "Territoriality: A Neglected Sociological Dimension":

> Home territories are areas where the regular participants have a relative freedom of behavior and a sense of intimacy and control over the area. Examples include makeshift club houses of children, hobo jungles, and homosexual bars. Home and public territories may be easily confused. In fact "the areas of public places and the areas of home territories are not always clearly differentiated in the social world and what may be defined and used as a public place by some may be defined and used as a home territory by others" [Cavan 1963]. Thus, *a home territory that also may be used as a public one is defined by its regular use by specific persons or categories of persons and by the particular "territorial stakes" or "identity pegs" that are found in such places.* (1967:238–38, emphasis added)

As this extract makes clear, Lyman and Scott by no means restricted home territories to public space and they recognized, drawing upon the work of their colleague and contemporary Sherri Cavan (1963, 1966), that when home territories did exist in public space, the exact character of the setting might become somewhat fuzzy. This is, of course, the point mentioned above: if home territory relationships to a space are established by people who also have intimate-secondary relationships with one another (which is frequently the case), and if the density of those relationships gets very high, the space—however legally defined—is no longer in the public realm.[25] However, as the Cavan quotation also makes clear, "what may be defined and used as a public place by some may be defined and used as a home territory by others." That is, at any given moment in a public realm locale people may be present who are in the locale for the first time, people who occasionally enter it, people who use it regularly but not frequently, people for whom it is very much a home territory, and all kinds of folks "in between."

The kinds of space that can serve as home territories are remarkably varied: multiple blocks of New York's West 42nd Street for the areas' hustlers, dealers, touts, and con men (Kornblum 1988);[26] street corners (Liebow 1967; Whyte [1943] 1993); a cafeteria for the regulars at *Slim's Table* (Duneier 1992); pornographic bookstores (Stein 1990); and, of course, bars (Anderson 1978; Cavan 1966) and coffee houses (Nathe 1976; Shapira and Navon 1991), among many other possibilities. What appears to be *not* variable is the emotional strength of the relationship; a home territory linkage is among person-to-place connections what an intimate-secondary relationship is among person-to-person connections:

> "I've been coming here [a long-established coffeehouse on Berkeley's Telegraph Avenue threatened by the loss of its lease] twice a day for 20 years. It's my office away from City Hall," said City Councilwoman Carla Woodworth, as she walked out the door, cappuccino in hand. "There's something about this place that feels like home to all of us. A lot of poets and politicians have held court here. Other coffee shops just don't foster that." . . . "This place" [said Landmark Preservation Commissioner Pamela Grove] "has provided an anchor in the community. All of the issues that have been important to the city have been discussed at the Med. It's been a forum for people. It has a resonance of intellectual pursuit. . . . I was stunned to hear they were moving. It was like hearing that the Campanile was going to be torn down." (Wells 1993)

*   *   *

We will be hearing much more of home territory connections as well as of other components of the public realm's relational web when, in the next chapter, we turn our attention to the topic of the realm's available pleasures. For now, however, as a last matter in this chapter, we want briefly to consider what effect space and time—culture and history—might have on person-to-person and person-to-place connections.

OPPORTUNITY AND THE RELATIONAL WEB:
TIME, SPACE, AND CHANGE

Most simply put, culture and history alter the "opportunity structure" for the development of both person-to-person and person-to-place connections. For example, if in Culture A or Time Period X, people spend a smaller proportion of their everyday life out in public than do the people in Culture B or Time Period Y, then they simply have less opportunity to develop public realm relationships. And such variations most certainly do occur. As we saw in Chapter 1, pre-eighteenth-century city dwellers appear to have been "out and about" in public far more frequently and regularly than are their modern counterparts (especially those in the so-called "developed nations") and thus were far more available for fleeting and other forms of relationships. On a less sweeping historic scale and looking only at the data for northern Europe and North America, we can note that with industrialization, daily toil was first lengthened and intensified—in many settings thereby reducing the time available for being anyplace but at work (Thompson 1963). But as the laboring day was gradually shortened, young working men and women increasingly used their "leisure time" not to return to the private spaces of family life, but to enjoy the pleasures of the street, the amusement park or fair, the saloon, beer garden, cabaret, the music hall, or the movies.[27] As such, the opportunity structure for participating in the relational web available to them was much enlarged. Similarly, as we move through space, that is, as we encounter differing cultural groups, we will again find differences in opportunity structures. Thus, again as we saw in Chapter 1, the historian Donald Olsen's argument in *The City as a Work of Art* (1986) that nineteenth-century London was far more "domestic" than were Vienna and Paris in the same period is another way of saying that in these latter cities, for whatever reason, private space represented a smaller proportion of the "everyday life space" of the inhabitants than it did in London—and consequently, for the Viennese and Parisians, the possibilities for public realm relationships were larger than they were for Londoners.

The sheer possibility for participation in the relational web may vary historically and culturally not simply in quantitative terms, as in the above discussion, but qualitatively, as well. That is, possibilities may vary because some kinds of spaces are differentially available, either in general or to particular populations. Thus, the quasi-primary relationships established among mostly unacquainted elderly women that Ruth Stumpe Brent (1981) found in public restroom lounges in "a northern midwestern city" (discussed above) could not emerge until restroom lounges appeared, and restroom lounges did not appear until nineteenth-century European and North American bourgeois merchants, interested in attracting middle-class women to consumerism, invented the department store with all its various amenities (Barth 1980; Hutter 1987; Miller 1981).

When we find a feature of human social life that is culturally and historically highly variable, we may also be witnessing a feature that is highly vulnerable. Thus, scholars like Ramon Oldenburg and Dennis Brissett who value such phenomena as "hangouts" (1980, 1982; Oldenburg 1989) and the relationships (and pleasures) they make possible also worry about their extinction:

> Once upon a time, American society seems to have had equivalents of the coffeehouse, places where ordinary people—men, at least—could find the conviviality Addison described, the "innocent and cheerful conversation," the "very useful" something that offered respite from work. There were, for instance, the long benches that small midwestern business places used to provide on either side of their entrances for the "sunshine club." There was the local tavern, as well as the small-town express office and the corner drugstore. Today, the neighborhood tavern survives, but most other places of its type are gone. . . . The hangout is important for what it symbolizes to us; a kind of pure, freewheeling sociability, uncontaminated by status, special purposes or goals. If there is a malaise in America, we believe it can be partially attributed to the lack of such places. (Oldenburg and Brissett 1980, p. 82)

Oldenburg and Brissett have reason to be concerned. The Anglo-American historical record is replete with locales that no longer exist or exist only in very altered form, as for example, the amusement park (Kasson 1978), the pleasure garden (Wroth [1896] 1979), the beer garden (Peiss 1986), the cabaret (Erenberg 1981), the saloon (Duis 1983; Noel 1982), and the music hall (Bailey 1986). We will have more to say about threats to the relational web in Chapters 6 and 7. But now, let us turn to a consideration of the sociability pleasures Oldenburg and Brissett extol and as well as of pleasures of other sorts.

NOTES

1.   I am here using the term *web* rather than the more familiar *network* because the latter—as a consequence of the careful work of "network analysts"—has moved from the status of loose adjective that would be applicable here to precise technical term that is not—but see Cohen (1980) and Miller (1986). On network analysis more generally, see Fischer 1982b), Wellman (1988), and Wellman and Leighton (1979).

2.   Students of intimate or private relationships have also encountered difficulties with the dichotomy, as in Helena Lopata's (1965) discussion of the "the secondary features of a primary relationship."

3. Davis's "fleeting relationships" are, in the terms used here, "routinized relationships." Similarly, what Stone meant by "quasi-primary," I refer to as "intimate-secondary."

4. The importance of knowledge of interactional "rules" applicable to routinized relationships *in such relationships* is emphasized by Leidner's account of the problems McDonald's had when they first opened an outlet in Moscow in 1990:

> Moscow's citizens did not find the system immediately comprehensible. They had to be persuaded to get in the shortest lines at the counter, since they had learned from experience that desirable goods were available only where there are long lines. (1993:75)

5. The literature on routinized relationships in parochial realm settings is abundant. See, for example, Czepiel, Solomon, and Surprenant (1985), Danet (1973), Jackall (1977), Katz and Danet (1973a, 1973b), Mennerick (1974), Prus (1989a, 1989b), Prus and Vassilakopoulos (1979), Stinchcombe (1990), and Valdez (1984).

6. On the waitress and the customer, see Butler and Snizek (1976), Spradley and Mann (1975), and Whyte ([1949] 1973a, [1946] 1973b). On street prostitutes and "johns," see Carmen and Moody (1985), Miller (1986), and Riccio (1992). On the beat patrolman and citizen, see Delano (1984) and Rubinstein (1973). On bartenders and drinkers, see Cavan (1966). On beggars and donors, see Gmelch and Gmelch (1978), Lee and Link (1995), and Snow and Anderson (1993). On street cons and their marks, see Mauer (1962) and Miller (1986). On checkout clerks and grocery buyers, see Ogbonna and Wilkinson (1988), Rafaeli (1989), and Tolich (1993). On vendors and purchasers, see Bennet (1984), Fields (1984), and Spalter-Roth and Zeitz (1986). On paramedics and victims, see Palmer (1983). And on the "squeegee man" and the driver, see Kaplan (1994).

7. Sometimes street performers or other public "events" generate something more complex than mere sociable dyads. When larger groups are involved, they may create what Clark McPhail (1994) calls "temporary gatherings," which form themselves into "arcs and rings."

8. Kenen's description of laundromat interaction is eloquent testimony to the complexities of understanding the relational web in presumptively public space. Some of her interactants are neighbors who also know one another in other neighborhood settings. When these relationships dominate, the laundromat is, of course, a piece of the parochial realm. But she also observed interactions among people who had not met before and who were not neighbors to one another. When these relationships dominate, the laundromat is a piece of the public realm.

9. I have previously labeled the interactions in such relationships "conventional encounters" ([1973] 1985:168–73). However, in an analysis of "warm relationships" among strangers in Amsterdam, Thaddeus Muller (1995) has demonstrated that stranger encounters may take on a quasi-primary character even when there is no verbal exchange between the interactants and that these exchanges often transcend the boundaries of what many people would describe as "conventional." See his discussion of the "touching relation" and the "eye contact relation."

10. See, for example, Glaberson (1990) and Johnson (1987a, 1987b).

11. Of course, many drinking establishments cater to a parochial realm clientele; in some instances (a neighborhood bar, for example) such a clientele may

dominate the setting during all the hours the setting is open; in other instances it may do so only at certain periods of the day or night (at the end of shifts, for example, in taverns located next to manufacturing plants). Perhaps because of societal concerns with alcohol "abuse," perhaps because of a general distrust of public realm "playfulness" (see Chapter 5), perhaps simply because they are easy to study, drinking establishments and the relationships that develop within them are the subjects of innumerable researches. See, for example, Cavan (1966), Clark (1981), Clinard (1962), Gottlieb (1957), Katovich and Reese (1987), LeMasters (1973, 1975), Kingsdale (1973), Macrory (1952), Mass Observation (1943), Popham (1978), Reitzes and Diver (1982), Richards (1963/64), Roebuck and Frese (1976), Roebuck and Spray (1967), Smith (1985), Sulkunen (1985), Thomas (1978), and Thomas and Kramer (1985).

12.   A small item in a Herb Caen column in the *San Francisco Chronicle* of December 4, 1991, provides a wonderfully wacky example of such a relationship, apparently in the early stages of formation:

> Scott McKellar heard this cosmopolitan superette dialogue in a mom'n'pop grocery store on Nob Hill, Mr. Woo at the cash register. Enter breadman, saying, "Como esta?" Mr. Woo: "Mezza mezza." Breadman: "Samo-samo, eh?" Mr Woo: "Just like downtown." Breadman: "Ten today?" Mr. Woo: "Right on, brother."

13.   On the general complexities of conceptualizing stranger relationships, see Karp et al. (1977:Chapter 4, 1991:Chapter 4) and Lofland ([1973] 1985:Chapter 1).

14.   See, further, Alexander (1973:245–46), Lofland (1983 and the references therein), Lynch (1989), and Watson (1958)).

15.   While network analysts have certainly uncovered evidence for the utility of weak ties [e.g., Warren (1981), Wellman (1981), Wellman and Wortley (1990), but see Gans (1974) for a contrary view], they have taught us less than we might expect about their emotional weighting. This seems largely a function of the methodology itself: the complexities involved in laying out networks of close and not-so-close relationships is considerable; to be able to identify nonintimate but personally meaningful others would be a formidable task indeed (Barry Wellman, personal communication).

16.   Many of the settings Oldenburg designates as "third places" are, in my terminology, "locations"—small pieces of the parochial realm—rather than those small pieces of the public realm I have called "locales." But the case he makes for nonintimate relationships is relevant to both locations and locale.

17.   This is a sparse literature, primarily, I suspect, because—similar to the situation relative to primary relationships and primacy—social scientists have tended to grant far more social psychological import to private (and, to a lesser degree, parochial) settings than to public ones. James Duncan's almost "off hand" assertion, "Private spaces are the most closely associated with an individual's identity. The home is an important part of one's self. Impersonal, highly public places do not usually constitute an integral aspect of an individual's identity" ([1978] 1983:96) provides a casebook example. But see Proshansky (1978).

18.   A simpler, but to me less satisfactory definition of place is provided by Setha Low and Irwin Altman: "Place . . . refers to space that has been given meaning through personal, group or cultural processes" (1992:4). The problem here is

that it is hard to imagine any space that a human might encounter not being given meaning by that human. Without the imputation of meaning, there can be no action since humans have to define objects (including pieces of space) in order to act in or toward them. So, from an interactionist point of view, the only space without meaning is space that no human being has ever either encountered or imagined—and that is certainly not what the geographers are talking about. Rather, as the quotes from Relph and Tuan suggest, the critical component of "place" is sentiment. On place, placelessness, and place attachment, in addition to the works already cited, see Altman and Low (1992), Altman and Zube (1989), Datel and Dingemans (1984), Guest and Lee (1983), Hiss (1990), Jackson (1994), Milligan (1998), Steele (1981), and Walter (1988). On person-physical environment linkages more generally, see Stokols and Shumaker (1981) and Weigert (1991).

19. Oddly enough, in the extant literature, the emotions associated with "place" are generally positive ones [but see Ahrentzen (1992) for an important exception]. Of course, memorial or "commemorative places" may represent events involving great suffering and horror, but the feelings such settings are presumably intended to evoke are far more positive: honor for the sacrificed dead, resolution that such horrors will not occur again, awe at the human capacity to survive, pride over expressions and acts of courage, and so forth.

20. Interestingly enough, among environmentalists and even among some geographers, the term *place* is largely restricted to pieces of the natural environment. As the urban ecologist Alan Durning has commented,

> Deep ecologists like Wendell Berry write beautifully about "place," and about how, if we can reconnect to a particular place, we can regain an immediate sense of responsibility for our natural environment.... But they're always writing about rural or wilderness areas. Most people are in cities and suburbs. So what does "place" mean for us? (quoted in P. Roberts 1996)

21. On neighborhood as place, see also Feldman (1990) and Rivlin (1982).

22. The literature on "sacred places" per se—especially war and other nation-state-level monuments (for example, the Vietnam Memorial)—is, of course, considerable (see, for example, Hubbard 1984; Reynolds 1988; Steele 1981; Tuan 1974, 1977; Walter 1988, and the extensive references contained therein). But most of this work is concerned with matters of architectural style, artistic intent, or semiotically derived "meaning" and only to a lesser extent with the connections that are forged between place and person. The exceptions are mostly represented by geographers who have shown considerable interest in pieces of the natural environment that have been imputed auras of sacredness. However, the kinds of everyday, small-scale, non-tourist-oriented public realm spaces (locales) I have in mind here have largely been ignored.

23. The market was certainly the setting in which intimate-secondary relationships developed between employees and customers—as the language used in the above quotes testifies. It was also a setting in which encounters between people connected in the private or parochial realm might take place. Nonetheless, given the dominance of stranger and categorical relations within it, the market was very much a locale—very much a piece of the public realm.

24. See also Baxter and Hopper (1981), Duncan ([1978] 1983), Levine (1990),

Rowe and Wolch (1990), Spradley (1970), Stein and McCall (1994), and Wolch and Rowe (1992b).

25.   Cavan's 1963 publication, "Interaction in Home Territories" (which is what Lyman and Scott are quoting), as well as her 1966 *Liquor License* and my own *A World of Strangers* ([1973] 1985) discuss this transformational possibility. See also Katovich and Reese (1987), LeMasters (1973, 1975), and Roebuck and Frese (1976).

26.   This is an area that has recently been "sanitized" (see Chapter 7) precisely for the purpose of destroying its many home territory connections.

27.   See, for example, Bailey (1986), Erenberg (1981), Kasson (1978), Peiss (1986), Rosenzweig (1983), and Walton and Walvin (1983).

4

A City "Garden of Earthly Delights"
Esthetic and Interactional Pleasures

INTRODUCTION: PLEASURES IN PUBLIC?

Within Anglo-American thought, there exists a very strong and persistent theme of antiurbanism (to be discussed in Chapter 5) and nestled within *that* theme is a subtheme expressing a particular animus toward public space. Anticipating the argument of the following chapter just a bit, let me suggest that among people who "buy into" the long-standing Western tradition of antiurbanism, the coupling of the words "pleasures" and "public" is oxymoronic—unless, of course, by "pleasures" we refer exclusively to those that are "sinful" and "depraved" or unless, as some do, we simply define *all* public pleasures *as* sinful and depraved. Nonetheless, whether because they are oblivious to or because they take added pleasure from the disapproving stares of the critics, many people do, in fact, find the city—especially the city's public realm—to be a "garden of earthly delights."[1] We have already seen some of this in preceding chapters. When people "use" the legal system of the public realm to initiate sociable interactions, they presumably do so because they find those interactions pleasurable. Similarly, many quasi-primary relationships and all intimate-secondary connections of which we have knowledge would simply not exist if they were experienced as painful or distasteful or disgusting. And, of course, spaces that become places are mostly, though admittedly not exclusively, associated with enjoyment, with satisfaction, with gratification—associated, in short, with pleasure. The goal of this chapter, then, is to build upon what has been said in preceding chapters, but to explore this matter of public realm pleasures more directly and in greater detail than I have done up until now.

Just as relational forms that are actually native to other realms can be found within the public realm, so can forms of pleasure. But our interest here is not in exogenous pleasures; rather we shall concentrate on forms for which the public realm seems to provide an especially favorable environment. Five of these—(1) perceptual innuendo, (2) unexpectedness, (3) whimsy, (4) historical layering/physical juxtaposition, and (5) crowding/stimulus diversity/spectacle—are best understood as forms or sources of *esthetic pleasure*.[2] Four others—(1) public solitude, (2) people-watching, (3) public sociability, and (4) playfulness/frivolity/fantasy—are forms or sources of *interactional pleasure*. After reviewing these forms, I conclude with some remarks about links between such pleasures and the character of the built environment.

SOURCES OF ESTHETIC PLEASURE

By esthetic pleasure, I am referring to the experience of enjoyment occasioned by certain (mostly) visual qualities of the built environment.[3] This is hardly unexplored terrain. Designers, architects, landscape architects, urban planners, environmental psychologists have all sought to understand why some human-made landscapes seem to attract while others seem to repel. What is it about modernist architecture, for example, that causes so many people to describe it as "bleak," "inhuman," "boring," "unfriendly"? Conversely, as another example, what is it about extant pre-twentieth-century, especially pre-nineteenth-century, urban forms that accounts for so many people describing them as "warm," "inviting," "human-scale," "interesting"? Why are Paris and Rome tourist meccas while Brasilia (see Illustration 7.6) is not? Why do the hard surfaces of medieval towns and cities strike many of us as "softer" (see Illustration 4.1) than the hard surfaces of contemporary megastructures (see Illustrations 7.4 and 7.11)? Are these differences in esthetic perception historically and culturally shaped and, if so, what is the character and extent of the shaping? Given the range of scholars asking such questions, we should not be surprised to find that the literature that attempts to answer them is enormous.[4] Some of that literature is highly technical and prescriptive and some of it starts with assumptions about the pan-human applicability of esthetic principles that those of us attuned to cultural and historical variation find troubling, to say the least. Much of it is also deductive: prescribed designs are simply applications of the "universal esthetic principles."

Happily for those discomforted by space- and time-transcendent claims, within the larger genre there is also a considerable body of work that begins not with assumptions about universal esthetics but by observing pieces of the built environment that people seem to enjoy and then attempting to *infer* esthetic principles from those observations. Given its grounding in specific times and spaces, it is not surprising that this work tends also to be relatively humble about the time-space reach of its inferred principles. Two exemplars of this latter approach are Jane Jacobs and William H. Whyte. Jacobs, as many will recall, suggested in *The Death and*

Illustration 4.1. Rue des Chanoines, Le Mas, France. By Lee Snider/ Photo Images, New York.

Life of Great American Cities that one secret to "successful parks" was to be found in esthetics, and she proposed four design elements essential for such parks: intricacy, centering, sun, and enclosure (1961:103–6). In a similar vein, William H. Whyte, in *City: Rediscovering the Center*, advanced numerous means by which available water, wind, trees, and light could contribute to the design of plazas that would be well-frequented (1988:Chapters 8, 17, and 18). In the following specification of five forms or sources of esthetic pleasure, I am attempting to follow the lead set by people like Jacobs and Whyte. My hypotheses about esthetic pleasures are inferences from my observations of persons in public space who were reacting to some aspect of the built environment and who overtly expressed emotions that I coded as delight, joy, happiness, and so forth. And, since my observations are limited *by* time (ca. 1980 to present) and space (sections of North America and northern Europe) and limited *to* a specific set of persons (the ones I saw), so must my hypotheses be.

Perceptual Innuendo

By "perceptual innuendo, " I refer to the pleasure that arises from glimpsing a small piece of the built environment, a glimpse that suggests that an interesting, exotic, weird, enticing, possibly enchanting social world exists just outside one's range of vision. Illustration 4.2 suggests one kind of architectural feature that may encourage the experience, in this case a tunnellike walkway leading from the street into a more private world. Illustration 4.3 suggests another: a fence and shrubbery shielding most of a private garden from the eyes of those passing by on the street. The presence of alleyways and of narrow streets leading away from major thoroughfares also seems to encourage the experience, especially if the built environment of the alley or side street is sufficiently complex to be only partially graspable when seen from a distance.

I can imagine that sometimes passersby are dissatisfied with mere glimpses and, if they can, penetrate into the "beckoning space," but I have recorded no such instances in my notes. The people I observed simply

Illustration 4.2.   Glimpse from the sidewalk, Tampare, Finland. (photo by author)

Illustration 4.3. Glimpse from the sidewalk, London. (photo by author)

stopped, looked, expressed pleasure over the scene (by facial expression or other quiet sign if alone, in words when with a companion), and then walked on. For some people, at least, perceptual innuendo seems to be the esthetic equivalent of people-watching (see below): one takes pleasure in the very incompleteness of the information one is able to gather exactly because incompleteness gives reign to imagination.

Unexpectedness

There is research suggesting a fairly strong preference for urban places that are "familiar"—if not a familiarity that emerges out of firsthand knowing, at least that which comes from "knowing about" (see, for example, Herzog, Kaplan, and Kaplan 1976). Without in any way challenging the validity of such findings, I want to suggest that, for some individuals at least, the opposite of the quality of familiarity—unexpectedness—seems also to appeal. There is nothing startling in this assertion. As many commentators have pointed out (e.g., Fischer 1976), in discussions of values or preferred qualities it is not always accurate to depict paired opposites as being *in opposition*. Rather, it may be that both are seen as desirable—community and individuality, for example—and the issue becomes not one *or* the other, but how much of one, how much of the other, and in

Illustration 4.4.   Street scene, Bend, Oregon. (photo by author)

what contexts. In any event, unexpectedness does seem to please. Of course, what is surprising to one person is "old hat" to another, so we must recognize that while all five of the esthetic pleasure sources discussed here exist primarily in the eye of the beholder, this seems especially true of the quality of unexpectedness. And that means that the range of physical objects and arrangements that can seem pleasurably unexpected is enormous. Let me mention just a few that I have encountered: a large and extremely fat cat (named "Tiddly") who resided full time in the "ladies loo" in London's Paddington Station; lush rooftop gardens glimpsed from street level in Manhattan and London; a small mews, just off a busy London traffic artery, which was literally erupting in flowers; prostitutes visible through the "picture" windows of their brothels in Amsterdam (especially astonishing to tourists who just "happened upon" an outer edge of the famous red-light district); and the arrival of a cruise boat at a dock outside a restaurant on the Sacramento River.

Whimsy

My *Webster's Seventh Collegiate Dictionary* (Merriam 1971) defines whimsy as "whim, caprice, a fanciful or fantastic device, object, or creation

Illustration 4.5. Prince Albert Memorial, London. (photo by author)

especially in writing or art." That begins to get at what I mean by the term, but Rodale's *The Synonym Finder* (1978) comes even closer. It suggests that appropriate synonyms for whimsy include frivolity, eccentricity, kookiness, nuttiness, capriciousness, oddness. Those words seem to capture the idea pretty well. In my observations, sometimes the whimsical object or arrangement was merely fanciful or frivolous, as in Bend, Oregon's wonderful "street furniture," depicted in Illustration 4.4. But sometimes the terms *eccentricity, fantastic, kookiness* seemed more apropos, or at least that

Illustration 4.6.   Street scene, London. (photo by author)

is what one might infer from viewing the comically disrespectful responses
of American tourists to London's Prince Albert Memorial (Illustration 4.5).

Historical Layering/Physical Juxtaposition

A fourth source of esthetic pleasure appears to be created when urban
areas develop slowly and incrementally and over relatively long periods
of time. When that happens, we see a kind of "jumbling" in the environment. For example, historical periods may become "layered" one on

Illustration 4.7. London square. (photo by author)

another, as when buildings of one era are to be seen cheek-by-jowl with buildings of a very different era and form a kind of panorama of overlapping architectural styles (see Illustration 4.6). One of the most interesting instances of this kind of jumbling that I have ever seen (impossible to convey by photograph) is to be found in the City of London, where a fifteenth- or sixteenth-century (possibly even earlier) church and its burial ground has been almost completely surrounded by twentieth-century office buildings—it can be reached only via a narrow alleyway between two of the modern structures.[5] Jumbling is also to be found wherever physical objects of one sort—those composing the natural environment, say—are juxtaposed with physical objects of another sort—those composing the built environment. I once had the pleasure of touring the waterway system of Stockholm by boat and was struck by the responses of tourists to one "scene" along the way. I assumed at the time (and it still seems reasonable at this writing) that it was the pairing of a very rurallike river, river bank, and bridge with the implicit knowledge that we were, in fact, in the middle of a major and quite high-density city that caused the "oohs" and "aahs." The "things" jumbled do not have to have the strong physicality suggested by these prior examples, however. In Illustration 4.7, for example, what is juxtaposed is not simply the accoutrements of a London city square with the seemingly out-of-place tombstones. My notes suggest, rather, that what many people found pleasurable in scenes of this sort (and

Illustration 4.8.   Street scene, Amsterdam. (photo by Thaddeus Müller, reprinted with permission.

there are many such scenes in London) was the juxtaposing of the world of the living, as it were, with the world of the dead.

Crowding/Stimulus Diversity/Spectacle

Finally, some parts of the built environment seem to evoke pleasure because in their crowding together of people and things and elements and in the diversity of stimuli and the spectacle that are created by this crowd-

ing, there is to be found—at least by some unknown number of persons—
a kind of *visual excitement*, a quality of *electric invigoration*. The range of
scenes with this quality is, as you might expect, numerous and the components that go to make up the scenes are, also as you might expect, varied, as Illustrations 4.8 and 4.9 attempt to convey. What I find especially
interesting about these scenes is their commonplaceness. There is nothing
outre, nothing grand, nothing monumental about them; they are the products of ordinary people going about their ordinary lives in ordinary settings. Despite their ordinariness, however, my notes record that some persons respond to such scenes with expressions reflecting pleasurable
excitement. Of course, the outre, the magnificent, the monumental (e.g.,
Moscow's ornate subway stations, Paris's Eiffel Tower, London's West-
minster Abbey, Agra's Taj Mahal) may also evoke visual excitement. Presumably they actually do so or the "wonders of the world" would not be
so widely visited by tourists. But the point here is that pleasure is not the
exclusive province of grandeur: it resides as well in humble spaces. It also
resides in the commonplaces of everyday interaction. And those commonplaces are our next topic.

Illustration 4.9.   After the market, Helsinki. (photo by author).

SOURCES OF INTERACTIONAL PLEASURES

Some of the pleasures of the public realm, as we have just seen, are esthetic. They derive from a primarily visual apprehension of both the built environment and those who are populating it. These latter also provide another kind of pleasure: that which derives from human interaction. We will here consider four forms or sources of interactional pleasure: public solitude, people-watching, public sociability, and the clustering of playfulness/frivolity/fantasy.

Public Solitude

Writing of the Los Angeles freeway system, David Brodsly points to an interesting feature of the experience of driving it:

> While it may appear far-fetched to compare a peak-hour commute with a stroll down a country road, the freeway has a certain quality that makes driving it the nearest equivalent to such an experience the average Angeleno is likely to have on a typical day. For here, rather than in Griffith Park or along the beach, one receives a daily guarantee of privacy. Safe from all direct communication with other individuals, on the freeway one is alone in the world. You can smoke, manipulate the radio dial at will, sing off key, belch, fart or pick your nose. A car on the freeway is more private than one's home. (Brodsly 1981:42–43)

Automobiles most certainly provide cocoons of privacy—private realm bubbles with a hard shell—but it is not quite true, I think, to suggest that "a car on the freeway [or any high-speed street] is more private than one's home." As we saw in Chapter 2, even solitary drivers are interacting with other drivers—total strangers to them—to create cooperative motility. It *is* true, however, that it is quite possible to find solitude in public. More importantly, it is also true that it is not necessary to be encased in a steel and glass container in order to do so. As we also saw in Chapter 2, one of the things strangers produce in their interactions with one another is privacy. Give off the right "signals" and you can come close to guaranteeing that, however public the setting, however dense the body of surrounding bodies, you can be "alone." What is relevant to our purposes here is the fact that some people appear to take pleasure in this.

I do not know of any study that provides definitive data on people's reasons for choosing to be alone in public but I do know that many observers judge such activity to be "pathetic." A judgment of this sort bears a remarkable similarity to Gregory Stone's assumption that his "personalizing consumer" wouldn't be so if she had any "real" social life (see Chapter 3) and to the views of the urban critics Jane Jacobs describes, who assume people are "on the street" only because they don't have "decent homes" to go to (see Chapter 5). But if we grant that there are real pleasures to be had in creating intimate-secondary relationships out of routinized ones and that there are esthetic pleasures available on the street that are not to be found at home, then it seems reasonable to allow for the possibility that people seek public solitude because for one or another of a variety of reasons they find it enjoyable.

The pleasure may reside in the comfort of being surrounded by the hum of conversation. This is certainly one of the reasons I like to be alone in public and it might very well be the reason some people go to such highly sociable public settings as cafes and bars but remain aloof from the spoken interaction. For example, some years ago two of my undergraduate students did an observational study of a local twenty-four-hour restaurant. They chose this locale for their (course-required) research because they were already in the habit of frequenting it in the late evening (after 10:00 P.M.) to "study."[6] In fact, the place was quite a hangout for students who came there most every night to drink coffee, "study," and socialize. The scene they depicted in the report of their research was a lively one—much calling back and forth between booths, much banter between student-customers and waitresses, much stopping at tables for chats. But there was one behavior pattern in the setting that they found to be anomalous: lone individuals who came to the restaurant every evening, who sat by themselves, and who ignored or turned away all interactional overtures. "Why," they inquired rhetorically, "did such people bother to come in?" After all, they suggested, "If they wanted to be alone, they could simply stay home." Unfortunately, my students did not take this opportunity to ask, but it is not unreasonable to speculate that in this instance, these individuals "bothered" because when one is home alone one cannot be awash in waves of human voices.

Pleasure may also be derived from a sense of oneness with the other inhabitants of a setting. The "joy" that is to be found in some collective behavior episodes or crowd experiences (Lofland 1982) seems linked to such a sense and it was clearly a motivation for customers of a Tel Aviv cafe studied by Rina Shapira and David Navon:

A special group atmosphere pervades the cafe on Israeli Memorial Day. . . . The particular significance of this day stems from the tragic suffering that has fallen upon many families in Israel since the Jewish people renewed its settlement in the area and began its struggle for independence. On Memorial Day sirens are sounded for the public to rise in silent tribute to the fallen.

There are customers who come to Afarcemon especially to be there when the siren sounds. As one of them explained:

> That's great, I managed to get here right on time, before the siren is sounded. I come here every year. Here I have a feeling of togetherness. At home I am alone, and the same happens in the street. It's very important for me to be with other people and to stand with them [when the siren is sounded]. It gives me a feeling of being part of the entire country (Shapira and Navon 1991:113).

A third reason for finding pleasure in public solitude is that when one is alone, one can concentrate all one's attention on another source of pleasure: people-watching (or listening). It is, for example, much easier to engage in unobtrusive eavesdropping (by pretending to be reading a newspaper or book) if there is no companion to provide distracting conversation, as is suggested by one of Thaddeus Muller's Amsterdam informants:

> I like to listen to arguments and predict the way they react. I can be totally involved. I try to move as close as possible to hear everything. Sometimes a sentence will stick with me for a long time. I heard a young man say to his girlfriend: "I do my best, but I can only act the way I feel, follow my instincts." And I thought that makes some sense. (1992:6)

Let us look at this form of "voyeurism" in more detail.

People-Watching

Being alone may facilitate more concentrated people-watching, but one does not have to be alone to enjoy it. For example, in her study of the Lovejoy and Forecourt fountains in Portland, Oregon, Ruth Love found that 54 percent of those who came to the fountains alone and 56 percent who came with others reported "people-watching" as a major activity (1973:191). Similarly, Dutch sociologist Jan Oosterman reports:

> Apart from drinking, relaxing and enjoying the sunshine, people in sidewalk-cafes [in Utrecht] are involved in a lot of activities that have to do with the public character of the setting. The first and by far most important favorite activity of people in the sidewalk-cafe is to *watch people go by*, to be entertained by street life and to inhale the atmosphere of the city. The chairs are always placed toward the street, like the chairs in a theatre are placed toward the stage. Some respondents in my research themselves even compared the street with a theatre. Most users of the cafe are accompanied by a friend and practically all of them like to discuss the appearances of other people who pass by. Generally speaking, one doesn't want to get involved

with anybody passing by. It's mainly the *spectacle* in front of the eye that people come for. (Oosterman 1992:11, emphasis in the original; see also 1993)

The theater metaphor, as we saw in Chapter 2's discussion of the principle of "audience role prominence," is widely used. And it is an apt metaphor. In fact, some locales seem designed to create "audience" and "performers" (see Campbell 1980; Gehl [1980] 1987; Lennard and Lennard 1984, 1987, 1995). The long balcony outside London's National Portrait Gallery, for example, looks down on Trafalgar Square, and in the summer the balcony is thronged with observers keeping a close eye on the hordes of tourists who, gathered together on the "stage" below, are feeding the square's ever-present pigeons.

Some of what seems to be involved in the pleasure of people-watching was suggested above in my discussion of perceptual innuendo and again in the words of Thaddeus Muller's informant. We overhear or oversee just enough to catch a glimpse of enticing real-life dramas; the filling out of the drama is a work of the imagination. Recently a companion and I shared an evening restaurant meal sitting by a window that looked out directly on the sidewalk and street. During our meal, we watched two young people, a male and a female, repeatedly exit and enter a parked car, apparently search portions of the car's interior and trunk, and stand on the sidewalk looking "odd." We amused ourselves that evening by weaving an elaborate story involving drug sales and other nefarious activities that "explained" to our happy satisfaction all the behaviors we had witnessed. Our conversation even attracted diners at another table, who added their own embellishment to the drama. Of course, we were probably 100 percent wrong in our interpretations, but that too is part of the pleasure. These leaps of imagination engendered by people-watching seem to be quite common. One of the difficulties I have when I send my students out to observe in public is that many of them are not content to record what they see. They tend also to record what they "see" with the mind's eye.

Given the widely shared principle of "audience role prominence" and given the ubiquity of people-watching as an activity, it is hardly surprising that for some people, the pleasure of seeing is intensified by the pleasure of *being seen.* Thus, the social occasion known as *the promenade.* Penelope Corfield describes its operation in eighteenth-century England:

Walking . . . was not only a utilitarian necessity but an agreeable form of informal entertainment in its own right. The urban promenade was the occasion for the citizens to sally forth to view the sights and each other: "to see and be seen," in the famous phrase. It was an integral part of city social life. Indeed, it remains so in many urban cultures today. . . . [I]n eighteenth-century [English] towns . . . the main occasions for social walking were on Sun-

★ reclaims some of the wonder + positive aspects of the publicsphere and democracy here for me

days, on holidays, and at special festivities, although the new pastime of window-shopping was enjoyed more frequently. Meanwhile, in London and in the specialist spas and resorts, fashionable society promenaded daily in the season, both in the mornings and the afternoon. (Corfield 1990:135; see also Laver 1958; Lyle 1970; Sennett 1977b)[7]

People-watching—seeing and being seen—may be a ubiquitous activity but it is not, as my somewhat ironic use of the term *voyeurism* was intended to convey, universally approved. The Parisian *flaneur* as a social type, for example, that loiterer, observer, and people-watcher par excellence, generated criticism in the nineteenth century and continues to do so today. And he is the object of criticism exactly *because* he is the detached observer, the rootless outsider who watches the scene but does not participate, the voyeur, eavesdropping on other people's lives (Wilson 1991). Or, as another example, when the people-watching is "girl"-watching, it can be and increasingly seems to be interpreted as harassment. William H. Whyte's depiction of a common New York street scene involving female office workers and men for whom watching them is their "main lunchtime recreation" (1974:28) is, for many feminists, simply one more piece of evidence of women's ill-treatment in public space (e.g., Gardner 1995).[8] Fortunately or unfortunately, depending upon one's social location and consequent point of view, criticisms do not seem to have much effect. As I suggested at the outset, not only does the reproachful stare of the critic not dissuade public realm pleasure seekers, it may even add to their enjoyment.

Public Sociability

Public solitude is, by definition, a lone pleasure. People-watching may be. But public sociability—by definition—involves spoken interaction between and among persons in dyads, triads, and even larger groupings. It is one of the pleasures of the public realm that has been written about extensively. In fact, much of the literature cited in Chapter 3 dealing with quasi-primary and intimate-secondary relationships is about the topic of public sociability.[9] Most studies of drinking establishments, for example, whether written from a disapproving, approving, or dispassionate point of view, spend a good deal of time documenting the sociability that permeates these locales. One such study, Louis Erenberg's *Steppin' Out* (1981), provides a particularly rich portrait of New York City's extensive nightlife scene between the years 1890 and 1930. In this scene, the cabaret, in particular, seemed to encourage interaction among strangers to a degree that middle-class Americans found both new and exciting:

Dining, drinking, talking, and flirting at their seats with members of their own party or with those at other tables, patrons were relaxed and could see

(handwritten margin note: is it really voyeurism? voyeurism? by degrees?)

the performance in a more informal way. . . . The dance floor, the absence of large proscenium arch stages, and the closeness of the audience seated at tables made the room a scene of expressive activity. The entire restaurant became the setting for performance, and customers themselves could not escape becoming involved in the action and spontaneity of the moment. . . . Under these conditions, the definition of the cabaret slowly and subtly expanded from a group of entertainers who worked close to an audience to being a distinctive environment different from a theatrical one. The setting became, as one columnist wrote of a particular establishment, "a friendly environment" where "there isn't a chance of feeling dull or grouchy." (ibid.:124)[10]

Similarly, Ray Oldenburg has argued that one of the major pleasures—perhaps the major pleasure—of the "third place" is verbal interaction. Although, as I have noted earlier, he tends to focus on parochial realm locations like neighborhood taverns and small-town coffee shops, Oldenburg's analysis of that pleasure is equally applicable to locales:

> The cardinal and sustaining activity of third places everywhere . . . is conversation. Nothing more clearly indicates a third place than that the talk there is good; that it is lively, scintillating, colorful, and engaging. The joys of association in third places may initially be marked by smiles and twinkling eyes, by hand-shaking and back-slapping, but they proceed and are maintained in pleasurable and entertaining conversation. A comparison of cultures readily reveals that the popularity of conversation in a society is closely related to the popularity of third places. . . . The rate of pub visitation in England or cafe visitation in France is high and corresponds to an obvious fondness for sociable conversation. American tourists [economist, Tibor] Scitovsky notes, "are usually struck and often morally shocked by the much more leisurely and frivolous attitude toward life of just about all foreigners, manifest by the tremendous amount of idle talk they engage in, on promenades and park benches, in cafes, sandwich shops, lobbies, doorways, and wherever people congregate." And, in the pubs and cafes, Scitovsky goes on to report, "socializing rather than drinking is clearly most people's main occupation." (Oldenburg 1989:26–27)

Whether Oldenburg and Scitovsky are correct about cultural variation in public sociability—or at least about the way in which they have phrased their assertions—is certainly subject to debate. But that many people do, in fact, find it pleasurable seems beyond question.

Playfulness/Frivolity/Fantasy

I suggested above that people-watching, what many would see as that most innocent of human pleasures, is not without its critics. To make the same statement about the triple package of playfulness/frivolity/fantasy is to be guilty of a massive understatement. As we will see in Chapter 5, the play, the frivolity, the fantasy available to inhabitants of the public realm strike many moralists as downright sacrilegious. If I understand these moralists correctly, it strikes them in this way, at least in part, because in their view such pleasures involve a release from "real" identities and responsibilities—from the serious stuff of everyday social life. Now the human tendency to program in such release through carnivals, festivals, fairs, spectacles, spectator-oriented sporting events, and so forth has been extensively studied by anthropologists, social historians, folklorists, and others.[11] Certainly, these out-of-the-ordinary events constitute a segment of the playfulness/frivolity/fantasy pleasures to be found in the public realm. And most certainly, critics have had much to say about the decadence they encourage. But what is of special interest to us here is not the out-of-the-ordinary, but the commonplace. Not the wondrous but infrequent pleasures, but the wondrous and constant ones.

We must grant the critics their due. Even commonplace pleasures—perhaps especially commonplace pleasures—do involve release from everyday selves and everyday duties. For example, given the stranger-filled character of the public realm, it is quite possible to "play" with who one is; quite possible to be involved in relationships in which one or both (or more) parties are not "really" what they seem. For example:

> To play the game [of pretending], one may or may not plan to do so ahead of time. . . . Often, the opportunity to play "just happens" but even when it does, the individual is under no particular obligation to take advantage of it. And since the game is always played with strangers and always in public space, one can often, if things go poorly, simply leave the scene. The essence of the game is a kind of "Walter Mitty" wish-fulfillment. The individual expresses in public for the ratification of surrounding strangers an identity or an aspect of identity that he or she feels cannot be expressed among personally-known others. Thus, for example, the individual may "pretend" to belong to some admired occupational group . . .

> In the friendly darkness of the anonymous bar, how easily does the teaching assistant become a professor; the clerk an executive; the lowly private out of uniform a man of substance. One informant told me that during his stint as an enlisted man in the air force, he would occasionally make dinner reservations under the name of Dr. ———— . Arriving at the restaurant early, he would wait in the bar until the speaker system announced that the "doctor's" table was ready and then walk into the dining room, the oppression of his "actual" status momentarily lifted. Sometimes the game is played in a more subtle, a more inward manner. I refer here to the expression of identity that accompanies being present in the appropriate location and/or dressing for the part. Here the individual makes no verbal claim to the identity in

question. . . . The shy young man, ill at ease and unsuccessful with women, can, at least for a moment, "be" the swinger of his secret dreams by the simple expedient of standing about in a body bar "looking cool." The adolescent female could, in the 1960s, don her "hippie" outfit on a Saturday afternoon and parade the streets of [San Francisco's] Haight-Ashbury, with the certain knowledge that the gawking tourists would take her to be one of the area's exotic inhabitants. (Lofland [1973] 1985:164–65; see also Proshansky 1978)

Beyond the possibility and the reality that the public realm will lure otherwise sober citizens into being someone they are not, critics castigate it for tempting otherwise responsible citizens into activities that distract them from doing things they ought to be doing. And again, the critics are right. Exactly because it is full of diverse people doing diverse things, the public realm can and does offer the pleasure of playing when one "ought" to be working, of being frivolous when one "ought" to be serious, of engaging in fantasy and daydreams when the workaday world beckons. No wonder adults, as we shall see in Chapter 5, are so anxious to keep children "off the streets." Writing of the play of poor children in the United States at the turn of the century, David Nasaw does not romanticize their playgrounds—but he also appreciates the lure of those playgrounds:

The streets . . . "were the true homes of small Italians, Irish, and Jews." The children shared these "homes" with others. The street was their playground, but it was also a marketplace, meeting ground, social club, place of assignation, political forum, sports arena, parade grounds, open-air tavern, coffeehouse and thoroughfare. The life on the street was the life of the city. . . . [T]he streets provided constant fun, games, and companions. There was always something to do or watch. Just when it was getting a bit dull, a horse might drop dead in the gutter, fire engines and ambulances appear from nowhere, teamsters and pushcarts do battle for the right-of-way, a stray cat creeps out of the basement to be tortured. (Nasaw 1985:20, 30; see also Dargan and Zeitlin 1990; Lynch 1977)

Adults, of course, may and do enjoy some of the same playful and frivolous and fantasy-inducing scenes and activities as small children. They may also, as may older children, find a physiologically more "mature" pleasure there as well. In 1960, Kevin Lynch characterized the urban environment as having a "sensuous" impact (p. 193) but he did not go on to spell out the implications of that characterization. Of course, since then, scholars (as well as fiction writers) have documented the reality of physical sexual activity in public (e.g., Davis 1983; Delph 1978; Humphreys 1970) but this particular pleasure, while undoubtedly occurring more frequently than most of us realize, also probably occurs far less frequently that fiction writers might lead us to believe. More ubiquitous, as the Danish sociologist Henning Bech has persuasively argued—and he is, to my knowledge, one of the first social scientist to make this specific argument—are the indirect pleasures of sexual playfulness and sexual fantasy:

> [It is] misleading [to place too much] emphasis on relations of an immediately tactile character [i.e., involving direct physical activity]. . . . Although such things no doubt do happen once in a while, and particularly in some spaces of the city, I believe that they should be seen in relation to a more basic and universal form of urban tactile sexuality. This is characterized by the simultaneous presence of closeness and distance. . . . [T]he importance of the visual in the sexuality of the city . . . is connected with the fact that in the social world of strangers people are only surfaces to one another, and that therefore the surface becomes an object to be evaluated and styled according to aesthetic criteria. . . . Now, the gaze which sees the surfaces of others, and which is active in the design of one's own, sees and evaluates on sexual criteria as well. Thus, surfaces are styled with a view of their potential signification of sexuality; and gazes are attracted to them for that very reason. (1994:9–10; see also Muller 1992)

We know from social histories that this sort of sexual enjoyment played an important part in the attractiveness of such locales as pleasure gardens (e.g., Conan and Marghieri 1989). We also know that it has evoked and continues to evoke a kind of choked fury among moralists of various stripes—but that is another story. And that is the story that we go to next, a story about all the various reasons for hating and disdaining cities and, most especially, for hating and disdaining their public realms. But before we shift to a detailed discussion of the opponents of the public realm, and as a partial transition to that shift, we should note the link between pleasures of the public realm and characteristics of public space.

DESIGNING FOR PLEASURE

Some locales, as I have already noted, seem to have been designed specifically for people-watching, though we know from the historical record that their creators did not, in fact, have such a use in mind: the locale formed by the balcony of London's National Portrait Gallery and Trafalgar Square is a case in point. Similarly, a pleasure like public sociability can be encouraged by quite intentional design, as Louis Erenberg's (1981) detailing of the architecture of the "cabaret" (discussed again in Chapter 7) makes clear. Conversely, environments that will ensure esthetic pleasures may not be all that easy to fabricate. Granted that the pleasure of crowding, stimulus diversity, and spectacle is probably the exception here—witness any Nevada gambling casino or recently constructed mega-mall—other esthetic pleasures seem beyond the abilities of designers-developers. Faux historical layering is within their ken, of course, but incorporating the "real" thing into a large-scale project is not. What *is* easy to create, as a stroll through any city in the world will quickly inform you, are environments that make esthetic pleasures *impossible*. What such a stroll will also inform you is that many environments appear (whatever the actual intention of their creators) to have been built to discourage pleasures of an interactional sort as well.

The question, then, is why. Granted that some pleasures may be beyond the direct control of the people who create the built environment, why do so many pieces of that environment exclude even those esthetic pleasures that can be designed for? Why are so many pieces of public space empty of the people or empty of the diversity of people that give rise to interactional pleasures? And even if developers cannot ensure that we will, for example, encounter the unexpected, why do so many places seem to be designed to ensure that the unexpected cannot intrude even unexpectedly? One answer, I believe—as I have suggested repeatedly in all that I have already said—lies in a widespread animus toward the public realm and, by implication, toward any pleasures it might induce. It is to the subject of that animus that we now turn.

NOTES

1.   As will become apparent in the next chapter, I selected this phrase for its irony.

2.   It is important to emphasize at this early juncture that historical layering or physical juxtaposition, for example, may create scenes that are pleasurable not simply because of those characteristics but also or alternatively because they are "unexpected" or "whimsical." Similarly, one person's scene of perceptual innuendo may be another's scene of whimsy and a third's scene of both. That is, some scenes may cause pleasure to pile upon pleasure or may be viewed as pleasurable by differing people for very different reasons.

3.   It seems highly likely that olfactory and auditory qualities of a given setting may also provide the occasion for esthetic pleasure, but I have no observational data dealing with this possibility. But see Sommer 1975.

4.   See, for example, Alexander, Ishikawa, and Silverstein (1977), Alexander, Neis, Anninou, and King (1987), Bourassa (1990), Breines and Dean (1974), Carp, Zawadski, and Shokrkon (1976), Carr (1967), Carr, Francis, Rivlin, and Stone (1992), Deasy (1985), Eldred (1990), Francis (1987b, 1989), Gehl ([1980] 1987), Gruen (1973), Harvey and Henning (1987), Heckscher (1977), *Landscape Architecture* (1989), Lennard and Lennard (1984, 1987, 1995), Longo, Tatge, and Fishman (1983), Lynch (1960, 1972, 1976, 1981), Mehrabian (1976), Nasar (1989, 1990), Peters (1984),

Prak (1985), Rapoport (1977), Relph (1981, 1987), Share (1978), Sommer (1972, 1974), Tuan (1974, 1978), Walmsley (1988:Chapter 3), Walter (1988), Webb (1990), Williams (1980), Weisman (1992), Wohlwill (1966), and Wolfe (1981).

5. Of course, to many historical preservationists, this and the setting depicted in Illustration 4.6 represent a desecration of the built environment—one of the reasons, perhaps, why when preservationists hold sway over a fairly large area, the resulting neighborhood tends to strike some observers as having a frozen, museumlike quality.

6. I did not at the time and I will not now comment on the appropriateness of such a setting for college-level "homework."

7. It is useful, I think, to understand teenage "cruising" as a vehicular version of the urban promenade.

8. I will deal with this topic in some detail in Chapter 6.

9. In addition to that literature, see Barrows and Room (1991), Butsch (1990), Calkins (1901), Fabian (1990), Girouard (1975), Gray (1978), Haavio-Mannila (1981), Kotarba (1977), Moore (1897), Nasaw (1993), Pin (1985), and Single and Storm (1985), Storm and Cutler (1985).

10. Long-time San Francisco columnist Herb Caen has documented many such scenes of public sociability in that city. The documentation is, of course, scattered throughout several thousands of daily columns and therefore difficult to retrieve. However, some sense of what those columns in their totality would reveal can be gleaned from published collections of them. See, for example, Mecchi (1992).

11. See, for example, Adelman (1986), Bristol (1985), Caillois (1961), Da Matta (1984), Gonzalez ([1970] 1980), Guttman (1986), Judd (1983), Lawrence (1982), MacAloon (1984), Orloff (1981), Piette (1992), Riess (1989), Strong (1984), and Turner (1982).

II
OPPONENTS OF THE PUBLIC REALM
Assaults on a Social Territory

The goal of Part I was to sketch a portrait of the public realm. The goal here is to understand something of the forces that seem to be arrayed against it. These forces—cultural imagery, personal fears, architectural and developer practices—are simultaneously independent of and interrelated with one another. I do not argue grand conspiracy here. But I do argue for a situation of mutual reinforcement.

Much of the material used to build the chapters that form Part II will be familiar to many readers: the strong strain of antiurbanism in Anglo-American thought, fear of crime and of "difference," and the history of urban development in the United States since 1945. What is hopefully new in these chapters is my use of this material for a single purpose: to illuminate the hostile environment confronting the public realm.

5

Antiurbanism and the Representational War on the Public Realm

Despite its ordered character, despite the richly diverse relationships that inhabit it, and despite is manifold pleasures and esthetics, the public realm is *not* a social territory well-beloved by one and all. More accurately, it appears to be a territory actively disliked by many. In this chapter, we begin the task of exploring this widespread and many-formed animus toward the public realm by looking at words and visual images, that is, by looking at assaults of a *representational* character. Chapter 6 will explore *emotional* and *behavioral* forms of this animus and Chapter 7 will focus on its *concrete embodiment* in the built environment.

CAIN'S CREATION: THE LONG TRADITION OF ANTIURBANISM

What do the following ten items have in common?

1. This sentence, which opens a newspaper story on a planned up-scale "gated" development outside Sacramento: "You'd think a pastoral setting 30 minutes from the evils of city life would provide enough peace of mind, but Bill Parker [the developer] is taking no chances."[1]
2. The American painter George Tooker's *The Waiting Room* (see Illustration 5.1).
3. A "Hi and Lois" comic strip (see Illustration 5.2).
4. A full-page magazine advertisement for LeisureWorld (see Illustration 5.3)
5. A 1993 book edited by Edward O. Wilson and Stephen Kellert, which advances the hypothesis that humans are genetically ill-adapted to urban settings.
6. A classroom film distributed by PennState Audio-Visual Services entitled "The City and the Self," which is advertised as "demon-

Illustration 5.1. George Tooker, *The Waiting Room*, 1959. National Museum of American Art, Smithsonian Institution. Gift of S.C. Johnson & Son, Inc. Reproduced with permission.

strat[ing] the anonymity, aloofness, and indifference of city life by examining city dwellers' perceptions of their city and their behavior in created [read, "experimental"] situations."[2]

7. The frontispiece to John Helmer's and Neil A. Eddington's *Urbanman: The Psychology of Urban Survival* (see Illustration 5.4).

8. Extracts from a page from the 1997–1998 UC, Davis General Catalogue (see Illustration 5.5).

9. A letter to the editor of *Mother Jones*, which asserts that "dense populations lead to centralized, authoritarian police states, with or without a facade of civil liberties."[3]

10. A May 1994 cover photograph and story from *Parade* (see Illustration 5.6)

The answer to the question of commonality, obviously, is that all ten are illustrative of a strong and long-lasting theme in Western thought and in Anglo-American visual and rhetorical productions in particular: the theme of antiurbanism. The artist, cartoonists, scholars, journalists, adver-

Illustration 5.2. Brian and Greg Walker, "Hi and Lois." Published in the *Sacramento Bee*, October 22, 1995. Reprinted with special permission of King Features Syndicate.

tiser, and letter writer whose words and images are reproduced here seem to share with the seventeenth-century English poet and essayist, Abraham Cowley, the certain view that *"God the first garden made, and the first city Cain"* ("The Garden," [1666] 1906; emphasis added).

Cowley's epigram tells us why some scholars have traced the Western tradition of urban animus to the first book of the Old Testament. As Sidney Aronson has suggested, our view of the city might be very different

> had the Jewish scribes who wrote the Book of Genesis been urban dwellers rather than members of a nomadic, desert tribe; had they located paradise amid the marketplace or the theatre of a thriving town rather than in a pastoral Garden of Eden; had they not held up to an impressionable posterity the "cities of the valley"—Sodom and Gomorrah—as archetypal images of appalling evil. (1977:253)

Other scholars have pointed to a current of antiurbanism even among the city-building Romans and to the escalation of that current in the Christian theology of St. Augustine (Hadden and Barton 1973). Certainly the current was flowing briskly in late eighteenth-century America when Thomas Jefferson wrote that "I view great cities as penitential to the morals, the health, and the liberties of man." And yet, in some sense, up until the end of the eighteenth century in both Europe and America, such hostility probably did not matter very much. Few people lived in cities. Most of those who did could neither read nor write, so what they thought of their environments would have been shaped far more by direct experience and face-to-face conversation than by the rhetorical productions of intellectuals and political and religious leaders. But with the "industrial" and "urban" revolutions of the late eighteenth and nineteenth centuries and with their continuing consequences throughout the twentieth, not only did more and more people come to live in urban settlements, but more and more of them learned to read and write. And with that, more and more people prepared

LEISURE WORLD. FOR PEOPLE WHO AREN'T BIG ON BIG-CITY LIVING.

IF BEING ANOTHER FACE IN THE CROWD ISN'T YOUR IDEA OF ADULT LIVING, COME TO OUR SMALL FRIENDLY WORLD–LEISURE WORLD.

Instead of a sprawling retirement city, we're a friendly, close-knit community of 2,600. With two golf courses. Tennis. Swimming. Shuffleboard. Lawn bowling. Plus a beautiful indoor recreation center.

For complete privacy we maintain 24-hour security patrol seven days a week. And we offer the option

of Monitor 6, a security, fire and medical-alert system.

You can have that system in your choice of energy-efficient 1- and 2-bedroom twinhomes from the mid 40's, and 2- and 3-bedroom homes priced from the mid 60's.

These Leisure World homes are just blocks from Mesa's banks, restaurants, retail stores, and Valley Lutheran Hospital. And they're practically next door to the spectacular Superstition Mountains.

But the real beauty here is the friendly, secure environment of our small world.

908 S. Power Rd., Mesa • 832-3232
(between Southern & Broadway)

LeisureWorld
Our big difference is we're not too big.
A development of Western Savings & Loan Association

Illustration 5.3. Full-page magazine advertisement for LeisureWorld. *Phoenix Home/Garden*, March 1984.

more and more words and images reflecting the centuries-old tradition of urban hostility. And then that tradition came to matter very much indeed.[4]

Look again at Illustrations 5.2, 5.3, 5.5, and 5.6. As you can see, expressions of antiurbanism rarely stand alone. Their counterpointal theme, as Cowley's epigram and Aronson's commentary presages, is the celebration of wilderness, village, rurality.[5] The "Hi and Lois" cartoon, for example,

URBANMAN

Anti-power failure headlamp for use in subway tunnels, unlighted streets, etc.

Air-pollution mask

Snowshoes in event of unpredicted heavy snowfall

Scaling rope for lowering self from office buildings during power shutdown

Identification

Briefcase containing emergency cash for sudden tax hikes, fare and toll increases. Also, midtown travel permit, draft card

Emergency drought supply

Change-maker for exact change for buses, pay toilets, tipping waiters, bartenders, etc.

Anti-mugger chain for briefcase

Belt containing skate key and spare skate wheels

Pistol, holster, and ammunition for citizen's arrest, if witness to a crime

Books to read during next newspaper strike and tutoring children during school strike

Aids for getting through demonstrations

Travel aids during transit shutdown

Curb feelers

Illustration 5.4. Urbanman. Reprinted with permission of the Free Press, a division of Simon & Schuster from *Urbanman: The Psychology of Urban Survival* edited by John Helmer and Neil Eddington. Copyright © 1973 by the Free Press.

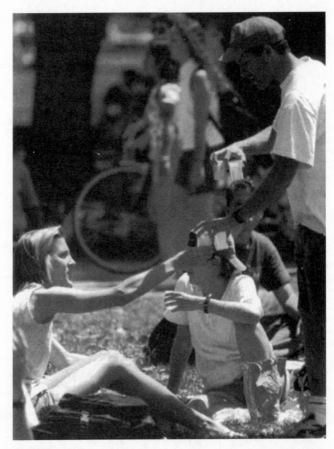

Illustration 5.5.   From the 1997–1998 UC, Davis General
Catalogue.

contrasts the congestion and pollution of the city with the simplicity and
cleanliness of nature. LeisureWorld evokes the village by offering an environment that is small, friendly, and secure. My campus's General Catalogue magically transforms the actual small city of Davis into a "small
town" and its actual agra-business and metropolitan surroundings into
"countryside." And as *Parade* tells us, the answer to urban stress and danger is the serenity and safety of the farm. Similarly, in sociologist David
Hummon's research on community ideology, the talk of self-described
"small town enthusiasts" is replete with counterpointal city imagery. Two
examples:

> We had friends we had met in St. Louis who came to Valleytown[6] to visit
> for a week. He had been born and raised in St. Louis. And it was interesting,

Illustration 5.6.   Cover from *Parade*, May 15, 1994.

his reaction. He'd sit in the backyard—he couldn't fathom the quietness of it. There was a street out in front and there wasn't all the noise from the traffic. (1990:51; see also 1980, 1986a, 1986b)

In cities, there's too much riff-raff. You have to protect your back all the time. . . . I feel pretty safe in a small town and strictly safe in the wilderness. There's crime in a small town but it's penny ante stuff. Only a few murders once every year or two. In small towns, people control their own crime. If people are friendly, honest, you shouldn't have any crime. And in a small town, people are concerned. (1990:59)

Note also the "pairing" method used by Coalinga, California, amateur poet Alice Dale to celebrate her small town:

Big cities can be exciting,
With so many places to go,
Big stores, and fine museums,
Parks, and theatres, I know.

But I guess I am not the type
To live a cosmopolitan life.
I would rather live in a small town,
Away from traffic and strife.

I like the place I live,
With its hills around the town
Where people smile and greet you,
And very seldom frown.

I like the friendly churches,
And nice people whom I meet,
And I like being able to park,
Anywhere along the street.

I like to know my neighbors,
And have friends whom I can call,
And I guess if I had a choice,
I wouldn't change my life at all.

(*Coalinga Record*, Wednesday, June 23, 1993)

This juxtapositioning of the moral and physical virtue and purity of small towns and villages and their rural or wilderness surroundings against the moral and physical vileness and pollution of the city is so common a device[7] that each can be evoked by the other *even in the absence of the other*. The power, for example, of a Dore etching of a London street (Illustration 5.7) is intensified by its contrast to, for example, a well-known Constable landscape (Illustration 5.8). Or, in a contemporary magazine advertisement, the beauty of what is depicted is emphasized by the "obvious" ugliness of the unseen cityscape that is evoked (Illustration 5.9).

To speak of the antiurbanism theme in Anglo-American culture is not to suggest that no countercurrents exist.[8] Among Americans, in particular, city "boosterism" has been and continues to be a lively presence (Prus and Fleras 1989; Strauss 1961, 1968) and a steady current of cityphilia is readily discernible in the past and contemporary productions of American and Northern European intellectuals: a phenomenon we will explore at the end of this chapter and again in Chapter 8. Nonetheless, what almost all observers of antiurbanism have remarked on is the extraordinary vigor of the theme and its domination in so many areas of discourse. The American geographer Yi-Fu Tuan has written, "It has become an unthinking reflex for Americans to see the city as the farmer and intellectual see it: Babylon—den of iniquity, atheistic and un-American, impersonal and

Illustration 5.7.   A City Thoroughfare. Gustave Doré and Blanchard Gerrold, *A Pilgrimage,* Grant, London, 1872.

destructive" (1974:193). Sociologist Claude Fischer makes an even broader generalization:

> Citizens of the Western world are heirs to millennia of legend, literature, and art focused on cities and city life-styles. The messages conveyed by those cultural expressions have not always been consistent or uniform, *but the themes that repeat themselves are largely negative ones.* (1976:15, emphasis added)

If, as Tuan suggests, Americans—and Westerners more generally—tend to be unreflectively antiurban, the reason, as Fischer suggests, is to be found in the sheer *ubiquity* of the antiurban message. I have tried to convey some of this in the diversity of the illustrations presented above, but before concluding this section, let me pile on a few more examples. Consider American political rhetoric. Criticism of the city comes from both the Left and the Right (Berger 1978). From the point of view of the Left, cities (at least modern cities) are necessarily alienating, inhuman, unnatural environments because they are the creations of evil capitalism. That is, even though the ultimate villain for the Left is the economic system and *its operation*, cities per se (rather than, say, excessive individualism) become

Illustration 5.8. John Constable, *The Hay Wain*, 1824. Copyright © Reproduced with permission. National Gallery, London.

Illustration 5.9. Advertisement from *Newsweek*, April 22, 1985.

[handwritten annotations: "Somewhat unfair? isn't Harvey looking @ industry and such — your sight is different here —"]

the "intervening villains" as in David Harvey's assertion that "cities . . . are founded upon the exploitation of the many by the few. An urbanism founded upon exploitation is a legacy of history. A genuinely humanizing urbanism has yet to be brought into being" (1973:314).[9] This often leads to a nostalgia for the imaginary ideal life of the small town or village or farm or to organizational efforts that have as their goal the transformation of some piece of urban space into a version of the ideal (see, for example, Kotler 1969; Gerloff 1992). From the point of view of the Right, cities are simply blamed in a relatively straightforward manner (they are the "independent villains") for the failings that might otherwise be attributed to the economic system. Thus the existence of a black underclass, poverty in general, and crime are all defined as *urban problems* and, as such, not worth "throwing money at." As Richard Nixon's secretary of agriculture Earl L. Butz explained over twenty years ago,

> One of the problems . . . has been the exodus of rural people to downtown Baltimore, Philadelphia, Detroit, St. Louis and New York, without the skills to be a productive citizen, without the cultural background to live there. They constitute a breeding ground for crime and delinquency and cause welfare rolls to skyrocket. We should have kept them in the country. We could keep them much cheaper out there, much more productive out there than we have them in the ghettos of the inner cities. (*New York Times Magazine*, April 16, 1972; see also Sternlieb 1972)[10]

Or, as Senator Joseph Biden remarked in accounting for Congress's resistance to New York City's pleas for financial help, "Cities are viewed as the seed of corruption and duplicity, and New York City is the biggest City" (*New York Times*, May 25, 1975, quoted in Fischer 1976:15).

Consider also the scholarly obsessions of generations of social scientists. The sheer amount of time and energy that has been devoted to questions about the ill-effects of one or another aspect of "city life" is astounding. There is, for example, a gigantic literature devoted solely to the study of the negative effects of high-density living [reviewed in Baldassare (1983), Choldin (1978b) and Freedman (1975)]. Similarly, the problems of social-psychological "well-being" (e.g., relational density, stress levels, overload, alienation, inauthenticity) among urban residents has kept innumerable researchers busy and "in print" (see, for example, Deutsch 1961; Klapp 1969:Chapter 3; Newman and McCauley 1977; Webb and Collette 1977). And the widespread assumption among collective behavior-social movement scholars that "city" was the independent variable that "explained" such phenomena as protest, conflict, and violence went unchallenged until tested empirically by Charles Tilly (1974).[11]

Consider too the U.S. environmental movement. Spokespeople for the movement certainly differ as to exactly what kind of a symbol they conceive the city to be—some, for example, would claim not to be against all cities, only against really large cities. Nonetheless, there is an important line of thought in environmentalism that is clearly reflected both in the Earth First cry, "Down with all high-rises! Out with all malls! Dream back the forests and the prairies!"[12] and in anarchist Ernest Callenbach's observation that

> it is hard for people who grow up in cities to have what you might call a fundamentally, biologically-oriented way of looking at people. . . . The fact that most of us, in our society, are now urbanites is very scary to me. It seems to me that it leads us away from a trust in the land. It's hard to have a feel for a bioregion if you haven't really lived in contact with the earth, or what we can legitimately call an agricultural way of life. (1981:12)

Or, finally, consider calendars and tourist advertising. First as to calendars, each year I send my students out to perform the same task: review all the calendars that feature landscapes of one or another sort and report back on what they have found. With predictable regularity, they find "nature" and village (especially European) photographs and sketches in abundance; cityscapes (almost always skyline or airplane views) represent a miniscule proportion of the total. Second as to advertising, let me quote David Hummon's description of one of the findings in his study of state-sponsored tourist advertising:

> [N]o state pamphlet with a single image on its cover used a cityscape in its presentation; words that are symbols of the metropolitan context—neighborhood, street, suburb—seldom appear in the Welcoming Statement of the governor or in the state Identity Passages. When cities are mentioned in tourist advertising, the antiurbanism of American culture may even lead state promotional literature to note that their cities are "unurban":
>> But don't misunderstand—Arkansas cities are equally special. Visitors have enjoyed the hospitality of Eureka Springs and Hot Springs for over a century. Little Rock, Fort Smith and Helen have been significant since the westward trek was started. Regardless of size, Arkansas cities manage to retain a certain small town comfort and friendliness.
> (Hummon 1985a:12)

Granting the widespread indictment of the city, just what is it about urban settlements that makes them the target of so much animus? The poverty that is to be found in them, you say. The meanness of London and New York's nineteenth-century rookeries and tenements, for example, or the drugged desolation of the contemporary South Bronx. And yet, exposés of agricultural and small-town poverty—the photographs of Walker Evans or Dorothea Lange, for example—do not provide the occasion for denunciations of rural life. Preachers do not thunder from their pulpits nor editors from their columns about the sin and wickedness of "the garden." Well, you say, then it must be that we hate cities because they are so often the settings for unspeakable working environments—like sweatshops, for example. But why is it, then, that the plight of farmworkers does not lead us to hate the land? Alright, you say, it is because city settings are so often the scenes of violence and brutality. And I answer, so are wilderness settings, but that doesn't lead to condemnation by the Sierra Club.

No, I do not believe we despise the city for any of these oft-mentioned reasons. Rather, I would like to offer the hypothesis that we despise the city largely *because it is the only settlement form that has a public realm*. I want to propose that our animus is primarily aimed not so much at the homes or residential neighborhoods or workplaces of the city—it is not really the city's private and parochial realms that is the target of our scorn. What we despise (and, as we will see, what we fear) are the city's "streets"—its public realm.

THE DEPRAVITY OF THE CITY'S "STREETS": GANGING UP ON THE PUBLIC REALM

I usually begin my urban courses by asking students to write down any words that come to mind when I say the word *city*. That the words they use are overwhelmingly negative should not surprise you, given what we know of antiurbanism among Americans. But what is surprising—or at least it was to me when I first noticed it—is the extent to which the qualities they attribute to the city are not qualities that could logically be attributed to all parts of the city, to most homes or workplaces, for example. Rather, they are qualities that, logically speaking, seem only applicable to public space: to streets, sidewalks, parks, plazas, alleyways, buses, and—to a lesser degree—bars, stores, and restaurants. Cities, my students tell me, are frenetic, crowded, loud, smelly, dangerous, indifferent, anonymous, dirty, filled with hostile strangers, and littered with the unsightly homeless and the unsightly poor. In a similar vein, a 1990 *Time* cover story on "The Decline of New York," detailed, among other of the city's problems, mounting economic injustice, soaring housing costs, and governmental ineptitude. The story's headlines, however, proclaimed "crime" and hinted "street crime," and the accompanying photographs, documenting neither corporate moguls in plush executive suites nor overpriced two-bedroom apartments nor uncaring bureaucrats, focused, as can be seen in Illustrations 5.10 and 5.11, on the city's "mean streets."

Perhaps the responses of my students should not have surprised me. Nor should I have expected anything different from the *Time* cover story.

Illustration 5.10.   Time, September 17, 1990. Photo: Kenneth Jarecke/Contact.

Illustration 5.11.   Time, September 17, 1990. Photo: Kenneth Jarecke/Contact.

After all, some thirty-five years ago Jane Jacobs noted that what really bothers urban reformers is not the city per se but the city's "streets." Reformers, she said,

> have long observed city people loitering on busy corners, hanging around in candy stores and bars and drinking soda pop on stoops, and have passed a judgment, the gist of which is: "This is deplorable! If these people had decent homes and a more private or bosky outdoor place, they wouldn't be on the street!" (1961:55)

And I might have remembered this homily from my youth:

> Fools' names and fools' faces are always seen in public places.

Or, I should have kept in mind that while antiurbanism centrally celebrates wilderness, rurality, and village, it also celebrates domesticity and neighborliness—and often celebrates them even when they these qualities have a city address. In other words, it should have come as no surprise to me that an important—if not the most important—component of urban animus is actually hostility toward the public realm, toward the world of "the street."[13] For most of the rest of this chapter, it is this component of antiurbanism that we will explore in detail. I will begin by posing the hypothesis that we judge the public realm as harshly as we do at least partly as a consequence of viewing it through the moral lens—that is, with the moral standards—of the parochial and private realms, especially the latter. We will then consider a number of the direct and indirect assaults that have been launched against it during the last several hundred years.

Through a Moral Lens Darkly

Over the years I have paid a great deal of attention to the statements of my students and my colleagues who "hate cities" and to the innumerable expressions of antiurbanism in Anglo-American visual and rhetorical representations. And as I have compared those views with what the research record actually tells us, I have begun to wonder if at least some of the reasons for the "bad odor" in which the public realm is held might have something to do with standards people are using to judge it. Is it possible that we give moral privilege to, especially, private and domestic territories (a possibility we will consider in more detail in Chapter 6) and thus devalue other sorts of social space?[14]

This idea does make a certain amount of sense. If, for example, we value private realm relationships because—at least ideally—they are personal and intimate, multifaceted, and diffuse, might we not, observing the fleeting and routinized character of so many public realm relationships, make the judgment that *the city is cold*? Or, as another example, might not my appreciation for the focused attention and mutual involvement of my private relations cause me to look upon such public realm normative principles as civil inattention and audience-role prominence with disapproval and thus to see *the city as uncaring*? What if the pleasures of intimate interaction and privacy that I find in my private world lead me to dismiss others' appreciation for public sociability or people-watching? Might I then make the judgment that *the city is invasive*? Or, if my private realm is—or at least I wish it to be—characterized by esthetic principles like harmony, serenity, utility, predictability, what am I to make of such sources of public realm esthetic pleasures as crowding/stimulus diversity/spectacle? Will I perhaps make the assessment that *the city is discordant*?

Definitive data on this issue do not currently exist. Nonetheless, as we explore some of the many direct and indirect representational assaults on the public realm, we will also encounter hints or whispers that strongly point in this direction.

Direct Assaults: The Public Realm as Moral Target

In the long history of the representational war against the public realm, the assaults launched against it display considerable variation. All, of course, draw upon the larger tradition of antiurbanism. But beyond that shared trait, there is much diversity. Some are subtle, some are heavy-handed; some damn with faint praise, some simply damn. The attack may be unseen—as in acts of omission—or highly visible to all—as in many acts of commission. Here I want to consider only one dimension of these many diverse formations: whether they are direct or indirect. In the next section, we will explore some examples of *indirect* assault, where the public realm is not target but rhetorical "warrant." At this juncture, let us consider four examples of assaults that have been quite *direct*—assaults in which the public realm itself is the moral target.

The Presence of the Unholy and the Unwashed. One direct assault involves the assertion that the public realm is somehow morally suspect because it contains within it the "unholy" and the "unwashed"—it is home to "the wrong kind of people"—however "wrong kind of people" may be defined. Eighteenth- and nineteenth-century London's defenders of domesticity (discussed below) warned women to stay at home in part because the streets were filled with men, but even more importantly because they teemed with the contaminating presence of the "lower orders" of both sexes. I use the word *contaminating* advisedly. Elizabeth

for all her specificity, are we still mixing scales here?

Wilson, among numerous commentators, has suggested that for British Victorians,

> excrement [was] a metaphor and a symbol for moral filth, perhaps even for the working class itself, and when they spoke and wrote of the cleansing of the city [streets] of filth, refuse and dung, they may really have longed to rid the cities of the labouring poor altogether. (1991:37; see also Winter 1989)

Similarly, in nineteenth- and early twentieth-century New York, "proper" men and women were encouraged to stay away from public places because of the disgusting ethnic character of their denizens. As an example, Bruce Bliven, a progressive intellectual and reformer, denounced Coney Island in a 1921 article in the *New Republic*, complaining that the hair on most heads along its beach was black. In this article and in other writings, Bliven expressed his disgust over the fact that "a new population was displacing 'native American stock'"; that Anglo-Saxon Puritanism, which he viewed as having historically formed "'the framework of American manners,' was being forced to yield before displays of 'love-making on the beach.' Established traditions, rules of conduct, values, all appeared, in his eyes, to be crumbling under the onslaught of a mongrel mass culture" (Kasson 1978:97–98)—and a mongrel mass culture that— and this is the crucial point—was showing itself "out in public."[15]

While twentieth-century discussions of the unholy and the unwashed are generally couched in a language that seems more discrete, more guarded than was nineteenth-century rhetoric, the theme of contamination has by no means disappeared. Publicly voiced complaints about the homeless, for example, often focus on the urine and feces they leave behind. This "foulness" motif is clearly evident in a 1990 *San Francisco Chronicle* news story, which reports than an activist, opposed to a shelter located in his neighborhood, claims that the homeless are "hanging around all day like rats."[16] Elizabeth Wilson's characterization of respectable Victorians as concerned with "cleansing" the streets hints at one recurring solution to the problem of contamination: *wash away* the offensive presence. The murders of street children, prostitutes, beggars, and others in Brazil and Columbia, for example, have been "justified" as an effort to "cleanse" Rio de Janeiro's or Bogota's public space, just as proposals for doubtfully legal measures against public inebriates in some American cities have as their goal the tidying up "required" by economic development goals.[17] And listen to the "good housekeeping" language embedded in this letter to the *San Francisco Chronicle*:

> A bum is a bum is a bum. Stop equating them with the homeless. It appears that the mayor and the Board of Supervisors will do nothing to *clean*

why no talk of who/what creates public space?

up the parks and streets. . . . We all care about the homeless. I am talking about bums. Bums that *dirty* our streets. Bums that have taken away our parks. Bums that insult us in every part of the city. Bums that have given us a bad name throughout the nation.

Why does the mayor and Board of Supervisors cater to this group? It is time that the citizens who want to live in a *clean environment* and want a city that is back under the control of the taxpayers do something. Let's use the liberals' methods and talk recall. Talk city initiatives to *clean up* our city. Let's talk about taking charge of the city and taking it back from the bums. Let's talking about everyone getting involved and *cleaning up* this city. (*San Francisco Chronicle*, July 5, 1990, emphasis added)

Another solution is to *segregate* the contaminants while at the same time creating sanitized public spaces—a solution we shall be exploring in Chapter 7 and that is foreshadowed in this letter to the *Chronicle*:

I spent a recent Friday in a foreign country that was *clean*, polite and good natured. The cafe was spotless and so was the *shopping center* and the only street person downtown was an elderly man in a wheelchair who was not abusive. I should add the children were polite too and everyone was helpful. Was this a daydream? No, it was San Rafael and a nasty shock to come back to San Francisco with the *foul smelling* streets, rude and inefficient civil servants and abusive beggars. (*San Francisco Chronicle*, July 6, 1990, emphasis added)

Or, perhaps most effective of all, one simply avoids the public realm altogether (an alternative we will consider in detail in Chapter 6).

Mixing the Unmixable. A second example assault is related to the first but is even broader in compass. The public realm is morally suspect not simply because the unholy and the unwashed can be found there, but because it is a social territory in which *many different kinds or categories of people are mixed up together*.

This particular attack, of course, is based on the premise that the public realm, at least theoretically, is that portion of social space to which everyone has access. In reality, of course, the right to be present may be seriously curtailed. Entire sections of cities may be defined as "belonging" to one or another racial, ethnic, or class grouping and thus be voluntarily avoided by nonmembers. Or, law or tradition may forbid the presence of specific "sorts" of persons (e.g., women, Jews, blacks) in ostensibly "public" spaces or in such spaces at certain times. And parochial "home territories" established within what is legally public space may sometimes prove inhospitable or even hostile to "outsiders." Granting such qualifications, it is nonetheless generally true that the public realm brings into copresence persons who might never otherwise encounter one another. Home and hearth offer the sedating security of homogeneity. Neighborhoods, workplaces, even voluntary organizations, can be made "exclusive." The "street," in contrast, jumbles together the chaste and unchaste, the respectable and the unrespectable, the dangerous and the benign, the rude and the polite, the "best people" and the outcasts, the domiciled and the homeless, the well-fed and the underfed, the righteous and the rebellious, and, of course, the "holy" and the "unholy" and the "washed" and the "unwashed." And, as I have said, it is precisely this characteristic that the opponents of the public realm seem frequently to find so troublesome and upon which they base their attack. The idea that there is a social territory in which various types or categories of people whom a deity, nature, tradition, etc., had intended to remain forever separate are allowed to mingle provides the occasion for much agonized hand-wringing and innumerable cries of alarm.

Lewis Erenberg's study of New York nightlife between 1890 and 1930 records many examples. Discussing "cabarets," he writes:

> In late 1912 and 1913 . . . , Mayor William J. Baynor and other concerned citizens were deeply disturbed by this boisterous public dancing, drinking, and *social mingling* now creeping out of lower-class dance halls and male saloons, and into the haunts of respectable urbanites. Most important, these haunts were public, *"open to everyone* . . . who chooses to come up and pay the entrance fee". . . . In this dangerously open environment . . . *respectable women could mix* promiscuously with people of un-specified moral character. . . . As "people of position have taken to frequenting the restaurants where dancing is the attraction," claimed author Julius Street, they created a social mixture never before seen in the United States, "a *hodge-podge* of people in which respectable young married and unmarried women and even debutantes dance, not only under the same roof, but in the same room with women of the town." (Erenberg, 1981:76–77, emphasis added)

Criticism of cabaret "tea dances" was even more pointed:

> In 1912 the cafes inaugurated a series of afternoon dances called the *dansants* or tango teas. For the price of a drink or a relatively small admission fee, single and married women could dance during the afternoon as well as at night. The management hired dancing partners or gigolos to take the unescorted women through their paces. . . . Here lay the fear: respectable women, seeking passion and excitement, would find them with men marked as disreputable by their sensuality and ethnicity, characteristics many people considered the same. In the heat of the dance, and the informal air of the cafe, the old gentility, which kept women in their place was forgotten. (Erenberg 1981:79)

As these quotations suggest, while mingling per se is viewed as abhorrent, it especially the *uncontrolled* character of that mingling that the public realm makes possible that many critics find especially noxious. For example, although turn-of-the-century reformers concerned with the recreation of working-class employed women considered sex-segregated leisure pursuits most appropriate and seemly for these "girls," such pursuits failed to attract the requisite numbers. As a consequence, reformers reluctantly came to include dances and other mixed-sex activities among their offerings. From their perspective, *supervised mingling* in semiprivate and controlled space was at least an improvement over the free and easy sociability of the dance hall, the pleasure garden, the Coney Island excursion, the nickelodeon, or the streets (Peiss 1986; see also Perry 1985).[18]

To late nineteenth- and early twentieth-century American moralists, at least, the evils associated with such public realm locales as cabarets, cafes, movie theaters, dance halls, and pleasure gardens did not reside merely in the possibility of respectable women being in the same room with women of "easy virtue" nor of unsupervised women being in the presence of men. An additional danger was to be found in the fact that these locales actually or potentially also brought together persons of the working, middle, and upper classes, blacks and whites, southern Europeans and northern Europeans (Erenberg 1981; Peiss 1986). In their concern with such indiscriminate shoulder rubbing, these moralists echoed the complaints of their eighteenth-century English counterparts who vented their spleen on the commercial "masquerade"—a social form in which participants were both costumed and masked and which granted participants considerable behavioral and verbal freedom. Referring to the masquerade's penchant for "promiscuously" bringing together men and women from all social ranks, a writer for the *Weekly Journal* of 1724 complains, "All state and ceremony are laid aside; since the *Peer* and the *Apprentice*, the *Punk* and the *Duchess* are, for so long a time, upon an equal Foot" (quoted in Castle 1986:30, italics in original).[19] According to the historian Terry Castle, while criticisms of the masquerade were many and varied, the "mingling" theme was always paramount:

> the dominant focus of anti-masquerade attacks throughout the century was never just the general theatricality of the occasion, or its effeminacy. The offense ran deeper; the masquerade seemed to such critics to challenge the symbolic order of eighteenth century culture. At its most profound level, antimasquerade rhetoric was *directed against the masquerade's unholy mixing of things meant to remain apart—its impulse, as it were, toward an incest of forms.* (Castle 1986:80, emphasis added; see also Jarrett 1974:Chapter 7)

To utilize eighteenth- and nineteenth-century examples is not to imply that attacks emphasizing mixing have disappeared in the twentieth. It is possible, however, that they have diminished. If so, it is probably not because "integration" is any more popular today than it was in the past. Rather, the cause is more likely to be found in the fact that many North American and some British and European cities have, in the twentieth century, achieved spatially an unprecedented degree of residential, functional, and life-style segregation (e.g., Lofland [1973] 1985:Chapter 4). If we complain less about commingling in public, it may be because so many of our public spaces so often contain only flocks of similarly feathered birds. Nevertheless, however diminished, contemporary complaints are by no means nonexistent—especially when it comes to the unappreciated presence of youth or to the unsuitable or unappreciated presence of children. Over the last ten years or so, for example, I have collected innumerable newspaper stories in which owners of bars, restaurants, and other adult-oriented businesses complain about teenage cruisers (whether in cars or on foot) on the grounds that the latter turn the streets into "amusement parks" and frighten away customers.[20] In a similar vein, some of the citizens of my city have publicly supported the proposed move of a planned shopping center from the middle to the periphery of a newly built subdivision because the original location put the center close to the elementary school. What is not clear is whether these residents disapprove of unaccompanied children in shopping centers because the children would be in the presence of nonparental adults or because adult customers would be in the presence of other peoples' children.[21]

The Sacrilegious Frivolity of Uncontrolled Play.　A third direct assault reproaches the public realm for the *irresponsible or even sacrilegious frivolity that characterizes its play activities*. In the public realm, the argument goes, the unquestioned virtues of sobriety, industry, rationality, diligence, and so forth are not only challenged, they are discarded. One example from criticisms of a public realm institution already discussed above provides some sense of the "flavor" of this particular critique. Describing the vision of the masquerade held by its critics, historian Terry Castle writes:

> At the classic eighteenth-century masquerade . . . a distinctly ungenteel liberty was the goal: liberty from every social, erotic, and psychological constraint. In this search after perfect freedom—a state of intoxication, ecstasy, and free-floating sensual pleasure—the eighteenth century masquerade demonstrated its kinship, however, distant, with those rituals of possession and collective frenzy found in traditional societies. . . . Ecstatic rituals transport their participants into another world, in which time and space are magically altered. In its most fervent stages, the masquerade held a similarly labile and convulsive power. With its scenes of manic, impetuous play, the masquerade often seemed to contemporaries to induce a kind of hallucinatory state. (Castle 1986:53)

In short, the public realm is suspect as a setting for disquieting exhibitions of frivolously *uncontrolled* playfulness—a charge that becomes the source of ever more distress when linked with the public realm's penchant for *uncontrolled mixing*. Once in one another's presence, who knows what frenzied activities this amalgamation of folks may get up to. Let us take a closer look at three of the numerous "frivolous play" activities that have enraged public realm critics: fantasy-play, sexual-play, and drinking-play.

As we saw above, Coney Island was, during its heyday, subjected to a great deal of moral criticism. In addition to the disgust that its working-class and "foreign-looking" hordes generated among "sensitive" observers, it was also condemned for permitting rowdy drinking and sexual abandon. But it was as the purveyor of *fantasy-play* that Coney Island most incensed the moralists (including Jane Addams). To quote from John Kasson:

> The response of James Gibbons Huneker [to Coney Island] is especially interesting. . . . An enthusiastic and iconoclastic critic, Huneker ranged freely over music, literature, art, and other subjects from the 1890's to the 1920's, often in vigorous defense of artistic novelty. But when he ventured to Coney Island in the 1910's . . . , most of what he saw moved him to despair.
>
> What disturbed Huneker, in fact, was precisely the surrender of reason, even of repression that Coney encouraged. "After the species of straitjacket that we wear in everyday life is removed at such Saturnalia as Coney Island," he observed dryly, "the human animal emerges in a not precisely winning guise." From this perspective, Coney's topsy-turvy entertainments and fantastic architecture were not harmless pleasures but evidence of cultural delirium. "Unreality is as greedily craved by the mob as alcohol by the dipsomaniac; indeed, the jumbled nightmares of a morphine eater are actually realized by Luna Park."
>
> In articulating these opinions, Huneker was not merely voicing idiosyncratic fears, but expressing concerns frequently advanced by leading behavioral scientists of the period. According to the dominant school of American psychiatry in the late nineteenth and early twentieth centuries, the genteel virtues of sobriety, diligence, thrift, and self-mastery safeguarded not only family and society but sanity itself. By encouraging sensuous self abandon, then, Coney Island in a very real sense promoted lunacy. (Kasson 1978: 95–96)

During the same period, a similar criticism was made of motion pictures (Peiss 1986; Richards 1983), of dance halls (Perry 1985), and of cabarets and nightclubs (Erenberg 1981). Somewhat earlier, concern had focused on such public celebrations as Philadelphia's rowdy Christmas festival (Davis 1982). And to Kasson's comment that "later critics would denounce rock concerts with their hallucinatory powers—and hallucinogenic drugs—in similar terms" (1978:101), I might add that they would also make a similar denouncement of video parlors and arcades.

Kasson's reference above to "sensuous self abandon" suggests an important reason for moralists' concern with fantasy: its linkage to sex (sensuous self-abandon) and to drink (self-abandon). In the early years of the twentieth century in the United States, criticism of *sexual-play* often focused on dancing:

> Of all the cabaret's activities, the public character of dancing aroused the bit-terest and most prolonged attacks. To reformers, the close physical contact and body expression connoted loss of self-control. The lifting of legs, the jerking of shoulders represented an unreserved demeanor on the part of youth and womanhood in general. . . . "Far from being 'new,'" a *Sun* editor-ial [of 1913] charged, "these dances are a reversion to the grossest practices of savage man." Indeed, they "are based on the primitive motive of orgies enjoyed by the aboriginal inhabitants of every uncivilized land." (Erenberg 1981:81)

In the same period the newly emergent motion picture theaters came under similar attack for the images of sexuality projected onto their screens and the effects of such images on impressionable youth. In 1909, a board of cen-sorship was established which, among other types of prohibitions,

> drew the line at what it considered suggestive behavior and heightened sen-suality in the movies—"the details of immoral sexual relations; over-pas-sionate love scenes; stimulating close dancing; unnecessary bedroom scenes in negligee; excessively low-cut gowns; undue or suggestive display of per-son." (Peiss 1986:160)

In their concern with public dancing and motion picture imagery, these critics were expressing fears over the more direct sexual activity that might later occur in private. More recent criticism of sexual-play has, of course, focused on public sexual activity per se, as in attempts to close or "sweep" such settings as "tearooms" (Humphreys 1970), parks (Delph 1978), or rest stops (Corzine and Kirby 1977), or to transform entire sections of cities (Boggs and Kornblum 1985; Kornblum et al. 1978). Whatever the specific fear, the linkage of public realm and sexual danger seems firmly ensconced in urban myth and legend and in urban imagery (Best and Horiuchi 1985; Brunvand 1981, 1984, 1986, 1989, 1993; Fine 1987):

> My mother is so fearful of the city. . . . She's all for these myths built up and yet she's lived in a city all her life. She was always fearful of having my sis-ter and I go into the downtown area, because everybody knows that young girls are carried away into white slavery. (quoted in Lofland [1973] 1985:102)

The public realm as the setting for fantasy-play and for sexual-play has received a great deal of attention from the guardians of public morality. But it is as the setting for *drinking-play* that seems to have generated the most concern. This aspect of public realm criticism is very well known. In the United States, enormous quantities of reformer energy have been expended in campaigns against saloons, taverns, cabarets, blind pigs, speakeasies, dives, nightclubs, and bars and, in more recent form, against the automobile drivers who emerge from such settings.[22] The temperance and prohibitionist movements have a long and well-documented history (see, for example, Gusfield 1963; Rosenzweig 1983) and we will shortly look more closely at their arguments against "demon rum" and the locales that dispense it. Similarly, in England, despite thorough integration of the "public house" into the transport, recreational, and political life of the country, the pub was not exempt from nineteenth-century temperance criticism. The burgeoning cities and the expanding industrial order generated both an urban working class of unprecedented numbers and working-class pubs in appropriate quantity to serve it, and moralists viewed the situation with considerable alarm. And as in the United States, the purported effect of drink on thrift, family life, work capacity, and so forth was a central rhetorical theme (see, e.g., Harrison 1973:178; Lees 1985) . More seriously and importantly, however, criticism of the public house in Britain concerned its role in fostering "revolutionary" activity. And that leads us into the fourth kind of attack on the public realm: its openness to uncontrolled politics.

Political Anarchy. That political activity located in the public realm should ipso facto be viewed with suspicion and dis-ease by guardians of the moral order—that is, should be thought of as *political anarchy*—is not at all unreasonable. The fact that the public realm, by definition and as we have seen above, involves space to which theoretically "everyone" has access (either for free or at minimal cost) means that it will seem particularly attractive as a site for politics to those who cannot command significant private space. That is, it will have particular appeal to the unmonied—the outcasts, the dangerous classes, the unworthy poor, the mob, the unwashed masses, the proletariat, the underclass—in short, to all those urban folks who (as we will discuss in Chapter 6) inspire fear in the hearts of authorities everywhere. Additionally, this same fact of accessibility means that public realm space is a natural stage and a powerful medium of communication. If the space chosen also happens to be one that is routinely heavily used, then it is guaranteed that spectators to the activity (if not an attentive audience) will be present. It is unsurprising, then, that public realm politics should excite concern or, as we learn from Hobsbawm, that since the French Revolution and the rise of Socialist movements, public authorities have become far more sensitive to crowds and disorder, especially in large or capital cities, than they were previously; and . . . , perhaps in consequence, the apparatus of public order has become increasingly large and efficient in the past one and a half centuries, even in the countries most suspicious of State action. (1959:110)

As we have seen above, in England some of the criticism of the urban working-class public house or "pub" was based on a perceived "cultural threat" (Harrison 1973:180) and in this the British temperance reformers shared a universe of discourse with their American colleagues. But the pub was also quite explicitly viewed as a direct political threat, a danger that seems not to have been associated with the American saloon:

[I]t was widely believed that pubs fostered revolutionary activity. Pubs assembled working people in *crowds* and encouraged them to consume an article which might subvert their customary rational appreciation of the Government's power: wine shops had indeed helped to transmit revolutionary ideas in France after 1789, and temperance reformers were eager to substitute a safe domesticity for the ominous public life of the working class. (ibid.:178)

Depending on exactly how one defines "revolutionary," one might well argue that the perceived threat from the pubs had considerable basis in fact. Many working-class public houses provided space for or sponsored debating clubs and these seem to have done much to generate and fortify radical opinion. Brian Harrison's description of the Sunday Evening Debating Society, which met in Birmingham's Hope and Anchor Inn, provides a single example that can stand for many:

[The] society met continuously from the mid-1850's to 1886. . . . From 8:30 to 11 every Sunday evening, almost without a break, twenty to forty members and (if the year 1864 was typical) over 150 spectators gathered to hear the topics introduced by regular speakers and then debated. . . . [B]etween 19 July 1863 and 6 November 1864 thirteen debates went on domestic politics, fourteen on foreign affairs, six on literary and cultural topics, five on religion, four each on labour questions, social problems and crime, two on science, and one on local affairs. . . . There was much to frighten the outside observer: the motion on 23 January 1859 for working-class enfranchisement was unopposed, and the monarchy lost by thirty nine votes to sixteen in a debate on republicanism. . . . On 6 February 1859 the motion "Has the Establishment and extension of Machinery tended to decrease the Wages of the employed" received unanimous support. (ibid.:179–180; see also Tilly and Schweitzer 1982)

Most criticism of the pub appears to have emanated from supporters of the political and economic status quo, but not all. Like labor activists in the United States who saw the saloon as standing in the way of a politically effective working class (Rosenzweig 1983), some British radicals supported prohibition because they believed that "only a *sober* radicalism could ever be really effective" (Harrison 1973:181; emphasis in the original). But it is not the enclosed locale like the pub that occasions most attacks on the polit- ical anarchy of the public realm. Rather, outdoor spaces—streets, parks, plazas, squares—are the major focus, as we will see in some detail in Chap- ter 7. At this juncture and as a hint of the link between moral concern and urban design, I will simply note that during the planning and construction of London's Trafalgar Square there were repeated expressions of official unease over "Leaving open so large a space in this particular quarter of the Metropolis" (Mace 1976:87). The cause of this concern: the urban "mob" and its revolutionary potential. Interestingly enough, John Nash's initial though unrealized plans for the square and for the entire Charing Cross area envisioned a street system that cut off easy access between the work- ing-class East End and the affluent West End.

Indirect Assaults: The Public Realm as Rhetorical "Warrant"

Not all attacks on the public realm are as direct as those we have been reviewing. Sometimes the attack is actually aimed elsewhere and the pub- lic realm simply gets drawn in as a handy piece of ammunition. This is the kind of situation we want to consider now. And it is a situation that is per- haps best introduced via the sad, sad story of Zerubbabel Green. The story is by a nineteenth-century popular writer named George Foster and was published in 1850 in his *New York by Gas-Light.* I am here quoting from a summary of that tale provided by Adrienne Siegel in her *The Image of the American City in Popular Literature*, (1981):

In [this story], the newcomer [to New York City] from upstate New York escapes cabmen, hotel runners, and pickpockets only to meet a gentleman who promises to introduce him to New York's "upper-ten-thousand." Taken to a place filled with beautifully dressed courtesans, he is plied with drink and led to believe that one of the harlots is the Countess of Astoria. His com- panion then suggests that, before sampling some of Gotham's exciting night life, they deposit their money in a safe with the "chief of police," an idea to which he readily agrees. Once in a bar, they realize that they lack money to pay for the drinks. Zerubbabel quickly draws upon the extra supply of cash in his secret money belt. After being aroused by scenes of naked women dancing, he is taken to an oyster bar, where a wager costs him his watch. He finally passes out in a drunken stupor and awakes the next morning in the

streets, robbed of everything. To compound his difficulties, a vigilant policeman hauls him to the Tombs for drunkenness and loitering. (ibid.:50–51)

This is, according to Siegel, a quite typical version of the "cautionary tale"
popular in the nineteenth century, which—among other uses—instructed
would-be urbanites in the potential perils of the big city. Such tales were
very widespread, emanating not only from pulp fiction writers like Foster,
but from ministers in their pulpits and editors in their business journals as
well. The point I want to emphasize here is not the cast of characters or the
plot of such tales but *their setting*. Take heed of just where this poor noodle
is when all these terrible things happen to him: Having escaped the dangerous types lurking about the railroad depot, Zerubbabel is now found in
some locale inhabited by courtesans (apparently not a brothel), then he
goes to a bar, then to an oyster bar, and finally, to the streets. That is, the
locus of his peril and travail is the city's public realm. Now in this story—
and in others like it—the author's goal is not the castigation of the public
realm per se. But in this story—and in others like it—that realm is the *setting* in which the action takes place, and as such it provides a "warrant" for
the lesson the author intends readers to understand from the narrative.

In using the term *warrant*, I am drawing here on Stephen Toulman's
(1958) discussion of the structure of an argument and especially on Joel
Best's use of that discussion to illuminate the rhetoric of claims- and
counter-claims-making in social movements and other political conflicts.
Briefly stated, a warrant is composed of "statements that justify drawing
conclusions from the grounds," drawing conclusions, that is, from the
"basic facts that serve as the foundation for" the argument (Best 1990:31,
25; see also 1987). For example—again using Joel Best's work—the *grounds*
in the child-victim movement are importantly composed of data on "missing children" leading to the *conclusion* that "something should be done."
But in between the grounds and the conclusion is the *warrant*, in this
instance, importantly (though not exclusively) composed of the sentimen-
tal value Americans place on children (see, for example Zelizer 1985).

What the value of children does for the rhetoric of the child-victim
movement, the public realm does for the nineteenth-century cautionary
tale. And what is true of nineteenth-century urban cautionary tales—that
is, their characteristic use of the public realm as warrant—is equally true
of the rhetorics of many social-movement and other political conflicts of
the nineteenth and twentieth centuries (including, as we will see, the
child-victim movement). When we look at the rhetorical productions emanating from class wars, race wars, moral-religious wars, cultural wars,
gender wars, and so on, we see that the public realm is frequently used to
justify the conclusions that are being drawn from the grounds. And in this
repetitious usage, all these various movements and political factions are—

whether intentionally or inadvertently—assaulting not simply their targeted enemies, but indirectly that realm as well. But why should the public realm be used in this manner? Given what has already been discussed
in this chapter, the answer should be clear. In crafting their arguments,
social-movement and other political spokespersons attempt to draw upon
ideas, themes, motifs, and meanings that will resonate with the largest
possible audience. At least in the United States and Great Britain, both the
theme of antiurbanism and its dominant motif of "street" depravity provide this desired quality of resonance. And as such, the public realm provides the obvious setting in which to espy social and political evils.[23] The
very fact that these "evils" occur in the setting proves that they *are* evil,
and thus grants the necessary warrant for doing something about them.

To get a better understanding of this use of the public realm as warrant,
let us examine some of the rhetoric emerging out of four cases of political-
social conflict: (1) the moral outcry at the increasing "emancipation" of
middle-class women in the late nineteenth century in England and the
United States; (2) the nineteenth-century antiprostitution movement,
especially as that developed in England; (3) the nineteenth- and twentieth-
century temperance/prohibition movement, especially as it developed in
the United States; and (4) nineteenth- and twentieth-century American
struggles over child "welfare" and "protection."

Preserving the Gentler Sex.   This first example, then, has to do with the
conflict over the appropriate conduct of women. From the point of view of
nineteenth-century moralists in both England and the United States, the
increasing presence of "respectable" women in urban public space[24]
served as especially vivid and provocative evidence of women's unnatural
and undesirable abandonment of hearth and home, of their unnatural and
undesirable abandonment of appropriate "place." Of course, poor women
had rarely, from the earliest cities, been barred from "the streets." And the
spatial freedom of privileged women has been culturally and historically
quite variable (Pipkin 1990). Thus, what these moralists—males and
females—were emphasizing was not so much the presence of *women* per
se in public places, but the presence there of *middle-class or "respectable"*
women. That is, one strategy the rhetoricians of gendered backlash used in
making their argument was to locate the "problem" out in public. Stated
crudely, such a rhetorical strategy employs the following logic: the number of uppity women is increasing, uppity women are to be seen in public
places, therefore something should be done about the problem of uppity
women.

One recurring theme was that "respectable women" who were shame-
less enough to go out in public were subject to great peril from men
because men's "normative sexuality" might unexpectedly transmutate

into abnormal and violent sexual expressions (Walkowitz 1992:212). For "unexplained" reasons, this transmutation seemed most likely to occur in public space.[25] The 1888 series of brutal "street" murders of poor women—mostly prostitutes—in the Whitechapel area of London, which were attributed to Jack the Ripper, provided both press and pulpit with repeated opportunities to hammer the lesson home. Let me quote from Judith Walkowitz's account (in *City of Dreadful Delight*) of newspaper coverage of the "Ripper Terror":

> [S]ensational newspaper coverage . . . blamed "women of evil life" for bring-ing the murders on themselves, though it warned elsewhere that "no woman is safe while this ghoul's abroad." The popular press seemed to glory in intensifying terror among "pure" and "impure" women by juxtaposing reports of less serious "attacks on women" [in public places] with an account of the Whitechapel "horror"; by featuring an illustration of a "lady fright-ened to death" by a Ripper impersonator on the cover of the *Police Illustrated News*; and by proposing that the Ripper might change his venue to the more respectable parts [of London] as Whitechapel became too dangerous for him. (ibid.:218; see also Jenkins 1994:102–6)

A second theme is not unrelated to the first: "respectable" women who went out in public were subject to peril because on the streets were also to be found "women of the streets" or "streetwalkers." The danger might reside only in the respectable woman being directly exposed to the immoral one, as we saw above relative to fears about "mixing." But the more serious danger was that respectable women might be misidentified as prostitutes. In London at least, this happened so often—or so reformers claimed—that the warning about it could be rendered as a joke. In an 1865 lithograph, "a well-dressed woman in the street is approached by an evan-gelical clergyman, who offers her a reforming tract. She rejects his attempt to rescue her and assures him, 'you're mistaken. I am not a social evil, I am only waiting for a bus'" (Walkowitz 1992:50; see also Wilson 1991:41).

Leading Men Not into Temptation. The same argumentive strategy used by critics of female "emancipation" was employed by the nineteenth-century English antiprostitution movement, a movement whose adher-ents included (interestingly enough) feminists as well as social-purity forces. The content differs, of course, but note the similarity of the form: Prostitution is flourishing in London, female prostitutes solicit on the streets, therefore prostitution should be outlawed. This is an especially "telling" use of the public realm as warrant because while nineteenth-cen-tury London certainly had many streetwalkers, a significant amount of the prostitution that serviced middle- and upper-class males—the major focus of reformer concern—was actually contained within brothels. Nonetheless, in many, many accounts of London's vice, prostitution appears either

> as disorderly behavior on the part of "soiled doves," sauntering down the city thoroughfares, dangerous in their collectivity; or as the isolated activity of the lone streetwalker, a solitary figure in the urban landscape, outside home and hearth, emblematic of urban alienation. (Walkowitz 1992:22)

We have seen above that the "street" prostitute imperiled chaste women, but this was as nothing compared to what she did to men. In the words of one evangelist, "[A young man] cannot pass along the street in the evening without meeting with and being accosted by women of the town at every step." Another evangelist claimed that a man's "path is beset on the right hand and on the left, so that he is at every step exposed to temptation from boyhood to mature age, his life is one continuous struggle against it." (quoted in Wilson 1991:39). And many reformers "complained of the physical and visual aggressiveness of the 'painted creatures,' with the 'gaudy dress,' aggressive gaze, and provoking deportment" (ibid.:23; see also Bullough and Bullough 1987).

Prohibiting Demon Rum. As with the arguments used against "modern" females and against prostitutes, the rhetoric of the temperance/prohibition movement often used the public realm as warrant. Again, the content differs, but the form of the argument is the same. Men drink alcoholic beverages and become drunk, alcoholic beverages are available in saloons open to male members of the public, therefore the sale of alcoholic beverages should be prohibited. In other words, the saloon—that public realm locale par excellence—proved a powerful symbol in the battle against "demon rum." Even today, the image of a hatchet-wielding Carry Nation laying ruin to the bar stools, kegs, and bottles of these male sanctuaries represents for many the essence of the temperance/prohibition movement (Day 1989). In fact, in his classic study of the movement, sociologist Joseph Gusfield has suggested that the formation of the Anti-Saloon League in 1896 instilled temperance forces with a momentum they had not previously achieved:

> Symbolically, the very title of the League suggests the movement away from the assimilative approaches of the WCTU or the political party approaches of the Prohibition Party. Both the singleness of purpose represented in the idea of the League and the sense of opposition suggested by the "anti" character of its name are dominant features of the Temperance movement in the period between 1900 and the passage of the Prohibition Amendment in 1920. The saloon was pre-eminently an urban institution. . . . For the small town native-American Protestant, it epitomized the social habits of

the immigrant population. To the follower of the Progressive movement, the saloon was a source of the corruption which he saw as the bane of political life. . . . Within the context of Populist antipathy to urban and Catholic communities, the saloon appeared as the symbol of a culture which was alien to the ascetic character of American values. Anything which supported one culture necessarily threatened the other. "The Anglo-Saxon stock is the best improved, hardiest and fittest . . . if we are to preserve this nation and the Anglo-Saxon type, we must abolish [saloons]."[26] (Gusfield 1963:99–100; see also Duis 1983)

Similar themes appear in the Reverend Josiah Strong's 1885 attack on drink and immigrants—the twin menace to civilization as we know it:

[T]he saloon, together with the intemperance and the liquor power which it represents, is multiplied in the city. East of the Mississippi there was, in 1880, one saloon to every 438 of the population; in Boston, one to every 329; in Cleveland, one to every 192; in Chicago, one to every 179; in New York, one to every 171; in Cincinnati, one to every 124. Of course the demoralizing and pauperizing power of the saloons and their debauching influence in politics increase with their numerical strength. (Strong 1968:127)

And the same ideas, more simply put, are to be found in the assertion of a spokesman for the Colorado Anti-Saloon League that the people of the state should give "their prayers, votes and money to fight the Un-American saloon" (Noel 1982:facing p. 110), in temperance posters that proclaimed such messages as "Drink Causes Most Crimes, Sorrow, and Unhappiness. The Saloon Must Go" (ibid.), and in a song taught by WCTU members in Colorado to the children of their "Little Temperance League" (or L.T.L.):

C-O-L-ORaDO Yell
Who are We? The L.T.L.
HO! HO! HO! Watch us Grow!
When we vote saloons must go!
(quoted in Noel 1982:113)

Protecting Innocent Children and Corruptible Youth

Recently in my small city a small group of citizens including members of the Substance Abuse Commission, police officers, school officials, and parents expressed support for the idea of a citywide, strengthened antiloitering ordinance[27] that would permanently ban students (or anyone else) from "hanging around" near school property. The newspaper story reporting this development contained little evidence of violent or other crimes that might have prompted citizen concern. It did, however, contain much evidence of suspicion. For example, a police sergeant is quoted as saying that "The *loitering itself*—whether by students or nonstudents—invariably brings problems. We see *more potential for* fighting, smoking, and drug handling. . . . And while there have *not been a lot of drug arrests made*, [the sergeant] said, the department is *concerned with the number of people who gravitate to Davis from out of town*. 'We haven't a clue why they come here,' he said, adding that visitors come from Sacramento and Woodland" (Ryen 1994, emphasis added).

I suppose there are many lessons to be learned from the example of these concerned citizens and their "suspicions." But the lesson that is of interest to us here is simply this: Just as reformers have used or continue to use the public realm as ammunition in their battles against "uppity" females, prostitution, and drinking, so too have they used and continue to use it to justify measures for the protection of innocent children and corruptible youth. To demonstrate that children and youth are "on the streets" is to demonstrate the seriousness of such "problems" as parental neglect, delinquency, child labor, youthful drug and alcohol use, preadult sexuality, and truancy, as well as "plain old" disobedience and truculence. Here are two illustrations of what I mean.

First, the strange case of the agent for the Children's Aid Society who, in the winter of 1856, encountered two small children on the streets of New York. According to historian Christine Stansall, who relates this story, the agent characterized the children as "tidy and sweet." When he accompanied them home, he met their widowed mother: "a stout, hearty woman" who was barely eking out a living for her small family by street peddling. At the end of his report to the society, the agent's perceptions took what Stansall calls "a curious turn":

> "Though for her pure young children too much could hardly be done, in such a woman there is little confidence to be put . . . it is probably, some cursed vice has thus reduced her, and that, if her children be not separated from her, she will drag them down, too." (quoted in Stansall 1986:193)

What, Stansall asks, can account for the curious turn? Why did the agent make such a harsh judgment of a woman who, from the earlier part of his report, he appeared to view as deserving and virtuous?

> The answer lies in a curious place—*the streets* where the agent . . . first met the children. Their presence there was to him prima facie evidence of their mother's vicious character. (ibid.:194, emphasis added)

A second strange case involves early twentieth-century American child labor reformers and their argument that children under the age of sixteen who were required to enter the work force would grow up "intellectually, and physically stunted." According to historian David Nasaw, this argument

> was not without merit when applied to the reformers' primary targets: the textile mills, coal mines, canneries, and berry fields. . . . In each of these workplaces, youngsters were forced to sit, stand, stoop, or lie on their bellies, hour after hour, day after day. They emerged in the end with twisted bodies, damaged eyesight, and senses numbed by inactivity and lack of stimulation. (1985:138–39)

But when the reformers turned their attention to street traders,

> their arguments lost their force and much of their validity. The street traders were not physically confined or constrained, nor were they deprived of sensory stimulation. . . . They were, on the contrary, freer to move on the streets than in the classrooms and no less stimulated. (ibid.)

How then account for the reformers' unabated zeal? The answer was

> a different order of evils: from too much, not too little freedom, stimulation and excitement. To the untrained eye, the *crowded downtown streets* might not appear particularly dangerous. But for the reformers, the sources of danger to unformed morals and awakening libidos were ubiquitous. (ibid.:140, emphasis added; see also Cahill 1990; Edwards, Oakley, and Carey 1987)

Let me not be misunderstood. I am in no way arguing that prostitution, child welfare, women's emancipation, drink, etc. are only defined as "problems" in terms of their publicness. I am arguing that however a minor a part it may be of the overall situation, public realm visibility per se gives special and especially meaningful ammunition to the foes of these problems—in fact, increases their very capacity to define them *as* problems. Returning again to Joel Best's study of the child victimization movement, we can note with him that most abducted children are taken by a parent. Nonetheless, in the rhetoric of the movement, tales of lurking strangers who pluck children "off the streets" provide a far more powerful warrant for doing something than do stories about mommies and daddies embroiled in custody disputes (Best 1990).

THE DEFENDERS STRIKE BACK

Antiurbanism more generally and the view of city streets as "depraved" in particular represent a torrent in the Anglo-American cultural

stream. Prourbanism and the celebration of "street"-life is better characterized, at least until quite recently (see Chapter 8), as a trickle. But trickle
or not, the representational works of cityphiles have, over a period of
many years, served as a constant and undoubtedly irritating challenge to
the hegemonic claims of cityphobes. In Chapter 1 and in Part I we have
already encountered a number of urban enthusiasts and apologists and we
will encounter even more of them in Chapter 8. My concern now is simply—in light of the unrelenting antiurbanism depicted in this and the subsequent two chapters—to remind readers that such a challenge exists: that
city life and street life have their defenders, and that the defenders provide
representations that, both directly and indirectly, "strike back." The easi-
est and most efficient way to do this reminding is, I think, to lay before you
a small sample of four paired contrasts, with one exception all involving
visual representations.

First, compare the message about the manifold dangers and unpleas-
antnesses of city life contained in the frontispiece to the Helmer and
Eddington volume (Illustration 5.4) to that contained in German architect
and art critic August Endell's 1908 essay:

> The astounding fact is that the big city, despite all the ugly buildings, despite
> the noise, despite everything in it that one can criticize, is a marvel of beauty
> and poetry to anyone who is willing to look, a fairy tale, brighter, more col-
> orful, more diverse than anything ever invented by a poet; a home, a mother,
> who daily bestows new happiness in great abundance upon her children.
> (quoted in Lees 1991:170)

Second, compare Dore's grim, almost oppressive London street scene
(Illustration 5.7) with the lightness and serenity of Gustave Caillebotte's
"Paris Street, Rainy Day" (Illustration 5.12). Third, look at how differently
Tooker (Illustration 5.13) and Reginald Marsh (Illustration 5.14) depict the
same subject: the New York subway. And finally, compare another Marsh
painting, this time of rush hour pedestrian traffic (Illustration 5.15), with
Irving Norman's starkly antithetic view (Illustration 5.16).

And yet, even in the face of significant challenge, the cityphobes usually
have their way. Reginald Marsh's paintings (Illustrations 5.14 and 5.15),
for example, convey to many viewers—and he himself was said to believe
that his work captured—the vitality and excitement and diversity of city
life (see Goodrich 1972). But note how an interpreter of his work, while
acknowledging the painter's perspective, manages to overlay it with her
own conventionally antiurban animus:

> Movies, dance halls, burlesque—these were all commercialized forms of
> recreation which developed to fill the needs of a new urban population. They

Illustration 5.12. Gustave Caillebotte, *Paris Street, Rainy Day*, 1876/77. Charles H. and Mary F.S. Worcester Collection, Art Institute of Chicago. Photograph © 1997, Art Institute of Chicago.

Illustration 5.13. George Tooker, *The Subway*, 1950. Collection: Whitney Museum of American Art. Of this painting, the artist said, "I was thinking of the large modern city as a kind of limbo. The subway seemed a good place to represent a denial of the senses and a negation of life itself. Its being underground with great weight overhead was important." (Garver, 1985:30)

Illustration 5.14. Reginald Marsh, *Subway Station,* 1930. Collection of Mr. and Mrs. Louis D. Cohen, Great Neck, New York. Reproduced in Goodrich (1972).

used sex and money to bring people together, providing *easy thrills* and excitement for people who *only temporarily shared any common interests. The tawdry halls and theatres came to epitomize the disorientation and dislocation, to evoke a hysteria that lay just beneath the surface.* And these were the activities Marsh chose to paint; he viewed them as colorful spectacles, and was drawn to their *crass* glamor, their *gaudiness,* their energy. (Cohen 1983:5, emphasis added)

If many contemporary humans fear and detest the city and its "streets," should we be surprised? And if they act on these emotions by encasing themselves inside private and parochial worlds, is this unexpected? Whether these emotions and actions feed or are fed by antiurbanism or whether each contributes to and reinforces the other, we cannot say definitively (though in the next two chapters I will hazard some guesses). What can be said is that the dominant representations of city life match harmoniously with the dominant feelings about and actions toward city life. And that is the topic of Chapter 6.

Illustration 5.15. Reginald Marsh, *BMT, Fourteenth Street,* 1932. Collection of Mr. and Mrs. Norman Schafler, New York City. Reproduced in Goodrich (1972).

Illustration 5.16.   Irving Norman, City Rush, 1941. Courtesy Jan Holloway Fine Art, San Francisco. Reproduced in Nash (1995).

NOTES

1.   Gary Delsohn, "A Pricey Preserve." *Sacramento Bee*, Sunday, October 22, 1995, p. I-1. Ironically enough, Delsohn is the *Bee* columnist-critic specializing in urban architecture, planning and design.

2.   From a film brochure entitled "Social Psychology Series" advertising four Stanley Milgram films that are distributed by PennState Audio-Visual Services. Received as an unsolicited mailer by the author in September 1990.

3. Letter from Edward Abbey of Oracle, Arizona, published in *Mother Jones*, April 1983, p. 4.

4. Overviews of the antiurbanism theme in Western thought include Aronson (1977), Fischer (1976:Chapter 2), Hadden and Barton (1973), Howe (1971), Karp, Stone, and Yoels (1977, 1991), Schorske (1968), and White and White (1962). It is interesting to note that Mount Holyoke, like many American colleges and universities, was built in rural Massachusetts for the express purpose of protecting its students from what were viewed as "the vices" of big cities (Horowitz 1984; reported in Spain 1992:4).

5. For discussions of this theme in American thought and letters, see Berger (1979), Goist (1977), Kirschner (1970), Lingeman (1980), McDermott (1972), Robertson and Robertson (1978), Ross (1994), Schmitt (1969), Smith (1966), Swanson, Cohen, and Swanson (1979), Taylor (1982), and Williams (1973).

6. Described by Hummon as "a rural small town in the central valley of California" (1990:41).

7. The device has sometimes incorporated unexpected or outre details. In eighteenth-century Europe, for example, the "savage" or "black"—an eighteenth-century symbol of inferiority—came also to stand, satirically, for "civilization" and was widely used to emphasize the artificiality and emptiness of urban culture, as in many Hogarth prints (Dabydeen 1987).

8. Certainly, David Hummon was able to locate a well-developed procity ideology among some of his California informants (Hummon 1990:Chapter 4) and there is a strong strain of procity/anti-small-town sentiment to be found in many novels of the early twentieth century: those of Sinclair Lewis and Thomas Wolfe are especially pointed in this regard. Additionally, the American phenomenon of "gentrification"—despite the fact that scholars interested in it probably outnumbered participants—stands as clear rebuke to anyone who would argue that Anglo-American culture is totally antiurban. And extant pre-1945 cities, in part because they carry the patina of historical significance, may evoke strong positive feelings (see, e.g., Bridger 1996; Maines and Bridger 1992). On the diversity of settlement imagery, see Bacon (1963), Beauregard (1993), Bender (1975), Coleman (1973), Fischer (1976), Glazer (1984a), Hansvick (1978), Hollister and Rodwin (1984), de Jonge (1962), Ladd (1969), Lees (1985), Pike (1981), Quandt (1970), Rodwin and Hollister (1984a, 1984b), Siegel (1981), Stern (1979), Strauss (1961, 1968), Tuan (1974), Warner (1984), and Wohl and Strauss (1958).

9. The Left's penchant for urban animus was nicely expressed in a 1989 review of Roberta Gratz's *The Living City* and William H. Whyte's *City*—both prourban books—in the *Nation*. Despite the reviewer's generally positive descriptions of the works, he could not help but express his concern over the failure on the part of both authors to give sufficient attention—to paraphrase him a bit—to what truly god-awful places cities were (Gottlieb 1989). Apparently, when the cityphiles dare to "peep" in response to the "roar" of the cityphobes, they need to be squished.

10. In the United States, the continuing use of the city-suburb distinction long after its descriptive value has dissolved should perhaps be understood as a distancing-mechanism. "If the inner cities are in trouble, well, what can you expect of

'cities' and their residents. It's not the suburban taxpayer's problem." On some of the consequences of this distancing, see Davis (1992) and McKenzie (1994).

11. On some of the consequences of antiurbanism for social theory and vice versa, see Jacobs (1969:Chapter 1), Karp et al. (1977, 1991), Smith (1979), and Tilly (1984).

12. Printed on a 2-3/4 × 3-3/4 card distributed by Earth First. Collected by the author in the fall of 1994.

13. Consider, for example, Claude Fischer's finding that urbanites in his survey were not estranged from "close associates or from familiar groups such as neighbors" but they are estranged from "the inhabitants of the 'world of strangers'" (1981:315). Interestingly enough, sustained critiques of urban *residences* often focus on characteristics more usually associated with the public realm, as when "hotel life" is castigated for its sexual and other license (see, e.g., Groth 1994:Chapter 7). Nonetheless, I do not want to be understood as saying here that antiurbanism is exclusively focused on the public realm. A focus on population size and on urbanization's association with industrialization are additional components of the sentiment.

14. A prime example of social analysis that does just that is Joanne Finkelstein's "Dining Out: The Self in Search of Civility" (1985).

15. On the coupling of immigrants with "dirty birds," see Fine and Christoforides (1991).

16. See, for example, Carl Nolte, "Support Drying Up for 'Urban Oasis'," *San Francisco Chronicle*, July 10, 1989, p. A2; Marc Sandalow, "Neighbors Don't Want Showroom as Shelter," *San Francisco Chronicle*, March 2, 1990, p. A6.

17. Associated Press, "Marchers in Rio Protest Murders of Street Kids," *San Francisco Chronicle*, November 30, 1991, p. A7; Leslie Wirpsa, "Death Squads Target 'Disposable' Columbians," *San Francisco Chronicle*, November 13, 1993, p. A13; Bob Sylva, "The Planner and the Planned," *Sacramento Bee*, December 22, 1988, p. E-1.

18. Even when mixing in a public setting is deemed desirable, close supervision is seen as the key to a positive outcome. For example, recreation workers in what Galen Cranz labels "the reform park" era (1900–1930) saw this newly emergent park form as an explicit agent of social and cultural (but *not* racial) integration, with themselves as the direct interpreters to children and their parents of the American assimilation experience (Cranz 1982; see also Rosenzweig 1983). As we will see in Chapter 7, I conceptualize such highly regulated supposedly "public" spaces as counterlocales.

19. On the development of class-segregated theaters and other performance settings in the United States in the last half of the nineteenth century, see Levine (1988). It may be that the emergence in the latter part of the nineteenth and early part of the twentieth centuries of commercial institutions that encouraged class and other mingling were viewed with particular concern exactly because they ran counter to the segregation that had been established between highbrow and lowbrow. On the development of internal class segregation in British music halls, see Earl (1986).

20. See, for example, Nikki Rexroat, "Rowdy Teenagers in Berkeley: Trouble on Telegraph Ave.," *San Francisco Chronicle*, August 22, 1986, p. 4; Mike Dunne, "Cruise City," *Sacramento Bee*, March 1, 1990, Scene, p. 1; R. V. Scheide, "Cruise

Control: Exile on Broadway," *Sacramento News and Review*, August 26, 1993, p. 14. See also "Foothills Teens to Hip to Handle: Rebel Somewhere Else, Tourist Businesses Ask," *Sacramento Bee*, October 30, 1996, p. B1. Complaints of this sort would seem to have a long history (see, e.g., Nasaw 1985:Chapter 10) and to cross national boundaries. In 1907, for example, free chamber music concerts were offered to the English working class in part, so as to get the courting young off the streets (Russell 1983).

21. Author's field notes and archives on Davis's politics.

22. On MADD (Mothers Against Drunk Driving) see McCarthy (1994) and McCarthy and Wolfson (1996).

23. Note the way in which street activities are equated with bad activities in the following letter to the editor of the *Davis Enterprise*. At issue here is a debate over the value of a city-built and city-funded "teen center" The thirteen-year-old writer is responding to an earlier letter in which the center was said to be inhabited exclusively by a small number of "punk skateboarders":

> I would like to let [the prior letter-writer] know that I attend the center regularly, and have natural hair, with only two earring holes. There are approximately 15 skateboarders that come in to the center every day, and they are perfectly normal people, as all skaters are. If they weren't at the teen center, they *would be on the streets, skating illegally on sidewalks, and supposedly being "bad" kids.* I just happen to have two brothers who skate and another who used to. They are not by any means "bad" people. The new seventh grade class has brought quite a large amount of teen-agers to the center this summer, all of whom are nice clean individuals who like having a place to go in the summer. Just this past Wednesday, 64 people came to the teen center, *staying off the streets where they could be doing "bad" things.* (July 20, 1995, emphasis added)

24. There were many reasons for this increase, including the development of new types of "feminine-friendly" spaces like department stores and tearooms, the increasing involvement of middle-class women in various forms of "hands-on" philanthropy, and the growing employment opportunities available to "respectable" women. See for example, Hutter (1987), Miller (1981), Walkowitz (1992), and Wilson (1991). But even before these changes brought more and more respectable women out in public, the intersection of women and town was thought to be an explosive one. Derek Jarrett describes *England in the Age of Hogarth*:

> Whatever else they disagreed about, almost all men were agreed that towns were the destroyers of feminine virtue. Women were thought to be peculiarly susceptible to the fashionable fripperies and time-wasting amusements of the town: even physicians were advised solemnly to think twice before sending their patient to take the water [at such resort towns as Bath, for example], for fear that this should 'please his wife and daughters by sending them to a scene of fashionable amusement.' Only in the country could a man be sure that his wife was his and his alone. (1974:194; see also Castle 1986:32–33)

25. Ironically enough, this theme has also been a recurring one in feminist discourse—both in the nineteenth century and currently—including the discourse emanating from sociologists and other social scientists. We will pursue this ironic convergence in Chapter 6.

26.   Gusfield is here quoting from the journal of the Anti-Saloon League—
American Issue—January 1912.

27.   The proposed ordinance would replace a current statute that "forbids nonstudents from loitering on or about school property for unlawful purposes or no
purpose at all" but that has a mere seventy-two-hour limit (Ryen 1994).

6
Fear, Loathing, and Personal Privatism

The overall goal of the three chapters making up Part II of this work is to attain some degree of understanding of the animus in which some individuals hold the public realm. In the prior chapter, we explored publicly available visual and verbal *representations* of that realm and of its "parent"—the city—and we saw that such representations are often strongly negative. Here, the focus shifts to the private feelings and activities of individual human beings, that is, to *emotional and behavioral* forms of the animus. The general argument, as the chapter title suggests, is that, in many individuals, the public realm has historically evoked and continues currently to evoke the emotions of fear and loathing and that, especially in the contemporary setting, those feelings may contribute to a penchant for privatism.

We will begin this chapter by looking at privatism per se: defining it, examining the conditions that might make its existence possible, and evaluating evidence for the reality of that existence. Then we will look at individual "feelings" that, given the possibility of privatism, might make it desirable. As a last matter, we will consider the possibility that privatism—as a life-style choice that some individuals make—may, in part, be a creature of antiurbanism and may, once created, loop back and feed the cultural theme that helped give it birth.

ENABLING AND EVALUATING PRIVATISM

In recent discussions, both the word *privatization* and the word *privatism* have been used to connote the movement of human activity from commonsensically understood "public" space into commonsensically understood "private" space—or, in the language of this study, the movement of activity out of the public or parochial realms and into the private (e.g., Lofland 1989; Popenoe 1985; Sennett 1970, 1977a, 1977b). My preference here is for "privatism" rather than "privatization" because I want to emphasize the personalistic and individualistic aspects of the phenomenon—its "property," as it were, of life-style choice—and because I want to reserve "privatization" for a phenomenon to be discussed in Chapter 7.[1]

Regardless of the specific word used, however, the idea conveyed is similar: that in portions of the contemporary world, some things that humans used to do outside their private spaces in the presence of their neighbors, their acquaintances, or strangers, they now do exclusively or mostly or increasingly inside their private space in the presence—if of anyone at all—of intimates. And the first question we need to ask about this phenomenon is a simple one: Regardless of whether it is desirable to some set of people, is privatism possible?

Making Privatism Possible: Enabling Conditions

The simple answer to the simple question of whether privatism is possible is "yes." The evidence for its possibility—that is, for the existence of conditions that would enable it—is ubiquitous and unequivocal.

Think back to Chapter 1 and to the discussion of changes in city form wrought by the Industrial Revolution. As I said there,

> [The] two characteristics [of the new form]—enlargement and enclosure—together made possible the separation of workplace from place of residence, made possible the development of highly specialized and large workplaces (e.g., factory districts), made possible the development of homogeneous and large areas of residence (e.g., working-class neighborhoods), made possible the siting of much round-of-life activity within the place of residence or neighborhood, and eventually, with the introduction and widespread personal ownership of the automobile, made it possible for an individual to connect pieces of widely dispersed space without the necessity of actually being, in any socially meaningful sense, in the intervening spaces. That is, it truly became *possible* for large numbers of late eighteenth-, nineteenth-, and twentieth-century city people, as it had not been possible for preindustrial city people, to spend significant portions of their lives entirely in the private and/or parochial realms.

The background context of this description of the new city form involved a discussion of *technological* innovations—for example, sewage, water and heating systems, the telephone and telegraph, improved mail delivery, new building materials and techniques, the elevator, and ground transportation systems and vehicles—which made it possible for the emerging industrial city to both enlarge and enclose. And that enlargement and enclosure, as I argued, made withdrawal from participation in the public realm a genuine option. In the twentieth century, the incessant march of technology has not only intensified that option, it has broadened it to include some withdrawal from the parochial realm as well. Consider, for example, the role of refrigerators and freezers in allowing weekly or semiweekly rather than daily visits to the market. Or consider the role of air conditioners in removing people from their windows, front porches, and stoops on hot summer evenings. Similarly, in the United States at least, with the rise of televised speeches and debates, the political rally has shrunk in importance and in some political races has largely disappeared. More tellingly, perhaps, the increasing use of the absentee ballot is moving the act of voting from the polling place to the home.[2] For those interested in "being entertained," the increase in the private ownership of television sets, VCRs, and other electronic devices make attendance at films, concerts, and theaters unnecessary. For those wishing to "reach out and touch someone," this can be accomplished via telephone, electronic mail, or other computer-created venues. Computers are also making possible some degree of withdrawal from the workplace, as more and more employees "telecommute." With the expansion of credit cards and direct mail selling, a good deal of nongrocery shopping can also be accomplished without setting foot outside one's household. The private automobile with its "cocoon of privacy" (Lofland [1973] 1985) has not only abetted the decline in availability and use of public transport, it has, as reiterated above, "made it possible for an individual to connect pieces of widely dispersed [private and parochial] space without the necessity of actually being, in any socially meaningful sense, in the intervening [public] spaces." And, of course, the fuel for those cocoons of privacy can now be obtained—via automated gasoline pumps—quite "privately."

But not all of the enabling conditions are technological. There is a second set of conditions—best labeled "architectural" or "stylistic"—which will be dealt with in detail in Chapter 7. And there is at least one (equally ubiquitous but perhaps less unequivocal) *social-psychological* condition that deserves mention: the extremely high value modern Western humans in general, but Americans in particular, seem to place on intimate (read, "authentic") relationships. As we saw in Chapter 3 and will see again in Chapter 8, Richard Sennett has long argued not only that there is such a preference but that it leads to a dismissal of more impersonal public—and even parochial—relationships as unimportant and unworthy (1970, 1977a, 1977b; see also Lofland 1983). If he is right in this, then certainly that preference—eliminating as it does any resistance to the loss of nonintimate contacts—is important in making privatism possible. We touched on this issue in the previous chapter in the discussion of the counterpointal role that "home and family" play in antiurban representations and, of course, the purported link between American individualism and privatism is one that can be traced back at least to Alexis de Tocqueville:

> Individualism is a calm and considered feeling which disposes each citizen
> to isolate himself from the mass of his fellows and withdraw into the circle

of family and friends; with this little society formed to his taste, he gladly leaves the greater society to look after itself. . . . Individualism is of demo-cratic origin and threatens to grow as conditions get more equal. . . . [N]ot only does democracy make men forget their ancestors, but also clouds their view of their descendants and isolates them from their contemporaries. Each man is forever thrown back on himself alone, and there is danger that he may be shut up in the solitude of his own heart . . . . I see an innumerable multitude of men, alike and equal, constantly circling around in pursuit of the petty and banal pleasures with which they glut their souls. Each one of them, withdrawn into himself, is almost unaware of the fate of the rest. Mankind, for him, consists of his children and his personal friends. As for the rest of his fellow citizens, they are near enough but he does not notice them. He touches them but feels nothing. ([1850] 1988:505, 507–8, 691–692; see also Sennett 1979)

Some one hundred and fifty years later, Robert Bellah and his research team expressed a similar concern:

In our interviews, it became clear that for most of those with whom we spoke, the touchstones of truth and goodness lie in individual experience and intimate relationships. Both the social situations of middle-class life and the vocabularies of everyday language predispose toward private sources of meaning . . . . As we have seen, ours is a society in which the language of individualism allows people to develop loyalties to others in the context of families, small communities, religious congregations, and what we have termed lifestyle enclaves. Even in these relatively narrow contexts, recipro-cal loyalty and understanding are frequently precarious and hard to main-tain. It is thus natural that the larger interdependencies in which people live, geographically, occupationally, and politically, are neither clearly under-stood nor easily encompassed by an effective sympathy. [Bellah, Madsen, Sullivan, Swidler, and Tipton (1985:250–51); but see Brown (1995) for a rather different perspective on the issue][3]

Assessing Privatism's Reality: Evaluating the Data

It is one thing to point with considerable certainty to the existence of conditions that make privatism possible—that enable it. It is quite another to produce data that prove its reality. The prime difficulty is that the phe-nomenon at issue here is neither an attitude, an institution, a belief, a ver-bal or visual representation of something, a piece of the physical environ-ment, an enacted law, nor any of a myriad of other sorts of phenomena that social science can easily probe, measure, describe, dissect, determine. Privatism *is*, by definition, an *increase* in the amount of certain human activities in one social territory with a concomitant *decrease* in other social territories of those same human activities. And the problem is that, unlike the situation for a few activities such as voting, purchasing automobiles, or attending movies, the "traces" left by most are not readily discernible.[4] No one keeps very good track of where most people are located when they are doing whatever they are doing, much less keeping very good track of what they are doing in the first place. So even if I could demonstrate, for example, that fewer people now than in the past do activity X in public or parochial locations, I would have a hard time demonstrating *directly* that the overall level of activity in public or parochial locations has dropped since it is always possible that simultaneous with a drop in the level of activity X, there is a rise in the level of activity Y. That is, if one wishes to answer the question of whether privatism exists and to do so definitively, one needs to be able to demonstrate not only that private activities are increasing but that *all parochial and public activities are decreasing in relation to them*. To my knowledge, no one has yet made such a demonstration. And I am, frankly, hard-pressed to see how anyone ever could.

Nonetheless, scholars do assert the reality of privatism (or privatization). David Popenoe, for one has argued that

> privatization reaches its apogee in metropolitan communities *because of factors that are indigenous to those communities*. The many structural features of metropolitan communities . . . —their large and diverse populations, great geographic and functional differentiation of people and human activities, and weak local autonomy as political and social entities— make up a social and cultural climate in which there is a progressive diminution of public [and parochial] life and a magnification of private life to a degree that is both historically unprecedented and socially harmful. (Popenoe 1985:111, emphasis in original)

But on what do students of social life like Popenoe base such assertions? How, if privatism is not a phenomenon that can be observed directly, can anyone in good conscience say that it exists? The answer, of course, is that—as with many sorts of illusive "things" pursued by scientists and scholars—its existence is *inferred*.

Some of this, as the Popenoe quotation implies, simply involves logical deductions from the enabling conditions. For example, if indoor plumbing and water supplies mean that people do not have to go out in public to relieve themselves or to get water, then they do not do so, and thus, unlike their ancestors, at least some of the time when they need to go to the bathroom or to get a drink of water, they can just stay home. Or, as another example, given the human inability corporally to be in two places at the same time, the employee who, by means of a computer, does her work in her own home is—obviously—not doing her work in the public or parochial location—as she would necessarily have been in the precomputer age. Similarly, individuals who, in contrast to their grandparents or great-grandparents, own cars and drive to work—either alone or with friends and family—are not simultaneously rubbing shoulders with strangers on buses or trains.

But there is more to inferring privatism that mere logical deduction: There are data, indirect data to be sure, but data nonetheless. Any single piece or even any single type of this data is relative unimpressive, but when considered *en masse*, the data become—if not totally persuasive—at least suggestive. There are, for example, various sort of assertions—claimed or reported—by newspaper writers about American withdrawal from nonfamilial social contact. In 1992, for example, the *San Francisco Chronicle* ran a story headlined "One Step Beyond Cocooning: 'Burrowers' Dig In, Stay There," which argued that "Increasing numbers of Americans in the '90's are discovering the joy of burrowing [staying home and liking it]" and which pointed to such "facts" as the modest 2 percent increase in food dollars spent away from home since 1987 compared with the 30–50 percent annual increase enjoyed by a Bay Area delivery service "that brings restaurant meals to the home."[5] In the fall of 1995, as another example, the *Davis Enterprise* and the *San Francisco Chronicle* both reported the claims of clinical psychologist Lynn Henderson and psychologist Philip Zimbardo of Stanford that, at least in the United States, shyness is increasing and that the cause is to be found in decreasing opportunities for (or the necessity of) nonfamilial interaction.[6]

More convincing, at least to me, are the observations of social historians who, after developing richly detailed portraits of public or parochial realm social activity in other times and places, claim to find little that is comparable in their own. This is what Amada Dargan and Steve Zeitlin have to say about *City Play*:

> In the 1930's and '40's, Oscar and Ethel Hale compiled a thousand-page- single-spaced manuscript called "From Sidewalk, Gutter, and Stoop," about traditional games on the streets of New York. They documented hundreds of different games and hundreds of variations on each of those games. . . . Half a century later, we did not find anywhere near the number or variety of games played out of doors. In the 1980's, far fewer blocks preserve that confluence of lifestyle and urban geography that sustain the traditional games and outdoor play. . . . Today, when children gather after school and face the recurrent question of what to do, street games are only one possibility, which must compete with a wide range of organized sports and commercial amusements along with television and radio. (1990:166, 167; see also, Gaster 1991)

And this is David Nasaw's lament about *Going Out*:

We no longer "go out" as much as we once did. The newest, most techno-
logically advanced amusement sites are our living rooms. There is less
"need" to leave the home to be amused. . . . As the public amusement realm
is year by year impoverished, the domestic one is enriched. (1993:255)

Statistics tell a similar story. In 1988, for example, Louis Harris and
Associates released a survey showing important shifts in attendance at art
events in the brief period between 1984 and 1987. Attendance at dance performances dropped 14 percent, nonmovie theater attendance went down
25 percent, while classical/popular concerts and opera/musical theater
attendance was reduced by 26 and 38 percent, respectively. During the
same period, increases were reported in movie (+9 percent) and museum
(+24 percent) attendance. But what really interested the survey takers and
the media that reported their results was the fact that simultaneously with
these ups and downs, VCR ownership increased by 234 percent!
Newsweek's comment was that "America may be turning into a stay-at-
home society of culture potatoes."[7] Here is another set of interesting numbers: There are 8,760 hours in a year. On the assumption that most humans
are going to use up about one-third of those in sleeping, that gives us 5,840
hours per year in which to "do things." The 1994 *Statistical Abstract of the
United States* estimates that Americans over the age of eighteen spend
approximately 1,435 hours or 25 percent of that time watching television.
Even if we grant that some (probably a miniscule) proportion of this
watching takes place in bars or other public or parochial locales, we are
forced to conclude that contemporary Americans spend somewhere
between one-fifth and one-fourth of their yearly waking hours at home
and in front of their television sets. And according to a 1986 Roper poll, we
are quite satisfied to do so. The pollsters asked this question: "Here are
some things most people experience in their daily lives. Of course, they
may all be important, but which three or four of these things do you find
give you the most personal satisfaction or enjoyment day in and day out?"
The results may or may not be surprising, depending on how convinced
you already are of privatism's reality. "Family" came in first at 70 percent,
"friends" were third at about 43 percent, losing out narrowly for second
position to "television," which garnered about 45 percent. Interestingly
enough, "socializing" (with whom or where unspecified) managed only a
meager 20 percent.[8] You will have noticed that thus far I have only mentioned the United States, but the numbers data are not so geographically
restricted. In the summer of 1995 the *Economist* reported:

In 1960, when France had 46 million people, there were reputed to be over
200,000 cafes [or bistros]. . . . Today, in a France of 58 million, only 50,000
remain, and they are disappearing at a rate of around 3,000 a year. In Paris

alone, more than 1,500 cafes closed last year, bringing the total down to half what it was in 1980.[9]

Some of the change is attributed to the influx of fast-food restaurants, longer commutes and working hours, and the "desertification" of the countryside. But some is also attributed to an increasing preference among the French for spending their leisure time at home watching TV rather than socializing in the cafe.

Then there are the data generated by sociological researchers. For example, Barry Wellman, in his discussion of the personal networks of Toronto men has reported:

> Just as urbanization once fostered public community among men, suburbanization now draws them away from public community. . . . Community has become domestic, moving from accessible public spaces to private homes. Men's friendships are now tucked away in homes just as women's friendships always have been. . . . Toronto men's friendships tend to be even more private than their other active relationships, rooted in the private worlds of homes . . . , letters . . . , and vacation cottages. (1992:7, 8)

Similarly, M. P. Baumgartner in her ethnographic study of an affluent community she calls Hampton (a piece of the New York "metrosea"), reports that "people typically spend most of their time in the town in their own homes" (1988:21). She identifies Hampton's dominating ethic—with family members, neighbors and friends, and strangers—to be "moral minimalism," which involves in part the preferred strategy of avoidance in conflict situations (e.g., a persistently barking dog, the presence on the street of a "suspicious" person). What is particularly relevant for our purposes is that avoidance of neighbors and strangers is especially easily accomplished by these residents because they spend *so little time in either the parochial spaces of their neighborhoods or the public spaces of the encompassing town*. In fact, to foreshadow a line of thought to be developed in Chapter 7, Hampton would seem to be the kind of settlement that might be said to be largely bereft of both neighborhood-parochial and public *realms*. Remember, if there are no people in the spaces, there can be no realms. And in Hampton, as in many similar American communities, there are rarely people in the spaces:

> On their way to and from public locations, most people in the town ride in private automobiles. Indeed, comparatively few walk anywhere except to mail an occasional letter at a corner mailbox, to drop in on a near neighbor, or to exercise a dog; few make use of public transit. Partly because there are no destinations along most roads except private houses, and partly because residents drive when they have errands to do, there is very little street life in

Hampton. It is possible to ride in a car for blocks at almost any time of day without encountering pedestrians. Even downtown, the streets are usually quiet. (ibid.:102)

As I said above, any single piece or even single type of data concerning the reality of privatism seems unsubstantial. But as the evidence—all of it, granted, indirect—accumulates, it gathers solidity and force and, in my view, *begins* (and I emphasize, begins) to take on a compelling quality.[10] Given these data, especially when viewed in conjunction with the enabling conditions, I am inclined to think that privatism is a real phenomenon, albeit one whose magnitude I find impossible to assess. But whatever its magnitude, the very existence of privatism must be understood as another source of threat to the public realm.

Interestingly enough, most scholars who view privatism with some alarm do so not out of concern for the public realm but out of concern for the parochial. It is the consequences of "cocooning" and "burrowing" for voluntary associations, for community organizations, for political groupings, for social movements, and so forth that worries them (e.g., Popenoe 1985; Putnam 1995a, 1995b, 1995c),[11] not the impact on bars, buses, plazas, parks, coffeehouses, and streets. But, of course, it is precisely privatism's impact on bars, busses, plazas, parks, coffeehouses, and streets that interests me here. And following that interest, I now ask whether there is anything we know about the emotions individuals harbor toward the public realm that might help to account for privatism. If there are manifold conditions that make it *possible*—and we have seen that there are—is there evidence of private feelings that would make it *desirable*?[12] The answer once again is yes.

FUELING PRIVATISM? NEGATIVE EMOTIONS AND SECLUDED LIVES

There is considerable evidence that for at least the last two hundred years in the West "the streets" have generated negative emotions among some proportion of the population. Eighteenth- and nineteenth-century materials tell us primarily about elite sentiments. It is their voices we mostly hear in the historical record—issuing alarms, passing legislation, creating organizations for social control, and so forth. In the twentieth century, thanks to survey research and opinion polling, and to ethnographic and journalistic observation and interviewing, the voices of nonelites have been added to the chorus. But whether we are "picking up on" the feelings of contemporaries or of ancestors, the whats and whys of those feelings evince a remarkable similitude. The whats are fear and loathing. The whys are various types of strangers.[13]

The Fearsome Stranger: Mobs, Outcasts, Criminals, and Males

For some humans, the public realm is fearsome because it is populated by fearsome strangers: mobs who challenge "legitimate" rule; outcasts whose social marginality is equated with sinfulness; criminals who rob, rape, maim, and kill; and males whose prey is women. Not unexpectedly, in some times and places the categories of who is to be feared tend to cluster (mobs composed entirely of outcasts, men who are mostly if not universally criminal) or to amalgamate into a single source of peril (mobs composed of criminal male outcasts). More commonly, any possible association between the categories goes unremarked as the fearful focus upon their individual nightmares.

Fear of the *mob* has a long pedigree.[14] In fact, Yi-Fu Tuan identifies "fear of anarchy and revolution, that is, of the overthrow of an established order by unassimilable and uncontrollable masses" as one of five long-standing themes of urban violence that generate, in the words of his chapter title, "Fear in the City" (Tuan 1979:157).[15] In the introductory chapter to his *The Great Riots of New York: 1712–1873*, Joel Tyler Headley, an immensely popular and prolific nineteenth-century author, provides a classic example of the "overthrow" theme. Headley is explaining to his readers just why they owe such a debt of gratitude to the men who put down the Draft Riots of 1863:

> One thing only is needed to show how complete and irreparable the disaster would have been [had the riots not been quelled]; namely the effect it would have had on the finances of the country. With the great banking-houses and moneyed institutions of New York sacked and destroyed, the financial credit of the country would have broken down utterly. . . . Had the rioters got complete possession of the city but for a single day, their first dash would have been for the treasures piled up in its moneyed institutions. Once in possession of these, they, like the mobs of Paris, would have fired the city before yielding them up. . . . Doubtless the disastrous effects would have been increased tenfold, if possible, by uprisings in other cities, which events showed were to follow. . . . In this view of the case, these riots assume a magnitude and importance that one cannot contemplate without a feeling of terror, and the truth of history requires that their proper place should be assigned them. . . . It is also important, as a lesson for the future, and naturally brings up the question, what are the best measures, and what is the best policy for the city of New York to adopt, in order to protect itself from that which today constitutes its greatest danger—*mob violence?* ([1873] 1970: 19–20, emphasis in original)[16]

As a Whig with aristocratic pretensions, Headley's expressed fears are very much elite fears. And, unsurprisingly, most such expressions do seem to emanate from elites. But not exclusively. Rodney Mace speaks of the response of "panic" among shopkeepers and other middle-class folks to the February 8, 1886 ("Black Monday") demonstration in London's Trafalgar Square by the Social Democratic Federation, the London United Workers Committee and the unorganized unemployed; but he also points out that such elite institutions as the *Times*, which reported on February 9 that "The vagabondage of London, apparently associated by some mysterious sympathy, marched up Pall Mall," certainly helped to fuel middle-class fears (1976:161–65; see also Jones 1971:290–96).[17]

During the late nineteenth century, fear of the "mob" was given ever more legitimacy through the "scientific" writings of psychologists and, to a lesser degree, sociologists who assured their readers that their terrors were valid. In France, for example, crowd psychologists (led by Gustave LeBon) proffered a vision that

> was awesome, almost invariably terrifying. Their crowds loomed as violent, bestial, insane, capricious beings whose comportment resembled that of the mentally ill, women, alcoholics, or savages. (Barrows 1981:5)

Even as late as 1908, the American sociologist E. A. Ross devoted an entire chapter of his *Social Psychology* to "Prophylactics Against Mob Mind" in which he warned that the presence of too many of what he labeled "mob folk" in a nation could produce "a dangerous rhythm in the conduct of public affairs" (ibid.:83). One of his prophylactics, by the way, was "country life," since "[c]ity-bred populations are liable to be hysterical" (ibid.:87). Among contemporary scholars, of course, fear of the crowd or mob has mostly been replaced by admiration. It is not too much of an exaggeration to say that historians and sociologists, in particular, rarely encounter a mob they don't like.[18] But fear has certainly not disappeared, as reactions to urban uprisings from the late 1960s to the present testify. For example, following the Los Angeles riots in the spring of 1992, gun sales in California for the first eleven days of May increased by 50 percent over the same period in 1991 (Eckholm 1992). And a *Los Angeles Times* poll, also in early May, found that only 60 percent of those polled reported feeling "safe where they live," down from 75 percent when the same question was asked in April (Clifford and McMillan 1992).

Fear of *outcasts* is not unrelated to fear of the mob but it also appears somewhat less solidly welded to elite interests. Gareth Stedman Jones, in his *Outcast London: A Study in the Relationship between Classes in Victorian Society* (1971), for example, argues that anxieties generated by casual laborers, the unemployed, and the persistent poor (known variously as the "dangerous class" or the "residuum") were very widespread in Britain in the second half of the nineteenth century. London, in particular, was thought to be the mecca for this group, and their existence was in part explained by the "theory of hereditary urban degeneration"—the idea that "long life in the towns is accompanied by more or less degeneration of the race" (ibid.:128). The residuum's preference for "cheap excitements offered by the pubs, the low music-halls, and streets" (ibid.:286) was viewed both as a contributor to and as evidence of the inevitable degeneration. Clearly some of the fear had to do with the possibility (and the occasional reality) of these outcasts forming themselves into mobs; but much also had to do with their perceived potential for "infecting" others morally and physically and with the threat to personal property and bodily integrity posed by their presumed criminality. Art historian Susan P. Casteras has even suggested that such fears found their way into nineteenth-century social realist art: "The shadowy places where the poor were often placed in paintings [e.g., Illustrations 6.1 and 6.2] reflected not only the reality of the dank world of disease and defeat which they inhabited but also the way the poor were perceived as sinister and threatening" (1987:131). And the Dutch sociologist Lodewijk Brunt has demonstrated that in the period 1850 to 1914, even the reports of presumably dispassionate social researchers were permeated with what he calls "the rhetoric of fear:"

> A striking aspect of the language many social explorers used is its abundant display of symbols and images referring to the supposedly sinister and frightening qualities of the urban poor. It is as if the readers had to be constantly reminded that everybody who did not belong to their own bourgeois class was a (potential) danger to society, civilization, and humankind in general. Much of the social explorers' compassion for the sad lives of the urban poor and appreciation for their toughness and ability to survive was concealed behind this rhetoric of fear. In this rhetoric a close link was drawn between poverty, crime, filth, and disease and emphasis was laid on the lack of self-control, primitive and barbarian conduct, decay and death, and, in general, the animal element in man. (1990:80–81)

Fear of "degenerate" outcasts is, of course, not confined to Britain of the last century, nor even to urban settings. It can be located in many times and places, including Paris in the early part of the nineteenth century (Merriman 1991), sixteenth-century England (Beier 1985), "New France" (Quebec) in the seventeenth century (Scalberg 1991), and late twentieth-century urban America. As we will see in the next section, there is much evidence that contemporary American outcasts such as the homeless are viewed with loathing. But there is also evidence that for some, the loathing is

Illustration 6.1. Gustave Doré, *the Bull's Eye, 1872.* Private collection. Printed in Treuherz, 1987.

mixed with or even dominated by fear. A single example should suffice to make the point. Here is a letter to the editor of the *San Francisco Chronicle* in response to a judge's ruling that begging is protected by free speech rights:

> I am writing to express my distaste with [the] U.S. District Judge['s] . . . ruling on panhandlers. Judge . . . has compromised the rights and safety of the

Illustration 6.2.   Luke Fildes, *Houseless and Hungry,* graphic, 1872. Rijksmuseum
Vincent van Gogh, Amsterdam. Printed in Treuherz, 1987.

majority of the public. He has seen fit to give street people, panhandlers,
thugs and various wackos free reign over our streets and daily lives. We are
no longer safe from being harassed. We can be insulted, spat upon and generally threatened in our own neighborhoods by someone who is expressing
his freedom of speech. In the name of freedom, our wives, girlfriends and
daughters can be threatened daily with abuse. For freedom of speech our
children will no longer be able to go out on their own because we do not feel
safe having a drug addict or an alcoholic camped at the public playground.
And when we get angry at the derelict in the Financial District who is urinating on our car, ignoring our protests, we should remember that this is
done in the name of freedom. Judge ... has pointed out the numerous
statutes that protect us. I am sure he is assuming there is a policeman on
every corner who is actually interested in taking a report. In my experience,
however, the police are too busy to bother, and the offender is long gone. The
police treat assault and robbery as a low-priority crime. And the street people know this. Perhaps Judge ... should take the time to walk the public
areas by himself, alone at night. Perhaps then will he understand what rights
the majority of us have given up in the name of freedom. (October 3, 1991)[19]

Despite the distance of some eight thousand miles and more than a century, this San Franciscan letter-writer would certainly have recognized
many of the nineteenth century's commentators on the "plague of beggars" in London as intellectual and emotional soulmates:

"No-one who lived in the suburbs," wrote Thomas Beggs, "could help feeling that [when in London] they were in circumstances of considerable peril".
. . . "What" [asked the Reverend Henry Solly, in a public address] "could a
force of 8,000 or 9,000 police be against the 150,000 roughs and ruffians,
whom, on some sufficiently exciting occasion, the Metropolis might see
arrayed against law and order?" (Jones 1971:242–43)

We have seen above that fear of outcasts sometimes merged with elite
anxieties about the mob on the one hand or with more widespread fears
about criminals on the other. For reasons we will discuss in the next chapter, fear of the mob appears to have abated somewhat, at least in developed nations. In contrast, fear of *criminals* definitely has not, particularly
in the United States.[20] I have in my files two U.S. magazines with covers
featuring the same topic. One displays a black-and white photograph of a
shadowed profile looking out from a barred highrise window and pro-
claims, "The Cities Lock Up: Fear of Crime Creates a Life-Style Behind
Steel." The photograph on the second magazine cover is in color—the
object photographed is a residential lawn sign announcing that a property
is "Protected by Electronic Automatic Alarm System." Superimposed on
the photograph is the simple title of the cover story: "The Marketing of
Fear." These covers and cover stories are not surprising, of course. We all
know that crime and fear of criminals has recently been very "big" with
Americans. And the December 1993 issue of *Metropolis*, the magazine with
the sign on its cover, was responding to that fact. No, the coverage of fear
by major magazines is not surprising at all—except that the first magazine
is *Life* and its date of publication is November 19, 1971. If there is a lesson
to be learned here it is simply that the American obsession with crime was
not "born yesterday." While the fear of crime certainly ebbs and flows—
sometimes reaching peaks one might reasonably label "hysteria"—for the
last thirty years or so, its overall level has remained relatively high, as witness the findings in Table 6.1 from the Gallup poll organization.

When the question posed asks about general concern, rather than
specifically experienced fear, the percentage admitting "unease" rises
somewhat, but the results are consistent with the Gallup findings. For
example, in 1984, a Media General/Associated Press poll asked the following question: "We read in the newspapers and hear by other means
much about victims of crimes. I'll read a list of crimes which we often read
or hear about. Please tell me if you are concerned or not concerned about
each happening to you." Sixty-one percent expressed concern about their
homes being forcibly entered and their possessions stolen; 49 percent were
concerned about being robbed or mugged on the street and 62 percent
worried about themselves or a family member being raped (Flanagan and
McGarrell 1985:146). A 1993 Gallup poll found that 39 percent of respon-
dents reported feeling "somewhat unsafe" to "very unsafe" when at

Table 6.1   American Obsession with Crime According to
           Gallup Polls [a]

Year of poll	Afraid to walk alone at night (%)	Feel unsafe at home (%)
1965	34	NA
1967	31	NA
1972	42	17
1975	45	20
1977	45	15
1981	45	16
1983	45	16
1989	43	10

[a] Poll question: Is there any area near where you live—that is, within a mile—where you would be afraid to walk alone at night? How about at home at night—do you feel safe and secure, or not? (George Gallup, Jr., *The Gallup Report*, Reports Nos. 282–283, March/April 1989, p. 8. Princeton, New Jersey.

home. When driving, the figure was 46 percent, 63 percent when walking, 87 percent when on public transportation (McAneny 1993).

Another indicator of fear levels, the purchase of secured spaces and security devices, seems also either to have remained fairly high or to have increased. Gated communities, often with their own private security forces (Davis 1992; McKenzie 1994; Walters 1992; Wilson 1988) and "for hire" play spaces for children (Jacobs 1993), have burgeoned over the last decade, as has the use of private security guard services more generally.[21] Similarly, such items as window and door bars and home alarm systems, handguns and other less lethal personal weapons (e.g., Mace, pepper spray), and automobile alarms, antitheft devices (e.g., "The Club"), and inflatable "passengers" have become familiar features of the American social landscape (Kleinfield 1992; Roberts 1996; Serrano 1994). In the same issue referred to above, *Life* published a brief questionnaire on fear of crime and asked readers to fill out the form and send it in. The results were reported on January 14, 1972:

—78% sometimes feel unsafe in their own homes [as one reader wrote]: "While the junkie and the robber remain free, citizens can only try to remain safe by putting one more lock on the door and one more set of bars on the window."
—61% overall and 80% in big cities are afraid in the streets at night;
—30% keep a gun for self defense. (*Life* 1972:28A)

As these data, the cover stories in both *Life* and *Metropolis*, the opinion poll findings, and the evidence of "fortress" home and security equipment purchases would seem to suggest, while most fear of crime is fear of criminal strangers,[22] not all fear is of *criminal strangers in the public realm*. Much has to do with the possible invasion by those strangers of one's private space. Nonetheless, as the same data indicate, for many individuals, fear of the criminal *is* fear of "the street." And this is true whether we look backward in time, as we did above in the discussion of mobs and outcasts, or concentrate on our own era, as we are doing here.

Of course, fear of the criminal stranger in the public realm is not evoked by the thought of, or even the reality of, *all* strangers. As we will see in a moment, for many women, only men (sometimes *all* men) are threatening. More generally, danger is seen to reside in whatever group is currently most despised and (often) ill-treated by the majority. In the late twentieth-century United States, that group is composed importantly of black males, especially young black males, although Hispanic males are sometimes targeted as well (Lejeune and Alex 1973; Merry 1981; Staples 1986; Werthman and Piliavin 1967). For example, in her study of the folklore of crime in New York City, Eleanor Wachs found:

> Most often, crime-victim story narrators, the majority of whom are white, identify offenders by race. "A black kid, you know, did this," or "Two blacks came up to me and put a knife in my side," or "He was Hispanic, no shirt." (1988:84)

Similarly, in his ethnography of the adjacent "Norton" (poor and black) and "Village" (middle-class and integrated) areas of Philadelphia, Elijah Anderson tells us:

> [Y]oung black males, particularly those who don the urban uniform (sneakers, athletic suits, gold chains, "gangster caps," sunglasses and large portable radios or "boom boxes") may be taken as the embodiment of the predator. In this uniform, which suggests to many the "dangerous underclass," these young men are presumed to be troublemakers or criminals. (1990:167)

Ironically enough, the fear some of these young males evoke appears to be quite independent of their actual behavior:[23]

> In their campaign for respectability, some young black men have become crusaders, particularly in those city areas that whites and blacks share. In their quest for positive judgment, they have become some of the most generous, helpful, kind, and courteous people around, contributing, to an often unacknowledged degree, to public safety. Nonetheless, it is impossible for

them to overcome the pervasive stereotype. In the Village, no young black male has an easy time on the streets. The residents fear him. The police generally consider him out to rob people or insult passersby. Perceiving him as a threat, they view him as someone they must contain. (ibid.:189)

It is important here to emphasize the point made earlier: just "who" is thought eligible for classification as criminal stranger varies by time and space. In nineteenth-century London, it was the Anglo-Saxon lower class; in twentieth-century Dublin, it is the Celtic "tinkers" (Gmelch 1977). According to folklorist Bill Ellis, the contemporary American version of the urban legend "The Castrated Boy" (in which a young boy is kidnapped, mutilated, and—in some versions—killed) seems mostly to feature a white boy as victim, but the perpetrators are variously identified as "little black boys," Mexican-Americans, Native-Americans, or "hippies." Versions of the same legend, moving backwards in time, also display variations in their central characters. In the late medieval period, a Christian child is ritually murdered by Jews while in Ancient Rome, Christians sacrifice the children of pagans (Ellis 1983).

As we saw in Chapter 5, nineteenth-century efforts to keep women "in place" employed, among other strategies, the image of the sex-mad, violence-prone male lying in wait for any woman who ventured out in public. Given what we know about nineteenth- and twentieth-century trends in female employment, leisure activity, and political participation, it seems unlikely that such efforts kept any significant numbers of women cowering in their domestic "havens." Oddly enough, however, in the late twentieth century, feminist intellectuals and movement activists are evoking that same specter of the fearsome *male* and there is at least some suggestion, as we will see below, that *their* warnings are falling on more receptive ears.

To the degree that contemporary women do fear men, especially men who are strangers to them, that fear is certainly importantly a fear of the male criminal and it thus participates in the larger fear of crime expressed by both men and women. What is interesting to us here, however, is that women's fear of men seems not at all limited to fear of crime. Rather, the latter is accompanied, perhaps even buttressed and enlarged, by a fear of "harassment." If we are to believe feminist scholars and intellectuals, the gawking, groping male is a ubiquitous feature of life in the public realm. Karen Franck and Lynn Paxson's description of female travails on the "street" captures this abundantly populated genre of modern morality tale quite succinctly:

Less severe than physical attack but nonetheless significant in women's use of public space is the frequency with which women are approached by strange men. Such approaches range from friendly overtures to harmless exhortations to sexually explicit comments and actual touching. No thorough or systematic research exists on the frequency, location, or reasons for this behavior despite the fact that it is a daily occurrence in urban settings for many women. . . . The frequency of sexual attacks and sexual approaches of a purely verbal nature indicates how much women's sexuality makes them fair game to men in public spaces. Once they are in public, unaccompanied by men, women cannot claim as much right to privacy as men can. (1989:129, 130)

As Franck and Paxson admit, "no thorough or systematic research exists on the frequency, location, or reasons for this behavior." And, in fact, my own hundreds, perhaps thousands, of hours of observation in public space have revealed almost no evidence of this supposedly ubiquitous occurrence (Lofland 1994). But a paucity of evidence has proved no barrier to the flood of claims by modern feminists that the woman who ventures out on the street risks a terrible fate.[24] While I certainly grant that harassment "happens"—it is solidly documented by interview studies, for example—it seems to me that the magnitude of its occurrence has been wildly exaggerated.[25] Nonetheless, first-person and interview data suggest that at least some women believe feminist claims and perceive themselves as suffering from an unceasing barrage of verbal and visual assaults. Here, as one example, is Lindsay Van Gelder describing a few of what she claimed were many similar experiences during a trip to Europe with a female friend:

—In Nice, while I was sitting at an outdoor cafe, two Frenchmen at an adjacent table introduced themselves and asked me out. I told them I had other plans. One of them leaned over, still chatting, and casually plopped his hand on my thigh. I removed the hand with a bristling "*s'il vous plait!*" at which point Pamela came back from the ladies' room and I got up to leave. As I passed their table, the man reached out to cop a feel of my breast.

—In the border town of Ventimiglia, Italy, several different groups of men followed us relentlessly down the narrow streets in their cars.

—In Dijon, we were typical-touristing through the medieval streets, gaping up at the gargoyles, when a flasher suddenly leaped out from between two parked cars. I happened to be carrying an open bottle of mineral water, and without missing a beat, I dumped a quart of Perrier on his erect penis. The look on his face made our day. (1981, p. 17)

A similar sense of being relentlessly pursued permeates this passage from one of Carol Brooks Gardner's informants, an African-American woman:

It started in junior high at [a private school]. Boys slapping your butt when you walked down the hall, elbowing your breasts when you're in a crowd or at your locker, the teachers making remarks. . . . Then it continues in high school, even [an expensive private school]. There are lots of Blacks there, so it's not race. Same things go on. By the time you're ready for the world of work and going out in public places, you've been socialized. The man who slapped my butt on the Circle probably wasn't the same man who slapped my butt when we were both eleven years old in junior high. He could've been, and that's my point. (1995:58)[26]

The Loathsome Stranger:
Crowds, The Destitute, "Crazies," and Aliens

For some humans, the public realm is loathsome because it is populated by loathsome strangers: crowds, whose sheer size offends senses and sensibilities; the destitute, whose presence in affluent areas ruins the ambience; "crazies," whose behavior disturbs the "sane"; and aliens of all sorts, whose very presence is an affront. As with the categories of fearsome strangers, the various loathsome types may sometimes merge—in this case, into a single *despicable* object: a crowd composed of crazy and destitute aliens. But again as with fear, specialized loathing is what seems most frequently to be expressed. However, fear and loathing are not totally similar: the former leaves far more "traces" than the latter. Fear is readily expressed to pollsters and other researchers, loathing has a more stealth-like character. Fear can be measured through the proliferation of objects and services, but except at its most extreme (e.g., in hate groups or hate crimes), individual loathing rarely takes an externally visible form. But to say that evidence of loathing is less visible than evidence of fear is not to say that it is invisible. It may leave fewer traces, but that is not to say that it leaves none at all.

Crowds, for example, can be loathed quite openly. In fact, given the strength of antiurbanism in Anglo-American culture, the crowd—associated as it is with crowd*ing*, with noise, and with either speed or gridlock—would appear to be an especially acceptable object of repugnance. Over the years in my urban courses, the theme of the "the crowds in the crowded city" appears again and again as one of the major reasons to dislike urban areas. David Hummon's small-town and suburban apologists express similar views:

> The city has too many people, too much going on, all mixed in too fast. City people are too busy doing other things to be friendly. Country people sit back and enjoy. (1990:60)
> There's obviously the faster pace in cities—the intensity of the place, the crime. And I keep referring to my children: I wouldn't want them there. The traffic problems, congestion, pollution, all the things you read and hear

about. Cities drive me nuts. I like to enjoy them—maybe one evening, or if I've got something specific to do; going to a play or out to dinner, that's terrific. But living there on a day-to-day basis ... there's not an escape. (ibid.:99–100)

Certainly those who dislike public transit often use "the crowd" to justify their dislike, as cartoonist Phil Frank's jibe (Illustration 6.3) at North Bay (Marin and Sonoma County, California) residents who must cross the Golden Gate Bridge to reach their work in San Francisco suggests. Frank's commuters apparently share in the same folklore that sociologists Morris Davis and Sol Levine discuss. They report that among Americans, the folklore of public transit is "almost wholly negative. ... [P]assengers are packed in like sardines; the ride is slow and dirty and exhausting; the vehicles are places of crime and hooliganism" (1967:89). And the author of this letter to the editor of the *San Francisco Chronicle* is in full agreement:

[Name] is quite correct in his letter of the 22nd when he says "We must find alternatives to the endless proliferation of automobiles." Unfortunately, the only way this will ever happen is by reducing the inexorable (they say) tendency toward increasing population in the area. I, for one, despise riding on public transit, even BART [Bay Area Rapid Transit], because I am forced to be in the midst of strangers whose behavior I can neither predict nor control. When public transit runs from my door to my destinations (or within a block of [them]), provides me with a private, lockable compartment, is there when I want it, and costs no more than driving, I will use it. Until that magic day, we must accommodate the automobile or travel like cattle. I prefer the auto, thank you. (October 27, 1987)

The crowds on public transit that Phil Frank's North Bay commuters and the letter-writing resident of the East Bay are complaining about are mostly made up of the relatively affluent. But, of course, one of the "prob-

Illustration 6.3. Reprinted by permission of Phil Frank, "Farley." *San Francisco Chronicle*, May 14, 1991.

lems" with public transit vehicles, as with other public realm locales, is that the crowd that inhabits them may contain more than the respectable affluent: it may contain *the destitute* as well. For a people who make some public claim to viewing charity and compassion as virtues, loathing the down-and-out may, perhaps, cause some frisson of guilt. My own guess is that there are many more folks in whom the homeless, for example, evoke repugnance than would ever admit it. Nonetheless, humans long ago developed strategies for handling this situation, as innumerable scholars have taught us: one simply "blames the victim."[27] In the United States in the 1980s and 1990s, that blame resulted in numerous municipalities attempting to suppress, move, or hide the destitute by criminalizing them. For example, the San Francisco "Matrix" program, used (among other devices) an 1872 statute that "prohibits lodging in any building, structure, vehicle, or place, whether public or private, without an owner's permission" to prevent "public sleeping." San Francisco also prohibited "aggressive" panhandling and confiscated "shopping carts," and San Diego followed a vigorous policy of arresting "panhasslers." New York City prohibited both begging and sleeping in its subway system. Oakland, California used antiloitering laws to clear the area around its Federal Building of "street people." Santa Monica simply closed it parks from midnight to 5:00 A.M. Dearborn, Michigan went further and barred all nonresidents from its parks. In Newark, New Jersey the homeless were barred from the public libraries for "smelling bad," 'while Anaheim, California proposed requiring panhandlers to obtain a city business license. And Santa Ana, California simply banished the homeless from its borders by making it a crime to camp on public land.[28]

Many of these statutes and policies have not withstood initial court tests, but proponents have frequently appealed court decisions or recrafted statues in the face of rather limited rulings. However, criminalization is not the only blame-oriented solution to the presence of the destitute. Architecture can be used as well, creating what Mike Davis in his study of Los Angeles has called "sadistic street environments" (1992:232–36). In San Francisco, for example:

—Metal bars with spikes have been bolted down to some lower-level windows so people cannot sit or sleep on the ledges. The vacant Hibernia Bank building at Market and McAllister streets recently installed such bars.
—Public benches have been designed with multiple armrests so the homeless cannot stretch out. Every time an old bench wears out, it is replaced with the new "homeless-proof" one.
—Bus shelters have hard, narrow tilting seats to discourage people from using the shelters as a place to sleep.
—Planters outside buildings such as 555 Market Street are made too tall for anyone except Manute Bol to sit on the edge.

—Shrubbery is pruned in Golden Gate Park so police and gardeners can see whether anyone is bedding down or lurking there.

—Fences have been raised around other public places, such as the ramps to the Embarcadero Freeway, so the homeless would not be able to sleep in the area.

—Gates are being added to storefronts in neighborhoods that never before had them to prevent anyone from loitering in front of a building or using it as a lavatory.[29]

Notice that thus far my "indicators" of loathing toward the destitute involve attitudes and actions expressed by collectivities—in this case municipal governments—not by individuals. Local governments, more precisely, the persons who act for them, presumably design programs they believe will be "popular" with voters, that will reflect the latter's "will." But, of course, they may be wrong. In San Francisco, as one example, Mayor Frank Jordan's "get tough toward the homeless" policies did not prevent his being ousted (in the election of November 1995) from office after one term. The task of locating loathing at the individual level is made even more complex by the fact that, as one Sacramento store manager noted, "If you go on record as wanting something done about people sleeping or begging in front of your store, then everybody brands you an animal who has no feelings."[30] Similarly, a national survey conducted in July of 1993 for the newspaper insert *Parade* found that an unbelievable 82 percent said that the homeless should "*not* be prohibited from public places, such as libraries, parks and mass transit."[31] Nonetheless, as I indicated above, there *are* traces. In a 1991 survey of twenty-eight cities conducted by the U.S. Conference of Mayors, for example, "nearly half the cities reported evidence of a public backlash against homeless people. 'Public sentiment has gone from apathy to anger,' an unnamed official in Miami was quoted as saying."[32] Anger was certainly in evidence in 1990 in Santa Cruz, California, when a protest of some three hundred homeless and their allies was met by a "counterdemonstration of more than 1,000 angry business owners and residents who are fed up with what they call 'bums and vagrants' sleeping in parks, on the beaches, and even in the downtown U.S. Post Office." Speakers at the counterdemonstration rally called the homeless "lazy freeloaders" and participants carried signs proclaiming such messages as HOMELESS BY CHOICE HAVE NO VOICE, THE AMERICAN DREAM IS NOT FREE, and WE PAY THE BILLS WHILE YOU SIT STILL.[33] Evidence of similar sentiments can be found in the always reliable "Letters to the Editor" feature of the *San Francisco Chronicle*:

It is no surprise to me that your recent poll (*Chronicle*, October 22) showed that Bay Area residents have an aversion to coming into San Francisco for

turns to
socialist action/
culture!

shopping or entertainment. It appears that the city government is much more concerned with attracting the homeless and comforting the down-and-out than with encouraging visitors and shoppers from adjacent areas. Although helping the needy is a noble goal, my impression is that the city has institutionalized poverty and promoted dependency (and its resultant criminal activity), as it pursues discredited tax and spend, liberal, socialist and collectivist ideas of the past. (October 25, 1990)

*   *   *

If any San Francisco mayoral candidate makes the people of San Francisco three promises, not only will I vote for him/her, but will campaign night and day as well. Promise me:

1. That you will close all the soup kitchens and homeless shelters.
2. That you will make panhandling illegal in San Francisco.
3. That fences will be placed around our neighborhood parks and the gates will be locked at night.

I am sick of being panhandled on my way to the grocery store, at a bus stop, in front of a museum or in a movie line. When will all this homelessness end? The more government gives, the more homeless people will come from elsewhere for the free ride. (October 10, 1991)

Finally, we can find "traces" of loathing in the testimony of two sociological ethnographers who immersed themselves in the world of the destitute. Here is what David Snow and Leon Anderson have to say about the response of Austin, Texas, homeless to the "stigmatizing" attitudes and actions directed toward them by the domiciled:

> The task the homeless face of salvaging the self is not easy, especially since wherever they turn they are reminded that they are at the very bottom of the status system. As Sonny McCallister lamented shortly after he became homeless, "The hardest thing's been getting used to the way people look down on street people. It's real hard to feel good about yourself when almost everyone you see is looking down on you." Tom Fisk, who had been on the streets longer, agreed. But he said that he had become more calloused over time:
>
> > I used to let it bother me when people stared at me while I was trying to sleep on the roof of my car or change clothes out of my truck, but I don't let it get to me anymore. I mean, they don't know who I am, so what gives them the right to judge me? I know I'm okay.
> >
> > But there was equivocation and uncertainty in his voice. Moreover, even if he no longer felt the stares and comments of others, he still had to make sense of the distance between himself and them. (1993:202; see also Anderson, Snow, and Cress 1994)

Despite the comfort that some Americans seem to derive from believing in a "just world" (Lerner 1980) or from buying into their own cultural propaganda about equal opportunities for all, many seem not to find it all that easy to loathe the destitute—or at least to do so openly. How even more difficult is it publicly to profess hate for the hapless and helpless down-and-outers, to be overt about one's loathing of the *crazies* in the ranks of the poor? Of course, if such folks also "drink" or "drug" or engage in other disapproved behavior, difficulties evaporate and the "traces" of loathing become more visible. Thus, many public expressions of disgust, such as in the following portion of a letter to the editor, lump together "crazies" and "substance abusers," thus presumably removing whatever claim to compassion the former might enjoy:

> Unquestionably our family's biggest problem has been the deteriorating quality of life in our once wonderful city of San Francisco.
> In less than five years, vagrants, substance abusers, the mentally ill and graffiti vandals have come to literally rule the streets in many areas of our town. (*San Francisco Chronicle*, November 19, 1991)

As we know, in recent years Americans in particular have had whatever capacity for compassion they possessed severely challenged. The deinstitutionalization of the mentally ill that began in the mid 1960s, combined with the failed provision of community-based clinics and other forms of support for them, have resulted in a visible increase in the number of the "bizarrely behaved" on the streets of American cities (Isaac and Armat 1990; Javers 1979; Morganthau and Associates 1986).[34] In addition, many men and women who are not "crazy" at the time they become homeless, may certainly become increasingly so as the period they spend on the streets increases (Snow and Anderson 1993; Snow, Baker, and Anderson 1988; Snow, Baker, Anderson, and Martin 1986). Thus it seems likely that tolerance for the visibly deranged, never very high under the best of circumstances (Conrad and Schneider 1980; Goffman 1963b; Lofland [1973] 1985), has plummeted in recent years. And those who are not filled with loathing may very well be filled with fear. Many would probably agree with a *London Times* headline that proclaimed that the mentally ill in the United States represented a "Ticking Time-Bomb Who Stalk Streets" (John Barnes, July 24, 1983; see also Lewis and Reed 1985).

But there is yet another reason to loathe the public realm. The destitute and "crazies" are simply two categories of a much larger group of strangers who are likely to be found there: *aliens* of all sorts. The human penchant for despising those who are defined as "unlike me" is too well-known to require explication here. People who look different, who act different, who smell different; people whose sexual preferences or politics or religions confound home values; people whose language or music sounds discordant; all of these are people whose very existence offends. And the fact is—as we will discuss in detail in Chapter 8—if there is one place we are likely to encounter these folks it is "on the street." And that observation takes us right back to the matter of antiurbanism and its possible links to fear, loathing, and privatism.

FROM ANTIURBANISM TO FEAR AND LOATHING TO PRIVATISM AND BACK AGAIN?

Does antiurbanism have anything to do with privatism? Is it possible to trace a causal linkage between visual and verbal representations like those laid out in the previous chapter, negative emotions toward the public realm such as the fear and loathing we have just examined, and individuals' choices regarding where and with whom they will spend their time? The best answer I can give to that question is, "Maybe." Providing a direct connection between antiurban imagery at one end of a causal chain and life-style choices on the other end is far more difficult than it might seem at first glance. In this final section, I will attempt to make the connections, but as I go along I will also try to point up some of the myriad logical and evidential difficulties involved in doing so.

We begin with the first link in the chain: the connection between antiurbanism as an Anglo-American cultural theme on the one hand, and the individual experiences of fear and loathing toward the public realm on the other. On the surface, they would seem "obviously" linked. After all, don't people exposed from childhood to the teachings of bigotry "naturally" and "obviously" view the objects of that bigotry with fear and loathing and isn't this the same sort of thing? Well, possibly. But scholars and scientists tend to be unpersuaded by the obvious—even more to the point here, they tend to be suspicious of it. What, they will ask, is your evidence? One kind of evidence that might be adduced has to do with the curious disconnect, evidenced in modern Americans, between fear and likelihood of victimization of urban-located crime. As innumerable researchers have found, women and the elderly tend to be the most afraid; they also have— statistically speaking—the least to be afraid of.[35] Similarly, fear of violent crime among the population at large tends to be fear of the violent stranger. But the violent intimate is the statistically more probable enemy:

Fear of death (or violent assault) at the hands of a stranger is a common concern among Americans. People fear either a direct personal assault, such as a mugging or rape, or a random act of violence, such as being killed by a stray bullet. The data suggest, however, that most homicide victims knew their attacker. . . . Only 16 percent of male victims are known to have been killed by a stranger. Similarly, 9 percent of female victims were known to be killed by a stranger. (Mackellar and Yanagishita 1995:7)

There have been many attempts to understand this "anomaly" (see references cited in note 35). Much of the disconnect seems to have to do with views of self as especially vulnerable (among women and the elderly, for example) and with issues of control (intimates are seen as more predictable than strangers). Recent scholars have argued that fear levels should not be dismissed as "hysterical" or "unreasonable" but, in fact, represent (especially under conditions of actual high crime rates and relentless media coverage of violent crime) understandable assessments of risk, rationally arrived at.[36] I certainly have no quarrel with this line of thought. But I would want to stir in another element. Surely some of the disconnect has to do with the conceptions of their environments that individuals are using in developing their "definitions of the situation" (Thomas 1931). As we know from innumerable microsociological studies, definitions of the situation bring macrophenomena to the microlevel; they link such large-scale entities as ideologies with the cognitive and emotional processes of individual human actors. That is, as they go about trying to make sense of the situations in which they find themselves, humans are relying not only on "clues" currently available to them, nor only on their past experiences, nor only on a combination of the two. They are also drawing upon the lore of their social group: upon the cultural, political, and other "stories" that their "people" tell about various objects. And, as we have seen, many of the stories about settlements that Anglo-American people now tell and have told for many years are strongly antiurban. Which brings us to another piece of evidence. Based on his interviews with Californians residing in a variety of settlement types, David Hummon argues that as his informants attempt to understand and evaluate "what kind of a place they live in," they make heavy use of what he calls the "community ideologies" (or "cultural systems of belief") available to them. Regardless of where they, in fact, reside, those whose preferred settlement is the small town or the "suburb" filter their actual experiences of "communities" through the lens of antiurbanism. That is, they *see* small towns and suburbs as benign and beautiful while *seeing* cities as fearsome and loathsome (Hummon 1990).

Unfortunately, neither evidence of a disconnect nor Hummon's interpretation of his interview data comes anywhere near to drawing a direct and convincing connection between antiurbanism and negative emotions. We do not know, for example, whether people filled with fear and loathing are the *same* people carrying cityphobe ideology around in their heads. Nor do we know whether Hummon's informants, in their cognitive and emotional processes, are *representative* of any significant number of even Americans, must less Western humans more generally. But to say this is not to dismiss the proposition either. As a *hypothesis*, that first link in the chain seems worthy of retention.

What, then, of the connection between fear and loathing and privatism? Now things get even trickier. We *do know* that some number of persons have in the past and do now fear and loathe strangers who are situated in the public realm. Thus, inquiring into the causes of these emotions is a reasonable endeavor. But we *do not know* whether privatism even exists. To seek to understand why a phenomenon develops when the phenomenon itself may be a figment of the imagination is, at minimum, a somewhat whimsical activity. Still, As W. I. Thomas taught us, if humans "define situations as real, they are real in their consequences" (1931:41–50). And if fear and loathing are real definitions—which they are—then we ought to be able to find some real consequences. So, however whimsical, a brief look does seem justified. We do have some evidence that people who fear urban crime *say* that they curtail activities that would take them into the public realm. For example, in one study (Gordon, Riger, LeBailly, and Heath 1981), 75 percent of the women surveyed reported that they never go to the movies alone after dark and 46 percent claimed never to use public transit alone after dark (reported in Franck and Paxon 1989). Contemporary American females may, in fact, learn both to be fearful and to practice avoidance when they are children. Silvia Golombek's research on children's images of the city reveals that

> Girls in the study were likely to be concerned about their own personal safety in an urban environment. They did not feel secure unless they were surrounded by friends and family. . . . It was not very common for girls to move and know their way around in the city on their own which was associated to their fear of getting lost. This anxiety was compounded by their fear of strangers and "crazy" people that might harm them. (1993:121–22)

Another study found that city dwellers of both sexes tend to "stay off the streets at night, avoid strangers, curtail social activities" (Clemente and Kleiman 1977:519; see also Skogan 1986). Similarly, in his interview study of urban "danger" in Amsterdam, sociologist Lodewijk Brunt concluded that while

> [t]he elderly and women of all ages are apt of say they "never go out any more" . . . [the statement should not be taken literally] but is meant to describe a certain attitude rather than what actually happens. What the state-

ment indicates is that people *only go out if they absolutely have to,* for example, to go shopping, to go to the doctor or to relatives or friends. (1993:10–11, emphasis in original)[37]

There is yet another sort of evidence for the negative emotions–privatism link, which we will explore more fully in the next chapter but which should at least be mentioned here. This has to do with fear and loathing felt by middle-class white Americans toward the "aliens" in the older portions of the metrosea (the so-called "inner city") and the former's mass movement, after World War II, into the new low-density, automobile-dependent housing developments that were replacing open land (the so-called "white flight"). As we will see shortly, there are innumerable reasons for that outward rush (which transformed the North American urban landscape), and scholars continue to argue (e.g., Liska and Bellair 1995; Palen 1995) about the relative contribution of white flight. However, to the degree that it played *some* role, it may well have contributed to privatism. And that is because—again, as we will see in more detail in Chapter 7—low-density, automobile-dependent housing developments seem to encourage a family-oriented, domestically dominated style of life. Let us allow one of David Hummon's suburban apologists to make the case:

> A real city person likes walking in the city, going to stores, shops. They cannot move to a suburb. They don't like to drive and they are used to seeing more people. When we come from work, we go to the garage, close the garage, and come to the house, and our activities are inside the house—like personal hobbies. City people like to go out. They don't like to water the garden or work on the house. Some people in the city don't like to have a house at all. (1990:101)

Again, the accumulated evidence supporting the second link in the causal chain is anything but definitive. But I would judge that there is enough of it to allow me to say, as I did relative to the first link, that it can stand as a *hypothesis* worthy of retention.

Finally, what of the third piece of the chain? What of the possibility that privatism itself loops back and feeds antiurbanism? Here, I must admit, there is no evidence at all. I think it makes social-psychological sense to posit a connection between becoming habituated to a social life composed importantly of intimate interactions and domestic pursuits and an increasing dislike of nonintimate interactions and nondomestic pursuits. In 1993, I was asked to appear in an "Author Meets the Critics" session at the meetings of the American Sociological Association in Los Angeles. The book in question was Mike Davis's *City of Quartz: Excavating the Future in Los Angles* (1992). In my remarks, among other matters, I addressed a question

that seemed to float through every chapter of the book but that Davis
never confronted directly: the question of the consequences of the Southern California built environment for the values and beliefs of the residents
of that area. The argument I made then about that connection is the argument I would make now. This is what I said:

> There seems no doubt, as Davis and other historians of the area have argued,
> but that Southern California "sold" itself to the midwestern and southern
> "babbits" (Davis's characterization) who bought its real estate importantly
> as a "garden"—as a place in opposition to all that was associated with the
> traditional city, i.e., density, heterogeneity, public life. So perhaps one could
> hypothesize, again as many historians of the area have done, that the culture
> (including both the mind-set and the built environment) of contemporary
> Southern California home owners is—at least to some degree—simply a con-
> tinuation of the "culture" of those midwesterners and southerners who
> migrated here in the late nineteenth century through the mid-twentieth cen-
> tury. Yet what of the consequences of the built environment they found, rein-
> forced, and extended when they got here? Once ensconced in their large
> tracts of similarly priced single-family bungalows or mission-style hacien-
> das, once they had filled their gardens with shrubs and trees and grass and
> had tasted the sweet pleasures of private backyard picnics, is it possible that
> the built environment they initially sought began to act back upon them, to
> become not simply a product of their values and preferences, but a shaper of
> those values and preferences as well? What does it mean that by 1925, as
> Davis tells us, Southern Californians had already "attained a density [of]
> (one car per 1.6 persons) which the rest of the nation would not reach until
> the late 1950s" (ibid.:118)? Was it their preference for the garden that made
> the private car—that cocoon of privacy, that formidable barrier between one-
> self and the alien other—so irresistible? Or, is it possible that living in the
> garden helped shape the preference for a form of transport that could pro-
> vide a formidable barrier?
>   Davis tells us that in the Los Angeles region, and presumably in the rest of
> Southern California as well, "homeowners, like the Sicilians in *Prizzi's
> Honor*, love their children, but they love their property values more" and that
> community in the area "means homogeneity of race, class and, especially,
> home values" (ibid.:153). Again, are property values one's god because one
> prefers the single-family detached home? Or is it possible that the single-
> family detached home entices its occupant into the new religion with its new
> god and all the privatism, xenophobic parochialism, and paranoia the wor-
> ship of that god entails?

I didn't know the answer then to the general question I was posing. I
don't know the answer now. But I am also as convinced now as I was then
that it is reasonable to *hypothesize* that the antiurbanism that created the
privatistic built environment and life-style of Southern Californians is
now itself fed by that very privatism. And given Southern California's role

as the model for the postwar built environment in the rest of the nation, that seems a hypothesis well worthy of retention indeed. All of which leads us to the next chapter, because it is there that we are going to look closely at the postwar built environment for which Southern California provided the model.

NOTES

1. The term "privatization" also carries unwanted connotations. In the United States and Europe, at least, it is widely used to refer to the transfer of services historically provided by public agencies (e.g., garbage collection, postal service, the operation of schools and prisons) into private hands. "Privatism" has somewhat similar connotative baggage problems (see, e.g., Franklin 1989:93) but it has the advantage that the other meanings attached to it are less well known.

2. The state of Oregon, in an attempt to induce more citizens to vote, is experimenting with mail-only balloting. See, for example, Ellen Goodman, "Oregon to Try Voting at Home." *San Francisco Chronicle*, November 7, 1997, p. A19. Presumably if the experiment "works" in Oregon, the practice will be imitated nationally.

3. The literature on this topic includes Arendt (1958), Benn and Gaus (1983a), Bensman and Lilienfeld (1979), Etzioni (1995, 1996), Goldston (1970), Halmos (1953), Halttunen (1982), Hayden (1981:Chapters 13 and 14, 1984:Chapter 2), Jackson (1985), Ketcham (1987), McKenzie (1994), Popenoe (1985), Ryan (1982), and Schwartz (1968).

4. Two studies that make skillful use of these traces are Fischer (1992) and Franklin (1989).

5. Shann Nix, "One Step Beyond Cocooning," *San Francisco Chronicle*, August 12, 1992, p. B-3. See also Sylvia Run, "The New Stay-at-Homes," *San Francisco Chronicle*, September 2, 1987, People, p. 16).

6. Edward Epstein, "A Less Social Society Is Becoming Shy," *San Francisco Chronicle*, September 14, 1995, p. A-1); Karyn Hunt, "Technology, Violent Society Lead to More Shyness," *Davis Enterprise*, November 20, 1995.

7. "Americans and the Arts: VCR's Take Off," *Newsweek*, March 28, 1988, p. 69.

8. "Family Ties," *Washington Post National Weekly Edition*, August 11, 1986, p. 37. These figures are, of course, in keeping with the oft-noted preference of Americans for private, intimate relationships discussed above.

9. *Economist,* June 10, 1995, p. 50. See also Peter Mikelbank, "Cafes, a French Institution, Are on the Wane," *Sacramento Bee*, July 28, 1991, Travel, p. 1 [reprinted from *Washington Post*]; "Is France Bidding Adieu to the Bistro?" *Sacramento Bee*, July 19, 1995, p. B7. Something similar seems to be happening to British pubs but the reasons seem even more complex, including competition from wine bars (e.g., "British Pub Keepers Facing Tough Times," *San Francisco Chronicle*, September 18, 1984, p. 14; see also Vasey 1990).

10. I do need to acknowledge that two scholars who have looked very carefully at materials dealing directly with privatism have both concluded that the

data do not support the reality. However, both studies look at periods in which most of the conditions that I have identified as making privatism possible (e.g., television) did not exist. Claude Fischer (1992) looked at leisure activities in three towns in California in the period 1890 to 1940 and A. Franklin (1989) studied working-class activity in one neighborhood in Bristol, England, in the early part of the twentieth century.

11.   The reality of privatism *as it affects the parochial realm* is rather hotly debated in political science and Putnam's work, in particular, has come under attack. See, for example, Lemann (1996), Stengel (1996), and Jackman and Miller (1998).

12.   Privatism is unquestionably also being fueled by structural arrangements—as, for example, at least in North America and Europe, the aging of the population, and especially in North America, the increasing employment of women (see, e.g., Wellman 1985).

13.   A 1980s cross-cultural study of emotional experience in Belgium, France, Great Britain, Israel, Italy, Spain, Switzerland, and West Germany found that

> Strangers . . . seemed to be able to provoke only fear and anger and did so fairly frequently. Given this result, it is not surprising that in most cultures strangers are regarded with some diffidence and that strangeness is a partial source for the development of stereotypes and prejudice. Strangers very rarely provoke joy or happiness, so the most we can expect is that they will leave us alone. (Wallbott and Scherer 1986:73)

In reality, of course, fear and loathing (as this passage suggests) are compounded: I fear what I loathe and loathe what I fear. However, I am separating them here for analytic convenience.

14.   The terms *mob* and *crowd* are often used synonymously. Here I am violating that convention because I want to reserve the latter, somewhat less explosive term for my discussion of loathing.

15.   The others are (1) "violent conflicts among urban magnates and the creation of a fortified landscape of fear," (2) "danger from and anxiety about strangers in an urban milieu," (3) "distaste for and fear of the poor as a potential source of moral corruption and of disease," and (4) "urban fears in the lives of poor immigrants" (ibid.). Number 2, of course, is the focus of this entire chapter and number 3 will be discussed in the section on loathing.

16.   It is worthy of note that in their introduction to the 1970 reprint of *The Great Riots*, historians Thomas Rose and James Rodgers suggest that Headley's very negative assessment of "the mob" was part and parcel of his negative assessment of urban life more generally (Headley [1873] 1970:xiii). And in fact, in the book's second sentence, Headley makes quite explicit the connection between the "dangerous classes" and cities per se: "[The history of New York's riots] furnish a sort of moral history of that vast, ignorant, turbulent class which is one of the distinguishing features of a great city, and at the same time the chief cause of its solicitude and anxiety, and often of dread" (ibid.:17). Relative to the link between fear and loathing and privatism, it is also interesting to note that Headley spent the last forty years of his life on a country estate in Newburgh.

17.   Additional studies of fear of the mob include Davis (1986), Gilje (1987), and Merriman (1991).

18. See, for example, Feagin and Hahn (1973), Harris ([1975] 1987), Harrison (1988), Hobsbawm (1959), Krantz (1985), Parry, Moyser, and Wagstaffe (1987), Rubenstein (1970), Rude (1959, 1964), and Tilly (1986).

19. In the preceding chapter, I used letters to the editor as evidence of "representations" of antiurbanism. Here and later, I am using them as evidence of individual feelings. I think the two kinds of usages are fully justified. Once published in the press, letters do become "representations" available for public consumption. But as individually produced documents, like diaries (see, e.g., Rosenblatt 1983) they also serve as indicators of the emotional states of their authors.

20. The general literature on fear of crime and its correlates and consequences among Americans is extensive. For a small sample, see Archer and Erlich-Erfer (1991), Balkin (1979), Clemente and Kleiman (1977), Ferraro (1995), Fisher and Nasar (1992), Gates and Rohe (1987), Hartnagel (1979), Kail and Kleinman (1985), Lee (1981), Levine and Wachs (1986), Liska and Baccaglini (1990), Liska, Sanchirico, and Reed (1988), Newman and Franck (1981), Skogan (1981), *Utne Reader* (1993), Ward, LaGory, and Sherman (1986), Warr (1990), Yin (1980), and Wilson (1968).

21. See, for example, Diane Divoky, "This Bandwagon Picks Up Ads for Alarms, Videos, Draperies," *Sacramento Bee*, February 16, 1986; Peter Fimrite, "Private Security Business Booms: Americans Taking Control of Their Own Safety," *San Francisco Chronicle*, December 8, 1994, p. A1; Curt Guyette, "What Price Security? Crime: America's Growth Industry," *Sacramento News and Review*, October 31, 1991, p. 13–14; Rick Marin, "Please Panic," *New York Times*, July 26, 1992.

22. That the overwhelming fear of crime is fear of crime by strangers is very well documented. See, for example, Ferraro (1995), Hunter (1978, 1985), Mackellar and Yanagishita (1995), Merry (1981), Neumann (1991), Rand (1984), Riedel (1993), and Wachs (1988). See also Fischer (1981, 1984) on urban "distrust" of persons outside the family and neighborhood circle.

23. Such "exclusivity" of fear can have odd consequences. In their study of mugging events and their aftermath, Lejeune and Alex found that some victims did not "sense" the impending crime because their muggers did not "look" dangerous:

> He looked so clean-cut. I would never be afraid, wherever, in the darkest alley if I met any individual like that who is so clean-cut and so unlike the stereotype that people have in their minds. .... He looked so wonderful, so proper and conservative and square and clean. You know, his clothes, his hair, his face, and that ruddy complexion—handsome. Very, very Anglo-Saxon looking. (1973:271)

24. Other examples of the genre include Davis (1978), Gardner (1980, 1989, 1990b, 1995), Kantrowitz and Associates (1991), Mazey and Lee (1983), MacLeod (1989/90), Wekerle (1980), and many of the references to be found in Wilson (1991). Concern over physical and psychic safety has led many women to advocate female-friendly urban policies and designs. See, for example, Bruning and Wheeler (1995), Franck (1985), Garber and Turner (1994), Hayden (1980), MATRIX (1984:Chapter 4), Penrose (1987), Saegert (1985), Wekerle (1988), Wekerle, Peterson, and Morley (1980), and Whitzman (1992).

25. Once again, I suspect, the public realm is serving its recurring role as "warrant." As Elizabeth Wilson has observed, "Many women and much feminist writing have been hostile to the city, and recent feminist contributions to the discussion

of urban problems have tended to restrict themselves narrowly to issues of safety, welfare, and protection." (1991:10). It is also interesting to note that while "Take Back the Night" marches focus on the dangers of "the streets" to women, the rallies that precede them tend to focus on victim tales of acquaintance rape, incest, and childhood sexual abuse. On a similar theme, see Jenkins (1994:Chapter 7) on the rhetorical use of serial murder by feminists.

26.   See also Blair (1974) and Enjeu and Save (1974).

27.   There are many variants on this strategy. One perfected by British Victorians and used to advantage by Gingrich Republicans and "New" Democrats is to separate the "worthy" from the "unworthy" poor. A distinct advantage of this strategy is that, so often, so many poor conveniently arrange themselves in the "unworthy" category that the "need" for charity (whether of heart or purse) is kept manageably minute. On the general strategy of blaming the victim, see Lerner (1980) and Ryan (1971). Of course, because the strategy is well known *as a strategy*, spokespeople for the "victims" are quick to charge their opponents with using it.

28.   Associated Press, "Judge Rules Against Library That Barred Homeless," *San Francisco Chronicle*, May 23, 1991, p. A13; Associated Press, "Law Barring Non-residents from Parks Is Overturned," *San Francisco Chronicle*, September 30, 1986; Josh Brandon, "City Is Using 1872 Statute to 'Police' Homelessness," *San Francisco Chronicle*, April 24, 1991; Claire Cooper, "Court Tests Santa Ana's Move to Banish Homeless," *Sacramento Bee*, January 1, 1995, p. A1; Jim Doyle, "Anti-Panhandling Law Overturned," *San Francisco Chronicle*, September 26, 1991, p. A17; Kevin Fagan, "Crackdown at Oakland's Federal Towers," *San Francisco Chronicle*, July 12, 1993; Seth Faison, Jr., *New York Times*, "N.Y. Police Ordered to Tighten Policy on Homeless in Subway," *San Francisco Chronicle*, October 19, 1991; Manny Fernandez, "Hunger Strikers Won't Stomach Matrix," *San Francisco Chronicle*, June 22, 1995, p. A20; Elaine Herscher, "Mayor Jordan Puts Panhandling, Sanctuary Measures on Ballot," *San Francisco Chronicle*, August 6, 1992; John King, "San Diego Goes After 'Panhasslers,'" *San Francisco Chronicle*, January 16, 1993, p. A1; John King and April Lynch, "Matrix Program Stirs Up a Fight," *San Francisco Chronicle*, September 24, 1993, p. A1; Cherie Lebrun, "Park Closure Plan Is Unfair to Those Living on the Edge," [Santa Monica] *Daily Breeze* (Outlook Edition), June 27, 1993; April Lynch, "Anti-Panhandling Measure Passes in S.F.," *San Francisco Chronicle*, November 4, 1992; April Lynch and Clarence Johnson, "S.F. Police Confiscate Homeless People's Carts," *San Francisco Chronicle*, November 13, 1993, p. A17; Tom Philp, "S.F. 'Retaking' Streets from Homeless," *Sacramento Bee*, December 16, 1993, p. A1; Marc Sandalow, "S.F.'s Homeless Plan, Shelters Assailed," *San Francisco Chronicle*, July 27, 1990, p. A2; Terry Spencer, "Business Licenses for Panhandling Urged in Anaheim," *Los Angeles Time*, July 6, 1993.

29.   Chronicle Staff Report, "S.F. Design Trend: Making Homeless Feel Not at Home," *San Francisco Chronicle*, August 1, 1991, p. 1.

30.   Mark Glover, "Panhandlers Turn Public against All Homeless," *Sacramento Bee*, August 31, p. A1.

31.   "What Americans Say About the Homeless," *Parade* (January 9, 1994):4–6.

32.   Associated Press, "Homeless Problem Worsening: Survey of 28 Cities Shows GoodWill, Food in Short Supply," *San Francisco Chronicle*, December 17, 1991.

33.   David A. Sylvester, "Opposing Rallies on Homeless Issue," *San Francisco Chronicle*, July 5, 1990, p. A2. Santa Cruz was also one of the settings across the United States where loathing erupted into hate crime. "Troll busting," as the youth of the community called it, resulted in assaults on at least nineteen vagrants during the summer of 1984 and the wounding of another (with a homemade bazooka) the prior December. See Arnold Abrams, *Newsday*, "As the 'Grate Society' Grows, So Does Intolerance," *Sacramento Bee*, Sunday, January 6, 1985, p. E2.

34.   I suspect, entirely I must admit without data to support that suspicion, that modern humans, particularly those in developed countries, may be considerably more disturbed (certainly less amused) by the bizarrely behaved than were our ancestors. I have often wondered how Samuel Johnson, described here by Fanny Burney, would have fared in the twentieth century:

> Dr. Johnson was announced. He is, indeed, very ill-favoured; is tall and stout; but stoops terribly; he is almost bent double. His mouth is almost continually opening and shutting, as if he was chewing. He has a strange method of frequently twirling his fingers, and twisting his hands. His body is in continual agitation, *see-sawing* up and down; his feet are never a moment quiet; and, in short, his whole person is in *perpetual motion*. (quoted in Halliday 1968:108)

35.   See, for example, Franck and Paxson (1989), Office of the Solicitor General (1985), Ferraro (1995), Mackellar and Yanagishita (1995), Riger (1981), Riger and Gordon (1981), Ward et al. (1986), Warr (1990), and Yin (1980).

36.   Carol Zisowitz Stearns and Peter N. Stearns, in their book *Anger: The Struggle for Emotional Control in America's History*, posit one factor in explaining the anomaly that most researchers have overlooked:

> Recurrent tendencies in the twentieth century to exaggerate crime trends, though they have several sources, owe something to the new perception of the unacceptability of expressions of anger. Certain kinds of crime, and anxiety about crime, have become to some extent methods of defining anger as deviance. This is most obvious, again, in the transformation of certain acts of youthful hooliganism, once regarded as acceptable (though probably annoying) letting off of steam, into criminal acts; but it feeds the more general preoccupation with crime as well. (1986:221)

37.   This is a particularly nice example of the power of fearful "definitions of the situation" because the crime rate—particularly the violent crime rate—in Amsterdam is miniscule by American standards.

7

Control By Design
The Architectural Assault on the Public Realm

It would be easy to argue that the theme of antiurbanism is less ubiquitous and less substantial in Anglo-American culture than I have claimed. After all, measuring the frequency and magnitude of ideas and images in populations past and present—which is what is involved here—is a daunting, perhaps impossible task. This is also true regarding the link between privatism and negative feelings about the public realm; in fact, the very existence of privatism itself is a matter of inference involving the interpretation of data fragments. And such inferences and interpretations are certainly subject to disagreement and debate. In short, in the previous two chapters we have been dealing with phenomena of an elusive, insubstantial, intangible, perhaps chimerical character. Thus, I freely admit that I find the subject of *this* chapter—the animus toward the public realm expressed in the built environment—to be gratifying in its solidity, its concreteness, its palpability. As we will see, social scientists may argue about the causal efficacy of physical objects and their arrangements in space, but they cannot debate the existence, frequency, or magnitude of those arranged objects. Privatism may or may not be "real." Of freeway interchanges there can be no doubt.[1]

We will begin our investigation of assault by architecture by taking an excursus into sociology's long-standing agoraphobia and I will offer some arguments that attempt to counter it. In the second section—which provides a brief overview of various attempts to "control" the public realm—we will see that the people who actually design and build cities appear, in contrast to the sociologists who study *these people*, to suffer from no agoraphobic qualms. Rather, they seem deeply appreciative of the power of spatial arrangements to subdue the unruly public realm either by destroying or by sanitizing it. The last two major sections of the chapter explore in considerable detail these alternative strategies of control. I will conclude with some thoughts about the contributions of the built environment itself to ever more antiurbanism, to ever stronger feelings of fear and loathing toward the public realm, and to ever greater degrees of privatism.

COUNTERING SOCIOLOGY'S "AGORAPHOBIA": THE SPATIAL "STRUCTURING" OF INTERACTION

Agoraphobia is defined as a fear of open or public spaces and of crowds. To say that sociologists suffer from it is, admittedly, to take some liberties with that definition[2] because what I actually mean to convey here is the sociologists' fear of the *idea of space as a potential causal variable* (Choldin 1978a). To watch a room full of sociologists (and fellow travelers) when the "s" word is used is to witness a room full of "wicked witches of the west" who have just been doused with water. Well, perhaps I am exaggerating somewhat. But not much. At least since Emile Durkheim's denunciation of the "geographical" or "climatic" causes of *Suicide* ([1897] 1952), most of us have been fleeing from even a hint of geographical determinism in our work. Generations of us have avoided the shoals of such determinism as though avoiding the plague and, even in these enlightened times, any author accused of committing a "gd" may well face the discipline's equivalent of the stake: a humiliating drubbing in the book review section of one or another of its journals. In 1956, for example, Nathan Glazer wrote, "We must root out of our thinking the assumption that the physical form of our communities has social consequences" (quoted in Fowler 1987). A few years later in 1968, Herbert Gans accused Jane Jacobs (in *The Death and Life of Great American Cities*) of falling "victim to the Fallacy of Physical Determinism" (quoted in Fowler 1987). And almost thirty years later, J. John Palen (taking to task the admittedly deterministic excesses displayed by early critics of American suburban development) repeats the refrain: "Implicit in the developing myth regarding suburbanites and their lifestyles was a naive determinism *that assumed that the characteristics of the built environment changed how people believed and acted*" (1995:82, emphasis added). In sum, Winston Churchill's observation, "We shape our buildings, thereafter they shape us," that is, the idea that the spaces and places we create may, in turn, create us—a commonplace among geographers and environmental psychologists—is, for many sociologists, simply too "outrageous" to be taken seriously.

Let me not be misunderstood here. In the last ten or fifteen years, "space" has been as *au courant* a concept in sociology as it is possible to get—especially among those inclined toward "critical" or political-economic analyses. And of course, in urban sociology, land-use patterning and change (i.e., "spatial" arrangements) have been of dominating concern from the early days of the Chicago School. Oddly enough, however, all this interest is in the concept's nearly exclusive role as *dependent variable*. Space is shaped: by "natural selection" or "natural market forces" (e.g., Burgess 1925; Hawley 1950), by the machinations of "capital" and "capi-

ha! quotes!

talists" (e.g., Fainstein, Gordon, and Harloe 1992; Gottdiener 1985, 1989; Harvey 1973, 1985, 1989; Walton 1979, 1981; Zukin 1982, 1987, 1991, 1995), by the "production needs" of a "world economy" (e.g., Sassen 1991, 1994), and by local and regional "growth machines" (Logan and Molotch 1987; Molotch 1976). Space may also be the "recipient" of human emotional attachment or antipathy (Firey 1945; Fried 1963; Hummon 1990). But except in a few isolated works (e.g., Fowler 1987; Levitas 1978; McKenzie 1925; LaGory 1983; Maines, Bridger, and Ulmer 1996; Satler 1990; Schneider 1978; Snow, Leahy, and Schwab 1981; Spain 1992; Tilly and Schweitzer 1982), space does not itself shape, it does not give, it does not "cause."

Yet as I suggested at the end of Chapter 6, there are very good reasons to accept, at least as a working hypothesis, the idea that the character of the built environment (meaning the arrangement of physical objects in space) is connected to what humans do in that environment. As a prelude to the major business of this chapter then, let me sketch out three of these very good reasons. These have to do with the ways in which space *structures*— puts parameters around—human interaction. I would argue that it does so by affecting (1) how interaction occurs, (2) who interacts with whom, and (3) the content of the interaction.

Structuring How Interaction Occurs

The built environment certainly does not *determine* exactly how people are going to interact with one another, but it does amplify or constrain the range of interactional possibilities. The extraordinarily complex social relationship among drivers on a freeway or in crowded city streets that was discussed in Chapter 2 is one example of a particular form of interaction made possible by a particular form of physical structure. The replacement of the horse-drawn carriage by the railroad car as the principal mode of long-distance land transport in the nineteenth century is an example of the replacement of one interactional possibility by another:

> Travelers of the eighteenth century, prior to the railroads, formed small groups that, for the duration of the journey, were characterized by intensive conversation and interaction: the travel novels of the period testify to this quite eloquently. [In contrast] the travelers in the train compartment do not know what to do with each other, and reading becomes a surrogate for the [verbal] communication that no longer takes place. This connection between reading and the alienation of railroad travelers from one another is made by all authors dealing with the subject of travel reading. It appears in the following contribution to the medical congress of 1866, in which travel reading is cited as the general and sole activity of travelers:

Nowadays one travels so fast and sees, if the journey is of any duration, such a succession of new faces, that one frequently arrives at the destination without having said a single word. Conversation no longer takes place except among people who know each other, at least not beyond the exchange of mere generalities. . . . Thus one might say that the railroads have in this respect, too, completely changed our habits. Whenever, in the past, one knew that one was going to pass several hours, sometimes several days, in the company of others, one tried to establish a rapport with one's companions that often lasted beyond the duration of the journey. Today we no longer think about anything but the impatiently awaited and soon reached destination. The traveler one takes one's leave from may get off at the next station where he will be replaced by another. Thus reading becomes a necessity. (Schivelbusch 1979:71)

The German historian and social scientist Wolfgang Schilvelbusch is here describing the social situation of the typical European first- or second-class railway car: divided into separate compartments, each compartment seating three or four persons on one side who faced three or four persons on the other. It is *this* configuration, modeled after the horse-drawn carriage, which, under conditions of relatively brief travel time, appeared to affect the willingness of strangers to talk to one another. Less intimate physical arrangements, as in the railway cars in the United States and those European cars designed for "the lower orders" were the scenes of considerable sociability. As numerous nineteenth-century commentators observed:

Only the privileged classes undergo this experience of no longer speaking to each other and being increasingly embarrassed by their companions. In the carriages of the third and fourth class, which mostly *have not been divided into compartments but consist of one large space*, there is neither embarrassed silence nor general perusal of reading matter. On the contrary, the sounds emanating from these carriages can even be overhead in the compartments of the privileged. . . . The French novelist Alphonse Daudet gives his impression of the lively goings-on in the proletarian carriages . . . : "I'll never forget my trip to Paris in a third-class carriage . . . in the midst of drunken sailors singing, big fat peasants sleeping with their mouths open like those of dead fish, little old ladies with their baskets, children, fleas, wetnurses, the whole paraphernalia of the carriage of the poor with its odor of pipe smoke, brandy, garlic sausage and wet straw. I think I'm still there." (Schivelbusch 1979:81, 82, emphasis added)

Certainly we know from Jane Jacobs's classic *The Death and Life of Great American Cities* (1961) and from studies such as those William H. Whyte has done on small urban spaces (1980, 1988) that the built environment—space—can encourage or discourage people from "hanging about" and thus encourage or discourage interaction of a more than fleeting sort. That is, there is nothing "inevitable" about opportunities for the public realm pleasures we reviewed in Chapter 4. People watching can occur only if there are people to watch. Brief or prolonged verbal exchanges between strangers can occur only if people are in copresence long enough to initiate encounters. One has only to walk the parklike grounds of the Le Corbusier-inspired housing projects of England, Sweden, Russia, Finland, or the United States (see, for example, Illustrations 7.1 and 7.2), or to stroll the exterior of contemporary megastructures, like the Bonaventure Hotel in Los Angeles or London's South Bank Complex (see Illustrations 7.3 and 7.4), to encounter environments—to be explored in detail below—so devoid of people that interaction is simply foreclosed.[3]

Structuring Who Interacts with Whom

The built environment is no more fully determinant of who interacts with whom than it is of how that interaction takes place, but it is also no less powerful as a facilitator or hindrance. The privileged classes of Victorian England understood this very well. They had always designed their freestanding houses so as to incorporate totally separate quarters and entrances for servants and tradespeople. As they began in the nineteenth century to contemplate residence in luxury blocks of flats, the question of how to ensure that they and their servants would not meet in the build-

Illustration 7.1.   Roehampton Estate, outside London. (Photo by author)

Illustration 7.2.   Roehampton Estate, outside London. (photo by author)

Illustration 7.3.   Bonaventure Hotel, Los Angeles. Reprinted by permission of Robert D. Herman, Pomona College, Claremont, CA.

Illustration 7.4.   South Bank Complex, London. (photo by author)

ings' common areas taxed their ingenuity. A contemporary journal, the *Builder*, offered one solution:

> The provision of a separate servants' staircase with a servants' entrance on each flat would of course somewhat complicate the planning, but in houses on a tolerably large scale it could very well be managed; only it should be so placed as to be in the way of being a good deal overlooked by the residents, and not in a too removed and out-of-the-way corner, otherwise the facility for gossip, etc., would be almost as great as in the Parisian system. (quoted in Olsen 1976:118)

Owners of New York's newly emerging "cabarets" in the late nineteenth and early twentieth centuries also appreciated the power of the built environment. Unlike the builders of English apartment houses, however, their goal was integration rather than segregation: integration of audience and performer and integration of differing groups within the audience. They managed this, in part, architecturally:

> The layout of the cabaret . . . modified the formal boundaries that existed between audience and performers in the theatre. The floor . . . had to be located in the center of the room, to give "a good view to everyone in the place." Obstructing posts and the other sight-hindering features of a theatre

had to be eliminated. The closeness of the floor to the tables, moreover, placed patrons in the middle of the action rather than separating them from it. . . . In the cabaret, performers and audiences were in much closer proximity than in theatrical presentations. Performers appeared on the floor at eye level, standing or moving amid the diners seated in a semi-circle. (Erenberg 1981:124)

This extract is drawn from a book we have met before (in Chapters 4 and 5): Louis Erenberg's *Steppin' Out: New York Nightlife and the Transformation of American Culture, 1890–1930*. In it, Erenberg argues persuasively that the normatively and architecturally created *inclusiveness* of the cabaret environment made possible free interchanges between categories of persons— sexual, racial, ethnic, class—who had heretofore been rigidly segregated or severely limited in their interaction, and these new interaction possibilities, in turn, reshaped American culture and politics. However, as will soon become apparent, many contemporary and historic architectural forms seem to have more affinity with the segregative Victorian flat than with the integrative cabaret. For those who are discomforted by intercategorical mixing (and we have seen in Chapters 5 and 6 that many persons appear to be so), designers of the built environment have created an impressive range of solutions.

Structuring Interactional Content

We do not normally think of space or the built environment as a medium of communication. But I think it is reasonable and useful to do so because like other communication media—magazines, television, newspapers, radio, and so forth—space not only structures how communication will occur and who will communicate, it also has consequences for the content of that communication.[4] One of the more convincing demonstrations of this assertion is to be found in Susan Davis's *Parades and Power: Street Theatre in Nineteenth-Century Philadelphia*. Davis begins her argument with the straightforward assumption that persons who have something to communicate do not always have access to printing presses, posters, fliers, and other message devices, or if they do, such devices may not always prove as effective as they might wish. Under those circumstances, one alternative is the use of the streets (a possibility, you will recall, we encountered in Chapter 5 when we reviewed verbal attacks on the public realm because of its rich potential for political activity). Davis's description of the situation for nineteenth-century Philadelphia's union organizers can stand for the situation more generally:

> [In 1835], ten-hour-day advocates, led by the citywide General Trades'
> Union, organized a general strike. With employers, the party press, munici-
> pal authorities, and evangelical preachers ranged against them, unions
> needed a way to establish the morality of their cause before the city. The
> labor press was one way to reach the public; the "card" or poster placed in
> shop windows was another. Committees of vigilance organized their neigh-
> borhoods, *but the uses of public space played a central role. Parades, demonstra-*
> *tions, and mass meetings presented the strikers as a strong unified community*
> linked to a moral undertaking and made the city aware of the issue. (Davis
> 1986:134, emphasis added)

Davis argues that throughout the nineteenth century, the streets of
Philadelphia made possible the delivery and reception of a great many
political, protesting, and/or dissenting messages that might otherwise
never have reached an audience.[5] The urban form of Philadelphia, like that
of most other American and European cities of the time, made it an especially effective medium:

> The streets enabled workers, poor people, and racial minorities to broadcast
> messages to large numbers of people, which partly explains the vibrant pop-
> ularity of parades of all kinds and the variety of autonomously produced
> mobile performances. The street was *shared more equally than any other space.*
> A decision to strike, a meeting's outcome, or a festive gathering could move
> quickly from an assembly into a marching line that conveyed a message to
> coworkers, neighbors, and the city at large. *The grid of streets built for com-*
> *merce suited the circulation of important messages,* and parades fit the informal
> milieu of the street. . . . *Especially in the dense downtown area where work and*
> *domestic life were adjacent, parades took place within sight of home and neighbors,*
> *and within view of wide varieties of people.* (ibid.:33–34, emphasis added)

The density and small-scale segregation of the nineteenth-century city
made it, as I have indicated above, a particularly effective communication
medium, and one singularly hospitable to the messages of "outsiders." In
contrast, the low density and automobile-scale segregation of the typical
late twentieth-century city (metropolitan Los Angeles or Phoenix, for
example) make it particularly ineffective. The fact that contemporary
authorities in the United States seem to worry a great deal less about public political activity (especially activity by the dispossessed) and its attendant "subversive" messages than did their nineteenth-century counterparts would seem to be not unrelated to the simple fact that modern urban
densities greatly reduce the built environment's value as a medium for
dissenting political messages (Davis 1986:Chapter 6; Felshin 1995; Nielsen
1988).

Just how powerful the medium can be as a conveyer of nonestablish-ment messages, given the "right" architectural conditions, can be seen in those instances where authorities have found it expedient to "rebuild." In his exhaustive study of London's Trafalgar Square (construction of which began in 1842), Rodney Mace argues that the design of the square, as well as the designs of many of the "improvements" in London that preceded and followed its construction, were quite explicitly intended to forestall working-class penetration into upper-class territory, especially penetra-tion that had a political intent. For example, John Nash's (unrealized) street plan for the Piccadilly area in 1813 provided "a boundary and com-plete separation between the Streets and Squares occupied by the Nobility and Gentry [and the] narrow Streets and meaner houses occupied by mechanics and the trading part of the community. . . . It will be seen . . . that there would be *no opening* on the East side of the New Street all the way from the Opera House to Piccadilly . . . *and the inferior houses and the traffic from the Haymarket would be cut off from any communication with the New Street*" (quoted in Mace 1976:33, emphasis added). Nash, quite unabashedly, had mob control in mind. So did the various artists and architects who contributed to the eventual plan for Trafalgar Square.[6]

In sum, I am arguing here that there is very good reason to take seri-ously the "s" word's capacity to act as independent variable, to counter sociology's traditional agoraphobia, to consider the idea that the built environment may have genuine consequences for social life. If we do not do so, we will miss much that is crucial for an understanding of urban set-tlements and we will be unable to comprehend the role that architecture has played and continues to play in shaping public realm social life. But before turning to a close look at that role, we want first briefly to review two very different strategies that have been utilized, to varying effect, in attempts to control the public realm.

CONTROL BY REGULATION AND CONTROL BY DESIGN: A BRIEF OVERVIEW

As we have already glimpsed, the historical record of city life is replete with evidence of authorities' dismay over and dissatisfaction with public "goings-on." Not content to confine their "perversities" to hidden spaces, some humans seem actually to prefer to flaunt their "sins." Instead of dying quietly in their hovels, the poor often beg on the streets—sometimes even aggressively. Rather than "advancing" themselves quietly and in a ladylike manner, women have been known to participate in protest marches and to appear in public without male escorts. Children sometimes escape the total institutions into which they are properly confined and make nuisances of themselves to serious consumers. The sexual attraction between two males or two females may be expressed not only behind shaded windows but in a bar or theater or on a bus. The unwashed may intrude into the pristine precincts of the fashionable. Dark heads may penetrate into the playgrounds of the blondes and sometimes the two heads may be seen side by side. And even unscrupulousness has been known to seep out of the private offices of men of business and to infect lesser beings whose best chance for ill-gotten gain involves pickpocketing skills or the use of guns in alleyways. In the face of such ubiquitous debauchery then, is it any wonder that the historic record is also replete with evidence of authorities' attempts to control it?

The precise character of *what and who* are to be controlled has, naturally, varied a good deal across time and space. But the attempted *strategies* of control have shown considerably less diversification. In the main, most seem amenable to classification into one or the other of two categories: control may be attempted via the strategy of *regulation* or it may be attempted via the strategy of *design*. And as we shall see, of the two, this latter strategy appears the more efficacious.[7] Thus it is to this matter of regulatory impotence that we now turn.

The "Pathos" of Regulatory Control

Anyone who so much as dips a toe into the literature detailing the history and current status of public spaces in Britain and North America (and northern Europe more generally) cannot help but be struck by how persistent, how recurrent is the theme of regulatory control. Someone seems always to be attempting to get some category of persons or activities to absent itself from "the streets" altogether or, at minimum, to move to a location where the persons and/or the activities will be less noticeable and therefore less bothersome. Pick any year. You will find editorials editorializing, rulers ruling, legislative bodies legislating, police powers policing. Pick another, later year. Now you will find that new editorials are editorializing anew, new rulers are ruling anew, new legislatures are legislating anew, new police powers are policing anew. Oddly enough, however, none of this regulatory activity ever seems to meet with any appreciable success.[8]

We have seen some of this "pathos" in the preceding chapter, where I detailed attempts by municipalities to regulate away the homeless—and, of course, as we all know, homelessness, if not completely eradicated, has at least become totally invisible! Similarly, one would be hard-pressed to declare that either the several centuries' attempts to control prostitution by banning public solicitation or the efforts to control public drunkenness by outlawing saloons and taverns are unqualified successes. Or, as another example, between 1890 and 1940, Progressive Era activists struggled to remove from the streets of New York peddlers and other mobile merchants—identified by reformers as "the pushcart evil"—whose presence clashed with their conceptions of the "beautiful, clean, and efficient city" (Bluestone 1991:68):

> Proposals for banning pushcarts favored a modern ideal of the street as the exclusive province of smoothly circulating "traffic." This vision anticipated not only the eradication of street buying and selling but also the eclipse of earlier social uses of the street for political activity, gregarious socializing, and popular amusements. . . . [However] from the proposals of Progressive Era reformers it took decades to suppress pushcart trade. . . . In the end it was [not the proposals but] the depression crisis . . . that most effectively removed working-class pushcart commerce from the streets. (ibid.:69, 89)

Whatever the individual efficacy of regulations versus economic disaster in suppressing the "pushcart evil" during the late 1930s, neither, in fact, proved to have any permanent effect. Here is William H. Whyte, writing in 1988 about the street vendors of New York City:

> Street vendors sell everything. There are perennial staples: junk jewelry, watches, umbrellas, plastic raincoats, toys. But the vendors are always trying out new items and occasionally most of them will be riding one fad, or whatever the jobbers are loaded up with. . . . The vendors have been growing in numbers. They have been broadening the range of merchandise sold. To the aggravation of merchants, they have also been staking out more of the sidewalk space, that in front of stores especially. . . . Virtually all street vending is illegal. . . . The police do go after the vendors. But not very hard. Cops arresting vendors is one of the standard dramas of the street. (pp. 26–27; see also Beckett 1990; Blair 1995; Brown-May 1996)

If regulation alone could achieve the purification of the public realm, we would all currently live in a world from which not only the homeless, street prostitutes, peddlers, and drunkards had completely disappeared, but so had such diverse activities as panhandling and begging, loitering, rollerskating and skateboarding, singing, shouting, eating, soliciting, dancing, shilling, parading and protesting, miming, making music, politicking, courting, urinating, swearing or cursing, fighting, gambling, spitting, and game playing (see, e.g., Davis 1982, 1986; Inwood 1990; Parks, 1970; Perry 1985; Pimentel 1996; Spencer 1990; Staudt 1996; Walton 1983; Wortman 1977). That we are witness to no such purification tells us a great deal about the relative impotence of regulation as a mechanism of public realm control. It is important to emphasize that the ability to recognize this impotence is not unique to the historical vision. Contemporary regulators often appreciated the essential pointlessness of their activities. Mid-nineteenth-century London policemen, for example,

> understood that "the absence of crime," which they all promised to strive for, was not a practical possibility. At all levels, it was obvious that repression would not succeed, even if it was thought to be desirable. Vagrants and prostitutes would be back on the streets after their spell in prison, and there was no satisfactory punishment available for street urchins. Sunday markets and brothels would not disappear while there was demand for their goods and services. . . . Noise and indecency were natural [the police] thought, in poor neighbourhoods, and too deeply rooted in working-class life to be eradicated by policing. (Inwood 1990:144)

Yet surely we have all passed through sections of the urban landscape in which most, if not all bothersome persons and activities have been eliminated, in which a kind of moral and esthetic purification has been achieved. In the late twentieth century, such environments abound. They represent the fruits of much learning over the centuries about the efficacy of control by design; the fruits of much learning about the pathos of regulatory solutions versus the power of architectural ones.

Early Efforts at Architectural Solutions

The same historic literature that yields so much information about attempts to control the public realm via regulation also provides glimpses of occasional and sometimes unwitting activities that rein it in architecturally. I use the words "sometimes unwitting" because it is not always possible to discern whether these early creators (or would-be creators) of purified built environments fully or even partially intended that which they wrought. Some like British architect John Nash most clearly did—as we saw just above (and in Chapter 5) regarding his 1813 plans for London's Piccadilly area (Mace 1976). The designers and builders of Trafalgar Square were also unabashedly interested in creating a space that would discourage or disarm "the mob" (ibid.). Similarly, regardless of whether Baron Haussmann's massive reconstruction of Paris during the nineteenth century contained within it a "military" motive (which continues to be debated among historians), he most certainly intended one outcome to be a high level of "orderliness" on the city's streets (Jordan 1995; Saalman 1971). And the forerunner of the now ubiquitous enclosed mall—the shopping arcade—was designed specifically to facilitate the control of its entrances and thus the character of its clientele. London's Burlington Arcade was typical. Constructed in the early nineteenth century, it evinced the standard "form of a covered passageway with shops on . . . both sides, [forming] a private street of shops for pedestrians with its central space covered over [by skylights or a fully glazed roof] for protection from the weather" (MacKeith 1986:1). Beadles (minor officials whose tasks included the preservation of parish and civil order), stationed at each end of the passageway, carefully screened all who entered, making certain, for example, that perambulators and the nursemaids who pushed them were blocked "because it was known that soldiers would follow nursemaids and they would stand and gossip, thus obstructing the entrances to the shops" (ibid.:23).

Conversely, it is less clear whether the individual builders of such edifices as enclosed markets—like London's Smithfields and Billingsgate—were motivated only by profit or whether they also believed that it was their moral duty to render less visible and less "smellable" the sellers and selling of meat and fish. It is also a matter of some debate just how rigidly exclusive, how thoroughly class segregated early department stores were meant to be (e.g., Lawrence 1992). Certainly women of leisure formed their major clientele and, in the United States, the first zoning laws were crafted to keep foreign-born working-class women employed in the garment industry at a safe distance from the "tony" precincts of New York's Fifth Avenue with its luxury department stores and other upscale retail establishments (Toll 1969; see also Hendrickson 1980; Hutter 1987; Miller 1981; Olsen 1976:123–27). On the other hand, some historians have argued quite persuasively that the nineteenth- and early twentieth-century American department store was a truly democratic institution that "served large numbers of women from all segments of society" (Barth 1980:121; see also Boorstin 1973; Leach 1984).

Whatever the case regarding the intentions of their creators, these few and usually small-scale additions to the built environment's storehouse of design patterns—new street configurations and traffic patterns, shopping arcades, large enclosed markets, department stores—seem to have been far more successful than the voluminous and ubiquitous regulations in sanitizing the public realm. Historians and other social scientists have noted, for example, that the nineteenth-century changes in the physical structure of London did seem to have the consequence of "reserving" the West End for the respectable middle class and confining working- and lower-class Londoners (the "residuum") to the East End (e.g., Tilly and Schweitzer 1982). Similarly, the history of enclosed markets reveals no significant tendency on the part of the market denizens to "leak out" onto the street again. And both shopping arcades and department stories seem to have a remarkably successful record of keeping the "unholy" and the "unwashed" on the "appropriate" side of their entrances.

Nonetheless, neither in their size nor in their numbers were these innovations any real match for the sprawling disorder of nineteenth-century city "streets." What they could do, and what I believe they did, was to provide models for *how* to proceed *when* it became possible *to* proceed in a manner that would truly be effective.

Preconditions for Effective Control By Design

There are, it seems to me, four interrelated conditions that must be met before genuine control of the public realm can be accomplished architecturally: *First,* a specific set of political, economic, and legal arrangements must be in place and be accompanied by, *second,* cultural attitudes that support, *third,* a large number of construction projects that are, *fourth,* large in scale.[9] Stated differently: given political, economic, and legal arrangements and cultural attitudes that are conducive both to a massive construction effort and to the construction of massive projects, then should it be deemed desirable to rein in or purify the public realm, it will also be possible to do so and to do so effectively.

However, when the political, economic, and legal conditions are not met, desire alone will prove a weak reed. For example, if land is distributed into small holdings with legal arrangements making the acquisition of large tracts difficult, any desire on the part of anyone to create a different kind of city is likely to go unfulfilled. This was the situation in London in 1666 when a fire destroyed almost all of the city and Christopher Wren, astronomer and aspiring architect, saw in its rebuilding an opportunity to transform the old teeming, disorderly maze of medieval streets and crooked houses into a model of modern, rational, and orderly planning. Wren did get to build St. Paul's Cathedral, of course, as well as other churches, but the glorious new city he had in mind never quite got off the drawing board. Individual landholders, oblivious to dreams and desires of planners, simply rebuilt what they had had before the fire—though using brick and stone this time, instead of wood. And within a few years, London also became pretty much what it had been before the fire, albeit with generally wider and straighter streets. As the historian, Robert Gray has commented:

> The rejection of Wren's plan was a powerful demonstration of the way in which private ownership has always dominated London's development, rendering it, for all its size, a town of intimate rather than magnificent

appeal, a succession of many and various small-scale delights rather than one overwhelming and integrated spectacle. (Gray 1978:187–88)

Similarly, even in situations where the requisite political, economic, and legal conditions are in place, if the cultural attitudes are "wrong," desire again will be unquenched. The almost total destruction of many German cities by Allied bombing raids during the Second World War necessitated a massive postwar building effort and that, combined with supportive legal and other arrangements, certainly opened up the opportunity to "repair the mistakes of the past." However, sadly for those who, inspired by Le Corbusier, dreamed of creating "radiant cities" (see Illustrations 7.1, 7.2, and 7.10), some culturally "old fashioned" populaces chose—like the Londoners before them—to rebuild what they had had before (e.g., Diefendorf 1990).

There are, of course, many locations in which all the requisite conditions have come together: British rebuilding of the bombed-out sections of London's East End (see Illustration 7.5) is a case in point, as is the start-from-scratch construction of Brasilia, Brazil's "new" capital (see Illustration 7.6). But I think there is no place on earth where the conditions came together as powerfully as they did in the United States in 1945. Nor do I think there is any place on earth where the conditions have stayed together and stayed together as powerfully as in the United States from 1945 to the present. After all, if James Kunstler is correct in his assertion that "eighty

Illustration 7.5. Barbicon development, East End, London. (photo by author)

Illustration 7.6. Brasilia, capital of Brazil. (photo by Mike Andrews) From Toyn-bee (ed.), 1967.

percent of everything ever built in America has been built in the last fifty years" (1993:10), at minimum, the *canvas* on which the architectural brush could play has been an enormous one. And as they wielded that architec-tural brush, planners, architects, developers, and builders—unlike the London landholders Robert Gray described—showed a greater preference for "magnificent appeal" and "overwhelming and integrated spectacle" than for "intimate appeal" and "a succession of many and various small-scale delights." Thus, if we want to understand control by design—design that is destructive of the public realm and design that sanitizes it, we can find no case more promising than the American.

DESTRUCTIVE DESIGN: BUILDING THE "PRIVATE CITY"

American strategies for control of the public realm seem to have quite a bit in common with American strategies for dealing with crime: one can eliminate or destroy the offending object (incarceration or capital punishment) or one can transform it (rehabilitation). Our first concern here is with a control solution that may be understood as the design equivalent of incarceration and capital punishment in the criminal justice system. Recalling the distinction made in Chapters 1 and 2 between public (or physical) space and the social territory that is the public realm, we can appreciate that it is quite possible to build environments that have almost no public space—and thus have no areas available for the creation of a public realm—or that have public space that is of such a character that public realm formation is discouraged. It is quite possible to build, that is, a "private city."[10] And for the past fifty years, that is exactly what Americans have been doing. In the following section, we will begin with a brief summary of that activity and of some of the forces that fueled it and then we will go on to examine five design characteristics of the private city that, taken together, render it so thoroughly inhospitable to the public realm.

The Transformation of Postwar America

The story of the massive alteration of the American landscape after World War II is a story that has been told many times and from many angles and is undoubtedly so familiar to my readers that I need retell it only in capsule form. And I can convey much of the story with only three photographs. Illustration 7.7 captures something of the pace and the scale of the alteration as it registered itself at street or eye-level, and the paired photos in Illustration 7.8 let us see the larger landscape consequences of the multiples of these eye-level changes.

What happened is this. In the United States, the production of housing stock, automobiles, marriages, and children had been reduced or deferred by the depression of the 1930s and the war of the early 1940s. When the war ended the depression and then itself ended, the stage was set for an explosion of marriages, residential units, cars, and babies. Theoretically, it might have been possible to build the housing units needed for all those brides and grooms and babies by "filling in" the empty spaces of existing towns and cities ("urban infill"). But what was theoretically possible became practically impossible because of a series of conjoining conditions that overdetermined another outcome altogether. Among these "overde-termining" conjoint conditions, the following seem especially crucial: (1) automobile manufacturers (and their suppliers), who were once again producing domestic products and who tried to ensure the sale of those products by luring in customers with advertising and cheap prices; (2) a U.S. government that decided—for defense, as well as for economic rea-sons—to build a high-speed interstate highway system; (3) developers and contractors who had learned techniques of mass-housing construc-

Illustration 7.7. Moving day, Los Angeles, 1953. *Life:* J.R. Eyerman, Copyright © Time Inc.

tion during the war and were poised to try them out on all that not-that-far-from-the-city open land made or about to be made "commutable" by the new highways and all the newly purchased cars; (4) government and private plans for home mortgages that targeted their loans toward newly built homes only; (5) tax policies that favored home owners over renters; (6) a large-scale "urban renewal" effort that wiped out a substantial portion of the prewar urban housing stock; (7) decisions by municipality after municipality to modernize themselves by tearing up their light rail lines, shutting down their bus systems, and turning their streets over to the private automobile; (8) an ideology among urban planners that "privileged"

Illustration 7.8. San Fernando Valley, Los Angeles County, 1949 and 1963. Spence Collection, Air Photo Archives, Department of Geography, UCLA. Reprinted with permission

(to use a late 1990s trendy term) an environment of grass and trees over one of streets and buildings; and—as the coup de grace—(9) a strong theme of antiurbanism in the cultural baggage carried by both the builders and the buyers. In the face of the combined power of these conjoining conditions, it is no wonder that William H. Whyte was alarmed by the possibility of a "last landscape" (1968). Writing in 1957, Whyte described what was then just becoming visible but what we now take for granted—urban sprawl:

> Already huge patches of once green countryside have been turned into vast, smog-filled deserts that are neither city, suburb, nor country, and each day— at a rate of 3,000 acres a day—more countryside is being bull-dozed under. ([1957] 1993:133)

The initial outward movement was residential, but it was followed in a few years by service establishments that clustered together in strip malls, open shopping centers, and, of course, enclosed malls. And a few years later again, the houses and the stores were followed by jobs—offices, plants, warehouses. "At the end of the day," as the British say, the American urban environment is now a vast "metrosea" (Davis 1992:376) of housing developments, office, manufacturing, and warehouse parks, shopping centers and malls, freeways, parking lots, megastores, and fast-food outlet repetitions—most of it built at relatively low densities and located outside the boundaries of the cities and towns that existed in 1945. No wonder, as we saw in Chapter 1, that the Census Bureau, in its attempts to measure the urbanness of the population, has had to develop concepts like the SMA, the PMSA, and the CSMA. No wonder also that scholars and critics have struggled to find a language appropriate to the phenomenon: not only metrosea, but edge city, megalopolis, urban galaxy, postsuburban city, urban region, postmodern city, undifferentiated urban mass, urban agglomeration, conurbation, slurbia, McUrbia, and sprawl city.

Recent decades have witnessed newer environment-shaping conditions: for example, the globalization of investment in general and of real estate financing in particular; the globalization of the economy and of ideas, institutions, and cultural practices (including architectural styles); and the transformation of the organization and scale of developers (the emergence of the megadeveloper). Interestingly enough, these new conditions have not contributed to significant changes in the portrait I have just sketched for the United States. Rather, they have merely intensified its extant features. Residential housing developments, retail structures, office buildings, and office parks simply grew larger in scale, becoming megadevelopments and megastructures. Megadevelopments and megastructures, of course, inevitably contributed to the creation of megametroseas. Writing of the Southern California urban region, Sacramento-based political columnist Dan Walters speaks of "one uninterrupted, sprawling megalopolis, expanding into Orange and Ventura counties and, in more recent years, to San Bernardino and Riverside counties. They are, in effect, *the burroughs of one continuous city that is nearly 100 miles long and 75 miles wide*" (1992:26, emphasis added). And the megametroseas have spawned ever more super highway systems, which then have spawned ever more megadevelopments and megastructures along their routes.[11]

That is the bare-bones story of the creation of the "private city" in the United States after World War II.[12] But we need to go beyond this tale if we are to understand why and how the private city *is* the private city. We need, that is, to look closely at the way it was put together; we need to grasp some critical elements in its design.

Critical Design Elements

The five elements in the design of the "private city" that seem to me to be central to an understanding of its hostility toward the public realm have—individually and collectively—received a hefty dollop of attention in recent writings on the built environment. Much of this attention has been critical. Architects and scholars identified with the "new urbanism,"[13] for example, have focused on the destructive consequences of one or more of the elements for "neighboring" or "community identification" (for, in my language, the "parochial realm"). Others, like social critics James Howard Kunstler (*The Geography of Nowhere* 1993) and Mike Davis (*City of Quartz* 1992) and political scientist Evan McKenzie (*Privatopia* 1994), while echoing this concern, have, in addition, pointed to negative esthetic, environmental, and political consequences.[14] While what I have to say about these design elements is not unlike what such critics have said, the emphasis is different. My focus here is exclusively on the consequences of five design elements—megamononeighborhoods, autoresidences, autostreets, antiparks, and megastructures—for the public realm.

Megamononeighborhoods.   Specialized and segregated land use is not a postwar invention. Tendencies in that direction could be discerned even in compact, jumbled preindustrial cities (Lofland [1973] 1985:49–52), though, as we saw in Chapter 1, it took the industrial revolution and the geographical expansion of the city it made possible to transform a tendency into a characteristic. Nonetheless, areas of specialized land use in postwar America—because they were automobile rather than mass-transit based—achieved a physical size unseen in the late eighteenth, nineteenth, or early twentieth centuries. In the decades following 1945, more and more monochromic (i.e., single-use) neighborhoods were constructed and more of more of them were constructed on a megascale. Some of these megamononeighborhoods are devoted to warehouses and light industry (industrial parks), some to health care institutions (medical complexes), some to research institutions (research parks), and some to corporate headquarters or branch offices (office parks), but probably the majority are devoted to single-family homes (residential developments, subdivisions, or tracts). Additionally, within each residential subdivision, houses tend to be identical or nearly identical in style and price range.

Most if not all of these neighborhoods[15] have within them areas that qualify as legally designated public space (e.g., streets, roadways and their grass verges, an occasional park). But few have areas that qualify as public realm. To the degree that interaction occurs at all in their public spaces, it is likely to occur between fellow workers or between neighbors, not between strangers. And that is because, in the main, strangers have no reason to be present or at least no reason to be present in a way that facilitates interaction. Any neighborhood draws to itself primarily people who have a "legitimate reason" to be present. Monochromic enclaves largely restrict the "legitimates" to people who live or work in them or who are visiting residents or workers. And given the scale at which they have been built, even those megamononeighborhoods that attract outsiders (because of, for example, unusual esthetic features) attract primarily those who, because they are automobile-encased, are available only for highly delimited interaction.[16]

Autoresidences.   A second design feature that contributes to the private city's inhospitality to the public realm is to be found within mega-mononeighborhoods of the residential variety. I refer here to the peculiar fact that a significant proportion of houses built since 1945 have as their dominant feature the prominence of the garage. That is, from the street, these houses appear to have been designed for the sole purpose of housing automobiles. As the "new urbanist" architect and developer Andres Duany has remarked, if you are walking along the streets of many U.S. neighborhoods looking at the structures, the information most readily available to you is that "cars live here"—or, in the case of double-garages, that "cars are 'shacking up' here" (Duany 1990). Recalling our discussion of public realm pleasures and esthetics in Chapter 4, it is not difficult to see why so many residential developments attract so few pedestrians—outsiders or residents—and thus do so little to create or sustain even a parochial realm, much less a public one. Street after street after street of autoresidences offer few opportunities for public sociability, people-watching, public solitude or playfulness, frivolity, and fantasy and they provide little in the way of layering, juxtaposition, crowding/stimulus diversity/spectacle, perceptual innuendo, unexpectedness, and whimsy as esthetic features. Or, in the words of the geographer Edward Relph, such neighborhoods have "reduced the likelihood of idiosyncratic developments and the 'happy accidents' of juxtaposition . . . which make the older parts of cities so interesting visually" (1987:143).

Autostreets.   In a nation where automobiles appear to have their own houses, it is both logical and unsurprising that they should also have nearly exclusive claim to so many traffic arteries—that is, that streets should be or become autostreets.[17] I speak here not only of great interurban highway systems (whose entrances proclaim that pedestrians, bicycles, and motor-driven cycles are forbidden) but of intraurban roadways as well. As European visitors so frequently comment, in the United States the pedestrian is expendable, the car is king. I will let the following single illustration of this car-is-king principle stand for all the hundreds of thousands of similar illustrations that could be pulled from the record of postwar urban planning and development. From a story in the *Los Angeles Times* of November 9, 1983:

> In the city's reaffirmation last week of its intent to narrow a busy sidewalk and cut down four mature shade trees downtown, the real power behind such pernicious decisions that misshape the Los Angeles cityscale became apparent. . . . According to sources in and close to City Hall and by investigation, it seems the power rests with the general manager of the city's Transportation Department, Donald Howery, a career civil servant. . . . [T]here is concern that as long as Howery's planning theories favoring cars over people persist, Los Angeles will never achieve its goal of becoming a world-class city with a vibrant downtown. And this despite a public and private investment of billions of dollars to make downtown attractive. . . . Howery dismissed the problems that the narrowing of the sidewalk might generate. "We need to widen Flower and other streets if the city is to handle the expected increase in vehicular demands from all the new developments going up in Bunker Hill and elsewhere in the west side of the CBD (central business district)," he declared. . . . Howery's planning theories to relieve congestion rely heavily on street widenings, to a point where he has declared that sidewalks downtown might eventually just exist either in the air as pedways or on private property as plazas. He dismissed the importance of pedestrian life as a critical element in the city's quality of life and all but ignored the fact that walking also is a form of transportation. He repeated that his "top priority is to move cars." (Kaplan 1983:1, 8)

As of this writing, downtown Los Angeles still has its sidewalks but it also still has a plethora of streets that are far from pedestrian friendly. And—with few exceptions—the traffic arteries of the Southern California urban region more generally, like those of most of America's metroseas, appear to have been designed under the aegis of the Donald Howery School of Street Planning. Interestingly enough, automobiles and unencased people seem quite capable of coexisting, and where street design allows them to do so—as in Manhattan (e.g., Whyte 1988)—a public realm is likely to be found. In fact, in many cities in the United States at least, turning streets over to the exclusive use of pedestrians has turned out to be almost as devastating to public realm development as turning the streets over to the exclusive use of cars (see, e.g., Houston 1990; Robertson 1990). In the former instance, a perception that parking is inconvenient keeps people from coming to the area; in the latter instance, the perception that walking is inconvenient does the same. And public spaces deserted by people or populated only by encased people are spaces with an anemic or absent public realm.

But autostreets are not inhospitable to the public realm merely because they make walking difficult or dangerous—by timing traffic lights to maximize automobile flow rather than to facilitate pedestrian street crossing, for example. Autostreets are inhospitable, as well, because they, like mega-mononeighborhoods and autoresidences, discourage pedestrian traffic by making walking boring. Even if they have spacious sidewalks (which is rare), autostreets are often also what Edward Relph calls "prairie-spaces, characterised by a sort of horizontal vacuity. . . . Wide roads are lined by parking lots and low, no-frill modernist plazas, or by neat houses" (1987:244) or, I might add, by walls (see Illustration 7.9).[18]

Antiparks. We saw above that many nonresidential megamononeighborhoods are conventionally known as "parks": industrial parks, research parks, business parks, and so forth. This is an odd, perhaps even ironic use of the word. The *Random House Dictionary* (Random House 1987) provides as its first definition, "an area of land, usually in a largely natural state, for the enjoyment of the public, having facilities for rest and recreation, often owned, set apart, and managed by a city, state, or nation"—a far cry from the reality of industrial, research, or business parks. And while there are

Illustration 7.9.   Fifth Street, Davis, California, 1996. (photo by author)

certainly other meanings of the noun, almost all of those meanings carry the "rest and recreation" connotation. Industrial and other such "parks" are better understood as antiparks. In this genre of built environment form, buildings are situated amidst trees and bushes and grass but none of the "open space" is intended for the "enjoyment of the public" (frequent signs remind visitors that this is privately owned space) and, if my observations and those of my students are accurate, neither is it much frequented by "park" employees. In fact, the landscaping often seems to be designed precisely to discourage use by anyone: very narrow strips of grass, impenetrable bushes, berms thick with ivy or other ground cover. These landscapes have something of a museumlike quality. One gazes at them from afar—through the glass of a car window or the glass of an office window—but one does not touch them. And like many landscape paintings hung in museums, they contain no people. And where there are no people, of course, there can be no public realm.

Megastructures. The fifth design feature that helps to make the private city private is the megastructure. William H. Whyte calls them the "ultimate expressions of the flight from the street" and defines them as "huge, multipurpose complexes combining offices, stores, hotels, and garages, and enclosed in a great carapace of concrete and glass. . . . Their distinguishing characteristic is self-containment" (1988:206; see also Relph 1987:243). Megastructures often contain those spaces I call "counter-locales" and, as such, are crucial pieces of the second major strategy for successful control of the public realm. We shall thus be looking at them again in the following section on "Sanitary Design." For the moment, our interest in this design element is in its capacity to reduce, destroy, or inhibit the creation of street life outside its walls. Illustration 7.3 helps us to understand why this should be so. As we can see from it, megastructures, like the other design elements I have been discussing, create visually deficit environments. However interesting they may be on the inside (and, as we will see, designers have often been quite successful at creating visually exciting interiors), from the outside they have all the charm that we would expect of a large blank space.[19]

In 1961 in *The Death and Life of Great American Cities*, Jane Jacobs provided a series of quite specific suggestions for creating a "lively street life" or, in my terms, for ensuring the presence of a public realm. What is needed, she said, are (1) mixed primary uses (i.e., no megamononeighborhoods), (2) small blocks [i.e., no autostreets or megastructures (which create "border vacuums")], (3) differently aged buildings (i.e., no megamononeighborhoods, autoresidences, megastructures, or antiparks), and (4) population concentrations or high densities (i.e., no autostreets, antiparks, or megamono-detached-housing-neighborhoods). Since 1945, a substantial portion of the urban environment in the United States has been built following principles that are the exact opposite of what Jacobs prescribed. In the place of a "lively street life" we have millions of adult Americans who have as an option a round of life consisting of (1) leaving their autoresidences—which are located in megamononeighborhoods of similarly priced and designed detached houses, (2) driving through autostreets to the antiparks or megastructures where they work, (3) stopping at the counterlocale shopping mall (see below) after work, and then (4) returning via autostreets to the autoresidences they call home. This is an option for a life of privatism. As we saw in Chapter 6, the extent to which contemporary Americans actually choose (or, less consciously, give in to) this option is difficult to determine. But there can be no question but that the architectural features of the contemporary American urban environment make it possible.

But was this intentional? Before we turn to the second strategy for control by design—the counterlocale—let me attempt, briefly, to answer this question.

Design and Intentionality?

I suggested earlier that it was difficult to determine whether late eighteenth- and nineteenth-century architectural "solutions" were always designed as "solutions"—that is, whether their builders had public realm control firmly in mind. What has been happening in the United States since 1945, however, is far less mysterious. While planners and architects and developers and others who have been shaping the built environment may not have set out specifically to do the opposite of what Jane Jacobs suggested, many of them did set out to create the opposite of a lively street life. And while it is unlikely that they wished to generate the sense of danger or menace that nearly empty urban spaces seem to elicit, it is quite likely that they fully intended to create empty spaces. The evidence for this assertion is both varied and voluminous. We have seen some of it in preceding chapters and earlier in this chapter: the "street" and the motley collection of human types who inhabit it have long been the bane of elites, reformers, and to a greater or lesser degree, ordinary citizens. Since at least the turn of the century, planners have, as we saw earlier in this chapter, yearned to rid the streets of pushcarts and pedestrians and to dedicate them to the exclusive use of "traffic" and modern city officials, like Los Angeles's Donald Howery, make no secret of harboring exactly these intentions.

But the evidence is far more extensive than has yet been conveyed. There seems to be no question, for example, that the great French architect

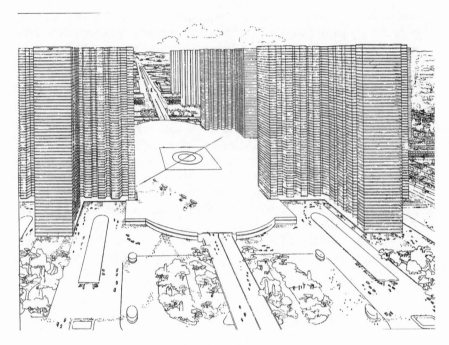

Illustration 7.10.   Sketch of "Radiant City" (from Le Corbusier 1929:190–92).

Le Corbusier, whose 1920s utopian cityscapes (see Illustration 7.10) have been an important source of inspiration for builders of autostreets and megastructures around the world, hated the polyglot street. He yearned for order and efficiency and, above all, speed:

> [Skyscrapers in the city of tomorrow] will contain the city's brains, the brains of the whole nation. They stand for all the careful working-out and organization on which the general activity is based. Everything is concentrated in them: apparatus for abolishing time and space, telephones, cables and wireless; the banks, business affairs and the control of industry; finance, commerce, specialization. The station is in the midst of the skyscrapers, the Tubes run below them and the tracks for fast traffic are at their base. And all around are vast open spaces. There need be no limit to the number of motor vehicles for immense covered parking areas linked up by subterranean passages would collect together the host on wheels which camps in the city each day and is the result of rapid *individual* transit. The airplanes too would land in the centre, on the roof of the station, and who knows whether soon it will not be equally possible for them to land on the roofs of the sky-scrapers. . . . From every point of the compass the main railway lines come straight to the centre.

This is the ideal city. A model city for commerce! . . . [T]he city which can achieve speed will achieve success—and this is an obvious truth. (Le Corbusier 1929:187–91)

Similarly, Ebenezer Howard's "Garden City" vision—one source of inspiration for the now ubiquitous residential megamononeighborhood—was designed precisely in opposition to the "disorder," "crowding," and "impurity" of the nineteenth-century city. In the introduction to his 1898 classic *Garden Cities of Tomorrow*, Howard tells his readers, "It is wellnigh universally agreed by men of all parties, not only in England, but all over Europe and America and our colonies, that it is deeply to be deplored that the people should continue to stream into the already over-crowded cities, and should thus further deplete the country districts" ([1898] 1946:42). He then goes on to quote with great approval the opinions of a number of his more elite contemporaries:

Lord Rosebery, speaking some years ago as Chairman of the London County Council, dwelt with very special emphasis on this point.

"There is no thought of pride associated in my mind with the idea of London. I am always haunted by the awfulness of London: by the great appalling fact of these millions cast down, as it would appear by hazard, on the banks of this noble stream, working each in their own groove, and their own cell, without regard or knowledge of each other, without heeding each other, without having the slightest idea how the other lives—the heedless casualty of unnumbered thousands of men. Sixty years ago a great Englishman, Cobbett, called it a wen. If it was wen then, what is it now? A tumor, an elephantiasis sucking into its gorged system half the life and the blood and the bone of the rural districts" . . .

Dean Farrar says: "We are becoming a land of great cities. Villages are stationary or receding; cities are enormously increasing. And if it be true that great cities tend more and more to become the graves of the physique of our race, can we wonder at it when we see the houses so foul, so squalid, so ill-drained, so vitiated by neglect and dirt?" (Howard 1965:42–43)

In selecting out Le Corbusier and Howard for attention, I am hardly being original. They made their debut as major villains in the story of the postwar transformation quite early on—in Jane Jacobs *The Death and Life of Great American Cities*—and ever since they have done yeoman service as nicely immobile targets for the many critics of the built environment. But, of course, neither Le Corbusier nor Howard was the actual creator of the private city. What they "intended" is not important in itself but only because the innumerable post-1945 planners, developers, and architects whom they inspired were taken not only by their designs but, even more importantly, by their visions of the private city those designs made possible.

And Le Corbusier and Howard and their followers are merely a tip of one ideological iceberg floating amidst many other similarly configured icebergs. Postwar creators of the American built environment have drawn inspiration from—and been themselves—the generators of a plethora of anti–public realm/pro–private city ideas: ideas about romantic suburbs, ideas about the political quiescence of the owners of single-family residences with yards, ideas about rescuing or shielding children from peril and corruption, ideas about ordered neighborhoods and responsible workers, ideas about women's domestic duties, ideas about segregated space use and rational lives, ideas about grass and trees and wholesome relationships, ideas about domesticity and morality. In my judgment, enough evidence is in to make the case that in building the private city and thus in creating an environment inhospitable to the public realm, postwar agents of transformation knew exactly what they were doing.[20]

As did those who worked with a different strategy: the strategy of the counterlocale. To that second strategy for controlling the public realm "by design" we now turn.

SANITARY DESIGN: THE CREATION
OF THE COUNTERLOCALE

In Chapter 5, I quoted the following passage from a letter to the editor of the *San Francisco Chronicle*:

> I spent a recent Friday in a foreign country that was clean, polite and good natured. The cafe was spotless and so was the shopping center and the only street person downtown was an elderly man in a wheelchair who was not abusive. I should add the children were polite too and everyone was helpful. Was this a daydream? No, it was San Rafael and a nasty shock to come back to San Francisco with the foul smelling streets, rude and inefficient civil servants and abusive beggars. (July 6, 1990)

The letter writer does not tell us exactly where in San Rafael she was, nor—beyond vague mentions of a "cafe," "shopping center," and "downtown"—does she characterize the kinds of spaces she visited. And we know nothing of the physical relationship between the cafe, the downtown, and the shopping center or of her physical relationship to the settings: Was the cafe a part of the shopping center? Were the downtown and the shopping center separated by many blocks or miles? How much time did she spend in the cafe and in the shopping center? And did she walk though "downtown" or traverse it in an automobile? Nonetheless, despite all we don't know, we do have two pieces of quite definite information.

First, she liked the spaces she was in—she found them pleasant and unthreatening. And second, she found them pleasant and unthreatening because they were purified or sanitized—no abusive streetpeople or beggars, no dirty, impolite, and ill-natured denizens, no foul-smelling streets. In sum, we do not know whether this letter writer was, in fact, in a "counterlocale." But we do know that she was in spaces that exhibited some important "counterlocale" characteristics.

To understand what I mean by counterlocale and why it represents the second major successful design strategy for controlling the public realm, we need to go back to an idea I discussed initially in Chapter 1: the idea of the "locale." Borrowing from and extending Anselm Strauss's (1961) conceptualization, I there defined locales as bounded or identifiable portions of nonprivate space in which the inhabitants are likely to be dissimilar and to be strangers or merely categorically known to one another. The difference between locales and counterlocales is not the presence of strangers—both are settings in which most of the people present are likely to be personally unknown or only categorically known to one another. The difference, rather, is in the extent and character of "dissimilarity" between and among these strangers. Counterlocales, then, may be defined as *locales to which both entry and behavior are monitored and controlled so as to reduce the possibility for discomforting, annoying, or threatening interactions*. Stated another way, counterlocales are "purified" or "sanitized" locales. Exactly *who* is thought to be responsible for such *verboten* interactions and exactly *what behaviors* are so categorized will, of course, vary from setting to setting. What remains constant is the power of the monitors and controllers to establish the governing definitions.

We have already met early examples of the counterlocale in our discussion of shopping arcades and department stores. But these were relatively weak forms of the phenomenon and, in contrast to the larger urban environments in which they were embedded, they were also relatively insignificant. Again, it took the massive postwar building program in the United States to transform a weak and insignificant strategy for taming the public realm into a colossus. Inhabitants of the private city do need now and again to venture outside their private and parochial spaces. What the proliferation of the counterlocale makes possible is the limiting of such excursions exclusively to those portions of the public realm that have been—and I am here going back to the criminal justice analogy introduced earlier in this chapter—thoroughly rehabilitated.

Although they have not used the term, the proliferation of counterlocales has certainly not gone unnoticed by critics of the postwar transformation. For example, architect and writer Michael Sorkin's widely reviewed and cited edited collection, *Variations on a Theme Park* (1992), is subtitled *The New American City and the End of Public Space*. Mike Davis, as another example, writes about "pseudo public space" and its designers, who "attack the crowd by homogenizing it. They set up architectural and semiotic barriers to filter out 'undesirables'" (1992:257). Recall also that William H. Whyte described those packages for counterlocales par excellence—megastructures—as the "ultimate expression of the flight from the street" (1988:206). He then goes on to suggest that such settings "screen out people . . . by keeping out undesirables, the . . . guards provide regular customers with a more secure and pleasant environment. They are public, but not *too* public" (ibid.:208). My goal here, then, is not simply to reiterate what has already been so well described and persuasively argued by so many other scholars.[21] What I want to do instead—and rather briefly—is, first, to detail some mechanisms that are frequently used in counterlocales to ensure (or to try to ensure) that the public realm is, in fact, in rehabilitated form, and second—again briefly—to comment on why it is that so many, especially newer counterlocales do not always "feel" like the highly controlled environments they actually are.

Mechanisms for "Rehabilitation"

Locales can be rehabilitated (i.e., sanitized) in many different ways. Here I want to draw attention to only four mechanisms or tactics that seem to me to be especially widely used: privatization, shadow privatization, the "panopticon" approach, and the "hideaway" approach.

Privatization. The term "public space" covers a diversity of legal connections between the public and the space. Space that actually belongs to the "public" does so by dint of being the property of some government entity—though, of course, not all such public property allows of public access. On the other hand, much space that is legally in the hands of private owners is "open to the public" in the sense of access—saloons, restaurants, malls, theme parks are examples. Government-owned territory that is open to public access is the most public of public space. Privately owned territory that is open to public access is less "public"—though how much less is always a matter for empirical determination. The mechanism of privatization, then, refers to bringing ever more publicly accessible space under the control of private ownership.[22] Throughout most of human history, most privately owned public places (shops and pubs, for example) have been relatively small in size and their relationship to that most public of government-owned space, the street, was a highly permeable one. With the explosive growth of megastructures of all sorts—enclosed malls, gallerias, hotel-shopping complexes, underground shopping centers— what was once permeable has become impermeable. Once inside the megastructure, the individual is fully in privately owned space and, to whatever degree the owners wish it and the law allows, fully under the control of those owners.[23] As William H. Whyte tells us:

> Much has been made of malls as the new town centers. They are not. . . . They reject many of the activities of a true center. They do not welcome— indeed do not tolerate—controversy, soapboxing, passing of leaflets, impromptu entertaining, happenings, or eccentric behavior, harmless or no . . .
> In Toronto's Eaton Centre, police hand out trespass tickets for a fine of fifty-three dollars for undesirable behavior. In 1985 they forcibly removed about 30,000 people, mostly derelicts, teenagers, and other "undesirables." . . . Sometimes even ordinary people can cause problems. Taking pictures with a camera is one of the most frequent of public-place activities, yet for some reason it upsets mall management. This has been an occupational hazard for me; I've found that even a small Olympus camera will bring up a worried guard in short order. (1988:208–10)

Similarly, William Kowinski, author of *The Malling of America*, has noted:

> [T]he mall was designed to control a protected fantasy environment, and that means controlling not only what is included but also what is excluded. . . . I started noticing that aspect of mall control early in my odyssey, and I was reminded of it often. The manager of Westmoreland Mall told me bluntly, "Nothing gets in here unless we let it in." In Washington D.C., Tysons Corner and other Lerner Company malls post explicit notices at their entrances: "Areas in Tysons Corner Center used by the public are not public ways, but are for the use of tenants and the public transacting business with them. Permission to use said areas may be revoked at any time." There are similar notices in malls all over America. (1985:354–55)

Shadow Privatization. Recent public-private partnerships in urban America have made possible a second mechanism for public realm rehabilitation, which, for lack of a better term, I have called "shadow privatization." By this I refer to numerous odd arrangements whereby (1) publicly owned space is transferred to private or semiprivate control with the understanding that the space is "sort of" public or (2) in exchange for one or another consideration from government, privately owned space is declared to be "sort of" public. Examples of the former arrangements include redevelopment trade-offs in some cities and—with increasing frequency—"business improvement districts" (or BIDs). An example of arrangements of the latter type is "incentive zoning."

(1) In attempts to reclaim or revitalize their central business districts (CBDs), many prewar municipalities have entered into "faustian bargains" with developers. Los Angeles, for example, has given over much of its old downtown property to private interests—as Illustration 7.11, a plaque on the "public" sidewalk outside the Bonaventure Hotel, testifies (see also Davis 1992:Chapter 4). Similarly, skyway or skywalk systems that connect downtown buildings above street level (and that are intended to "replace" the street) are sometimes (as in Minneapolis) privately owned, but whether privately or publicly owned (as in St. Paul), they are very much privately controlled. Jeffrey and Anedith Nash describe both the St. Paul and Minneapolis systems:

> In many ways skyways seem more like private entities than public ones since they are governed by an extensive set of ordinances to prohibit many behaviors commonly engaged in outdoors. For example, inside the skyway one may not sit, kneel, lounge, lie or otherwise recline on floors or stairs. One may not stand upon any radiator, seat or other fixture, or commit any act that tends to create or incite an immediate breach of the peace. Prohibited conduct also includes running, obscene language, and noisy or boisterous behavior which might be constituted as abusive, offensive, disgusting, or insulting. . . . There are further prohibitions against animals, littering, sales, and unauthorized performances. (Nash and Nash 1994:172)

Business improvement districts (or BIDs) also give control of publicly owned space to private interests. As Sharon Zukin tells us, "the concept originated in the 1970's as special assessment districts; in the 1980s, the name was changed to a more upbeat acronym" (1995:33). BIDs—associations of area business and property owners—may take over street cleaning and trash pickups, they may also hire their own security police. The sanitizing (Boggs and Kornblum 1985) of New York's Times Square, for

Illustration 7.11. "Public" sidewalk outside the Bonaventure Hotel, Los Angeles. (photo by author)

example, is importantly being financed by a BID (Gallagher 1995; Gladwell 1995) and when BIDs set out to "clean up" an area, they may do so enthusiastically:

> Generally, discussion of BIDs is buried in the dry notices of the business pages, but in April, the story took a turn toward the picaresque when four fellows known on the street as Bubba, Big Black, Kizer and Red claimed they had beaten up homeless individuals while in the employ of the Grand Central partnership, a Manhattan BID. The partnership's management was, of course, shocked by the charges. "It's fiction," claimed executive director Jefrey Grunberg. "None of it happened." But the charges were backed up by five other employees, and when a subsequent review found that the partnership had been hiring scores of untrained homeless people at $10 a day to guard up to eight A.T.M.s, Chase Manhattan Bank declined to renew a $450,000 security contract. (Gallagher 1995:788)

(2) Although theoretically moving control not from public to private but from private to public, arrangements such as those involved in "incentive zoning" may also allow for shadow privatization. In New York City, for example, developers have been allowed to build "higher" or "denser" than zoning regulations permitted with the understanding that their projects would include "trade-off" public amenities—including privately owned but publicly accessible plazas. In some instances, lively public sites were produced. In others, and perhaps more commonly, the result was plazas that were so hidden (see below), so empty, so uninviting, or so fortresslike that they were "publicly accessible" in name only (see, for example, Davis 1992; Goldberger 1989; Whyte 1988:Chapter 16).

The "Panopticon" Approach.   Numerous methods of human rehabilitation involve the use of caretakers or guards to monitor and restrain behavior. Unsurprisingly then, a third mechanism for ensuring that locales are and remain rehabilitated also involves the use of surveillance: the "panopticon" approach,[24] to borrow Foucault's (1977) use of the term. We have already had glimpses of this mechanism as, just above, when W. H. Whyte writes of police handing out trespass tickets to "undesirables" and guards accosting him when he attempted to use his camera. But unaided human monitors (usually members of private security forces) are a small part of the overall approach. Indoor and outdoor surveillance cameras, closed-circuit TVs, movement sensor devices, high fences with gates that can only be opened electronically, two-way mirrors, hidden microphones—all the paraphernalia we associate with the modern police state—are essential elements in the struggle (and it is a struggle)[25] to ensure that the rehabilitated condition is not jeopardized. Over a decade ago, William Kowinski described the increasingly sophisticated security efforts of the typical large enclosed regional mall. But what he had to say applies equally well today—and not only to malls but to counterlocales of all sorts:

> With its antiseptic fantasy and its bright distraction, its enclosed and selective universe, the mall is a shelter from fear. . . . By creating a secure environment in which buying is the whole point, the mall psychologically links the idea of safety with the idea of shopping. But it must do more than that; it must take practical steps to ensure the mall's actual security. And that is becoming an increasingly difficult task. . . . Most malls use to favor the Neighborhood Cop image, a low-keyed, friendly approach, which worked fine as long as security's main activities were finding lost children and giving directions to lost adults. Now many malls have combined this image with something a little sterner: an image of highly visible police authority, designed to deter crime. The guys in blazers have been replaced by uniformed guards, their belts full of intimidating stuff, including guns. They use official-looking cruisers and other police technology. It all adds up to the image of the Big Neighborhood Cop. (Kowinski 1985:360, 362; see also Davis 1992:240–44; Hazel 1992; Davis, Lundman, and Martinez 1990; Meredith 1996; Titus 1990).

The "Hideaway" Approach. I quoted Mike Davis above critiquing what he calls "pseudo public spaces" on the grounds that the designers of such spaces "attack the crowd by homogenizing it. They set up architectural and semiotic barriers to filter out 'undesirables'." As I understand him, by "architectural and semiotic barriers" Davis is describing the same phenomenon I am conceiving of as the "hideaway" approach—the fourth and final rehabilitative mechanism to be discussed here. That is, as I mentioned in describing "incentive zoning," it is possible to create presumptively publicly accessible spaces that are sufficiently "hidden" so as to discourage their use by any but the "appropriate people." In redeveloped downtown Los Angeles, for example, there are "public" plazas tucked away behind clusters of imposing high-rise office buildings that seem to be used almost exclusively by workers in the buildings—a consequence of the fact that outsiders would have a difficult time finding them. (Of course, should anyone who is "inappropriate" accidently happen upon the "public" plazas, the omnipresent security guards are available to rectify the mistake.) As another example, a few years ago on a trip to Spokane, Washington, a companion and I were walking through the nearly empty streets of the downtown. We had begun to wonder if there had been some emergency we hadn't heard about when we "looked up" and saw that Spokane has an extensive skyway system. Although we both consider ourselves quite adept at "reading" the city (Clay 1980), it took us some time to finally find a way to enter the skyway from street level. Spokane's system, like many around the country, assumes that it will be approached by middle-class people who arrive in cars and park in the multistory garages that are integral to it. And it makes quite clear, architecturally speaking, that most of the people who might come into it off the street are not the sort of people who "ought" to be in it at all.

Similarly, many recently built hotels that are themselves, or that are embedded within, megastructures and that, given that they are after all *hotels*, we might expect to present a welcoming demeanor to the world (after all, the traditional doorman always kept out the riffraff) are oddly miserly with their entrances. Illustration 7.12 depicts one of the "hide-away" entrances to the Hyatt Regency Hotel in Los Angeles, and here is Frederic Jameson's slightly outdated (because of remodeling) but still largely accurate-in-spirit musings about finding one's way into the Los Angeles Bonaventure:

> There are three entrances to the Bonaventure, one from Figueroa and the other two by way of elevated gardens on the other side of the hotel, which is built into the remaining slope of the former Bunker Hill. None of these is

Illustration 7.12. Hyatt Regency Hotel, Los Angeles. (photo by author)

anything like the old hotel marquee, or the monumental porte cochere with which the sumptuous buildings of yesteryear were wont to stage your passage from city street to interior. The entryways of the Bonaventure are, as it were, lateral and rather backdoor affairs; the gardens in the back admit you to the sixth floor of the towers, and even there you must walk down one flight to find the elevator by which you gain access to the lobby. Meanwhile, what one is still tempted to think of as the front entry, on Figueroa, admits you, baggage and all, onto the second-story shopping balcony, from which you must take an escalator down to the main registration desk. What I first want to suggest about these curious unmarked ways in is that they seem to have been imposed by some new category of closure governing the inner space of the hotel itself. (Jameson 1991:39–40)

More generally, one can speak—as architect Michael Brill does—of "denial cues." Presumptively publicly accessible counterlocales that are being kept sanitized via the hideaway approach have design elements that communicate inaccessibility. These include, but are not limited to the quality of secrecy I have emphasized here. Other such cues, rather than hiding the space itself, hide the fact of its publicness, as in

the simple fact of having doors to a public place, as well as obviously lockable ones; the use of ornate private-sector materials; the social filter of the presence of "hosts," often armed private guards at the entrances; expensive shops rimming the public space; elegant furniture. (Brill 1989b:23)

Camouflaged Control: Counterlocales and "Carnival"

"Disneyland" or "Disneyworld" is often used as the prototypical example of the kinds of "public" spaces I have termed counterlocales. Michael Sorkin's concluding chapter in his edited volume, *Variations on a Theme Park* (1992), is titled "See you in Disneyland." Criminologists Clifford D. Shearing and Phillips C. Stenning, writing of shifts in methods of social control, title their article, "From the Panopticon to Disney World: The Development of Discipline" (1985). Sharon Zukin's (1991) *Landscapes of Power* is subtitled, *From Detroit to Disneyworld.* In her *The Cultures of Cities* 1995) Chapter 2 is "Learning from Disney World." Mark Gottdiener uses what he calls "sociosemiotic analysis" to dissect "Disneyland: A Utopian Urban Space" (1982).

What is going on here? What is it about Disney's "imagineered" spaces that resonates so strongly with analysts and critics of the American postwar urban environment? The answer is by no means complicated. Disney environments are tightly controlled and highly sanitized. They are also sufficiently entertaining, enticing, and engaging so that their users either don't notice or, if they notice, don't care about the degree to which they are being controlled. And (and this is what the critics and analysts are responding to) increasingly, counterlocales other than theme parks— malls, hotels, gallerias, underground amusement areas, and so forth—are striving to mimic the carnivallike atmosphere that (American) Disney installations have so successfully manufactured. In fact, many newly designed—and even some older—counterlocales incorporate most of the esthetic features we discussed in Chapter 4: whimsy, juxtaposition, crowding, spectacle, stimulus diversity.[26] The West Edmonton Mall, for example, in addition to more than eight hundred stores, a four-hundred-foot-long lake, and a Fantasyland Hotel, has

> several theme shopping areas, the Ice Palace skating rink, a Spanish galleon in its own lake, four submarines, and 37 animal displays and a petting zoo— birds, Siberian tiger cubs, miniature Arabian horses, reindeer, baby bears, baby moose and one baby elephant. (Kowinski 1986:35)

Minnesota's Mall of America is equally impressive, boasting five million plastic blocks in the "Lego Imagination Center," an "Underwater World" aquarium with 1.2 million gallons of water, a Spamland cookout area, and a seven acre Camp Snoopy with twenty-three rides.[27] If it is ever built, a Silver Spring, Maryland, mall (which its hopeful developers propose to call "The American Dream") would contain

> a 425-room hotel, and a 90,00-square-foot amusement park, and a wave pool with room for a couple of thousand people at a time, and a skating rink with seating for 1,000, and three levels of upscale stores, and perhaps a dozen restaurants, and two dozen movie theaters, and a fresh-food market, and who knows what else. (Finkel 1995:18)

Admirers of these controlled but carnivalesque spaces have no delusions about what they admire, but they do appear to be a bit naive about the mechanisms by which what they admire is accomplished. Mall of America, for example has a security command center that is fed by 120 zoom cameras (ibid.:20), yet Karal Ann Marling, a professor at the University of Minnesota, is quoted as saying about this particular panopticon space:

> There's a fear of urbanism in the Midwest. We're pretty skeptical of the city. . . . *Malls are cities, but cities better than you ever thought they could be because they are enclosed and manmade and everything is controlled.* It's also a city without government. We're a culture that's in the process of almost choking ourselves with government. From that point of view, it is the utopian city. ("Mall of America Banks on the Notion That Bigger Is Better," *Davis Enterprise*, August 2, 1992, p. C-1, emphasis added)

Along the same lines, *Chicago Tribune* columnist Bob Greene wanted to know why "America's real cities can't do" what the Mall of America does: provide

> a bright, vibrant, *secure-feeling* atmosphere where crowds of people congregate day and night, an *immaculate* and thriving shopping area where thousands of people . . . can spend time browsing, dining or going to the theater, *a clean and well-run place* that *while one is inside it*, seems to be the center of things. (Greene 1994, emphasis added)

Not to be outdone by malls parading as "cities better than you ever thought they could be," real prewar cities, via redevelopment agreements and BIDs and inspired perhaps by Universal Studio's "City Walk"[28] are importing the carnivalesque into their downtowns—often using the "same entertainment conglomerates that are creating" the new malls, aka "destination entertainment centers" (Kaufman 1995). Horton Plaza, for example, represents an apparent attempt to plop down a traditional Mediterranean village (albeit one that is in a perpetual state of festival) amid San Diego's megastructured and blank-walled high-rises (see Illustrations 7.13 and 7.14). Denver has installed an "old-fashioned amusement park" adjacent to its downtown. And New York has brought in the Walt Disney Company to "create on this notorious block [Times Square] what chairman Michael Eisner calls 'the cleaner, more friendly environment that customers expect because of Disney'" (Adler 1995; see also Galdwell 1995; Huxtable 1991; Kaplan 1996).

Even megastructure hotels that appear as hostile fortresses from the outside are transformed into gaiety itself once their ramparts have been breached. Or, as *Newsweek* columnist Meg Greenfield asked some years ago:

> [W]ho decided to bring the lake into the lobby? The water question is fundamental. Over the past several years I have stayed in newly constructed hotels in Texas, Michigan, Georgia, New York, Florida, Missouri and California. The undertow has followed me indoors and upstairs as far as the mezzanine. I have stayed in hotels with waterfalls in the lobby, with rivers, with canals and with what looked to be, in Georgia, an attempt at re-creation of the elaborate irrigation system of early Sumeria. I have been in hotels where you needed a kayak to get to the newsstand and could locate the coffee shop only by recalling that it was about a quarter of a mile upstream past the Eighth Cataract. I ask myself: how many weary, late-arriving American travelers have actually drowned in hotel lobbies? Does anyone know? Does anyone care? (Greenfield 1986:76)

In sum, as more and more critics are suggesting, Orwellian surveillance may be firmly in place in postwar America's counterlocales, but the inhab-

Illustration 7.13. Horton Plaza, San Diego, on a Saturday in April, 1994. (photos by author)

Illustration 7.14. Area just outside Horton Plaza, San Diego, on a Saturday in April 1994. (photo by author)

itants are apparently too busy enjoying the delights of Huxley's *Brave New World* to be even the slightest bit alarmed (Shearing and Stenning 1985; see also Postman 1985).

MORE LOOPING BACK: DESIGNED
SPACE AND CITYPHOBIA

Can designed space contribute to cityphobia? At the end of Chapter 6, I hypothesized that the "private city"—the design form that, though initially mostly confined to Southern California, metastasized in the postwar era and spread throughout the body geographic—might very well have done and continue to do so. After all, I argued, it makes social-psychological sense to posit a connection between becoming habituated to a social life composed importantly of intimate interactions and domestic pursuits and an increasing dislike of (or at least dis-ease with) the nonintimate interactions and nondomestic pursuits that characterize the quintessential city: the public realm. Here, let me proffer a complementary hypothesis relative to the contributions of the ubiquitous and unquestionably popular counterlocale. Analogies are always risky, of course, but one cannot help speculating that the consequences of prolonged exposure to sanitized social environments must be very similar to those of prolonged exposure to sanitized physical environments: in both, one develops a vulnerability to medical or psychological distress should one have the "misfortune" to encounter alien life forms. That is, it seems possible to me that counterlocales prevent the development of a robust psychological immunity to the rough-and-tumble reality of locales and, thus, increase in Americans a revulsion for such a reality should they ever come across it. Michael Eisner, the CEO of the Disney empire in the late 1990's, seems to agree:

> If you go to any public building in the U.S.—baseball stadiums, basketball arenas, fairs—*because of Disney-*,—the customer expects a cleaner, safer, more friendly environment. (quoted in Adler 1995:70, emphasis in original)

Michael Eisner ought to know.

$$*\qquad*\qquad*$$

All the above having been said, what possible difference can it make to anyone but a few social and architectural critics if the various assaults on the public realm succeed in weakening or even destroying it? Chapters 2, 3, and 4 have hopefully answered that question in part. In the final chapter, I will try to answer it more fully.

NOTES

1.   I think it is no coincidence that contemporary scholars most prone to the antirealism and nihilism of radical postmodernism seem frequently to be those whose primary objects of study have an insubstantial character, e.g., meanings, images, representations. As a "cure" for their delusions, I would prescribe a period of forced research concentration on either the natural or the built environment, or both.

2.   Come to think of it, to the degree that sociologists participate in antiurbanism and are particularly disdainful or fearful of the public realm, the term might be an apt one indeed.

3.   One of the qualities of space that has enormous power to encourage or discourage public realm interaction is light. As Wolfgang Schivelbusch has taught us, prior to the widespread installation of candle-, gas-, and especially electricity-powered street lighting, the coming of night was the signal to most city denizens to retreat into private space:

Each evening, the medieval community prepared itself for dark, like a ship's crew preparing to face a gathering storm. At sunset, people began to retreat indoors, locking and bolting everything behind them. First the city gates, which had been opened at sunrise, were closed. The same thing happened in individual houses. (1988:81; see also, Bouman 1987; on the "frontier" character of nighttime, see Melbin 1978, 1987)

4.   Interestingly enough, in recent decades, one communication medium—the built environment—seems clearly to be losing out to another communication medium—television—at least relative to messages about the character of commercial establishments. Discussing the "commercial strip," which emerged in the 1950s in the United States with the proliferation of automobiles, Kent MacDonald writes:

I contend that the commercial strip has entered a period in which our latest love—television—mediates our experience of the environment in a profoundly different way. Nowadays, as much as we like to drive, we like to watch. And through the "windshield" of our television screen we derive much of our information about the world. . . . On the Television Road, freestanding signs by the roadway are simply the corporation name. . . . Jack-in-the-Box, Arby's, Denny's, Wendy's, Carl's Jr., Sambo's, Exxon, Arco, and Mobil are names of strip enterprises as well as their trademarks in the landscape. They are only names—none indicates what the business does, what service or product it provides. No other signs visible from the road suggest this either. Nothing tells the driver that Denny's for example, is a family-oriented restaurant with clean rest rooms, friendly hostesses, and a dinner special at $4.99. The sign does not need to do this because information about the place has already been transmitted to the driver by television. (1985:12, 18)

But the decreasing communicatory effectiveness of the built environment relative to television and other electronic media (see, for example, Meyrowitz 1985; Popenoe 1985) probably extends well beyond messages about the character of commercial establishments. As we saw in Chapter 6 relative to the privatism issue, the political rally in the public square has largely been replaced by the television commercial or debate. Similarly, New York City's Times Square electronic newsboard, in the past the magnet for thousands of New Yorkers during periods of fast-breaking important events, now is of minor consequence for a population with access to individual radios and television sets. In fact, as Eric Rothenbuhler (1988) has persuasively argued, even on those occasions when communicatory events actually occur within the built environment, they frequently serve only as the stage or prop for the "real event," which is the television broadcast.

5.   Again, as the power of the electronic media, especially television, increases in providing an audience for political messages, that of the built environment declines. To have significant impact, contemporary mass political activity—marches, sit-ins, and so forth—must be televised. And to warrant the medium's attention, such activities must be extremely well "hyped" or involve enormous numbers of people. As anyone with any experience of public protest can testify, most such political messages go unseen and unheard (e.g., McCarthy, McPhail, and Smith 1996).

6.   Mace contends, in fact, that a most of the nineteenth-century reconstruction of London can be understood as being for the cultural, economic, and *military* benefit of the elite. By military benefit, Mace is referring to the fact that specific

street arrangements, building placements and design, and so forth came about because elites desired to ensure that state military apparatus would have strategic advantage in any political "street wars." A similar argument has been made about Baron Haussmann's reconstruction of Paris (see, for example, Jordan 1995; Saalman 1971).

7. To get ahead of the story a bit, it does look as if authorities interested in bringing the public realm to heel would be best advised to fire the lawyers and hire the architects.

8. One is reminded here of the similar failure of European aristocrats in the enforcement of "sumptuary" regulations against wealthy members of the bourgeoisie. For example, a French royal edict of 1294 proclaimed:

> No bourgeois shall have a chariot nor wear gold, precious stones, or crowns of gold or silver. . . . The bourgeois possessing two thousand pounds or more may order for himself a dress of twelve sous six deniers, and for his wife one worth sixteen sous at the most. (quoted in Lacroix [1876] 1963:86)

And yet one century later, France's Charles VII was "obliged to censure the excess of luxury in dress by an edict that was, however, no better enforced than the rest" (ibid.).

9. Attempts to purify the public realm by making small alterations in existing space seem mostly to be met with failure. The psychologist Robert Sommer and his student Franklin Becker have documented one instance—but one that I think is representative. In the late 1960s in Sacramento, planners were concerned that the old men (both alcoholics and sober "old-timers" who gathered each day in one of the city's parks) were alarming passing pedestrians by creating "an ominous crowd look." Hoping to disperse this user group and to open up the park to white-collar types, the city, among other "improvements," cut down sixteen large shade-producing elmwood trees. The results of the park redesign included a failure "to discourage the old-timers and alcoholics from using the park" and a failure to "encourage the downtown workers to use the park. Instead of relieving the 'ominous crowd look' through dispersion, [the redesign] added to it by crowding the men together under the remaining shade trees" (Sommer and Becker 1969; see also Becker 1968).

10. I am here adopting, and transforming for my own purposes, Sam Bass Warner's sobriquet for Philadelphia (see *The Private City: Philadelphia in Three Periods of Its Growth*, [1968] 1987). By "private city," Warner intended to convey the urban tradition of "privatism" or "liberal capitalism" that was the city's dominant ethos. By "private city" I intend to convey an environment largely devoid of public encounters—a rather different meaning from his. On the other hand, if we hark back to the discussion in the preceding chapter of "privatism" and its links to American individualism, perhaps we can entertain the possibility that my meaning and Warner's meaning have more in common than would appear, at first blush, to be the case.

11. This summary version of the story of the American transformation is drawn from, among other sources, Albrecht (1995), Beauregard (1993), Bennett (1990), Davis (1992), Fainstein (1994), Garreau (1991), Goldston (1970), Gottdiener (1977, 1985), Greer (1962, 1965, 1972), Huxtable (1972), Jacobs (1961), Kling, Olin,

and Poster (1991), Kunstler (1993), Logan and Molotch (1987), Lowe (1967), McKenzie (1994), Palen (1995), Pipkin, LaGory, and Blau (1983), Plotkin (1987), Popenoe (1977, 1985), Relph (1987), Sassen (1991, 1994), Siegel (1993), Tabb and Sawers (1984), Walters (1992), Warner ([1972] 1995), "Where Have All Our Cities Gone?" 1987), Whyte (1968, [1957] 1993), and Zukin (1991).

12. To varying degrees, the postwar "landscape" experience of Australia, Canada, and Britain has been similar—although the extent and the exact character of that similarity have been and continue to be subject to debate (for example, Garber and Imbroscio 1996; Lowe 1992b). What does seem undebatable is that (1) increasing automobile dependence is a worldwide phenomenon, (2) it has both been fueled by and fueled a tendency toward urban sprawl, (3) affluent nations—unlike poorer ones—have been able to counter and control some of the negative environmental consequences of automobile dependency and sprawl, and (4) a few affluent nations (The Netherlands and Denmark, for example) have also been relatively successful in countering and controlling automobile dependency and sprawl in the first place.

13. The "new urbanism" (sometimes called "neotraditionalism") is associated most closely with a set of architects and designers who, in opposition to the standard residential development of the past fifty years, advocate such prewar design features as sidewalks, street trees (rather than yard trees), front porches, minimal setbacks from the street, and rear-lot garages reached by alleys (see, for example, Bressi 1992; Calthorpe 1993; Christoforidis 1994; Duany and Plater-Zyberk 1992; Gerloff 1992, 1994; Katz 1994; Lowe 1992a; "Neighborhoods Reborn" 1996). Whether these features—incorporated partially or fully into newly created housing subdivisions (for example, Laguna West, just south of Sacramento, California)—will contribute to parochial realm creation is an open question. That they do nothing whatsoever for the public realm seems unarguable. A "new urbanism" housing tract is still a housing tract surrounded by other housing tracts: automobile dependent and linked to the rest of the metrosea via large road systems. More recently, the new urbanism label has been applied to critics of the American postwar transformation more generally, including people like Jane Jacobs and William H. Whyte, whose initial criticisms were expressed nearly forty years ago and whose interests were focused as much if not more on the public realm as on the parochial.

14. The critiques of the "private city" have apparently attained a magnitude such that they can no longer be ignored by developers and builders, who are beginning to strike back. In a recent issue of the *Sacramento Bee*, for example, Paul Campos, who is identified as general counsel for the Building Industry Association, contributed an opinion piece entitled "The Myths about Suburban Sprawl" (1996).

15. I say "most if not all" because in some instances, entire neighborhoods can be designated off-limits to all but residents and their guests. The streets of so-called "gated" communities, for example, are not open to the public and that restriction is frequently enforced by security guards. On the rise of the gated community in the United States, see Davis (1992), McKenzie (1994), Walters (1992), and Wilson (1988). On its late nineteenth- and early twentieth-century predecessors, see Beito and Smith (1990). On "democratic streets," see Francis (1987a) and Moudon (1987).

16.   When proposals threaten to bring in unencased outsiders—as with the plan for a monorail stop in Beverly Hills, California—opposition from residents seems a probable outcome (see, for example, Avent 1993).

17.   For an analysis of the consequences of automobile worship on a culture not unlike that of the United States, see Thompson (1975).

18.   An additional consequence of autostreets is that even those who savor the pleasures of public life may find those pleasures inconvenient or dangerous to pursue. A single example: As we have discussed in Chapters 4 and 5, social historian Lewis Erenberg's *Stepping Out* (1981) describes a lively nightclub "scene" that flourished in New York City in the 1910s and 1920s. Drinking was an important element in the scene, of course, but more crucial elements seemed to have involved the pleasures of public sociability, including brief encounters with strangers, many of whom were unlike oneself in class, ethnicity, and life-style. The vitality, indeed the very existence, of this scene was importantly linked to the fact that the New Yorkers who participated in it did not rely on personal automobiles for transport. When they went home, they walked, or rode a trolley or other public conveyance. In contrast, the situation of the urbanite in the dispersed settlement pattern of the American postwar city seems almost designed to preclude participation in such a scene. Limited public transport, the scale of housing tracts and thus the distances between a nightclub district and home, and, most crucially, the very high-speed highway systems (or autostreets) that link the various parts of the metrosea make public sociability involving drinking a very dangerous pleasure, indeed.

19.   One wonders why they don't attract more graffiti artists. Many such exteriors literally "cry out" for someone to paint something on them.

20.   The literature documenting the case for intentionality is enormous. For a small sample, see Albrecht (1995), Bottles (1987), M. C. Boyer (1983), P. Boyer (1978), Eells and Walton (1968), Findlay (1992), Fishman (1987), Gilbert (1991), Hayden (1981, 1984), Howard ([1898] 1946), Hutter, no date), Jackson (1985), Johnson (1976), Kling et al. (1991), Le Corbusier ([1946] 1971, [1929] 1987), Levering (1978), Lubove (1967), MacFadyen (1970), Mansfield (1990), Moudon (1990), Naylor (1968), Osborn and Whittick (1977), Relph (1987), Rydell (1993), Schaffer (1982), Tabb and Sawers (1984), Wright (1958), and Zim, Lerner, and Rolfes (1988).

21.   In addition to Davis, Sorkin, and Whyte, the relevant literature includes Brill (1989b), Glazer and Lilla (1987), Harris ([1975] 1987), Jacobs (1984), Judd (1996), Kowinski (1985), Loth (1966), Nash and Nash (1994), Ortiz (1994), Palmer (1985), *Progressive Architecture* (1978), Rathbun (1992), Ritzer (1993), and Zukin (1991, 1995). See also any issue of *Shopping Center Age* and *Chain Store Age Executive*. David Snow and Leon Anderson, with their useful distinction between "prime" and "marginal" space (1993:102–6), help us to understand something of what happens to those who are displaced by sanitation efforts: they are confined to marginal space.

22.   As discussed in Chapter 6, note 1, privatization is often used both as a synonym for the phenomenon I have labeled "privatism" and to connote the transfer of public services such as garbage collection from public to private agencies.

23.   Some court decisions have seemed to grant free speech and genuine public access rights to patrons of malls and other privately owned megastructures. But like the "right to die," the realization of such rights is highly problematic. In recent

years, numerous malls and other shopping centers have successfully banned Salvation Army bellringers during the Christmas season on the grounds that if they
let in the bellringers they might have to let in union organizers as well (Dirk Johnson, "Retailers Turning Away Salvation Army Ringers," *San Francisco Chronicle*,
December 18, 1995, p. A12). Similarly, in August of 1995 in Sacramento, California,
labor activists applied to picket a "Downtown Plaza" clothing store they claimed
contracted with factories whose workers were subjected to inhumane working
conditions. As reported by Diana Griego Erwin, columnist for *The Sacramento Bee*:

> *No can do,* Downtown Plaza told the activists of their public-information campaign.
> *Not here.*
> In other words, an application to distribute leaflets at the mall was denied. Court deci-
> sions have declared private shopping centers public places in the name of free speech,
> but Downtown Plaza General Manager Dennis Smith said the rulings don't cover this
> type request. (*Sacramento Bee*, August 1, 1995, p. A2)

Other court decisions have appeared to give greater weight to property rights
than to civil rights. For example, late in 1994 the New Jersey Supreme Court ruled
that political leaflets could be distributed in a privately owned mall, but then went
on to reassure

> mall operators that it was opening the mall doors only a crack, that its ruling "does not
> include bullhorns, megaphones or even a soapbox; it does not include placards, pick-
> ets, parades and demonstrations; it does not include anything other than normal
> speech and then only such as is necessary to the effectiveness of leafletting." (Sam
> Roberts, "Taking Liberty Inside the Mall," *Sacramento Bee*, January 8, 1995; originally
> published in the *New York Times*)

See further, Cole (1994), Harris ([1975] 1987), Warner (1985).

24. Technically, a "panopticon" is "a building, as a prison, hospital, library, or
the like, so arranged that all parts of the interior are visible from a single point"
(Random House 1987). Given the role that surveillance and security play in maintaining a counterlocale *as a* counterlocale, we should not be surprised to learn that
a university curriculum in mall management includes courses not only in engineering and traffic control, but in police science as well (Joe McDonald, "ABCs of
Mall Management," *Sacramento Bee*, December 5, 1988, p. C2).

25.   Some years ago, the American Sociological Association held its annual
meeting in that quintessential megastructure, the Detroit Renaissance Center.
Upon checking into the structure's hotel, guests were handed the following notice:

> Reminder . . .
> Please remember to exercise CAUTION when traveling about the Hotel and the sur-
> rounding area. There are Renaissance Center Security Personnel stationed throughout
> the Center; they will help you to find areas that may be difficult to locate. If you find
> it necessary to contact the Security Office, Dial 7-8175.

26.   See Francaviglia (1974), Lyndon (1984), Rybczynski (1993), and Shields
(1989); for examples of the sophisticated level of counterlocale design, see Rathbun
(1992).

27.   After her visit to this Minnesota marvel, Molly Ivins noted, "Once before
in my life I have had exactly the same feeling that the Mall of America gave me: the

occasion in upstate New York where I was privileged to see a 1,000-pound cheese go by in a parade. 'My,' I thought, 'that certainly is something.' There are many wonders in our great nation" (Ivins 1994).

28. "City Walk" is an adjunct to Los Angeles's Universal Studios with its famous Studio Tour and is owned and controlled by the MCA Development Corporation. It is a two-block uncovered pedestrian street lined with restaurants, theaters, and shops! See Adler (1995) and Latham (1994).

8
Uses of the Public Realm

As should be obvious by now, the root assumption of this book is that the public realm has social value. The burden of this final chapter, then, is to try to indicate just what that value might be. That such a chapter is needed, that the utility of the public realm is not obvious, tells us a great deal about the power of the combined efforts of "countryside," "small town," "city home," and "city neighborhood" to oppose "street." As we have seen in Chapter 5, paeans to rurality and small-town life litter the intellectual landscape like fast-food containers. Nor do most people have any doubts about the value of home and neighborhood—even city home and city neighborhood. While they would not use my precise terms, still "everyone" knows—or has known at least since the nineteenth-century idealization of domesticity and accompanying assertions about "home as haven" (Lasch 1977; Ryan 1982; Stearns and Stearns 1986)—how crucial the private realm is to the socialization of children and to the provision of emotional sustenance for both children and adults. Similarly, the enormous literature on "community," on neighborhood organizations (formal and informal) and neighborhood destruction,[1] and on friend- and kin-based support networks (Fischer 1982a; Wellman and Wortley 1990) testifies to our certainty that the parochial realm gives us a degree of physical and emotional safety; enlarges, while still containing, the world of our growing young; provides us with affirmation of our personal worth; and "mediates" our linkages to the powerful nation-state (Berger 1977). Of course, we recognize that neither the private nor the parochial realm always performs as expected; each can be "dysfunctional." But the very intensity of our distress with failure is persuasive documentation of just how strongly we value their "functions." But "everyone" *doesn't know* about the value of the public realm. Thus, as I said above, it is the burden of this chapter to try to remedy that situation. Let us begin, setting the stage for the "utility inventory" to come, by looking briefly at a current of thought that, consistently over the years, has taken serious exception to the dominant rhetoric of antiurbanism.[2]

CITYPHILES AND THE EVOCATION OF VALUE

"When a man is tired of London, he is tired of life; for there is in London all that life can afford." So said Samuel Johnson. Or, at least, so James Boswell ([1791] 1979) said Samuel Johnson said. But, as we saw in Chapter 5, Johnson's is not the only voice to counter the antiurban refrain. Amidst its dominating clang and clatter, one can discern the voices of others who, like Johnson, love the city. These cityphiles seek to celebrate the city, especially the "great city"—places like London, Hong Kong, New York, San Francisco, Amsterdam, or Buenos Aires—and the reasons they give are various. Cities are said to be interesting places, for example, the sorts of places where, as the Johnson quote suggests, "things happen," where the rich array of humankind comes together in a kind of "carnival" or "bazaar" (for example, Jukes 1990; Langer 1984; Oosterman 1993; Wilson 1991). William H. Whyte, although writing some two hundred years after Johnson's famous utterance, sounds, in a passage I quoted in Chapter 1, an echoing refrain:

> More than ever, the [city] center is the place for news and gossip, for the creation of ideas, for marketing them and swiping them, for hatching deals, for starting parades. This is the stuff of the public life of the city—by no means wholly admirable, often abrasive, noisy, contentious, without apparent purpose. But this human congress is the genius of the place, its reason for being, its great marginal edge. This is the engine, the city's true export. (1988:341)

Another recurring theme is that cities allow a level of emancipation from ascribed statuses and the "space" to experiment with new identities that smaller settlements simply cannot match. This is a very old rationale, one that can be traced back at least as far as the medieval adage "Stadt luft macht frei" (City air makes man free), reflecting the fact that after a specified period of city residence, a European serf was freed of his feudal obligations (Clapp 1984:11).[3] And Elizabeth Wilson, countering recent feminist writings that focus exclusively on the dangers that cities pose for women, writes:

> The city offers women freedom. . . . Surely it is possible to be both pro-cities and pro-women, to hold in balance an awareness of both the pleasures and the dangers that the city offers women, and to judge that in the end, urban life, however fraught with difficulty, has emancipated women more than rural life or suburban domesticity. (Wilson 1991:7, 10)

But perhaps the most frequently encountered of cityphile rationales is the assertion that the great city is, in and of itself, a settlement form that generates cosmopolitanism among its citizenry; it is a settlement form that produces—by its very nature—a populace that is far more open to and accepting of human variability, far more inclined to civility and less to fanaticism and smug parochialism than are the residents of more homogeneous and intimate settlement forms like tribe, village, or small town. In a 1968 review of novelistic images of New York City, the American sociologist Anselm Strauss captured this rationale succinctly:

> One classic theme of the urban novel pertains to the diversity of every large city's social worlds and populations. Drawn from the four quarters of the earth . . . the city teems with the people of different races, origins, cultures, and beliefs. Diversity is celebrated for it gives rise to cosmopolitanism. The very multiplicity of populations permits and fosters worldliness—for the city itself and for those of its citizens who "get around." (1968:6)

Or to quote an earlier sociologist: "the juxtaposition of divergent personalities and modes of life," wrote Louis Wirth, "tends to produce a relativistic perspective and a sense of toleration of differences" (1938; quoted in Sennett 1969:155; see also Lennard and Lennard 1984).

While the writings of cityphiles provide powerful evocations of value, they are often rather unclear as to specifics. What is it (beyond being heterogeneous) that cities *do* to give birth to or—less grandly—to provide support for, these valued assets? How do they do it? Are all parts or segments of the city equally implicated? In the remainder of this chapter, we shall look at some of the answers to these questions proffered by those who have focused not on the value of whole cities, but on the narrower issue of utility and on the narrower social territory of the public realm. These scholars have, of course, drawn extensively upon the long tradition of city celebration; their work starts with a taken-for-granted assumption of city value. But they have also sought to do the detail work—to fill in the blanks, to dot the i's and cross the t's—left undone by the celebrants.

AN INVENTORY OF UTILITY

What, then, is the public realm good for? Does it do anything for us that is worth valuing? Is it—like the private and parochial realms—deserving of care and nurturing? Should we be alarmed by its weakening or demise? The answers are: many things, yes, yes, and yes. More specifically, one answer to the first question is a list of six "uses" of, or "functions" performed by, this social territory: The public realm offers a rich environment for learning, provides needed respites and refreshments, operates as center of communication, allows for the "practice" of politics, is the stage for the enactment of social arrangements and social conflict, and assists in the creation of cosmopolitans.

An Environment for Learning

In the first three chapters of Part One of *The Death and Life of Great American Cities* (1961:29–88), Jane Jacobs posits a triad of uses to which city sidewalks can be put: safety, contact, and assimilating children.[4] None of the three chapter titles specifically refers to the educational value of these sidewalks, but the content of the chapters is replete with examples. Huge expanses of grass are said to be boring to children, city sidewalks, in contrast, are intellectually stimulating. Here they can learn how to relate to nonkin women *and men*, how to seek help when needed, how to move among crowds, how to take responsibility for people to whom one has no friendship or family ties, how to find adventure in mundane niches, and how to feel comfortable with different kinds of people, among many other lessons. A. E. Parr, writing of the experiences of his own childhood, tells a similar story, though one more focused on learning from encountered "scenes":

> Until I reached the age of five we lived a short commuter distance outside of a town of about 75,000 on the west coast of Norway. Not as a chore, but as an eagerly desired pleasure, I was fairly regularly entrusted with the task of buying fish and bringing it home alone. This involved the following: walking to the station in five to ten minutes; buying ticket; watching train with coal-burning steam locomotive pull in; boarding train; riding across long bridge over shallows separating small-boat harbor (on the right) from ship's harbor (on the left), including small naval base with torpedo boats; continuing through a tunnel; leaving train at terminal, sometimes dawdling to look at railroad equipment; walking by and sometimes entering fisheries museum; passing central town park where military band played during mid-day break; strolling by central shopping and business district, or, alternatively, passing fire station with horses at ease under suspended harness, ready to go, and continuing past centuries old town hall and other ancient buildings; exploration of fish market and fishing fleet; selection of fish; haggling about price; purchase and return home. (Parr 1967; see also 1968)

Of course, as discussed in Chapter 5, the "learning potential" of the public realm has long been a hot poker on the flesh of reformers (see especially Nasaw 1985). And as we saw in Chapter 7, they have been quite successful in ensuring that modern children, at least modern American and English children, do not have experiences like those A. E. Parr describes. To paraphrase Jane Jacobs slightly, those who yearn "for the Organization

Child" have done a fine job of "incarcerat[ing] incidental play" (1961:85; see also Devereaux 1991).

Respites and Refreshments

Built into the assertion that the public realm is useful as a "learning environment" for children is the idea that this is so because it is also a stimulating "play" environment. But scholars who argue that the public realm has uses do not limit themselves to a concern for children. A second posited use, then, is as playground for both children *and adults*, where respites and refreshments attractive to both groups abound. We have already seen much of this in Chapter 4 and there is no need to reiterate those materials. The point to be emphasized here is not the availability of pleasures, but their utility; not the fact that we experience pleasure, but that the experienced pleasure *is good for us*. Ray Oldenburg, whose work we met in Chapters 3 and 4, has perhaps gone further than any other scholar in making this argument. The title of his 1989 book lays out the thesis: *The Great Good Place: Cafes, Coffee Shops, Community Centers, Beauty Parlors, General Stores, Bars, Hangouts, and How They Get You through the Day.* Certainly, as I suggested earlier, many of the settings Oldenburg discusses would be considered locations in my terminology—small, bounded pieces of the parochial realm. But many are also locales—small, bounded pieces of the public realm—and in Oldenburg's view, both locations *and* locales help to "get you through the day." How do they do this? They do this, he tells us, by means of their high level of sociability and the psychic rewards attendant to that high level:

> The essential and pervasive rewards attending third place involvement include novelty (which is characteristically in short supply in industrialized, urbanized, and bureaucratized societies), perspective (or a healthy mental outlook), spiritual tonic (or the daily pick-me-up attending third place visits), and friends by the set (or the advantages of regularly engaging friends in *numbers* rather than singly). (Oldenburg 1989:43–44, emphasis in original)

The presence of such settings in a settlement alters the "feel" of the settlement, and does so in a positive direction. In cities that have third places, "the stranger feels at home—nay, *is* at home—whereas in cities without them, even the native does not feel at home" (ibid.:xv).

A Communications Center

The high sociability level of the third place links such establishments to another posited use of the public realm—as a center of communication, especially communication between and among diverse individuals and groups. In northern Europe, in particular, this use is frequently invoked by governmental bodies to justify the building or the refurbishing of parks, plazas, pedestrian malls, and other urban amenities:

> City councils and architects attribute all sorts of positive characteristics to the urban public spaces they would like to create. The plazas in particular are thought of as the living room of the city community, where every city dweller can meet all other city dwellers. For example, the city council of The Hague created an ambitious inner city plan . . . with respect to public space. The document says that the city's public places should be societal territories and special meeting places. Policy documents of many other Dutch towns use similar terms. (Oosterman 1992:2)

As Dutch sociologist Jan Oosterman suggests in his first sentence above, the assertion of utility as communications center also provides architects, landscape architects, and other designers with a raison d'être for their professional services (Gehl [1980] 1987), a raison d'être by no means limited to Northern Europe. Thomas V. Czarnowski, for example, an American architect, calls the street "a communications artifact":

> It is the urban street that from the first origins of settlements has acted as principal place of public contact and public passage, a place of exchange of ideas, good, and services. . . . We contend that the urban street provides physically, probably uniquely, for a scale a range of communications vital to the life of society. (1978:207; see also Bender 1987)

But the argument regarding the public realm's communicative uses is not made only by those with political or pecuniary ends in mind. Disinterested scholars, too, have pointed to the essential role of the public realm, or some piece of the public realm, in promoting verbal and other exchanges. Joseph Rykwert, a British architect and historian, reviewing some of the transformations in streets during the past hundred years, warns, "The expectation of daily human contact that the street uniquely offers, and offers in a pattern of exchanges without which the community would break down, is inhibited at the risk of the increasing alienation of the inhabitant from his city" (1978:15).

The "Practice" of Politics

Given the thesis that the public realm is useful because it enables communication, it follows logically and unsurprisingly that a fourth proffered use should have to do with politics. Here, Richard Sennett's work is critical. As discussed in Chapter 3, initially in *The Uses of Disorder* (1970) and later in *The Fall of Public Man* (1977b), Sennett developed a complex psychosocial argument that linked the city experience—especially the experience of the city's public domain (in my terms, realm)—with emotional, intellectual, and—of relevance here—*political* maturity. What participation in the public domain can teach, what the interaction between and among strangers can teach, he proposed, is that "men can act together without the compulsion to be the same" (1977b:255) and the learning of *that* lesson is the bedrock—the sine qua non—of effective political action. If I interpret him correctly, Sennett's vision of the use of the public domain is strikingly similar to the "citizenship schooling" uses attributed by Sarah Evans and Harry Boyte to such groupings as "religious organizations, clubs, self-help and mutual aid societies, reform groups, neighborhood, civic, and ethnic groups and a host of other associations grounded in the fabric of community life" (1986:18)—what they, perhaps somewhat metaphorically, call "free spaces":

> [F]ree spaces are the environments in which people are able to learn a new self-respect, a deeper and more assertive group identity, public skills, and values of cooperation and civic virtue. Put simply, free spaces are settings between private lives and large-scale institutions where ordinary citizens can act with dignity, independence, and vision. (ibid.:17)

That is, involvement in the public life of cities, in the nonmetaphoric "free spaces" that constitute the public realm, also provides citizenship schooling and allows people to practice (either in the sense of "rehearsing" or in the sense of "doing") politics. As Ray Oldenburg has argued:

> If Americans generally find it difficult to appreciate the political value of third places, it is partly because of the great freedom of association that Americans enjoy. In totalitarian societies, the leadership is keenly aware of the political potential of informal gathering places and actively discourages them. I recall from childhood days some old-timers of German descent discussing Hitler's ban against the assembly of more than three persons on the street corners of German towns and cities. (1989:66)

The Enactment of Social Arrangements and Social Conflict

But the public realm does not merely allow for the practice of politics. It is also the stage upon which political realities may be enacted—may be given visual form. Streets and other open spaces of urban settlements have long been used by elites to "parade" extant social arrangements. Writing of the *procession generale* in Montpellier (France) in the eighteenth century, the historian Robert Darnton comments:

> A modern American might be tempted to compare this spectacle with a Rose Bowl or a Macy's Thanksgiving Day parade, but nothing could be more misleading. A *procession generale* in Montpellier did not stir up fans or stimulate trade; *it expressed the corporate order of urban society. It was a statement unfurled in the streets, through which the city represented itself to itself*—and sometimes to God, for it also took place when Montpellier was threatened by drought or famine. (1984:120, emphasis added; see also Schwartz 1987:96)

Similarly, sociologist Edward Gross (1986), after reviewing three forms of what he calls "public dramas" [(1) the Corpus Christi Pageants of England from the fourteenth to the sixteenth centuries, (2) diverse "community" pageants celebrating valued ideologies, and (3) pageants of the French Revolution] suggests that such public dramas were employed for one or another of six kinds of reasons—that is, they had six uses: They symbolized power, they presented the status order, they provided for demonstrations of loyalty, they symbolized tradition, they emphasized solidarity, and they helped to engineer social and cultural change (ibid.:191–95).

This last use reminds us that the fact that the public realm is such an effective setting for visualizing current arrangements *also* makes it an effective setting for the enactment of change or proposed change, for the enactment of social conflict. In speaking of the engineering of social and cultural change, Gross was actually still speaking of elite usage—one of his examples is Cromwell's destruction of the royal regalia costuming characteristic of English monarchical dramas and his attempt "to create [alternative] symbols appropriate to a republic" (ibid.:195). But, as we saw in some detail in Chapter 5, nonelites, challengers to the status quo, radicals, rebels, and "troublemakers" of all sorts have also appreciated the dramatic potential of "the street" (see, especially, Davis 1986; Mace 1976; see also Felshin 1995). To the degree that some of the alterations of the built environment detailed in Chapter 7 have vitiated this dramatic potential, they have done so for both elites and their challengers. The critical difference, of course, is that the former, unlike most of the latter, have the resources to use or create alternative media of communication and enactment.

The Creation of Cosmopolitans

The specific question of concern here is one that, as Richard Sennett tells us (1990:233), bedeviled classical Greece. It is also a question that unquestionably bedevils us yet today. To wit: How are people who, when within the privacy of their households or the community of their fellowships, pray to diverging or different gods—how are such people "to live together in one city"? Now, as we saw above, cityphiles have implicitly answered this question with the claim that city living—*by itself*—generated tolerance and civility, that city living—*by itself*—created cosmopolitans.[5] In fact, the claim of tolerance-production has been one of the linchpins in the argument that cities are good places to live (Hummon 1985b, 1990).

At one level, there would seem to be considerable truth to this claim. Our conventional wisdom tells us that as compared with small towns and villages, cities do seem to be "tolerant" sorts of places. In them, very diverse peoples do live in relative peace. There are, of course, many exceptions, but cities do appear—more than other sorts of places—to allow human variety to be openly expressed. In Robert Park's words:

> Because of the opportunity it offers, particularly to the exceptional and abnormal types of man, a great city tends to spread out and lay bare to the public view in a massive manner all the human characters and traits which are ordinarily obscured and suppressed in smaller communities. (1925: 45–46)

Nonetheless, anyone who has ever lived in a city or who has ever read a newspaper knows that there is considerable distance between the "imagery" of the city as the creator of cosmopolitanism and the reality. Cities may generate cosmopolitanism and tolerance, they may create civility in the face of heterogeneity, they may, as Park claimed, provide a stage for ways of being that are "obscured and suppressed in smaller communities," but they do not inevitably do so. But if they *do* sometimes manage to create civility in the face of heterogeneity, *how* do they do it? Echoing what was said earlier about cityphiles and their evocations of value, the answer to be proposed here is that cities per se don't do it. The hero of the story is not, of course, the entire city but the city's public realm. The argument here is that one of the most critical uses of the public realm is its capacity to teach its residents about tolerance—its capacity to transform its residents into cosmopolitans.[6]

Let me begin the discussion of this last item in my "inventory of utility" by describing some research findings and speculations that address the question of how cities per se generate civility. I will then offer a social-psychological—more specifically a symbolic interactionist—reinterpretation of these findings and speculations. And finally, I will link this reinterpretation to the public realm.

Findings and Speculations. Work on the relationship between urbanness and urbaneness—as the American sociologist Samuel Wallace (1980) has phrased it—provides a considerable range of "factors," "variables," or "conditions" that are thought to "contribute to," "make possible," "account for" urban cosmopolitanism, tolerance, and public civility. These conclusions are most easily summarized if we start by drawing a distinction between two types of tolerance: negative and positive. *Negative tolerance* is the capacity to "put up with" an other's difference from self because the different other is simply not perceived and/or because self and other do not intersect. For example, an American may "tolerate" what he believes to be disgusting changes in the liturgical practices of the Roman Catholic Church because he attends mass only at highly conservative churches. *Positive tolerance*, in contrast, is the capacity to "put up with" an other's *fully recognized* differences from self even under conditions of intersection and, perhaps, sometimes, to do so with a mild appreciation for or enjoyment of those differences. A nice example of positive tolerance is found in the responses of some of sociologist Leon Deben's domiciled informants who, describing the widely despised homeless encampment in the Artis Zoo area of Amsterdam, used such words as "freedom," "own identity," "interesting," and "free of shackles" (1990:16).

Accomplished research and the speculation from that research, then, suggest that *negative tolerance* is generated when

1. *People share a larger bounded space but not the smaller pieces of it.* Robert Park's contention, which I quoted earlier, that the great city "tends to spread out and lay bare . . . all the human characters and traits which are ordinarily obscured and suppressed in smaller communities" rested on a view of the city as a "mosaic" of social worlds that touched but did not interpenetrate (1925:40). More recent scholars have continued to echo this theme: the highly specialized space use of the modern city (Lofland [1973] 1985) segregates diversity into homogeneous enclaves, thus making it possible for diverse groups to "live together" in the same city because they are essentially invisible to one another[7] Concepts like "spatial myopia" (Karp et al. 1977:145, 1991:124) have been invented to describe the situation. The anthropologist Ulf Hannerz did not use the term, but he would seem to have been talking about "spatial myopia" when he wrote that the built environment of Amsterdam is "dense, unpredictable, unsurveillable, uncontrollable . . . allow[ing] some activities to go unseen, or at least allow[ing] the excuse that they are not seen, whenever one prefers not to see" (1993:166).

2. *People physically share smaller spaces within the larger space but segregate themselves from one another symbolically.* Thus, for example, the argument is made by people like Pierre van den Berghe (1970; see also Lofland [1973] 1985) that in the preindustrial city, given the clear visual signaling of identities and a rigidly controlled system of

hierarchy, diverse individuals and groups, despite sharing the same space at the same time, not only did not intersect socially, they often probably did not—in any meaningful sense—"see" one another. Similarly, many contemporary urban Americans, via the mechanism of nonperson treatment (Goffman 1963a:84), are able to render the homeless—ubiquitously present on the streets of most urban centers—largely invisible (Anderson et al. 1994).

Now, "out of sight, out of mind"—the essence of negative tolerance—is certainly not what city aficionados mean whey they celebrate their preferred settlement form as the mother of cosmopolitanism. Very much to the contrary, the central celebrative assertion about the city is that its citizenry is capable of living with human heterogeneity and doing so with civility and at least a modicum of appreciation. Work on the more positive alternative suggests a number of conditions for the generation of *positive tolerance*:

1. *Diverse people are not segregated into homogeneous enclaves and are forced to settle whatever conflicts arise among them without recourse to centrally imposed instruments of order.* This is Richard Sennett's argument, one he first promulgated in *The Uses of Disorder* (1970) and later developed in *The Fall of Public Man* (1977b). As we saw in the discussion on his work above, under these circumstances, people learn that they can act together without the necessity to be the same. He adds, however, an important proviso. If conflict is not to escalate into violence and thereby undercut the tolerance-producing capacity of the process, the stakes must not be so high that "winning" is crucial. Whatever conditions ensure that winning will not be crucial (for example, a decent and widely shared level of affluence) must be met.

2. *People have mastered the complexity of the urban environment sufficiently to move through it with a high degree of psychic safety.* The argument here is that, since widespread personal knowledge of others is impossible in the city (because of the sheer size and heterogeneity of the population), the mastery of shorthand methods for accurately interpreting who people are and what they are up to allows urbanites to conduct themselves in an appropriate manner under a wide variety of situations and thus allows them to confront the heterogeneity of the city with a minimum of distrust and fear (Anderson 1990; Lofland ([1973] 1985:Chapters 5 and 8). A proviso, often mentioned in this regard, is that the environment itself must offer sufficient physical safety to avoid the production of an urban guerilla or garrison-state mentality, even among the knowledgeable.

3. *The levels of community closest to the actor (the home, the immediate neighborhood) are secure and nonthreatening.* That is, people can learn to tolerate diverse (and thus potentially threatening) others only if they have available to them safe enclaves within which to withdraw (see, for example, Jacobs 1961; Rieder 1985; Wallace 1980).

4. *People are able to control the character and quality of their contact with diverse others.* The argument is that if close contact is forced, if persons must forgo their autonomy over the depth of involvement with the different other, tolerance will not be produced (Becker and Horowitz 1972; Love 1973; Karp et al. 1977, 1991).

5. *People possess certain demographic characteristics, those characteristics themselves generating a capacity for tolerance.* Characteristics mentioned in the literature include highly educated, high status, single, and childless.[8] Scholars making this sort of argument also point up the contribution of the contextual effect, that is, as persons are surrounded by others who are more tolerant, they themselves may become more tolerant (Smith and Peterson 1980; Stouffer 1955; Wilson 1985).

Now, with these data and speculations in mind, the next step is to interpret them in terms not quite identical to—though, I hope, not in violation of—those used by the authors themselves.

A Reinterpretation. The empirical base for these ideas about urban tolerance is considerably less than rock solid. Many arise not out of well-grounded observations of empirical regularities, but out of "impressions" about what is the case. Even when the indicators of tolerance are empirically grounded, they may not be ones that other scholars—or the researcher, for that matter—find totally satisfactory (verbal expressions rather than behavior, for example). And it is clear that what these various researchers mean by tolerance or cosmopolitanism is not always the same. Nonetheless, despite such drawbacks, there is much to be learned from this work.[9] However differently they may phrase it, the various scholars who have thought about these matters all can be read (or read into) as suggesting that the presence of urbanity, tolerance, civility, cosmopolitanism in oneself *is linked to a distance in the relationship between self and the relevant other or others. That is, the different other is tolerable, perhaps even worthy of appreciation only if, psychically or physically (that is, symbolically or spatially), he or she is sufficiently distant to pose no threat.*

When negative tolerance is at issue, the link between tolerance and distance is self-evident. By definition, negative tolerance implies psychic and/or physical space between self and other. But distance is a recurring element in discussions of positive tolerance as well. When Sennett suggests that conflicts that can be settled without recourse to centralized authority are those not involving "crucial" issues, he is implying the necessity for a certain amount of distance between perceived self-interest and the issues/persons with whom one is in conflict. Similarly, to say that shorthand methods of knowing are needed to master the urban environment is to say that persons will have knowledge of one another without being close to one another. The arguments about the necessity for home and neighborhood to be secure and about the utility of controlled contact do not even require translation to be read as saying that the persons and places closest to self must pose no threat and that potentially threatening others must not be allowed to come too close. So too, lines of thought regarding population characteristics and cosmopolitans may be understood as arguing that those persons whose family or other statuses allow them the freedom to "distance" themselves from unlike others (for example, their children are not required to play together, there is no necessity that they live at close quarters) are most tolerant.

From a social-psychological point of view, more specifically, a symbolic interactionist point of view, this hypothesized link between symbolic and spatial distance on the one hand and tolerance on the other is certainly not surprising. Interactionists take as a given the vulnerability of the self, its need for ongoing confirmation, validation, and support. Interactionists would also take as given the fact that the very existence of counterrealities (inherent in most human heterogeneity) poses a potential threat to that self. Further, interactionist understandings about the generation and maintenance of the self lead to a third given: that the most serious psychic assaults on oneself are likely to come from those most significant or closest to one. In short, serious differences between self and other in close or intimate relationships generate not tolerance but cleavage. Obviously, negative tolerance, by definition, is precluded in an intimate relationship. One is not having an intimate relationship with someone who is both "out of sight and out of mind." But positive tolerance is precluded as well. That is, if I may shift the language of the argument slightly, urbanity (cosmopolitanism) is generally not possible in the primary group. Intimate voluntary relationships (friendships, modern marriages, links between adult children and their parents), even not-so-intimate kin or community relationships, seem to require for their maintenance a good deal of similarity between or among the parties. As such, while intimate relationships may *preach* positive tolerance, they cannot *teach* it.

In this last assertion, I have, I think, violated commonsense understandings of these matters. What better teacher of cosmopolitanism can be imagined than the interethnic, intercultural, or subcultural friendship group? What better demonstrator of the creed of the worth and equality of all humans than the family that takes unto itself, via adoption or marriage, a new member from a different religion, class, life-style, race? Yet the point I wish to make is that what is being taught in such groupings has nothing to do with urbanity, tolerance, or cosmopolitanism. The lesson learned— both by participants and observers—from such "fusions of heterogeneity" is that some kinds of differences are unnecessary barriers to closeness. Put simply, the lesson is: Others may say that characteristic Y makes A very different from B, but experience teaches that A and B are very much alike and that Y is irrelevant. Translated into highly sexist but familiar language: this is the "brotherhood of man under the fatherhood of god" kind of idea. We're all human beings under the skin. The differences between and among us are superficial and should not get in the way of appreciating our mutual membership in the human family.

This is a very appealing notion, of course. And in some contexts it is a very useful one. But tolerance, cosmopolitanism, urbanity have nothing to do with such a notion. *Much to the contrary, tolerance, cosmopolitanism, urbanity are about the fact that humans differ significantly along important lines and that these differences matter to them. Tolerance, cosmopolitanism, urbanity have to do with living civilly with such a reality.*

The idea of relational "distance" pointed to so consistently, if not always explicitly, by those sociologists who have thought about the link between the urban and the urbane, between city living and urbanity, then may be phrased in another way. The learning of tolerance, the creation of cosmopolitanism may require the existence of and repeated experience with "nonintimate," "noncommunal" relationships. *Limited, segmental, episodic, distanced links between self and other may constitute the social situations that both allow and teach civility and urbanity in the face of significant differences.* And this assertion brings us to the matter of the public realm.

Cosmopolitanism and the Public Realm. The public realm is one of the very few kinds of social territories that, on a recurring basis, provides the opportunity for individuals to experience limited, segmental, episodic, distanced links between self and other. The public realm is, in fact, proba- bly the locus for a significant portion of all noncommunal, nonintimate relationships that humans form with one another.[10] When negotiating a crowded intersection, when managing civil inattention on a crowded tram or subway, when watching the human comedy play itself out on a plaza, when giving or receiving minor assistance, when purchasing a drink or a meal, in these and myriad other ways that we reviewed in Chapters 2, 3, and 4, persons can truly learn Sennett's lesson that "one can act together [more accurately, one can *interact*] without the necessity to be the same" (1970, 1977b). To learn that lesson is to become not only a more mature political actor, but a more cosmopolitan one as well.

Designing for Cosmopolitanism

Before I conclude this chapter, I would like to add a brief coda, one that links what I have been saying here with some of the speculations in the Epilogue to follow. I have been saying that physical urban public spaces *may* provide the settings for the learning of cosmopolitanism but that they do not inevitably do so. What, then, does my argument imply about what public space ought, ideally, to be like? Let me suggest four characteristics:

1. The city containing the space should be small in area and compactly settled—a pedestrian- or mass-transit-oriented city. This allows people, naturally, as a part of their daily lives, to be in the public realm just as a consequence of getting from point A to point B (see Dantzig and Saaty 1973).
2. If the city spatially segregates persons and functions (and almost all contemporary cities do this to some degree), the areas of segregation should be quite small-scale. This allows people, naturally, as a part of their daily lives, to encounter diverse others.
3. The differences between and among the citizens must be viewed by them as "meaningful" differences. That is, they must, in the normal course of their everyday lives, rub shoulders with—accomplish uneventful interactions with—persons of whom they disapprove, with whom they disagree, toward whom they feel at least mild antipathy, or who evoke in them at least mild fear. That means that any city that is capable of teaching urbanity and tolerance must have a hard edge. Cleaned-up, tidy, purified, Disneyland cities (or sections of cities) where nothing shocks, nothing disgusts, nothing is even slightly feared may be pleasant sites for family outings or corporate gatherings, but their public places will not help to create cosmopolitans.
4. I have just said that a city must have a hard edge; its public space must—at least occasionally—generate mild fear. But the crucial fourth and final characteristic is that a city's public space must not be viewed by its citizenry as "too" dangerous. Beyond some minimal level of fear, they will not venture forth and then, of course, no lessons can be learned.

In sum and put somewhat differently: To teach tolerance—to create cosmopolitans—a city must show a substantial amount of "anarchy." But if the anarchy is not to overwhelm and negate the lesson, it must be regulated. A city characterized by a "highly regulated urban anarchism," to use

Edward Soja's (1993:72) description of Amsterdam, should be a tolerant, a cosmopolitan city.

*   *   *

Assuming there is some validity to the various claims about the realm's utility outlined in this chapter, the realization of that utility is very much linked to the fate of the public realm per se. As we have seen in Chapter 7, ostensibly public space may or may not contain a public realm—in fact, it may not contain any realm at all. Realms, remember, are social, not spatial territories; they are created and defined by their predominating relational forms. Spaces that contain no relationships, spaces that are inhospitable to relationships, will be devoid of realms, and thus of whatever uses to which those realms might be put. In the Epilogue to follow, I will sketch out my vision of the future both for the public realm *and* for its "functions."

NOTES

1.   For a sample of this voluminous literature, see Abrahamson (1996), Anderson 1978), Anson (1981), Bayor (1982), Bestor (1989), Bullard (1990), Davies (1966), Gans (1962, 1967), Gratz (1989), Greer and Greer (1974), Hallman (1984), Hannerz (1969), Horowitz (1983), Hunter (1974), Keller (1968), Kotler (1969), Liebow (1967), Jacobs (1961:Chapter 6), Melvin (1987), Olson (1982), Palen and London (1984), Rieder (1985), Schoenberg and Rosenbaum (1980), Stack (1974), Suttles (1968, 1972), Whyte ([1943] 1993), Wylie (1989).

2.   Such writings are to be distinguished from the "save the cities" literature, which seems to emerge not out of any particular love for urban settlements but out of a kind of "resigned realism": Well, if a substantial population of the county/world is now or soon will be urban, then I guess we ought to do something about making cities more "livable." See, for example, J. Lowe (1967) and M. Lowe (1992a).

3.   See also Cox (1965, especially Chapter 2) and Park and Burgess (1921:56).

4.   Jane Jacobs's "laboratory," the area where many of her insights were born, was her own neighborhood of Greenwich Village in Manhattan. That this area is one where public realm and private realm *overlap* does not gainsay the validity of whatever it has to teach about both realms.

5.   I use the related terms tolerance, tolerant, cosmopolitan, cosmopolitanism, and civility in their essentially commonsense meanings; that is, in their standard dictionary senses. Thus, by *tolerance*, I mean "a permissive or liberal attitude toward beliefs or practices differing from or conflicting with one's own," a "breadth of spirit or of viewpoints." By *tolerant*, I imply the display of "understanding or leniency for conduct or ideas differing from or conflicting with one's own." Or, more delightfully put, to be tolerant is to "bear contrariety mildly." The *cosmopolitan* is defined as being "marked by interest in, familiarity with, or knowledge and appreciation of, many parts of the world." He or she is "not provincial,

local, limited or restricted by the attitudes, interest, or loyalties of a single section or sphere of activity." The cosmopolitan is "marked by sophistication and savoir faire arising from [presumably] urban life and wide travel." *Cosmopolitanism* is a "climate of opinion, distinguished by the absence of narrow, national loyalties or parochial prejudices and by a readiness to borrow from other lands or regions in the formation of cultural or artistic patterns." And, finally, *civility* may be understood simply as "civil conduct," in the sense of "decent behavior and treatment."

6.   Mention should be made of a rather thorny philosophical and ethical critique that is sometimes made about concerns such as those being expressed here. It can be argued that ideas like tolerance, cosmopolitanism, and civility and that serious concern with those ideas have a profoundly conservative character, that they are supportive to the status quo (see, for example, DeMott 1996). Thus, to be blasé about heterogeneity, for example, is to be blasé and unconcerned about the inequities of class and power, about the hegemony of dominant ideologies, about the cruelty of exploitation, about the dangers inherent in some perspectives and groups. (Within the United States uneasiness among some otherwise "liberal" groups over certain defenses of speech rights made by the American Civil Liberties Union reflects aspects of this critique.) Obviously I cannot here deal seriously with such a charge. Let me just say that I think it contains some kernels of truth. For moral people, there clearly must be limits to tolerance (presumably, for example, one must have an intolerance for intolerance). Perhaps there is need to differentiate among types of tolerance, forms of cosmopolitanism, and so forth. Perhaps these terms themselves are too broad, contain to many diverse images to be especially useful to the social scientist. But I would also argue that the history of the world seems not to suggest any great surfeit of tolerance or cosmopolitanism or civility. At least initially, until we can get to more sophisticated dissections of the phenomena, it seems to me fully justified, both sociologically and ethically, to be concerned with the production of what our philosophical forefathers of the Enlightenment hoped would be a new and better human being. As the historian Gérard De Puymège has noted in his excellent study of the emergence of the concept of fanaticism:

> The need for tolerance, consonant with nature, is a leitmotif of Enlightenment literature. . . . Voltaire went furthest on this path. In his view, fanaticism more than despotism, is the principal enemy of liberty, while tolerance for him is the "backbone of a civilized society." (1983:22)

7.   See, for example, Hall (1966), Horowitz (1987), Hurst (1975), Karp et al. (1977, 1991), and Lynch (1960, 1972).

8.   See, for example, Becker and Horowitz (1972), Fischer (1971), and Karp et al. (1977, 1991).

9.   Explicitly and, more frequently, implicitly, most of the work here reviewed tells us that any serious pursuit of questions about cities and cosmopolitanism cannot proceed purely at the social-psychological level. We need to ask further about the cultural, economic, historic, political, and ideological context within which a tolerance for diversity (of what sorts) may exist and/or flourish. Certainly the linkages are not simple ones, commonsensically given. Urban milieux that might be characterized as cosmopolitan—eighteenth-century London, Imperial Rome,

Berlin in the early 1930s—were themselves extant within societies characterized by great economic inequalities and/or political despotism (a reason, perhaps, for the dis-ease in some quarters about the value of tolerance). And even within the framework of totalitarian religious ideologies, glimmerings of urbaneness may be found (contemporary Teheran, for example). Let me emphasize, then, my recognition of the fact that in talking about urban relationships and urbane people without mention of their highly complex macrocontext, I am omitting what are certainly crucial elements of the story. On the other hand, given the strong tendency of macro-oriented scholars to ignore social-psychological realities and to see no need to apologize for having done so, perhaps this omission is equally justified.

10.   It is theoretically possible that some workplace (parochial realm) settings may also be the locus for such relationships, but I know of no research that would allow one to assess the proposition.

Epilogue
The Future of the Public Realm

In the Prologue, I suggested that the public realm is best understood as a *regio incognita*. Here, I want to muse just a bit about whether it will remain with us long enough ever to become anything else. I will limit my musing to the same geographic area that has been the focus of this book: North America, England, and to a lesser extent, other parts of northern Europe. Since I know next to nothing about the character of the public realm in the rest of the world, it strikes me as just a bit foolhardy to try to move directly from ignorance to prediction.

The bottom line on what I am going to say is simple: I am not sanguine, especially not sanguine relative to North America, and even more especially, relative to the United States. The forces arrayed against the public realm, many of which we have encountered in the preceding chapters, seem to me to be so powerful relative to the forces that support or nurture it that, barring a miracle, the outcome must be a foregone conclusion. It is not my intent here to reiterate everything I have said previously that might be relevant to the subject at hand. Rather, I want simply to "talk" briefly about three aspects of the current situation that loom large in my calculations regarding future possibilities: technology, tourism, and timidity.

As we saw in Chapter 1, *technologies* associated with the Industrial Revolution made possible—at least for some—a round of life that could be confined almost entirely to the private or parochial realms. Technological "advances" since that time—some of which were reviewed in Chapter 6—have extended that possibility to ever larger numbers. In contrast to the situation of most city dwellers throughout human history, who had to spend time in the public realm whether they wanted to or not, most of us now have considerable choice in the matter. And given what we can now glimpse of both the newer and the probable technologies, that level of choice seems destined only to increase.

Technology, of course, only provides a choice. It does not determine what that choice will be. What adds to the likelihood that the choice will not favor the public realm are the unrelenting demands of *tourism*. Tourism, I suggest, increases pressures for sanitized locales. Some cities may actually transform their downtowns into theme parks for the benefit of the locals, but most, I would wager, have another population in mind. For example, much of the impetus for the "improvement" of New York's Times Square area (discussed in Chapter 7) emerged out of a concern that visitors to the city were avoiding the area and thus avoiding the theaters that are concentrated there. An equally telling, if more humble example of the power of the "tourist gaze" (Urry 1990) is to be found in my own state. The city council of Nevada City—a Sierra foothills town that represents the epitome of what historic preservation can do for tourism—has recently approved an ordinance banning sitting or lying down on downtown sidewalks:

> Fed up with complaints from merchants and some local residents about colorful bands of young people and older denizens who aimlessly hang out in town, the City Council adopted an ordinance with fines of $100 and up to anyone who obstructs the sidewalks and refuses an order to move. . . . George Dyer, owner of the South Pine Cafe, said many merchants fear that the young people who congregate in crowds outside their doors are bad for business and the downtown ambience.
>
> "Some of the kids can look intimidating or freaky with their crazy hairdos," said Dyer. "They haven't caused me any trouble but they do leave trash everywhere." (Hecht 1997)

The New York and Nevada City examples are representative of hundreds of such cases documented in my files. In fact, many of the efforts to segregate and to sanitize discussed in preceding chapters seem to have at their base a concern for the sensitivities and preferences of tourists.

When we combine technology's support of privatism with tourism's preference for sanitized locales, we have a potent recipe for either the destruction of the public realm, or its enfeeblement—or, combining individually occurring outcomes, both. And when we add to these elements the intrusive imperatives of *timidity*, we move, it seems to me, well beyond the mere "potent" to the "overpowering." As I hypothesized at the end of Chapter 7, the less we are exposed to the rough and tumble of the public realm diversity, the less frequently we encounter its "hard edge," the more we are likely to be upset when exposure does occur and the greater the probability that we will avoid the public realm if we can. This is not *just* a matter of hypothesizing. I take very seriously Donald Reitzes's finding (based on a survey of 735 metropolitan Atlanta residents) that

> people who are more familiar with the role of stranger are more likely to be attracted to downtown, have less fear of crime, and hold a more positive downtown evaluation. Learning the role of stranger enables a person to better anticipate the responses of others, adjust to the social setting, and develop a broader range of alternative lines of action. Mastery of the stranger

role is one of the important keys to satisfactory participation in downtown exchanges and encounters. (1986a:178; see also 1986b)

Surely, if familiarity with the public realm (even the pale version to be found in downtown Atlanta)—which is how I interpret what Reitzes is saying—leads to lessened fears of and increased pleasures in it, then it is not unreasonable to expect that the reverse might also be true. Less familiarity (less exposure) can lead to greater fear, less pleasure (real and anticipated), and, in the end, a preference for avoidance.

Working in unison then, the elements of technology, tourism, and timidity would seem to offer little hope for the future of a robust public realm. But if "real" public realm settings are in peril, might it not be that their "virtual" equivalents are even now being born? Are not such innovative interactional settings as radio talk shows and the internet the public realm of the future? Some would certainly so argue (e.g., Brill 1989a), but I find myself unpersuaded by their arguments. What social forms will eventually be created in "virtual" space remains unknown. But the emergent forms that are currently visible seem to partake more of the private (e.g., Kendall 1998) and the parochial (e.g., Wellman and Gulia 1998) realms than they do of the public. And even in those electronic situations where strangers remain strangers, interactions take place between and among ethereal intellects, between and among beings without bodies— sterile versions of the palpably corporeal interactions characteristic of the public realm.

In 1973, I ended *A World of Strangers* with the words, "For most of us, the world of strangers is a permanent home. For most of us, the world of strangers must become routine. I hope we shall be equal to the task." Almost thirty years later, I end this book by observing that, at least in my home country, that hope remains unfulfilled.

References

Abrahamson, Mark. 1996. *Urban Enclaves: Identity and Place in America*. New York: St. Martin's.

Abrentzen, Sherry Boland. 1992. "Home as a Workplace in the Lives of Women." Pp. 113–38 in *Human Behavior and Environment: Advances in Theory and Research*, Volume 12, *Place Attachment*, edited by Irwin Altman and Setha M. Low. New York: Plenum.

Adelman, Melvin L. 1986. *A Sporting Time: New York City and the Rise of Modern Athletics, 1820–70*. Champaign: University of Illinois Press.

Adler, Jerry. 1995. "Theme Cities." *Newsweek* (September 11), pp. 68–70.

Al-Kodmany, Kheir. 1996. "Traditional Arab-Islamic Attitudes to Privacy." Pp. 113–16 in *Public and Privates Places: Proceedings of the Twenty-Seventh Annual Conference of the Environmental Design Research Association*, edited by Jack L. Nasar and Barbara B. Brown. Edmond, OK: EDRA.

Albrecht, Donald (ed.). 1995. *World War II and the American Dream: How Wartime Building Changed a Nation*. Cambridge, MA: MIT Press, Washington, DC: National Building Museum.

Alexander, Christopher. 1973. "The City as a Mechanism for Sustaining Human Contact." Pp. 239–74 in *Urbanman: The Psychology of Urban Survival*, edited by John Helmer and Neil A. Eddington. New York: Free Press.

Alexander, Christopher, Sara Ishikawa, and Murray Silverstein, with Max Jacobson, Ingrid Fiksdahl-King, and Shlomo Angel. 1977. *A Pattern Language: Towns, Buildings, Construction*. New York: Oxford University Press.

Alexander, Christopher, Hajo Neis, Artemis Anninou, and Ingrid King. 1987. *A New Theory of Urban Design*. New York: Oxford University Press.

Alexander, Katherine C. and Andrew Federhar. 1978. "Crosswalk Behavior and Attitudes." Pp. 59–67 in *New Directions in Environmental Design Research*, edited by Walter E. Rogers and William H. Ittelson. Washington, DC: Environmental Design Research Association.

Altman, Irwin. 1975. *The Environment and Social Behavior: Privacy, Personal Space, Territory, Crowding*. Monterey, CA: Brooks/Cole.

Altman, Irwin and Setha M. Low (eds.). 1992. *Human Behavior and Environment: Advances in Theory and Research*, Volume 12, *Place Attachment*. New York: Plenum.

Altman, Irwin and Ervin H. Zube (eds.). 1989. *Human Behavior and Environment: Advances in Theory and Research*, Volume 10, *Public Places and Spaces*. New York: Plenum.

Amato, Paul R. 1981. "Urban-Rural Differences in Helping Behavior in Australia and the United States." *Journal of Social Psychology* 114(August):289–90.

———. 1990. "Personality and Social Network Involvement as Predictors of Helping Behavior in Everyday Life." *Social Psychology Quarterly* 53(1, March):
31–43.

Amato, Paul R. and Julie Saunders. 1985. "The Perceived Dimensions of Help-
Seeking Episodes." *Social Psychology Quarterly* 48(2, June):130–38.

Anderson, Elijah. 1978. *A Place on the Corner*. Chicago: University of Chicago Press.

———. 1990. *Street Wise: Race, Class and Change in an Urban Community*. Chicago:
University of Chicago Press.

Anderson, Leon, David A. Snow, and Daniel Cress. 1994. "Negotiating the Public
Realm: Stigma Management And Collective Action Among the Homeless."
Pp. 121–43 in *Research in Community Sociology*, edited by Dan C. Chekki, Sup-
plement 1, *The Community of the Streets*, edited by Spencer E. Cahill and Lyn H.
Lofland. Greenwich, CT: JAI.

Anderson, Stanford (ed.). 1978. *On Streets*. Cambridge, MA: MIT Press.

Anson, Brian. 1981. *I'll Fight You for It! Behind the Struggle for Covent Garden*. London: Jonathan Cape.

Archer, Dane and Lynn Erlich-Erfer. 1991. "Fear and Loading: Archival Traces of
the Response to Extraordinary Violence." *Social Psychology Quarterly* 54(4,
December):343–52.

Arendt, Hannah. 1958. *The Human Condition*. Chicago: University of Chicago Press.

Arensberg, Conrad M. 1980. "The Urban in Crosscultural Perspective." Pp. 37–51
in *Urban Life: Readings in Urban Anthropology*, edited by George Gmelch and
Walter P. Zenner. New York: St. Martin's.

Argyle, Michael and Mark Cook. 1976. *Gaze and Mutual Gaze*. Cambridge: Cambridge University Press.

Aronson, Sidney H. 1977. "The City: Illusion, Nostalgia, and Reality." Pp. 253–64 in
Readings in Introductory Sociology, 3rd edition, edited by Dennis H. Wrong and
Harry L. Gracey. New York: Macmillan. [Originally published in *Dissent*, 1971.]

Ashcraft, Norman and Albert E. Scheflen. 1976. *People Space: The Making and Break-
ing of Human Boundaries*. Garden City, NY: Anchor.

Avent, G. Jeanette. 1993. "City Backs Out of Monorail Study: Beverly Hills Won't
Pay Share of Study." *Los Angeles Times* (July 8), p. J1.

Bacon, Edmund N. 1963. "The City Image." Pp. 25–32 in *Man and the Modern City*,
edited by Elizabeth Geen, Jeanne R. Lowe, and Kenneth Walker. Pittsburgh:
University of Pittsburgh Press.

Bahrdt, Hans Paul. 1966. "Public Activity and Private Activity as Basic Forms of
City Association." Pp. 78–85 in *Perspectives on the American Community: A Book
of Readings*, edited by Roland L. Warren. Chicago: Rand McNally.

Bailey, Peter (ed.). 1986. *Music Hall: The Business of Pleasure*. Milton Keynes, UK:
Open University Press.

Bakeman, Robert and Stephen Beck. 1974. "The Size of Informal Groups in Public."
Environment and Behavior 6(3, September):378–90.

Baldassare, Mark. 1983. "Residential Crowding and Social Behavior." Pp. 148–61 in
Remaking the City: Social Science Perspectives on Urban Design, edited by John S.
Pipkin, Mark E. LaGory, and Judith R. Blau. Albany: State University of New
York Press.

Balkin, Steven. 1979. "Victimization Rates, Safety and Fear of Crime." *Social Problems* 26(3, February):343–58.

Barefoot, John C., Howard Hoople, and David McClay. 1972. "Avoidance of an Act Which Would Violate Personal Space." *Psychonomic Science* 28(4, August 25):205–6.

Barker, Roger (ed.). 1963. *The Stream of Behavior: Explorations of Its Structure and Content*. New York: Appleton-Century-Crofts.

———. 1968. *Ecological Psychology*. Stanford, CA: Stanford University Press.

Barker, Roger G. and Associates. 1978. *Habitats, Environments and Human Behavior*. San Francisco: Jossey-Bass.

Barrows, Susanna. 1981. *Distorting Mirrors: Visions of the Crowd in Late Nineteenth-Century France*. New Haven, CT: Yale University Press.

Barrows, Susanna and Robin Room (eds.). 1991. *Drinking Behavior and Belief in Modern History*. Berkeley: University of California Press.

Barth, Gunther. 1980. *City People: The Rise of Modern City Culture in Nineteenth-Century America*. New York: Oxford University Press.

Baumgartner, M. P. 1988. *The Moral Order of a Suburb*. New York: Oxford University Press.

Baxter, Ellen and Kim Hopper. 1981. *Private Lives/Public Spaces: Homeless Adults on the Streets of New York City*. New York: Community Service Society.

Bayor, Ronald (ed.). 1982. *Neighborhoods in Urban America*. Port Washington, NY: Kennikat.

Beauregard, Robert A. 1993. *Voices of Decline: The Postwar Fate of U.S. Cities*. Oxford: Blackwell.

Bech, Henning. 1994. "CitySex: Representing Lust in Public." Unpublished paper. Department of Sociology, University of Copenhagen.

Beck, Bernard. 1977. "Face-Saving at the Singles Dance." *Social Problems* 24(5, June):530–44.

Becker, Franklin D. 1968. "Redsigned Plaza, Study Claims Is 'Planned Failure.'" *Sacramento Bee*, September 1, p. B4.

———. 1973. "Study of Spatial Markers." *Journal of Personality and Social Psychology* 26(June):439–45.

Becker, Howard and Irving Louis Horowitz. 1972. *Culture and Civility in San Francisco*. New Brunswick, NJ: Transaction.

Beckett, Jamie. 1990. "Bureaucracy in the Hot-Dog Trade." *San Francisco Chronicle*, September 27, p. C-1.

Beier, A. L. 1985. *Masterless Men: The Vagrancy Problem in England 1560–1640*. London and New York: Methuen.

Beito, David T. with Bruce Smith. 1990. "The Formation of Urban Infrastructure Through Nongovernmental Planning: The Private Places of St. Louis, 1869–1920." *Journal of Urban History* 16(3, May):263–303.

Bellah, Robert N., Richard Madsen, William M. Sullivan, Ann Swidler, and Steven M. Tipton. 1985. *Habits of the Heart: Individualism and Commitment in American Life*. Berkeley: University of California Press.

Bender, Ross. 1987. "Getting Nowhere Fast: Abundant Life with Public Transit." *The Other Side* (March):42–43.

Bender, Thomas. 1975. *Toward an Urban Vision: Ideas and Institutions in Nineteenth-Century America*. Lexington: University of Kentucky Press.

Benn, Stanley I. and Gerald F. Gaus (eds.). 1983a. *Public and Private in Social Life*. London: Croom Helm.

——— . 1983b. "The Public and the Private: Concepts and Action." Pp. 3–27 in *Public and Private in Social Life*, edited by Stanley I. Benn and Gerald F. Gaus. London: Croom Helm.

——— . 1983c. "The Liberal Conception of the Public and the Private." Pp. 31–65 in *Culture and Ideology in Ireland*, edited by *Public and Private in Social Life*, edited by Stanley I. Benn and Gerald F. Gaus. London: Croom Helm.

Bennet, Don. 1984. "Maggie Feathers and Missie Reilly: Hawking Life in Dublin's City Quay." Pp. 136–53 in *Culture and Ideology in Ireland*, edited by Chris Curtin, Mary Kelly, and Liam O'Dowd. Galway: Galway University Press.

Bennett, Larry. 1990. *Fragments of Cities: The New American Downtowns and Neighborhoods*. Columbus: Ohio State University Press.

Bensman, Joseph and Robert Lilienfeld. 1979. *Between Public and Private: The Lost Boundaries of the Self*. New York: Free Press.

Berger, Bennett M. 1979. "American Pastoralism, Suburbia and the Commune Movement: An Exercise in the Microsociology of Knowledge." Pp. 235–50 in *On the Making of Americans: Essays in Honor of David Riesman*, edited by Herbert Gans, Nathan Glazer, Joseph R. Gusfield, and Christopher Jencks. Philadelphia: University of Pennsylvania Press.

Berger, Peter. 1977. *Facing Up to Modernity: Excursions in Society, Politics and Religion*. New York: Basic Books.

——— . 1978. "In Praise of New York: A Semi-Secular Homily." Pp. 28–31 in *Focus: Urban Society, An Annual Editions Reader*. New York: Dushkin.

Berger, Peter and Hans Kellner. 1964. "Marriage and the Construction of Reality." *Diogenes* 45:1–25.

Berkowitz, William. 1971. "A Cross-National Comparison of Some Social Patterns of Urban Pedestrians." *Journal of Cross-Cultural Psychology* 2:129–44.

Best, Joel. 1987. "Rhetoric in Claims-Making: Constructing the Missing Children Problem." *Social Problems* 34(2, April):101–21.

——— . 1990. *Threatened Children: Rhetoric and Concern about Child-Victims*. Chicago: University of Chicago Press.

Best, Joel and Gerald T. Horiuchi. 1985. "The Razor Blade in the Apple: The Social Construction of Urban Legends." *Social Problems* 32:488–99.

Bestor, Theodore C. 1989. *Neighborhood Tokyo*. Stanford: Stanford University Press.

Blair, Gwenda Linda. 1974. "Standing on the Corner." *Liberation* 18(9, July/August):6–8.

Blair, Maude. 1995. "City Seeking to Put Brakes on 'Mobile' Businesses." *Sacramento Bee*, August 4, p. B1.

Bluestone, Daniel M. 1991. "'The Pushcart Evil' Peddlers, Merchants, and New York City's Streets, 1890–1940." *Journal of Urban History* 18(1, November):68–92.

Blumer, Herbert. 1969. *Symbolic Interactionism: Perspective and Method*. Englewood Cliffs, NJ: Prentice-Hall.

Boggs, Vernon and William Kornblum. 1985. "Symbiosis in the City: The Human Ecology of Times Square." *Sciences* (January/February):25–30.

Boorstin, Daniel. 1973. *The Americans: The Democratic Experience*. New York: Random House.

Boswell, James. [1791] 1979. *The Life of Johnson*. Hammondsworth: Penguin.

Bottles, Scott L. 1987. *Los Angeles and the Automobile: The Making of the Modern City*. Berkeley: University of California Press.

Bouman, Mark J. 1987. "Luxury and Control: The Urbanity of Street Lighting in Nineteenth-Century Cities." *Journal of Urban History* 14(1, 7–37).

Bourassa, Steven C. 1990. "A Paradigm for Landscape Aesthetics." *Environment and Behavior* 22(6, November):787–812.

Boyer, M. Christine. 1983. *Dreaming the Rational City: The Myth of American City Planning*. Cambridge: MIT Press.

Boyer, Paul. 1978. *Urban Masses and Moral Order in America 1820–1920*. Cambridge, MA: Harvard University Press.

Breines, Simon and William H. Dean. 1974. *The Pedestrian Revolution: Streets without Cars*. New York: Vintage.

Brent, Ruth Stumpe. 1981. "Usage of Public Restroom Lounges as Support Systems by Elderly Females." *Qualitative Sociology* 4(1, Spring):56–71.

Bressi, Todd W. 1992. "The Neo-Traditional Revolution." *Utne Reader* (May/June): 101–4.

Bridger, Jeffrey C. 1996. "Community Imagery and the Built Environment." *Sociological Quarterly* 37(3):353–74.

Brill, Michael. 1989a. "An Ontology for Exploring Urban Public Life Today." *Places* 6(Fall):24–31.

———. 1989b. "Transformation, Nostalgia, and Illusion in Public Life and Public Place." Pp. 7–29 in *Human Behavior and Environment: Advances in Theory and Research*, Volume 10, *Public Places and Spaces*, edited by Irwin Altman and Ervin H. Zube. New York: Plenum.

Bristol, Michael D. 1985. *Carnival and Theater: Plebeian Culture and the Structure of Authority in Renaissance England*. New York: Methuen.

Britton, Rob. 1983. "The Australian Pub: Best Mates, Good Cheer, Cold Beer." *Landscape* 27:1–9.

Brodsly, David. 1981. *L.A. Freeway: An Appreciative Essay*. Berkeley: University of California Press.

Brower, Sidney, N. 1980. "Territory in Urban Settings." Pp. 179–207 in *Human Behavior and Environment: Advances in Theory and Research*, Volume 4, *Environment and Culture*, edited by Irwin Altman, Amos Rapoport, and Joachim F. Wohlwill. New York: Plenum.

Brown, David. W. 1995. *When Strangers Cooperate: Using Social Conventions to Govern Ourselves*. New York: Free Press.

Brown-May, Andrew. 1996. "A Charitable Indulgence: Street Stalls and the Transformation of Public Space in Melbourne, c. 1850–1920." *Urban History* 23(1, May):48–71.

Bruning, Nany and Stephen Wheeler. 1995. "Designing Cities As If Women Mattered: An Interview with Clare Cooper Marcus." *Urban Ecologist* 1:1, 3–4.

Brunt, Lodewijk. 1990. "The Ethnography of 'Babylon': The Rhetoric of Fear and the Study of London, 1850–1914." *City and Society* 4(June):77–87.

——— . 1993. "Coping with Urban Danger." Pp. 19–40 in *Urban Anthropology and the Supranational and Regional Networks of the Town*, edited by Zdenek Uherek. Prague: Academy of Sciences of the Czech Republic.

Brunvand, Jan Harold. 1981. *The Vanishing Hitchhiker: American Urban Legends and Their Meanings*. New York: W.W. Norton.

——— . 1984. *The Choking Doberman and Other "New" Urban Legends*. New York: W.W. Norton.

——— . 1986. *The Mexican Pet: More "New" Urban Legends and Some Old Favorites*. New York: W.W. Norton.

——— . 1989. *Curses! Broiled Again! The Hottest Urban Legends Going*. New York: W.W. Norton.

——— . 1993. *The Baby Train and Other Lusty Urban Legends*. New York: W. W. Norton.

Bullard, Robert D. 1990. *Dumping in Dixie: Race, Class and Environmental Quality*. Boulder: Westview.

Bullough, Vern and Bonnie Bullough. 1987. *Women and Prostitution: A Social History*. Buffalo, NY: Prometheus.

Burgess, Ernest W. 1925. "The Growth of the City: An Introduction to a Research Project." Pp. 47–62 in *The City*, edited by Robert E. Park, Ernest W. Burgess, and Roderick D. McKenzie. Chicago: University of Chicago Press.

Butler, Suellen R. and William E. Snizek. 1976. "The Waitress-Diner Relationship: A Multimethod Approach to the Study of Subordinate Influence." *Sociology of Work and Occupations* 3(2, May):209–22.

Butsch, Richard (ed.). 1990. *For Fun and Profit: The Transformation of Leisure into Consumption*. Philadelphia: Temple University Press.

Cahill, Spencer E. 1985. "Meanwhile Backstage: Public Bathrooms and the Interaction Order." *Urban Life* 14(1, April):33–58.

——— . 1987. "Children and Civility: Ceremonial Deviance and the Acquisition of Ritual Competence." *Social Psychology Quarterly* 50(December):312–21.

——— . 1990. "Childhood and Public Life: Reaffirming Biographical Divisions." *Social Problems* 37(August):390–402.

——— . 1991. "Embarrassment, Embarrassability and Public Order: Another View of a Much Maligned Emotion." Unpublished paper.

——— . 1994. "Following Goffman Following Durkheim into the Public Realm." Pp. 3–17 in *Research in Community Sociology*, edited by Dan C. Chekki, Supplement 1, *The Community of the Streets*, edited by Spencer E. Cahill and Lyn H. Lofland. Greenwich, CT: JAI.

Cahill, Spencer E. and Robin Eggleston. 1994. "Managing Emotions in Public: The Case of Wheelchair Users." *Social Psychology Quarterly* 57(4, December): 300–12.

Caillois, Roger. 1961. *Man, Play, and Games*, translated by Meyer Barash. New York: Free Press of Glencoe.

Calkins, R. 1901. *Substitutes for the Saloon*. Boston: Houghton, Mifflin.

Callenbach, Ernest. 1981. Contributions to panel discussion, "Cities: Salvaging the Parts." *The Planet Drum Review* 1(3, Summer):12–13.

Calthorpe, Peter. 1993. *The Next American Metropolis: Ecology, Community, and the American Dream*. New York: Princeton Architectural Press.

Campbell, Robert. 1980. "Lure of the Marketplace: Real-Life Theater." *Historic Preservation* (January/February):47–49.

Campos, Paul B. 1996. "The Myths about Suburban Sprawl." *Sacramento Bee* (April 29).

Canavan, Peter. [1984] 1988. "The Gay Community at Jacob Riis Park." Pp. 67–82 in *The Apple Sliced: Sociological Studies of New York City*, edited by Vernon Boggs, Gerald Handel, and Sylvia Fava. Prospect Heights, IL: Waveland.

Carcopino, Jerome. 1940. *Daily Life in Ancient Rome: The People and the City at the Height of the Empire*, edited with bibliography and notes by Henry T. Rowell, translated by E. O. Lorimer. New Haven, CT: Yale University Press.

———. 1952. "Rome under the Antonines." Pp. 29–55 in *Golden Ages of the Great Cities*, edited by M. Bowra et al. London and New York: Thames and Hudson.

Carmen, Arlene and Howard Moody. 1985. *Working Women: The Subterranean World of Street Prostitution*. New York: Harper and Row.

Carp, Frances M., Rick T. Zawadski, and Hossein Shokrkon. 1976. "Dimensions of Urban Environmental Quality." *Environment and Behavior* 8(2):239–64.

Carr, Stephen. 1967. "The City of the Mind." Pp. 197–231 in *Environment for Man: The Next Fifty Years*, edited by William R. Ewald, Jr. Bloomington: Indiana University Press.

Carr, Stephen, Mark Francis, Leanne G. Rivlin, and Andrew M. Stone. 1992. *Public Space*. New York: Cambridge University Press.

Carroll, Raymonde. 1988. *Cultural Misunderstandings: The French-American Experience*, translated by Carol Volk. Chicago: University of Chicago Press.

Cary, Mark S. 1978. "Does Civil Inattention Exist in Pedestrian Passing?" *Journal of Personality and Social Psychology* 36(November):1185–93.

Casteras, Susan P. 1987. "'The Gulf of Destitution on Whose Brink They Hang': Images of Life on the Streets in Victorian Art." Pp. 131–34 in Julian Treuherz, *Hard Times: Social Realism in Victorian Art* (with contributions by Susan P. Casteras, Lee M. Edwards, Peter Keating, and Louis van Tilborgh). London: Lund Humphries and Mt. Kisco, NY: Moyer Bell, in association with Manchester City Art Galleries.

Castle, Terry. 1986. *Masquerade and Civilization: The Carnivalesque in Eighteenth-Century English Culture and Fiction*. Palo Alto, CA: Stanford University Press.

Cavan, Sherri. 1963. "Interaction in Home Territories." *Berkeley Journal of Sociology* 17–32.

———. 1966. *Liquor License*. Chicago: Aldine.

Chapin, F. Stuart. 1974. *Human Activity Patterns in the City: Things People Do in Time and in Space*. New York: Wiley.

Chermayeff, Serge and Christopher Alexander. 1963. *Community and Privacy: Toward a New Architecture of Humanism*. Garden City, NY: Anchor/Doubleday.

Choldin, Harvey M. 1978a. "Social Life and the Physical Environment." Pp. 352–84 in *Handbook of Contemporary Urban Life*, edited by David Street and Associates. San Francisco: Jossey-Bass.

———. 1978b. "Urban Density and Pathology." *Annual Review of Sociology* 4:91–113.

―――. 1985. *Cities and Suburbs: An Introduction to Urban Sociology.* New York: McGraw-Hill.

Christoforidis, Alex. 1994. "New Alternatives to the Suburb: Neo-traditional Developments." *Journal of Planning Literature* 8(4, May):429–40.

Clapp, James A. 1984. *The City: A Dictionary of Quotable Thought on Cities and Urban Life.* New Brunswick, NJ: Center for Urban Policy Research, Rutgers University.

Clark, Walter B. 1981. "The Contemporary Tavern." Pp. 425–70 in *Research Advances in Alcohol and Drug Problems,* Volume 6, edited by Yedy Israel, Frederick B. Glaser, Harold Kalant, Robert E. Popham, Wolfgang Schmidt, and Reginald G. Smart. New York: Plenum.

Clay, Grady. [1973] 1980. *Close-Up: How to Read the American City.* Chicago: University of Chicago Press.

Clemente, Frank and Michael B. Kleiman. 1977. "Fear of Crime in the United States: A Multivariate Analysis." *Social Forces* 56(2, December):519–31.

Clifford, Frank and Penelope McMillan. 1992. "The Times Poll: Most in LA Expect New Riots but Feel Safe." *Los Angeles Times,* May 14, pp. A1-3, T4–T5.

Clinard, Marshall B. 1962. "The Public Drinking House and Society." Pp. 270–92 in *Society, Culture, and Drinking Patterns,* edited by David J. Pittman and Charles R. Snyder. New York: Wiley.

Cloyd, Jerald W. 1976. "The Market-Place Bar: The Interrelation Between Sex, Situation and Strategies in the Pairing Rituals of Homo Ludens." *Urban Life* 5(October):293–312.

Cohen, Bernard. 1980. *Deviant Street Networks: Prostitution in New York City.* Lexington, MA: Lexington Books.

Cohen, Marilyn. 1983. *Reginald Marsh's New York.* New York: Whitney Museum of American Art in association with Dover.

Cole, David. 1994. "In Your Space." *Nation,* March 14, pp. 329–30.

Coleman, B. I. 1973. *The Idea of the City in Nineteenth-Century Britain.* London: Routledge and Kegan Paul.

Coleman, James. 1962. "Comment on Harrison White, 'Chance Models of Systems of Causal Groups.'" *Sociometry* 25:172–76.

Collett, P. and P. Marsh. 1974. "Patterns of Public Behavior: Collision Avoidance on a Pedestrian Passing." *Semiotica* 12:281–99.

Conan, Michel and Isabelle Marghieri. 1989. "A Walk in the Tuileries and Other Tales of Love." *Landscape* 30(2):1–8.

Congbalay, Dean. 1990. "A Generation That Hardly Leaves the Suburbs." *San Francisco Chronicle,* November 26, p. A1.

Conrad, Peter and Joseph Schneider. 1980. *Deviance and Medicalization: From Badness to Sickness.* St. Louis, MO: Mosby.

Cooley, Charles Horton. [1909] 1962. *Social Organization: A Study of the Larger Mind.* New York: Schocken.

Corfield, Penelope J. 1990. "Walking the City Streets: The Urban Odyssey in Eighteenth-Century England." *Journal of Urban History* 16(February):132–74.

Corzine, Jay and Richard Kirby. 1977. "Cruising the Truckers: Sexual Encounters in a Highway Rest Area." *Urban Life* 6(July):171–92.

Coser, Lewis A. 1978. "The Bridling of Affect and the Refinement of Manners" (review of Norbert Elias, *The Civilizing Process*, Volume 1, *The History of Manners*. *Contemporary Sociology* 7(September):563–70.

Cowley, Abraham. [1666] 1906. *Essays, Plays and Sundry Verses*, edited by A. R. Waller. Cambridge: Cambridge University Press.

Cox, Harvey. 1965. *The Secular City: Secularization and Urbanization in Theological Perspective*. New York: Macmillan.

Crader, Kelly W. and William M. Wentworth. 1984. "A Structural Reinterpretation of Responsibility, Risk and Helping in Small Collectives of Children." *American Sociological Review* 49(5, October):611–19.

Cranz, Galen. 1982. *The Politics of Park Design: A History of Urban Parks in America*. Cambridge, MA: MIT Press.

Czarnowski, Thomas V. 1978. "The Street as a Communications Artifact." Pp. 207–12 in *On Streets*, edited by Stanford Anderson. Cambridge, MA: MIT Press.

Czepiel, John A., Michael R. Solomon, and Carol F. Surprenant (eds.). 1985. *The Service Encounter: Managing Employee/Customer Interaction in Service Business*. Lexington, MA: D.C. Heath.

Da Matta, Roberto. 1984. "Carnival in Multiple Planes." Pp. 208–40 in *Rite, Drama, Festival, Spectacle: Rehearsals toward a Theory of Cultural Performance*, edited by John J. MacAloon. Philadelphia: Institute for the Study of Human Issues.

Dabydeen, David. 1987. *Hogarth's Blacks: Images of Blacks in Eighteenth Century English Art*. Manchester: Manchester University Press.

Danet, Brenda. 1973. "'Giving the Underdog a Break': Latent Particularism among Custom Officials." Pp. 329–37 in *Bureaucracy and the Public: A Reader in Official-Client Relations*, edited by Elihu Katz and Brenda Danet. New York: Basic Books.

Dantzig, George B. and Thomas L. Saaty. 1973. *Compact City: A Plan for a Liveable Urban Environment*. San Francisco: W. H. Freeman.

Dargan, Amanda and Steven Zeitlin. 1990. *City Play*. New Brunswick, NJ: Rutgers University Press.

Darley, John M. and Bibb Latané. 1968. "Bystander Intervention in Emergencies: Diffusion of Responsibility." *Journal of Personality and Social Psychology* 8:377–83.

Darnton, Robert. 1984. *The Great Cat Massacre and Other Episodes in French Cultural History*. New York: Basic Books.

Datel, Robin E. and Dennis J. Dingemans. 1984. "Environmental Perception, Historic Preservation, and Sense of Place." Pp. 131–44 in *Environmental Perception and Behavior: An Inventory and Prospect*, edited by Thomas F. Saarinen, David Seamon, and James L. Sell. Research Paper No. 209, Department of Geography, University of Chicago.

Davies, J. Clarence III. 1966. *Neighborhood Groups and Urban Renewal*. New York: Columbia University Press.

Davis, Dorothy. 1966. *Fairs, Shops, and Supermarkets: A History of English Shopping*. Toronto: University of Toronto Press.

Davis, Fred. 1959. "The Cabdriver and His Fare: Facets of a Fleeting Relationship." *American Journal of Sociology* 65(September):158–65.

Davis, Melissa G., Richard J. Lundman, and Rimairo Martinez, Jr. 1990. "Private Corporate Police." Paper presented at the Annual Meetings of the American Sociological Association, Washington, D.C., August.

Davis, Mike. 1992. *City of Quartz: Excavating the Future in Los Angeles*. New York: Vintage.

Davis, Morris and Sol Levine. 1967. "Toward a Sociology of Public Transit." *Social Problems* (Summer) Volume 15, No. 1, pp. 84–91.

Davis, Morris, Robert Seibert, and Warren Breed. 1966. "Interracial Seating Patterns on New Orleans Public Transit." *Social Problems* (Winter) 13:298–306.

Davis, Murray. 1983. *Smut: Erotic Reality/Obscene Ideology*. Chicago: University of Chicago Press.

Davis, Phillip W. 1991. "Stranger Intervention into Child Punishment in Public Places." *Social Problems* 38(2, May):227–46.

Davis, Sharon Kantorowski. 1978. "The Influence of an Untoward Public Act on Conceptions of Self." *Symbolic Interaction* 1(2, Spring):106–23.

Davis, Susan G. 1982. "'Making Night Hideous': Christmas Revelry and Public Order in Nineteenth-Century Philadelphia." *American Quarterly* 34(2, Summer):185–99.

———. 1986. *Parades and Power: Street Theatre in Nineteenth-Century Philadelphia*. Philadelphia: Temple University Press.

Day, Robert. 1989. "Carry from Kansas became a Nation All unto Herself." *Smithsonian* 20(1, April):147–48, 150, 152, 154–56, 158, 160, 162, 164.

de Jonge, Derk. 1962. "Images of Urban Areas." *Journal of the American Institute of Planners* (November):266–76.

De Puymege, Gerard. 1983. "From Priest to Philosopher: The Origins of the Concept." Pp. 17–33 in *Fanaticism: A Historical and Psychoanalytical Study*, edited by Andre Haynal, Miklos Molnar, and Gerard De Puymege. New York: Schocken.

Deasy, C. M., in collaboration with Thomas E. Lasswell. 1985. *Designing Places for People: A Handbook on Human Behavior for Architects, Designers, and Facility Managers*, New York: Whitney Library of Design.

Deben, Leon. 1990. "Urban Landsquatting: Another Way of Living in Amsterdam." University of Amsterdam Working Papers in Sociology.

Delano, Donald F. 1984. "The Bus Terminal: Cops, Mopes, and Skells on the Deuce." Pp. 271–90 in *The Apple Sliced: Sociological Studies of New York City*, edited by Vernon Boggs, Gerald Handel, and Sylvia Fava. Prospect Heights, IL: Waveland.

Delph, Edward William. 1978. *The Silent Community: Public Homosexual Encounters*. Beverly Hills, CA: Sage.

DeMott, Benjamin. 1996. "Political Manners and the Crisis of Democratic Values." *Nation* 263(9, December 9):11–19.

Deutsch, Karl W. 1961. "On Social Communication and the Metropolis." Pp. 129–43 in *The Future Metropolis*, edited by Lloyd Rodwin. New York: George Braziller.

Devereaux, Kathryn. 1991. "Children of Nature." *UCDavis Magazine* (Winter): 20–23.

Diefendorf, Jeffry, M. (ed.). 1990. *Rebuilding Europe's Bombed Cities*. New York: St. Martin's.

Distel, Anne, Douglas W. Druick, Gloria Groom, Rodolphe Rapetti, with Julia Sagraves, and an essay by Kirk Varnedoe, 1995. *Gustave Caillebotte: Urban Impressionist*. Musee d'Orsay, Paris; The Art Institute of Chicago; with Abbeville Press, New York.

Dogan, Mattei and John D. Kasarda. 1988. "Introduction: How Giant Cities Will Multiply and Grow." Pp. 12–29 in *The Metropolis Era*, Volume 1, *A World of Giant Cities*, edited by Mattei Dogan and John D. Kasarda. Newbury Park, CA: Sage.

Doob, Leonard W. 1952. *Social Psychology*. New York: Holt.

Duany, Andres. 1990. "Liveable Neighborhoods Lecture." Sponsored by the San Diego Planning Department and the Office of City Architect, San Diego, California (July 9).

Duany, Andres and Elizabeth Plater-Zyberk. 1992. "The Second Coming of the Small Town." *Utne Reader* (May/June):97–100.

Duis, Perry R. 1983. *The Saloon: Public Drinking in Chicago and Boston 1880–1920*. Urbana: University of Illinois Press.

Duncan James S. [1978] 1983. "Men without Property: The Tramp's Classification and Use of Urban Space." Pp. 86–102 in *Readings in Urban Analysis: Perspectives on Urban Form and Structure*, edited by Robert W. Lake. New Brunswick, NJ: Center for Urban Policy Research.

Duneier, Mitchell. 1992. *Slim's Table: Race, Respectability, and Masculinity*. Chicago: University of Chicago Press.

Durkheim, Emile. [1897] 1952. *Suicide: A Study in Sociology*, edited and with an introduction by George Simpson, translated by John A. Saulding and George Simpson. London: Routledge and Kegan Paul.

Earl, John. 1986. "Building the Halls." Pp. 1–32 in *Music Hall: The Business of Pleasure*, edited by Peter Bailey. Milton Keynes, UK: Open University Press.

Eckholm, Erik. 1992. "The Riots Bring a Rush to Arm and a New Debate." *New York Times*, May 17, p. 18.

Edelmann, Robert J. 1985. "Social Embarrassment: An Analysis of the Process." *Journal of Social and Personal Relationships* 2(2, June):195–213.

Edgerton, Robert B. 1979. *Alone Together: Social Order on an Urban Beach*. Berkeley and Los Angeles: University of California Press.

———. 1985. *Rules, Exceptions, and Social Order*. Berkeley: University of California Press.

Edwards, John, Robin Oakley, and Sean Carey. 1987. "Street Life, Ethnicity and Social Policy." Pp. 76–122 in *The Crowd in Contemporary Britain*, edited by George Gaskell and Robert Benewick. London: Sage.

Eells, Richard and Clarence Walton (eds.). 1968. *Man in the City of the Future: A Symposium of Urban Philosophers*. New York: Macmillan.

Eldred, Dale. 1990. "Place Defined by Time and Light." *Places* 6(4, Summer):34–41.

Elias, Norbert. [1939] 1978. *The Civilizing Process*, Volume 1, *The History of Manners*. New York: Pantheon.

———. [1939] 1982. *The Civilizing Process*, Volume 2, *Power and Civility*. New York: Pantheon.

Ellis, Bill. 1983. "De Legendis Urbis: Modern Legends in Ancient Rome." *Journal of American Folklore* 96:200–8.

Enjeu, Claude and Joana Save. 1974. "The City: Off-Limits to Women." *Liberation* 18(9, July–August):9–15.

Erenberg, Lewis A. 1981. *Steppin' Out: New York Nightlife and the Transformation of American Culture, 1890–1930*. Westport, CT: Greenwood.

Etzioni, Amitai (ed.). 1995. *Rights and the Common Good: The Communitarian Perspective*. New York: St. Martin's.

——. 1996. *The New Golden Rule: Community and Morality in a Democratic Society*. New York: Basic Books.

Evans, Sara M. and Harry C. Boyte. 1986. *Free Spaces: The Sources of Democratic Change in America*. New York: Harper and Row.

Fabian, Ann. 1990. *Card Sharps, Dream Books, and Bucket Shops: Gambling in 19th-Century America*. Ithaca, NY: Cornell University Press.

Fainstein, Susan S. 1994. *The City Builders: Property, Politics and Planning in London and New York*. Oxford: Blackwell.

Fainstein, Susan S., Ian Gordon, and Michael Harloe (eds.). 1992. *Divided Cities: New York and London in the Contemporary World*. Oxford, UK, and Cambridge, MA: Blackwell.

Farberman, Harvey and Eugene A. Weinstein. 1970. "Personalization in Lower Class Consumer Interaction." *Social Problems* 17(4, Spring):449–57.

Feagin, Joe R. 1991. "The Continuing Significance of Race: Antiblack Discrimination in Public Places." *American Sociological Review* 56(1, February):101–16.

Feagin, Joe R. and H. Hahn. 1973. *Ghetto Revolts: The Politics of Violence in American Cities*. New York: Macmillan.

Federal Committee on Standard Metropolitan Statistical Areas. 1979. "The Metropolitan Statistical Area Classification: Final Standards for Establishing Metropolitan Statistical Areas Following the 1980 Census." *Statistical Reporter* 80-3(December).

——. 1980. "Documents Relating to the Metropolitan Statistical Area Classification for the 1980s." *Statistical Reporter* 80-119(August).

Fei, Xiaotong. 1992. *From the Soil: Foundations of Chinese Society*, translation of *Xiangtu Zhongguo*, with an Introduction and Epilogue by Gary G. Hamilton and Wang Zheng. Berkeley: University of California Press.

Feigelman, William. 1974. "Peeping: The Pattern of Voyeurism among Construction Workers." *Urban Life and Culture* 3(April):35–49.

Feldman, Roberta M. 1990. "Settlement-Identity: Psychological Bonds with Home Places in a Mobile Society." *Environment and Behavior* 22(March):183–229.

Felipe, Nancy Jo and Robert Sommer. 1966. "Invasions of Personal Space." *Social Problems* 14(2, Fall):206–14.

Felshin, Nina (ed.). 1995. *But Is It Art? The Spirit of Art as Activism*. Seattle: Bay Press.

Ferraro, Kenneth F. 1995. *Fear of Crime: Interpreting Victimization Risk*. Albany: SUNY Press.

Fields, Allen B. 1984. "'Slinging Weed': The Social Organization of Streetcorner Marijuana Sales." *Urban Life* 13(2–3, July–October):247–70.

Findlay, John M. 1992. *Magic Lands: Western Cityscapes and American Culture after 1940*. Berkeley: University of California Press.

Fine, Gary Alan. 1987. "The City as a Folklore Generator: Legends in the Metropolis." *Urban Resources* 4:3–6, 61.

Fine, Gary Alan and Lazaros Christoforides. 1991. "Dirty Birds, Filthy Immigrants, and the English Sparrow War: Metaphorical Linkage in Constructing Social Problems." *Symbolic Interaction* 14(4, Winter):375–93.

Fine, Gary Alan, Jeffrey L. Stitt, and Michael Finch. 1984. "Couple Tie-Signs and Interpersonal Threat: A Field Experiment." *Social Psychology Quarterly* 47(3): 282–86.

Finkel, David. 1995. "Mall Is Beautiful." *Washington Post Magazine* (December 10):16–21, 30–35.

Finkelstein, Joanne. 1985. "Dining Out: The Self in Search of Civility." *Studies in Symbolic Interaction* 6:183–212.

Firestone, Ira J. and Irwin Altman. 1978. "Interaction Territory in Public Places: Studies of Active and Passive Defense." Pp. 98–108 in *Directions in Environmental Design Research*, edited by Walter E. Rogers and William H. Ittelson. Washington, DC: EDRA.

Firey, Walter. 1945. "Sentiment and Symbolism as Ecological Variables." *American Sociological Review* 10:140–48.

Fischer, Claude S. 1971. "A Research Note on Urbanism and Tolerance." *American Journal of Sociology* 76(March):847–56.

———. 1976. *The Urban Experience*. New York: Harcourt Brace Jovanovich.

———. 1981. "The Public and Private Worlds of City Life." *American Sociological Review* 46(March):306–16.

———. 1982a. "Rethinking Urban Life: Order and Disorder in the Public Realm." Paper presented at the Annual Meetings of the American Sociological Association, San Francisco, September.

———. 1982b. *To Dwell Among Friends: Personal Networks in Town and City*. Chicago: University of Chicago Press.

———. 1984. "On the Moral Disorder of City Life." Plenary Address, Urban Affairs Association, Portland, Oregon, March.

———. 1992. *America Calling: A Social History of the Telephone to 1940*. Berkeley: University of California Press.

Fisher, Bonnie S. and Jack L. Nasar. 1992. "Fear of Crime in Relation to Three Exterior Site Features: Prospect, Refuge, and Escape." *Environment and Behavior* 24(1, January):35–65.

Fishman, Robert. 1987. *Bourgeois Utopias: The Rise and Fall of Suburbia*. New York: Basic Books.

Flanagan, Timothy J. and Edmund F. McGarrell (eds.). 1985. *Sourcebook of Criminal Justice Statistics*. Albany, NY: Hindelang Criminal Justice Research Center.

Foster, George G. 1850. *New York by Gas-Light: With Here and There a Streak of Sunshine*. New York: Dewitt & Davenport.

Foucault, Michel. 1977. *Discipline and Punish: The Birth of the Prison*. New York: Vintage.

Fowler, E. P. 1987. "Street Management and City Design." *Social Forces* 666(2, December):365–89.

Francaviglia, Richard V. 1974. "Main Street Revisited." *Places* 1(3, October):7–11.

Francis, Mark. 1987a. "The Making of Democratic Streets." Pp. 23–39 in *Public*

Streets for Public Use, edited by A. Vernez Moudon. New York: Van Nostrand Reinhold.

―――. 1987b. "Urban Open Spaces." Pp. 71–106 in *Advances in Environment, Behavior and Design*, edited by E. Zube and G. Moore. New York: Plenum.

―――. 1989. "Control as a Dimension of Public-Space Quality." Pp. 147–72 in *Human Behavior and Environment: Advances in Theory and Research*, Volume 10, *Public Places and Spaces*, edited by Irwin Altman and Ervin H. Zube. New York: Plenum.

Franck, Karen A. 1985. "Social Construction of the Physical Environment: The Case of Gender." *Sociological Focus* 18(2, April):143–60.

Franck, Karen A. and Lynn Paxson. 1989. "Women and Urban Public Space: Research, Design and Policy Issues." Pp. 121–46 in *Human Behavior and Environment: Advances in Theory and Research*, Volume 10, *Public Places and Spaces*, edited by Irwin Altman and Ervin H. Zube. New York: Plenum.

Franklin, A. 1989. "Working-Class Privatism: An Historical Case Study of Bedminster, Bristol." *Environment and Planning D: Society and Space* 7:93–113.

Freedman, Jonathan L. 1975. *Crowding and Behavior*. San Francisco: W. H. Freeman.

Freudenburg, W. R. 1986. "The Density of Acquaintanceship: An Overlooked Variable in Community Research?" *American Journal of Sociology* 92(1, July): 27–63.

Fried, Marc. 1963. "Grieving for a Lost Home." Pp. 151–71 in *The Urban Condition: People and Policy in the Metropolis*, edited by Leonard J. Duhn. New York: Basic Books.

Friedmann, John. 1989. "Human Territoriality and the Struggle for Place." Unpublished paper.

Galdwell, Malcolm. 1995. "Times Square—Saved or Destroyed?" *Washington Post National Weekly Edition* (February 27–March 5):8.

Gallagher, Tom. 1995. "Trespasser on Main St. (You!)." *Nation* (December 18):787–90.

Gans, Herbert. 1962. *The Urban Villagers: Groups and Class Life of Italian-Americans*. New York: Free Press.

―――. 1967. *The Levittowners: Ways of Life and Politics in a New Suburban Community*. New York: Pantheon.

―――. 1974. "Commentary and Debate: Gans on Granovetter's 'Strength of Weak Ties,'" *American Journal of Sociology* 80(2, September):524–31.

Garber, Judith A. and David L. Imbroscio. 1996. "'The Myth of the North American City' Reconsidered: Local Constitutional Regimes in Canada and the United States." *Urban Affairs Review* 31(5, May):595–624.

Garber, Judith A. and Robyne S. Turner (eds.). 1994. *Gender in Urban Research* (Volume 42 of *Urban Affairs Annual Review*). Newbury Park, CA: Sage.

Gardner, Carol Brooks. 1980. "Passing By: Street Remarks, Address Rights, and the Urban Female." *Sociological Inquiry* 50(3–4):328–56.

―――. 1986a. "With Child: Opportunities for Speech and Interaction in Public for Women Accompanied by Children." Paper presented at the Annual Meetings of the American Sociological Association, Chicago, August.

―――. 1986b. "Public Aid." *Urban Life* 15(1, April):37–69.

————. 1988. "Access Information: Public Lies and Private Peril." *Social Problems* 35(4, October):384–97.

————. 1989. "Analyzing Gender in Public Places: Rethinking Goffman's Vision of Everyday Life." *American Sociologist* (Spring):42–56.

————. 1992. "Kinship Claims: Affiliation and the Disclosure of Stigma in Public Places." *Perspectives on Social Problems* 4:203–8.

————. 1994. "A Family among Strangers: Kinship Claims among Gay Men in Public Places." Pp. 95–118 in *Research in Community Sociology*, edited by Dan C. Chekki, Supplement 1, *The Community of the Streets*, edited by Spencer E. Cahill and Lyn H. Lofland. Greenwich, CT: JAI.

————. 1995. *Passing By: Gender and Public Harassment*. Berkeley: University of California Press.

Garver, Thomas H. 1985. *George Tooker*, 1st edition. New York: C.N. Potter: Distributed by Crown Publishers.

Gaster, Sanford. 1991. "Urban Children's Access to Their Neighborhood: Changes over Three Generations." *Environment and Behavior* 23(1, January):70–85.

Gates, Lauren B. and William M. Rohe. 1987. "Fear and Reaction to Crime: A Revised Model." *Urban Affairs Quarterly* 22(3, March):425–53.

Gehl, Jan. [1980] 1987. *Life between Buildings: Using Public Space*. New York: Van Nostrand Reinhold. [Originally published in Danish.]

Geographer's A–Z Map Company Ltd. 1995. *Inner London Atlas*. Kent, UK.

Gerloff, Robert. 1992. "Rediscovering the Village." *Utne Reader* (May/June):93–96.

————. 1994. "The New Urbanism Takes Hold." *Utne Reader* (May/June): 28–32.

Giddens, Anthony. 1984. *The Constitution of Society: Outline of the Theory of Structuration*. Cambridge, MA: Polity.

Gilbert, James. 1991. *Perfect Cities: Chicago's Utopias of 1893*. Chicago: University of Chicago Press.

Gilje, Paul A. 1987. *The Road to Mobocracy: Popular Disorder in New York City, 1763–1834*. Chapel Hill: University of North Carolina Press (published for the Institute of Early American History and Culture).

Gillis, A. R. and John Hagan. 1983. "Bystander Apathy and the Territorial Imperative." *Sociological Inquiry* 53(4, Fall):449–60.

Girouard, Mark. 1975. *Victorian Pubs*. London: Studio Vista.

Glaberson, William. 1990. "Hard Life of Urban Dwellers." *San Francisco Chronicle*, February 23, p. B3.

Gladwell, Malcolm. 1995. "Times Square—Saved or Destroyed?" *Washington Post National Weekly Edition* (February 27–March 5):8.

Glazer, Nathan. 1984a. "Notes on Sociological Images of the City." Pp. 337–44 in *Cities of the Mind: Images and Themes of the City in the Social Sciences*, edited by Lloyd Rodwin and Robert N. Hollister. New York: Plenum.

————. 1984b. "Paris—the View from New York." *Public Interest* 74(Winter):31–51.

Glazer, Nathan and Mark Lilla (eds.). 1987. *The Public Face of Architecture: Civil Culture and Public Spaces*. New York: Free Press.

Gmelch, George. 1977. *The Irish Tinkers: The Urbanization of an Itinerant People*. Menlo Park, CA: Cummings.

Gmelch, George and Sharon Bohn Gmelch. 1978. "Begging in Dublin: The Strate-gies of a Marginal Urban Occupation." *Urban Life* 6(4, January):439–54.

Goffman, Erving. 1959 *The Presentation of Self in Everyday Life*. Garden City, NY: Doubleday Anchor.

———. 1963a. *Behavior in Public Places*. New York: Free Press of Glencoe.

———. 1963b. *Stigma: Notes on the Management of Spoiled Identity*. Englewood Cliffs, NJ: Prentice-Hall.

———. 1971. *Relations in Public*. New York: Basic Books.

———. 1983. "The Interaction Order." *American Sociological Review* 48(Febru-ary):1–17.

Gmelch, George and Sharon Bohn Gmelch. 1978. "Begging in Dublin: The Strate-gies of a Marginal Urban Occupation." *Urban Life* 6(4, January):439–54.

Goist, Park Dixon. 1977. *From Main Street to State Street: Town, City and Community in America*. Port Washington, NY: National University Publications/Kennikat.

Gold, Harry. 1982. The Sociology of Urban Life. Englewood Cliffs, NJ: Prentice-Hall.

Goldberger, Paul. 1989. "The Lesson of New York." *Sacramento Bee*, July 9, Forum, p. 1.

Goldston, Robert. 1970. *Suburbia: Civic Denial*. New York: Macmillan.

Golombek, Silvia Blitzer. 1993. *A Sociological Image of the City: Through Children's Eyes*. New York: Peter Lang.

Gonzalez, Nancie L. [1970] 1980. "Social Functions of Carnival in a Dominican City." Pp. 238–48 in *Urban Life: Readings in Urban Anthropology*, edited by George Gmelch and Walter P. Zenner. New York: St. Martin's.

Goodrich, Lloyd. 1972. *Reginald Marsh*. New York: Harry N. Abrams.

Goodsell, Charles T. 1988. *The Social Meaning of Civil Space: Studying Political Authority Through Architecture*. Lawrence: University Press of Kansas.

Gordon, M. Y., S. Riger, R. K. LeBailly, and L. Heath. 1981. "Crime, Women and the Quality of Urban Life." Pp. 141–57 in *Women and the American City*, edited by C. R. Stimpson, E. Dixler, M. J. Nelson, and K. B. Yatrakis. Chicago: University of Chicago Press.

Gottdiener, Mark. 1977. *Planned Sprawl: Private and Public Interests in Suburbia*. Bev-erly Hills: Sage.

———. 1982. "Disneyland: A Utopian Urban Space." *Urban Life* 11(July):139–62. Albany: State University of New York Press.

———. 1985. *The Social Production of Urban Space*. Austin: University of Texas Press.

———. 1989. "Neo-Fordism, the Restructuring of Capital and the New Form of Settlement Space." Paper presented at the Annual Meetings of the American Sociological Association, San Francisco, August.

———. 1994. *The New Urban Sociology*. New York: McGraw-Hill.

Gottlieb, D. 1957. "The Neighborhood Tavern and the Cocktail Lounge: A Study of Class Differences." *American Journal of Sociology* 62:559–62.

Gottlieb, Martin. 1989. "Climbing Jacobs's Ladder." *Nation* (June 5):772–74.

Gouldner, Alvin. 1960. "The Norm of Reciprocity: A Preliminary Statement." *Amer-ican Sociological Review* 25(2, April):161–78.

Gowing, Lawrence, with Ronald Paulson. 1971. *Hogarth*. London: Tate Gallery.

Granovetter, Mark S. 1973. "The Strength of Weak Ties." *American Journal of Sociology* 78(6, May):1360–80.

———. 1982. "The Strength of Weak Ties: A Network Theory Revisited." Pp. 105–30 in *Social Structure and Network Analysis*, edited by Peter Marsden and Nan Lin. Beverly Hills, CA: Sage.

Gratz, Roberta Brandes. 1989. *The Living City: How Urban Residents Are Revitalizing America's Neighborhoods and Downtown Shopping Districts by Thinking Small in a Big Way*. New York: Simon and Schuster.

Gray, Kirk L. 1978. *Tavern-Based Leisure and Play in a Midwestern Working Class Community*. Santa Monica, CA: Rand.

Gray, Robert. 1978. *A History of London*. London: Hutchinson.

Greenblat, Cathy Stein, and John H. Gagnon. 1983. "Temporary Strangers: Travel and Tourism from a Sociological Perspective." *Sociological Perspectives* 26(January):89–110.

Greene, Bob. 1994. "Mall of America: Big, Showy—and It Works." *Sacramento Bee*, September 2, Scene, p. 2.

Greenfield, Meg. 1986. "Who Put the Lake in the Lobby?" *Newsweek* (January 13):76.

Greer, Scott. 1962. *The Emerging City: Myth and Reality*. New York: Free Press.

———. 1965. *Urban Renewal and American Cities*. Indianapolis: The Bobbs-Merrill Company.

———. 1972. *The Urbane View: Life and Politics in Metropolitan America*. New York: Oxford University Press.

Greer, Scott and Ann Lennarson Greer (eds.). 1974. *Neighborhood and Ghetto: The Local Area in Large-Scale Society*. New York: Basic Books.

Gregory, Stanford W. 1985. "Auto Traffic in Egypt as a Verdant Grammar." *Social Psychology Quarterly* 48(December):337–48.

Greifer, Julian L. 1945. "Attitudes to the Strangers: A Study of the Attitudes of Primitive Society and Early Hebrew Culture." *American Sociological Review* 10(December):739–45.

Groncki, Denise. 1989. "The Woman behind the Counter." *Farmer Bob's Sometimes News and Local Review* 1(4, April):13, 16.

Gross, Edward. 1986. "The Social Construction of Historical Events through Public Dramas." *Symbolic Interaction* 9(Fall):179–200.

Gross, Edward and Gregory P. Stone. 1964. "Embarrassment and the Analysis of Role Requirements." *American Journal of Sociology* 70(1, July):1–15.

Groth, Paul. 1994. *Living Downtown: The History of Residential Hotels in the United States*. Berkeley: University of California Press.

Gruen, Victor. 1973. *Centers for the Urban Environment: Survival of the Cities*. New York: Van Nostrand Reinhold.

Guest, Avery M. and Barrett A. Lee. 1983. "Sentiment and Evaluation as Ecological Variables." *Sociological Perspectives* 26(April):159–84.

Gulick, John. 1989. *The Humanity of Cities: An Introduction to Urban Societies*. Granby, MA: Bergin and Garvey.

Gusfield, Joseph R. 1963. *Symbolic Crusade: Status Politics and the American Temperance Movement*. Urbana: University of Illinois Press.

———. 1975. *Community: A Critical Response*. New York: Harper and Row.

Guttman, Allen. 1986. *Sports Spectators*. New York: Columbia University Press.

Haavio-Mannila, E. 1981. "Afternoon Dances: Drinking Contexts for Women." Pp. 85–102 in *Social Drinking Contexts*, edited by T. C. Harford and L. S. Gaines. Research Monograph #7. Washington, DC: NIAAA.

Habermas, Jurgen. [1964] 1974. "The Public Sphere: An Encyclopedia Article." *New German Critique* 3(Fall):49–55.

Hadden, Jeffrey K. and Josef J. Barton. 1973. "An Image That Will Not Die: Thoughts on the History of Anti-Urban Ideology." Pp. 79–116 in *The Urbanization of the Suburbs*, edited by Louis H. Masotti and Jeffrey K. Hadden. Beverly Hills, CA: Sage.

Haine, W. Scott. 1997. *The World of the Paris Cafe: Sociability among the French Working Class*. Baltimore: Johns Hopkins University Press.

Hall, Edward T. 1959. *The Silent Language*. Greenwich, CT: Fawcett.

——— . 1966. *The Hidden Dimension*. New York: Doubleday.

——— . 1974. *Handbook for Proxemic Research*. Washington, DC: Society for the Anthropology of Visual Communication.

Halliday, F. E. 1968. *Doctor Johnson and His World*. New York: Viking.

Hallman, Howard W. 1984. *Neighborhoods: Their Place in Urban Life*. Beverly Hills: Sage.

Halmos, Paul. 1953. *Solitude and Privacy: A Study of Social Isolation, Its Causes and Therapy*. New York: Philosophical Library.

Halttunen, Karen. 1982. *Confidence Men and Painted Women: A Study of Middle-Class Culture in America, 1830–1870*. New Haven, CT, and London: Yale University Press.

Hammond, Michael. 1987. "Evolution and Emotions." *Sociology of Emotions Newsletter* 2(2, July):2.

Handel, Gerald. 1986. "Taking Up Our Mandate, Using Our License: Qualitative Study of Families as Primary Groups." Paper presented at the Annual Meetings of the American Sociological Association, Chicago, August.

Hannerz, Ulf. 1969. *Soulside, Soulside: Inquiries into Ghetto Culture and Community*. New York: Columbia University Press.

——— . 1980. *Exploring the City: Inquiries toward an Urban Anthropology*. New York: Columbia University Press.

——— . 1993. "Cities as Windows on the World." Pp. 157–72 in *Understanding Amsterdam: Essays on Economic Vitality, City Life and Urban Form*, edited by Leon Deben, Willem Heinemeijer, and Dick Van Der Vaart. Amsterdam: Het Spinhuis

Hansvick, Christine L. 1978. "Comparing Urban Images: A Multivariate Approach." Pp. 109–26 in *New Directions in Environmental Design Research*, edited by Walter E. Rogers and William H. Ittelson. Washington, DC: Environmental Design Research Association.

Harman, Leslie D. 1988. *The Modern Stranger: On Language and Membership*. Berlin: Mouton de Gruyter.

Harris, Bruce, James E. R. Luginbuhl, and Jill E. Fishbein. 1978. "Density and Personal Space in a Field Setting." *Social Psychology* 41(4, December):350–53.

Harris, Neil. [1975] 1987. "Spaced Out at the Shopping Center." Pp. 320–31 in *The Public Face of Architecture: Civil Culture and Public Spaces*, edited by Nathan

Glazer and Mark Lilla. New York: Free Press. [Originally published in *New Republic*, December 13, 1975.]

Harrison, Brian. 1971. *Drink and the Victorians: The Temperance Question in England 1815–1872*. London: Faber and Faber.

———. 1973. "Pubs." Pp. 161–90 in *The Victorian City: Images and Realities*, Volume 1, edited by H. J. Dyos and Michael Wolff. London: Routledge and Kegan Paul.

Harrison, Mark. 1988. *Crowds and History: Mass Phenomena in English Towns, 1790–1835*. Cambridge: Cambridge University Press.

Harrison, Molly. 1975. *People and Shopping*. London: Ernest Benn.

Harrison, Sally. 1984. "Drawing a Circle in Washington Square Park." *Visual Communication* 10(Spring):68–83.

Harrison-Pepper, Sally. 1987. "Folk Heroes of the Urban Environment: Street Performers in the American City." *Urban Resources: Urban Folklore*. Volume 4, No. 3 (Spring), pp. 7–12.

Hartnagel, Timothy F. 1979. "The Perception and Fear of Crime: Implications for Neighborhood Cohesion, Social Activity, and Community Affect." *Social Forces* 58(1, September):175–93.

Harvey, David. 1973. *Social Justice and the City*. Baltimore: Johns Hopkins University Press.

———. 1985. *Consciousness and the Urban Experience: Studies in the History and Theory of Capitalist Urbanization*. Baltimore: Johns Hopkins University Press.

———. 1989. *The Condition of Postmodernity*. Oxford: Blackwell.

Harvey, Joan and Don Henning (eds.). 1987. *Public Environments: Proceedings of the Environment Design Research Association Conference*. Washington, DC: EDRA.

Hawley, Amos. 1950. *Human Ecology: A Theory of Community Structure*. New York: Ronald.

Hayden, Dolores. 1980. "What Would a Non-Sexist City Be Like? Speculations on Housing, Urban Design, and Human Work." *Signs* 5(3, Supplement): S170–S187.

———. 1981. *The Grand Domestic Revolution: A History of Feminist Designs for American Homes, Neighborhoods, and Cities*. Cambridge, MA: MIT Press.

———. 1984. *Redesigning the American Dream: The Future of Housing, Work and Family Life*. New York: W.W. Norton.

Hazel, Debra. 1992. "Crime in the Malls: A New and Growing Concern." *Chain Store Age Executive* (February):27–29.

Headley, Joel Tyler. [1873] 1970. *The Great Riots of New York: 1712–1873*. Indianapolis: Bobbs-Merrill [originally published by E. B. Treat].

Hecht, Peter. 1997. "Foes Won't Take This Law Lying Down." *Sacramento Bee*, June 13, p. B1.

Heckscher, August. 1977. *Open Spaces: The Life of American Cities*. New York: Harper and Row.

Henderson, Margaret R. 1975. "Acquiring Privacy in Public." *Urban Life* 3(January):446–63.

Hendrickson, Robert. 1980. *The Grand Emporiums: The Illustrated History of America's Great Department Store*. New York: Stein and Day.

Henley, Nancy M. 1977. *Body Politics: Power, Sex and Nonverbal Communication*. Englewood Cliffs, NJ: Prentice-Hall.

Henslin, James M. 1973. "Trust and the Cab Driver." Pp. 338–56 in *Bureaucracy and the Public: A Reader in Official-Client Relations*, edited by Elihu Katz and Brenda Danet. New York: Basic Books.

Herzog, Thomas R., Stephen Kaplan, and Rachel Kaplan. 1976. "The Prediction of Preference for Familiar Urban Places." *Environment and Behavior* 8(4, December):627–45.

Hillery, George A. 1963. "Villages, Cities, and Total Institutions." *American Sociological Review* 28(October):779–91.

Hiss, Tony. 1990. *The Experience of Place: A New Way of Looking at and Dealing with Our Radically Changing Cities and Countryside*. New York: Vintage.

Hobsbawm, E. J. 1959. *Primitive Rebels: Studies in Archaic Forms of Social Movements in the 19th and 20th Centuries*. New York: W. W. Norton.

Hohendahl, Peter. [1964] 1974. "Jurgen Habermas: 'The Public Sphere.'" *New German Critique* 3(Fall):45–48.

Hollister, Robert M. and Lloyd Rodwin (eds.). 1984. *Cities of the Mind: Images and Themes of the City in the Social Sciences*. New York: Plenum.

Hong, Lawrence K. and Marion V. Dearman. 1977. "The Streetcorner Preacher: Sowing Seeds By the Wayside." *Urban Life* 6(April):53–68.

Horowitz, Helen Lefkowitz. 1984. *Alma Mater: Design and Experience in the Women's Colleges from Their Nineteenth Century Beginnings to 1930*. Boston: Beacon.

Horowitz, Ruth. 1983. *Honor and the American Dream: Culture and Identity in a Chicano Community*. New Brunswick, NJ: Rutgers University Press.

———. 1987. "Community Tolerance of Gang Violence." *Social Problems* 34(December):437–50.

House, James and Sharon Wolf. 1978. "Effects of Urban Residence on Interpersonal Trust and Helping Behavior." *Journal of Personality and Social Psychology* 36:1029–43.

Houston, Lawrence O., Jr. 1990. "From Street to Mall and Back Again." *Planning* (June):4–10.

Howard, Ebenezer. [1898] 1946. *Garden Cities of Tomorrow*. Edited, with a Preface by F. J. Osborn. London: Faber and Faber.

Howe, Irving. 1971. "The City in Literature." *Commentary* 51(May):61–68.

Hraba, Joseph and Renata Siemienska-Zochowska. 1983. "Shopping in Poland: Queues and Queuing Tactics." Paper presented at the Annual Meetings of the American Sociological Association, Detroit.

Hubbard, William. 1984. "A Meaning for Monuments." *Public Interest* 74(Winter):17–30.

Hummon, David. 1980. "Popular Images of the American Small Town." *Landscape* 24(4):3–9.

———. 1985a. "Selling Places: The Cultural Presentation of States in Tourist Advertising." Paper presented at the Annual Meetings of the Popular Culture Association, Louisville, Kentucky, April.

———. 1985b. "Urban Ideology as a Cultural System." *Journal of Cultural Geography* 5(2, Spring/Summer):1–15.

———. 1986a. "City Mouse, Country Mouse: The Persistence of Community Identity." *Qualitative Sociology* 9(1, Spring):3–25.

―――― . 1986b. "Urban Views: Popular Perspectives on City Life." *Urban Life* 15(April):3–36.

―――― . 1990. *Commonplaces: Community Ideology and Identity in American Culture.* Albany: State University of New York Press.

Humphreys, Laud. 1970. *Tearoom Trade: Impersonal Sex in Public Places.* Chicago: Aldine.

Hunter, Albert. 1974. *Symbolic Communities.* Chicago: University of Chicago Press.

―――― . 1978. "Persistence of Local Sentiments in Mass Society." Pp. 133–62 in *Handbook of Contemporary Urban Life*, edited by David Street and Associates. San Francisco: Jossey-Bass.

―――― . 1985. "Private, Parochial and Public Social Orders: The Problem of Crime and Incivility in Urban Communities." Pp. 230–42 in *The Challenge of Social Control: Citizenship and Institution Building in Modern Society*, edited by Gerald D. Suttles and Mayer N. Zald. Norwood, NJ: Ablex.

Hurst, Michael. 1975. *I Came to the City.* Boston: Houghton Mifflin.

Hutter, Mark. 1987. "The Downtown Department Store as a Social Force." *Social Science Journal* 24(3):239–46.

―――― . No date. "Spacial Segregation, The Cult of Domesticity, and the Architectural Setting of the American Suburb." Unpublished course materials. Glassboro State College, New Jersey.

Huxtable, Ada Louise. 1972. *Will They Ever Finish Bruckner Boulevard? A Primer on Urbicide.* New York: Collier.

―――― . 1991. "Re-Inventing Times Square: 1990." Pp. 356–70 in *Inventing Times Square: Commerce and Culture at the Crossroads of The World*, edited by William R. Taylor. New York: Russell Sage Foundation.

Imray, Linda and Audrey Middleton. 1983. "Public and Private: Marking the Boundaries." Pp. 12–27 in *The Public and the Private*, edited by Eva Gamarnikow, David H. J. Morgan, June Purvis, and Daphne Taylorson. London: Heinemann.

Inwood, Stephen. 1990. "Policing London's Morals: The Metropolitan Police and Popular Culture, 1829–1850." *London Journal* 15(2):129–46.

Isaac, Rael Jean and Virginia C. Armat. 1990. *Madness in the Streets: How Psychiatry and the Law Abandoned the Mentally Ill.* New York: Free Press.

Issel, William. 1986. "Politics, Culture, and Ideology: Three Episodes in the Evolution of San Francisco's 'Culture of Civility.'" Paper presented at the Annual Meetings of the California American Studies Association.

Ivins, Molly. 1994. "Democracy Abounds in Mall of America's Maison du Popcorn." *Sacramento Bee*, May 17, p. B7.

Jackall, Robert. 1977. "The Control of Public Faces in a Commercial Bureaucratic Work Situation." *Urban Life* 6(3, October):277–302.

Jackman, Robert W. and Ross A. Miller. 1998. "Social Capital and Politics." *Annual Review of Political Science* 1.

Jackson, John Brinkerhoff. 1994. *A Sense of Place, A Sense of Time.* New Haven, CT: Yale University Press.

Jackson, Kenneth. 1985. *Crabgrass Frontier: The Suburbanization of the United States.* New York: Oxford University Press.

Jackson, L. E. and R. J. Johnston. 1972. "Structuring the Image: An Investigation of the Elements of Mental Maps." *Environment and Planning* 4:415–27.

Jacobs, Jane. 1961. *The Death and Life of Great American Cities.* New York: Vintage.

———. 1969. *The Economy of Cities.* New York: Random House.

Jacobs, Jerry. 1984. *The Mall: An Attempted Escape from Everyday Life.* Prospect Heights, IL: Waveland.

Jacobs, Karen. 1993. "The Marketing of Fear." *Metropolis* (December):34, 50–53.

James, John. 1951. "A Preliminary Study of the Size Determinant in Small Group Interaction." *American Sociological Review* 16:474–77.

———. 1953. "The Distribution of Free-Forming Small Group Size." *American Sociological Review* 18:569–70.

Jameson, Fredric. 1991. *Postmodernism, or, the Cultural Logic of Late Capitalism.* Durham, NC: Duke University Press.

Jarrett, Derek. 1974. *England in the Age of Hogarth.* Frogmore, St. Albans, Herts.: Paladin, Granada.

Jason, Leonard A., Arnold Reichler, and Walter Rucker. 1981. "Territorial Behavior on Beaches." *Journal of Social Psychology* 114(June):43–50.

Javers, Ron. 1979. "Bizarre Behavior on S.F.'s Streets." *San Francisco Chronicle,* April 26, p. 22.

Jenkins, Philip. 1994. *Using Murder: The Social Construction of Serial Homicide.* Hawthorne, NY: Aldine de Gruyter.

Johnson, Kenneth. 1976. *The Book of Letchworth: An Illustrated Record.* Chesham, Buckinghamshire: Barracuda.

Johnson, Lonn. 1987a. "Road Warriors Make Freeways a Battlefield." *San Francisco Chronicle,* July 22, p. 4.

———. 1987b. "Two More Hurt in South State Freeway Attack." *Sacramento Bee,* July 27, p. A3.

Jones, Gareth Stedman. 1971. *Outcast London: A Study in the Relationship between Classes in Victorian Society.* London: Oxford University Press.

Jordan, David P. 1955. *Transforming Paris: The Life and Labors of Baron Haussmann.* New York: Free Press.

Judd, Dennis R. 1996. "Enclosure, Community, and Public Life." Pp. 217–36 in *Research in Community Sociology: New Communities in a Changing World,* edited by Dan A. Chekki. Greenwich, CT: JAI.

Judd, Mark. 1983. "'The Oddest Combination of Town and County': Popular Culture and the London Fairs, 1800–60." Pp. 10–30 in *Leisure in Britain 1780–1939,* edited by John K. Walton and James Walvin. Manchester: Manchester University Press.

Jukes, Peter. 1990. *A Shout in the Street: An Excursion into the Modern City.* Berkeley: University of California Press.

Kail, Barbara Lynn and Paula Holzman Kleinman. 1985. "Fear, Crime, Community Organization, and Limitations on Daily Routines." *Urban Affairs Quarterly* 20(3, March):400–8.

Kammann, Richard, Richard Thomson, and Robyn Irwin. 1979. "Unhelpful Behavior in the Street: City Size of Immediate Pedestrian Density?" *Environment and Behavior* 11(June):245–50.

Kantrowitz, Barbara and Associates. 1991. "Striking a Nerve." *Newsweek* (October 21):34–40.

Kaplan, David A. 1994. "These Guys Do Windows." *Newsweek* (January 17):48.

Kaplan, Fred. 1996. "Face Lift on 42nd Street: Times Square Sheds Its Sleaze." *Sacramento Bee*, December 29, Travel, p. 1.

Kaplan, Sam Hall. 1983. "Street Planner Favors Cars over People." *Los Angeles Times*, November 9, p. 1.

Karp, David A. 1973. "Hiding in Pornographic Bookstores: A Reconsideration of the Nature of Urban Anonymity." *Urban Life* 1(January):427–51.

Karp, David S., Gregory Stone, and William C. Yoels. 1977. *Being Urban: A Social Psychological View of Urban Life*. Lexington, MA: D.C. Heath.

––––––. 1991. *Being Urban: A Sociology of City Life*. New York: Praeger.

Karp, David S. and William C. Yoels. 1986. *Sociology and Everyday Life*. Itasca, IL: F.E. Peacock.

Kasson, John F. 1978. *Amusing the Million: Coney Island at the Turn of the Century*. New York: Hill and Wang.

––––––. 1990. *Rudeness and Civility: Manners in Nineteenth-Century Urban America*. New York: Hill and Wang.

Katovich, Michael A. and William A. Reese II. 1987. "The Regular: Full-Time Identities and Memberships in an Urban Bar." *Journal of Contemporary Ethnography* 16(3, October):308–43.

Katz, Elihu and Brenda Danet. 1973a. "Petitions and Persuasive Appeals: A Study of Official-Client Relations." Pp. 174–90 in *Bureaucracy and the Public: A Reader in Official-Client Relations*, edited by Elihu Katz and Brenda Danet. New York: Basic Books.

––––––. (eds.). 1973b. *Bureaucracy and the Public: A Reader in Official-Client Relations*. New York: Basic Books.

Katz, Peter. 1994. *The New Urbanism: Toward an Architecture of Community*. New York: McGraw Hill.

Kaufman, Leslie. 1995. "That's Entertainment: Shopping Malls Are Borrowing Ideas from Theme Parks to Survive." *Newsweek* (September 11):72.

Keller, Suzanne. 1968. *The Urban Neighborhood: A Sociological Perspective*. New York: Random House.

Kendall, Lori. 1998. "Meaning and Identity in 'Cyberspace': The Performance of Gender, Class, and Race Online." *Symbolic Interaction* 21(3).

Kenen, Regina. 1982. "Soapsuds, Space, and Sociability: A Participant Observation of the Laundromat." *Urban Life* 11(2, July):163–84.

Ketcham, Ralph. 1987. *Individualism and Public Life: A Modern Dilemma*. New York: Basil Blackwell.

Khuri, Fuad I. 1968. "The Etiquette of Bargaining in the Middle East." *American Anthropologist* 70(August):698–706.

Kingsdale, J. M. 1973. "The 'Poor Man's Club': Social Functions of the Urban Working-Class Saloon." *American Quarterly* 25(October):472–89.

Kirschner, Don S. 1970. *City and Country: Rural Responses to Urbanization in the 1920's*. Westport, CT: Greenwood.

Klapp, Orrin E. 1969. *Collective Search for Identity*. New York: Holt, Rinehart and Winston.

Kleinfield, N. R. 1992. "This Long Island Industry Is Beating the Recession." *New York Times*, April 8, p. B1.

Kleinke, Chris L. and David A. Singer. 1979. "Influence of Gaze on Compliance with Demanding and Conciliatory Requests in a Field Setting." *Personality and Social Psychology Bulletin* 5(3, July):386–90.

Kleinman, Sherryl. 1981. "Making Professionals Into 'Persons': Discrepancies in Traditional and Humanistic Expectations of Professional Identity." *Sociology of Work and Occupations* 8(1, February):61–87.

Kling, Rob, Spencer Olin, and Mark Poster (eds.). 1991. *Postsuburban California: The Transformation of Orange County Since World War II.* Berkeley: University of California Press.

Kornblum, William. 1988. "Working the Deuce." *Yale Review* 77(3, Spring):356–67.

Kornblum, William and the West 42nd Street Study Team. 1978. "West 42nd Street: The Bright Light Zone." Unpublished manuscript. Graduate School and University Center of the City University of New York.

Kotarba, J. A. 1977. "The Serious Nature of Tavern Sociability." Paper presented at the Annual Meetings of the Society for the Study of Social Problems, Chicago.

Kotler, Milton. 1969. *Neighborhood Government: The Local Foundations of Political Life.* Indianapolis: Bobbs-Merrill.

Kowinski, William Severini. 1985. *The Malling of America: An Inside Look at the Great Consumer Paradise.* New York: William Morrow.

———. 1986. "Endless Summer at the World's Biggest Shopping Wonderland." *Smithsonian* (December):35–43.

Krantz, Frederick (ed.). 1985. *History from Below: Studies in Popular Protest and Popular Ideology in Honor of George Rude.* Montreal: Concordia University Press.

Krygier, Martin. 1983. "Publicness, Privateness and 'Primitive Law'." Pp. 307–40 in *Public and Private in Social Life*, edited by Stanley I. Benn and Gerald F. Gaus. London: Croom Helm.

Kunstler, James Howard. 1993. *The Geography of Nowhere: The Rise and Decline of America's Man-Made Landscape.* New York: Simon and Schuster.

Lacroix, Paul. [1876] 1963. *France in the Middle Ages.* New York: Frederick Ungar. [Originally published as *Manners, Customs and Dress During the Middle Ages and During the Renaissance Period.*]

Ladd, Everett Carll, Jr. 1969. *Ideology in America: Change and Response in a City, a Suburb, and a Small Town.* Ithaca: Cornell University Press.

LaGory, Mark. 1983. "The Social Consequences of Spatial Structure." Pp. 180–96 in *Remaking the City: Social Science Perspectives on Urban Design*, edited by John S. Pipkin, Mark E. LaGory, and Judith R. Blau. Albany: State University of New York Press.

Landscape Architecture. 1989. "International Urban Plazas" (special section; August):29–67.

Langer, Peter. 1984. "Sociology—Four Images of Organized Diversity: Bazaar, Jungle, Organism, and Machine." Pp. 97–117 in *Cities of the Mind: Images and Themes of the City in the Social Sciences*, edited by Lloyd Rodwin and Robert N. Hollister. New York: Plenum.

Lasch, Christopher. 1977. *Haven in a Heartless World.* New York: Basic Books.

Latané, Bibb and John M. Darley. 1968. "Group Inhibition of Bystander Intervention in Emergencies." *Journal of Personal and Social Psychology* 10:215–21.

———. 1970. *The Unresponsive Bystander.* New York: Appleton-Century-Crofts.

———. 1973. "Bystander 'Apathy.'" Pp. 62–91 in *Urbanman: The Psychology of*

Urban Survival, edited by John Helmer and Neil A. Eddington. New York: Free Press.

Latham, Aaron. 1994. "City Walk: L.A.'s Fantasy Village for Serious Shoppers, Diners." *Sacramento Bee* (November 9), Scene, p. 5.

Lau, S. and B. F. Blake. 1976. "Recent Research on Helping Behavior: An Overview and Bibliography." *APA: JSAS, Catalogue of Selected Documents in Psychology*, ms. 1289.

Laver, James. 1958. *Edwardian Promenade*. London: E. Hulton.

Lawrence, Denise. 1982. "Parades, Politics, and Competing Urban Images: Doo Dah and Roses." *Urban Anthropology* 11(2):155–76.

Lawrence, Jeanne Catherine. 1992. "Geographical Space, Social Space, and the Realm of the Department Store." *Urban History* 19(1, April):64–83.

Le Corbusier. [1946] 1971. *Looking At City Planning*. New York: Grossman. [Originally published in French.]

———. 1929. *The City of Tomorrow and Its Planning*. New York: Payson & Clarke Ltd.

Leach, W. R. 1984. "Transformations in a Culture of Consumption: Women and Department Stores, 1890–1940." *Journal of American History* 71(2, September):319–42.

Lee, Barrett A. 1981. "The Urban Unease Revisited: Perceptions of Local Safety and Neighborhood Satisfaction among Metropolitan Residents." *Social Science Quarterly* 62(4, December):611–29.

Lee, Barrett A. and Bruce G. Link. 1995. "Gender Differences in Contact with the Homeless." Paper presented at the Annual Meetings of the American Sociological Association, Washington, D.C.

Lees, Andrew. 1985. *Cities Perceived: Urban Society in European and American Thought, 1820–1940*. New York: Columbia University Press.

———. 1991. "Berlin and Modern Urbanity in German Discourse, 1845–1945." *Journal of Urban History* 17(2, February):153–80.

Leidner, Robin. 1993. *Fast Food, Fast Talk: Service Work and the Routinization of Everyday Life*. Berkeley: University of California Press.

Lejeune, Robert. 1977. "The Management of a Mugging." *Urban Life* 6(July):123–48.

Lejeune, Robert and Nicholas Alex. 1973. "On Being Mugged: The Event and Its Aftermath." *Urban Life* 2(October):259–87.

Lemann, Nicholas. 1996. "Kicking in Groups." *Atlantic Monthly* (April):22, 24–26.

LeMasters, E. E. 1973. "Social Life in a Working-Class Tavern." *Urban Life* 22(1, April):27–52.

———. 1975. *Blue-Collar Aristocrats: Life-Styles in a Working-Class Tavern*. Madison: University of Wisconsin Press.

Lennard, Suzanne H. Crowhurst and Henry Lennard. 1984. *Public Life in Urban Places*. Southhampton, NY: Gondolier.

———. 1987. *Livable Cities: People and Places: Social and Design Principles for the Future of the City*. New York: Center for Urban Well-Being.

———. 1995. *Livable Cities Observed: A Source Book of Images and Ideas for City Official, Community Leaders, Architects, Planners and All Others Committed to Making Their Cities Livable*. Carmel, CA: Gondolier.

Lerner, Melvin J. 1980. *The Belief in a Just World: A Fundamental Delusion*. New York: Plenum.

Levering, Thomas R. 1978. "Information in Form: A Study of How Values Are Manifested in the Built Environment." Pp. 458–79 in *New Directions in Environmental Design Research*, edited by Walter E. Rogers and William H. Ittelson. Washington, DC: Environmental Design Research Association.

Levine, Bettijane. 1990. "The Unseen Homeless Women." *San Francisco Chronicle*, December 11, p. B3.

Levine, Donald N. 1979. "Simmel at a Distance: On the History and Systematics of the Sociology of the Stranger." Pp. 21–36 in *Strangers in African Societies*, edited by William A. Shack and Elliott P. Skinner. Berkeley: University of California Press.

————. 1985. *The Flight from Ambiguity: Essays in Social and Cultural Theory.* Chicago: University of Chicago Press.

Levine, Janey, Ann Vinson, and Deborah Wood. 1973. "Subway Behavior." Pp. 208–16 in *People in Places: The Sociology of the Familiar*, edited by Arnold Birenbaum and Edward Sagarin. New York: Praeger.

Levine, Lawrence W. 1988. *Highbrow/Lowbrow: The Emergence of Cultural Hierarchy in America.* Cambridge, MA: Harvard University Press.

Levine, Ned and Martin Wachs. 1986. "Bus Crime in Los Angeles: II—Victims and Public Impact." *Transportation Research-A* 20(4):285–93.

Levitas, Gloria. 1978. "Anthropology and Sociology of Streets." Pp. 225–40 in *On Streets*, edited by Stanford Anderson. Cambridge, MA: MIT Press.

Lewis, Dan A. and Susan Reed. 1985. "Urban Danger and Mental Illness: From a Clinical to a Social Construction." Paper presented at the Annual Meetings of the American Sociological Association, Washington, D.C., August.

Liebow, Elliot. 1967. *Tally's Corner: A Study of Negro Streetcorner Men.* Boston: Little, Brown.

Life Magazine. 1972. "Readers Speak Out." January 14, pp. 28–31.

Lilly, J. Robert and Richard Ball. 1980. "Challenges to Situated Morality: Maintaining Respectability in a Sexual Rendezvous." *Qualitative Sociology* 3(Fall): 204–22.

————. 1981. "No-Tell Motel: The Management of Social Invisibility." *Urban Life* 10(July):179–98.

Linder, Darwyn E. 1974. *Personal Space.* University Programs Modular Studies. Morristown, NJ: General Learning Press.

Lingeman, Richard. 1980. *Small Town America: A Narrative History 1620 to the Present.* Boston: Houghton Mifflin.

Liska, Allen E. and William Baccaglini. 1990. "Feeling Safe by Comparison: Crime in the Newspapers." *Social Problems.* Volume 37, No. 3 (August), pp. 360–74.

Liska, Allen E. and Paul E. Bellair. 1995. "Violent-Crime Rates and Racial Composition: Convergence Over Time." *American Journal of Sociology* 101(3, November):578–610.

Liska, Allen E., Andrew Sanchirico, and Mark D. Reed. 1988. "Fear of Crime and Constrained Behavior: Specifying and Estimating a Reciprocal Effects Model." *Social Forces* 66(3, March):827–37.

Lofland, John. 1982. "Crowd Joys." *Urban Life* 10(4, January):355–81.

Lofland, Lyn H. 1972. "Self Management in Public Settings: Parts I and II" *Urban Life and Culture* 1(April and July):93–108, 217–31.

———. 1983. "Questioning the Primacy of the Primary: An Analysis of Human Bonding." Pp. 447–61 in *Family, Self, and Society: Emerging Issues, Alternatives, and Interventions*, edited by Douglas B. Gutknecht, Edgar W. Butler, Larry Criswell and Jerry Meints. Lanham, MD: University Press of America.

———. 1984. "Women and Urban Public Space." *Women and Environments* 6(2, April):12–14.

———. [1973] 1985. *A World of Strangers: Order and Action in Urban Public Space.* Prospect Heights, IL: Waveland.

———. 1989. "Social Life in the Public Realm: A Review." *Journal of Contemporary Ethnography* 17(4, January):453–82.

———. 1990. "Is Peace Possible? An Analysis of Sociology." *Sociological Perspectives* 33(3, Fall):313–25.

———. 1991. "The Urban Milieu: Locales, Public Sociability, and Moral Concern." Pp. 189–206 in *Social Organization and Social Process: Essays in Honor of Anselm Strauss*, edited by David R. Maines. Hawthorne, NY: Aldine de Gruyter.

———. 1993. "Urbanity, Tolerance and Public Space: The Creation of Cosmopolitans." Pp. 93–109 in *Understanding Amsterdam: Essays on Economic Vitality, City Life and Urban Form*, edited by Leon Deben, Willem Heinemeijer, and Dick Van Der Vaart. Amsterdam: Het Spinhuis.

———. 1994. "Observations and Observers in Conflict: Field Research in the Public Realm." Pp. 19-32 in *Research in Community Sociology*, Supplement 1, *The Community of the Streets*, edited by Spencer E. Cahill and Lyn H. Lofland. Greenwich, CT: JAI.

———. 1995. "Social Interaction: Continuities and Complexities in the Study of Non-Intimate Interaction." Pp. 176–201 in *Sociological Perspectives on Social Psychology*, edited by Karen S. Cook, Gary Alan Fine, and James S. House. Boston: Allyn and Bacon.

Logan, John R. and Harvey L. Molotch. 1987. *Urban Fortunes: The Political Economy of Place.* Berkeley: University of California Press.

Longo, Gianni, Jean Tatge, and Lois Fishman. 1983. *Learning from Galveston.* New Brunswick, NJ: Transaction.

Lopata, Helena Znaniecki. 1965. "The Secondary Features of a Primary Relationship." *Human Organization* 24(2, Summer):116–23.

Loth, David. 1966. *The City Within a City: The Romance of Rockefeller Center.* New York: William Morrow.

Love, Ruth Leeds. 1973. "The Fountains of Urban Life." *Urban Life and Culture* 2(July):161–209.

Low, Setha M. and Irwin Altman. 1992. "Place Attachment: A Conceptual Inquiry." Pp. 1–12 in *Human Behavior and Environment: Advances in Theory and Research*, Volume 12, *Place Attachment*, edited by Irwin Altman and Setha M. Low. New York: Plenum.

Lowe, Jeanne R. 1967. *Cities in a Race with Time.* New York: Vintage.

Lowe, Marcia D. 1992a. "How to Make Cities More Humane." *Utne Reader* (May/June):104–6.

———— . 1992b. "Shaping Cities." Pp. 119–37 in *State of the World*, Worldwatch Institute, Project Director, Lester R. Brown. New York: Norton.

Lubove, Roy. 1967. *The Urban Community: Housing and Planning in the Progressive Era*. Englewood Cliffs, NJ: Prentice-Hall.

Lyle, John T. 1970. "People-Watching in Parks: A Report from France and California." *Landscape Architecture* 61(October):31, 51–52.

Lyman, Stanford M. and Marvin B. Scott. 1967. "Territoriality: A Neglected Sociological Dimension." *Social Problems* 15(Fall):236–249.

Lynch, Kathleen. 1989. "Solidary Labour: Its Nature and Marginalisation." *Sociological Review* 37(1, February):1–14.

Lynch, Kevin. 1960. *The Image of the City*. Cambridge, MA: MIT Press.

———— . 1972. *What Time Is This Place?* Cambridge, MA: MIT Press.

———— . 1976. *Managing the Sense of a Region*. Cambridge, MA, Massachusetts: The MIT Press.

Lynch, Kevin (ed.). 1977. *Growing Up in Cities: Studies of the Spatial Environment of Adolescence in Cracow, Melbourne, Mexico City, Salta, Toluca, and Warszawa*. Cambridge, MA: MIT Press.

———— . 1981. *Good City Form*. Cambridge, MA: MIT Press.

Lyndon, Donlyn. 1984. "Public Buildings: Symbols Qualified by Experience." *Public Interest* 74(Winter):77–97.

MacAloon, John J. 1984. "Olympic Games and the Theory of Spectacle in Modern Societies." Pp. 241–80 in *Rite, Drama, Festival, Spectacle: Rehearsals Toward a Theory of Cultural Performance*, edited by John J. MacAloon. Philadelphia: Institute for the Study of Human Issues.

MacCannell, Dean. 1973. "Staged Authenticity: Arrangements of Social Space in Tourist Settings." *American Journal of Sociology* 79(November):589–603.

MacDonald, Kent. 1985. "The Commercial Strip: From Main Street to Television Road." *Landscape* 28:12–19.

Mace, Rodney. 1976. *Trafalgar Square: Emblem of Empire*. London: Lawrence and Wishart.

MacFadyen, Dugald. 1970. *Sir Ebenezer Howard and the Town Planning Movement*. Cambridge, MA: MIT Press.

MacKeith, Margaret. 1986. *The History and Conservation of Shopping Arcades*. London and New York: Mansell.

Mackellar, F. Landis and Machiko Yanagishita. 1995. "Homicide in the United States: Who's at Risk!" Report Number 26 in the series, *Population Trends and Public Policy*. Washington, DC: Population Reference Bureau.

MacLeod, Linda. 1989/90 "The City for Women: No Safe Place." *Women and Environments* 12(1, Fall/Winter):6–7.

Macrory, Boyd E. 1952. "The Tavern and the Community." *Quarterly Journal of Studies on Alcohol* 14(4):609–73.

Madge, Charles. 1950. "Private and Public Spaces." *Human Relations* 3:187–99.

Maines, David R. 1989. "Further Dialectics: Strangers, Friends, and Historical Transformations." *Communication Yearbook* 12:190–202.

Maines, David R. and Jeffrey C. Bridger. 1992. "Narratives, Community and Land Use Decision." *Social Science Journal* 29(4):363–80.

Maines, David R., Jeffrey C. Bridger, and Jeffrey T. Ulmer. 1996. "Mythic Facts and Park's Pragmatism: On Predecessor-Selection and Theorizing in Human Ecology." *Sociological Quarterly* 37(3):521–49.

Maisel, Robert. 1974. "The Flea Market as an Action Scene." *Urban Life* 2(January):488–505.

Mann, Leon. 1969. "Queue Culture: The Waiting Line as a Social System." *American Journal of Sociology* 74(November):340–54.

———. 1973. "Learning to Live with Lines." Pp. 42–61 in *Urbanman: The Psychology of Urban Survival*, edited by John Helmer and Neil A. Eddington. New York: Free Press.

Mansfield, Howard. 1990. *Cosmopolis: Yesterday's Cities of the Future*. Rutgers: Center for Urban Policy Research, State University of New Jersey.

Marris, Peter. 1974. *Loss and Change*. New York: Pantheon.

Martin, Judith. 1991. *Miss Manners' Guide To Excruciatingly Correct Behavior: The Ultimate Handbook on Modern Etiquette*. New York: Galahad.

Mass Observation. 1943. *The Pub and the People: A Worktown Study*. London: Victor Gollancz.

MATRIX. 1984. *Making Space: Women and the Man-Made Environment*. London and Sydney: Pluto.

Mauer, David W. 1962. *The Big Con*. New York: New American Library.

Mazey, Mary Ellen and David R. Lee. 1983. *Her Space, Her Place: A Geography of Women*. Washington, DC: Association of American Geographers.

Mazur, Allan, Eugene Rosa, Mark Faupel, Joshua Heller, Russell Leen, and Blake Thurman. 1980. "Physiological Aspects of Communication via Mutual Gaze." *American Journal of Sociology* 86(1, July):50–74.

McAneny, Leslie. 1993. "The Gallup Poll on Crime." *The Gallup Poll Monthly* (December):18–27.

McCall, George and J. L. Simmons. 1982. *Social Psychology: A Sociological Approach*. New York: Free Press.

McCarthy, John D. 1994. "Activists, Authorities, and Media Framing of Drunk Driving." Pp. 133–67 in *New Social Movements; From Ideology to Identity*, edited by Enrique Larana, Hank Johnson, and Joseph R. Gusfield. Philadelphia: Temple University Press.

McCarthy, John D., Clark McPhail, and Jackie Smith. 1996. "Images of Protest: Dimensions of Selection Bias in Media Coverage of Washington Demonstrations, 1982 and 1991." *American Sociological Review* 63(3, June):478–99.

McCarthy, John D., and Mark Wolfson. 1996. "Resource Mobilization by Local Social Movement Organizations: Agency, Strategy, and Organization in the Movement Against Drinking and Driving." *American Sociological Review* 61(December):1070–88.

McDermott, John J. 1972. "Nature Nostalgia and the City." *Soundings* 1(20, Spring):1–21.

McKenzie, Evan. 1994. *Privatopia: Homeowner Associations and the Rise of Residential Private Government*. New Haven, CT: Yale University Press.

McKenzie, Roderick D. 1925. "The Ecological Approach to the Study of the Human Community." Pp. 63–79 in *The City*, edited by Robert E. Park, Ernst

W. Burgess, and Roderick D. McKenzie. Chicgao: University of Chicago Press.

McPhail, Clark. 1987. "Social Behavior in Public Places: From Clusters to Arcs and Rings." Paper presented at the Annual Meetings of the American Sociological Association, Chicago.

———. 1991. "Pursuing the Pedestrian: From Ethnography to Computer Simulation of the Interaction Order." Unpublished paper.

———. 1994. "From Clusters to Arcs and Rings: Elementary Forms of Sociation in Temporary Gatherings." Pp. 35–57 in *Research in Community Sociology*, edited by Dan C. Chekki, Supplement 1, *The Community of the Streets*, edited by Spencer E. Cahill and Lyn H. Lofland. Greenwich, CT: JAI.

McPhail, Clark and Ronald T. Wohlstein. 1982. "Using Film to Analyze Pedestrian Behavior." *Sociological Methods and Research* 10:347–75.

———. 1986. "Collective Locomotion as Collective Behavior." *American Sociological Review* 51(4, August):447–63.

Mecchi, Irene. 1992. *Herb Caen's San Francisco 1976–1991*. San Francisco: Chronicle.

Mehrabian, Albert. 1976. *Public Places and Private Spaces: The Psychology of Work, Play, and Living Environments*. New York: Basic Books.

Melbin, Murray. 1978. "Night as Frontier." *American Sociological Review* 43(February):3–22.

———. 1987. *Night as Frontier: Colonizing the World After Dark*. New York: Free Press.

Melvin, Patricia Mooney. 1987. *The Organic City: Urban Definition and Neighborhood Organization 1880–1920*. Lexington: University Press of Kentucky.

Mennerick, Lewis A. 1974. "Client Typologies: A Method of Coping with Conflict in the Service Worker-Client Relationship." *Sociology of Work and Occupations* 1(4, November):396–418.

Meredith, Robyn. 1996. "Teen Patrons Face Curfews, Other Curbs at Mall of America." *New York Times*, September 4.

Merriam, G. & C. 1971. *Webster's Third New International Dictionary of the English Language*, unabridged. New York: Author.

Merriman, John M. 1991. *The Margins of City Life: Explorations on the French Urban Frontier, 1815–1851*. New York: Oxford University Press.

Merry, Sally Engle. 1981. *Urban Danger: Life in a Neighborhood of Strangers*. Philadelphia: Temple University Press.

Messer, John G. 1982. "Spontaneous Behavior in Emergencies." Paper presented at the Annual Meetings of the American Sociological Association, San Francisco.

Meyer, Julie. 1951. "The Stranger and the City." *American Journal of Sociology* 56(March):476–83.

Meyrowitz, Joshua. 1985. *No Sense of Place: The Impact of Electronic Media on Social Behavior*. New York: Oxford University Press.

Milgram, Stanley. [1970] 1973. "The Experience of Living in Cities." Pp. 1–22 in *Urbanman: The Psychology of Urban Survival*, edited by John Helmer and Neil A. Eddington. New York: Free Press.

———. 1977. *The Individual in a Social World*. Reading, MA: Addison-Wesley.

Milich, Nick. 1987. "The Flying 43rd: Riders Share Their Lives during the Daily Davis-Sacramento Run." *Davis Enterprise*, November 2, p. A10.

Miller, Eleanor M. 1986. *Street Woman*. Philadelphia: Temple University Press.

Miller, Michael B. 1981. *The Bon Marche: Bourgeois Culture and the Department Store, 1869–1920*. Princeton, NJ: Princeton University Press.

Milligan, Melinda. 1998. "Interactional Past and Potential: The Social Construction of Place Attachment." *Symbolic Interaction* 21(1).

Molotch, Harvey. 1976. "The City as a Growth Machine." *American Journal of Sociology* 82(September):309–30.

Monkkonen, Eric H. 1981. "A Disorderly People? Urban Order in the Nineteenth and Twentieth Centuries." *Journal of American History* 68(3, December):539–59.

Moore, E. C. 1897 "The Social Value of the Saloon." *American Journal of Sociology* 3(1, July):1–12.

Moore, Ellen Wedemeyer. 1985. *The Fairs of Medieval England: An Introductory Study*. Toronto: Pontifical Institute of Medieval Studies.

Morganthau, Tom and Associates. 1986. "Abandoned." *Newsweek* (January 6):14–19.

Mote, F. W. 1977. "The Transformation of Nanking, 1350–1400." Pp. 101–53 in *The City in Late Imperial China*, edited by G. William Skinner. Stanford, CA: Stanford University Press.

Moudon, Anne Vernez. 1987. *Public Streets for Public Use*. New York: Van Nostrand Reinhold.

Moudon, Anne Vernez, with Bill Wiseman and Kwang-joong Kim (eds.). 1990. *Master-Planned Communities: Shaping Exurbs in the 1990s*. Seattle: Urban Design Program, College of Architecture and Urban Planning, University of Washington.

Muir, Donal E. and Eugene Weinstein. 1962. "The Social Debt: An Investigation of Lower-Class and Middle-Class Norms of Social Obligation." *American Sociological Review* 27(4, August):532–38.

Muller, Thaddeus. 1992. "Amsterdam Inner-City Life: Intimate Aspects of Social Interactions in the Public Domain." Paper presented at the Congress, "European Cities: Growth and Decline," The Hague, April 13–16.

———. 1995. "The 'Extra-Quality' or the Added Dimension of Urban Life: Interactions with Fascinating, Friendly, and Intimate Strangers." Paper presented at the Qualitative Research Conference on "Studying Social Life: Ethnography in Cross-Cultural Perspective," Hamilton, Ontario: McMaster University, May 30–June 5.

Nasar, Jack L. 1989. "Perception, Cognition, and Evaluation of Urban Places." Pp. 31–56 in *Human Behavior and Environment: Advances in Theory and Research*, Volume 10, *Public Places and Spaces*, edited by Irwin Altman and Ervin H. Zube. New York: Plenum.

———. 1990. "The Evaluative Image of the City." *Journal of the American Planning Association* 56(1, Winter):41–53.

Nasar, Jack L. and A. Rengin Yurdakul. 1990. "Patterns of Behavior in Urban Public Spaces." *Journal of Architectural and Planning Research* 7(Spring):71–85.

Nasaw, David. 1985. *Children of the City: At Work and at Play*. Garden City, NY: Anchor/Doubleday.

———. 1993. *Going Out: The Rise and Fall of Public Amusements*. New York: Basic Books.

Nash, Jeffrey. 1975. "Bus Riding: Community on Wheels." *Urban Life* 4(1, April):99–124.

———. 1981. "Relations in Frozen Places: Observations on Winter Public Order." *Qualitative Sociology* 4(3, Fall):229–43.

Nash, Jeffrey and Anedith J. Nash. 1994. "The Skyway System and Urban Space: Vitality in Enclosed Public Places." Pp. 167–81 in *Research in Community Sociology*, edited by Dan C. Chekki, Supplement 1, *The Community of the Streets*, edited by Spencer E. Cahill and Lyn H. Lofland. Greenwich, CT: JAI.

Nash, Steven A. 1995. *Facing Eden: 100 Years of Landscape Art in the Bay Area*. Berkeley: University of California Press.

Nathe, Patricia A. 1976. "Prickly Pear Coffee House: The Hangout." *Urban Life* 5(April):75–104.

Naylor, Gillian. 1968. *The Bauhaus*. London: Studio Vista/Dutton Pictureback.

"Neighborhoods Reborn." 1996. *Consumer Reports* (May):24–30.

Neumann, A. Lin. 1991. "Fear in Our Hearts: Thoughts on Crime, Security and Dread." *Sacramento News and Review*, October 31, p. 12.

Newman, Joseph and Clark McCauley. 1977. "Eye Contact with Strangers in City, Suburb, and Small Town." *Environment and Behavior* 9(4, December):547–58.

Newman, Oscar and Karen A. Franck. 1981. "The Effects of Building Size on Personal Crime and Fear of Crime." Paper presented at the Annual Meetings of the American Sociological Association, Toronto (August).

Nielsen, Elizabeth. 1988. "The Public Sphere: Nuclear-Freeze Posters in a Commodity Culture." *Monthly Review* (June):43–52.

Noel, Thomas J. 1982. *The City and the Saloon: Denver, 1858–1916*. Lincoln: University of Nebraska Press.

Office of the Solicitor General, Research and Statistics Group. 1985. *Female Victims of Crime: Canadian Urban Victimization Survey*. Ottawa: Author.

Ogbonna, Emmanuel and Barry Wilkinson. 1988. "Corporate Strategy and Corporate Culture: The View from the Check-Out." *Personnel Review* 17:10–14.

Oldenburg, Ray. 1989. *The Great Good Place: Cafes, Coffee Shops, Community Centers, Beauty Parlors, General Stores, Bars, Hangouts, and How They Get You through the Day*. New York: Paragon House.

Oldenburg, Ray and Dennis Brissett. 1980. "The Essential Hangout." *Psychology Today* (April):82–84.

———. 1982. "The Third Place." *Qualitative Sociology* 5(Winter):265–84.

———. 1994. "The Urban Staging of Public Incivility." Pp. 145–64 in *Research in Community Sociology*, edited by Dan C. Chekki, Supplement 1, *The Community of the Streets*, edited by Spencer E. Cahill and Lyn H. Lofland. Greenwich, CT: JAI.

Olsen, Donald J. 1976. *The Growth of Victorian London*. Harmondsworth, England: Penguin.

———. 1986. *The City as a Work of Art*. New Haven, CT: Yale University Press.

Olson, Philip. 1982. "Urban Neighborhood Research: Its Development and Current Focus." *Urban Affairs Quarterly* 17(June):491–518.

Oosterman, Jan. 1992. "Welcome to the Pleasure Dome: Play and Entertainment in

Urban Public Space: The Example of the Sidewalk Cafe." *Built Environment* 18(2):155–64.

———. 1993. *Parade Der Passanten: De Stad, Het Vertier En De Terrassen.* Utrecht: Uitgeverij Jan van Arkel.

Orloff, Alexander. 1981. *Carnival: Myth and Cult.* Worgl, Austria: Perlinger.

Ortiz, Steven M. 1994. "Shopping for Sociability in the Mall." Pp. 183–99 in *Research in Community Sociology*, edited by Dan C. Chekki, Supplement 1, *The Community of the Streets*, edited by Spencer E. Cahill and Lyn H. Lofland. Greenwich, CT: JAI.

Orum, Anthony M. and Joe R. Feagin. 1991. "A Tale of Two Cities." Pp. 121–47 in *A Case for the Case Study*, edited by Joe R. Feagin, Anthony M. Orun, and Gideon Sjoberg. Chapel Hill: University of North Carolina Press.

Osborn, Frederick J. and Arnold Whittick. 1977. *New Town: Their Origins, Achievements and Progress.* London and Boston: Leonard Hill and Routledge and Kegan Paul.

Palen, J. John. 1995. *The Suburbs.* New York: McGraw-Hill.

Palen, J. John and Bruce London (eds.). 1984. *Gentrification, Displacement and Neighborhood Revitalization.* Albany: State University of New York Press.

Palmer, C. Eddie. 1983. "'Trauma Junkies' and Street Work: Occupational Behavior of Paramedics and Emergency Medical Technicians." *Urban Life* 12(2, July):162–83.

Palmer, Parker J. 1985. *The Company of Strangers: Christians and the Renewal of America's Public Life.* New York: Crossroad.

Park, Robert E. 1925. "The City: Suggestions for the Investigation of Human Behavior in the Urban Environment." Pp. 1–46 in *The City*, edited by Robert E. Park, Ernest W. Burgess, and Roderick D. McKenzie. Chicago: University of Chicago Press.

———. 1928. "Human Migration and the Marginal Man." *American Journal of Sociology* 33:888–96.

Park, Robert E. and Ernest W. Burgess. 1921. *Introduction to the Science of Sociology.* Chicago: University of Chicago Press.

Parks, Evelyn L. 1970. "From Constabulary to Police Society: Implications for Social Control." *Catalyst* (Summer):76–97.

Parr, A. E. 1967. "Urbanity and the Urban Scene." *Landscape* 16(Spring):3–5.

———. 1968. "The Five Ages of Urbanity." *Landscape* 17(Spring):7–10.

Parry, Geraint, George Moyser, and Margaret Wagstaffe. 1987. "The Crowd and the Community: Context, Content and Aftermath." Pp. 212–54 in *The Crowd in Contemporary Britain*, edited by George Gaskell and Robert Benewick. London: Sage.

Pateman, Carole. 1983. "Feminist Critiques of the Public/Private Dichotomy." Pp. 281–303 in *Public and Private in Social Life*, edited by Stanley I. Benn and Gerald F. Gaus. London: Croom Helm.

Paulson, Ronald. 1975. *The Art of Hogarth.* London: Phaidon.

Pearce, Philip L. 1980. "Strangers, Travelers, and Greyhound Terminals: A Study of Small-Scale Helping Behaviors." *Journal of Personality and Social Psychology* 38(June):935–40.

Peiss, Kathy. 1986. *Cheap Amusements: Working Women and Leisure in Turn-of-the-Century New York*. Philadelphia: Temple University Press.

Pellow, Deborah. 1993. "Chinese Privacy." Pp. 31–45 in *The Cultural Meaning of Urban Space*, edited by Robert Rotenberg and Gary McDonogh. Westport, CT: Bergin and Garvey.

Penrose, Jan. 1987. "Women and Man-Made Environment: The Dutch Experience." *Women and Environments* (Winter):12–13, 26.

Perry, Elisabeth I. 1985. "'The General Motherhood of the Commonwealth': Dance Hall Reform in the Progressive Era." *American Quarterly* 37(5, Winter):719–33.

Peters, Richard C. 1984. "Light and Public Places." *Places* 1(2, Winter):41–47.

Piette, Albert. 1992. "Play, Reality, and Fiction: Toward a Theoretical and Methodological Approach to the Festival Framework," translated by Mary Delahaye. *Qualitative Sociology* 15(1):37–52.

Pike, Burton. 1981. *The Image of the City in Modern Literature*. Princeton, NJ: Princeton University Press.

Pimentel, Benjamin. 1996. "Burlingame to Ticket Public Spitters." *San Francisco Chronicle*, April 18, p. A17.

Pin, Emile Jean, in collaboration with Jamie Turndorf. 1985. *The Pleasure of Your Company: A Socio-Psychological Analysis of Modern Sociability*. New York: Praeger.

Pipkin, John S. 1990. "Space and the Social Order in Pepys' Diary." *Urban Geography* 11(March/April):153–75.

Pipkin, John S., Mark E. LaGory, and Judith R. Blau (eds.). 1983. *Remaking the City: Social Science Perspectives on Urban Design*. Albany: State University of New York Press.

Pitkin, Donald. 1993. "Italian Urbanscape: Intersection of Private and Public." Pp. 95–101 in *The Cultural Meaning of Urban Space*, edited by Robert Rotenberg and Gary McDonogh. Westport, CT: Bergin and Garvey.

Plotkin, Sidney. 1987. *Keep Out: The Struggle for Land Use Control*. Berkeley: University of California Press.

Popenoe, David. 1977. *The Suburban Environment: Sweden and the United States*. Chicago: University of Chicago Press.

———. 1985. *Private Pleasure, Public Plight: American Metropolitan community Life in Comparative Perspective*. New Brunswick, NJ: Transaction.

Popham, Robert E. 1978. "The Social History of the Tavern." Pp. 225–302 in *Research Advances in Alcohol and Drug Problems*, Volume 4, edited by Yedy Israel, Frederick B. Glaser, Harold Kalant, Robert E. Popham, Wolfgang Schmidt, and Reginald G. Smart. New York: Plenum.

Postman, Neil. 1985. *Amusing Ourselves to Death: Public Discourse in the Age of Show Business*. New York: Viking.

Prak, Niels L. 1985. *The Visual Perception of the Built Environment*. Delft: Delft University Press.

Pratt, Lois V. 1986. "Social Integration of Age Groups in Public Settings." Unpublished manuscript. Jersey City State College, Jersey City, New Jersey.

Price, T. Douglas and James A. Brown (eds.). 1985. *Prehistoric Hunter-Gatherers: The Emergence of Cultural Complexity*. Orlando, FL: Academic.

Progressive Architecture. 1978. Special section on "Shopping Malls." December, pp. 49–74.

Proshansky, Harold. 1978. "The City and Self-Identity." *Environment and Behavior* 10(June):147–69.

Prus, Robert C. 1986/87. "Developing Loyalty: Fostering Purchasing Relationships in the Marketplace." *Urban Life* 15(October-January):331–66.

———. 1989a. *Making Sales: Influence as Interpersonal Accomplishment.* Newbury Park, California: Sage.

———. 1989b. *Pursuing Customers: An Ethnography of Marketing Activities.* Newbury Park, California: Sage.

Prus, Robert C. and Augie Fleras. 1989. "'Pitching' Images to the Generalized Other: Promotional Strategies of Business Development Officers." Paper presented at the Meetings of the Canadian Sociology and Anthropology Association, Quebec City (June).

Prus, Robert C. and Steve Vassilakopoulos. 1979. "Desk Clerks and Hookers: Hustling in a 'Shady' Hotel." *Urban Life* 8(1, April):52–71.

Putnam, Robert D. 1995a. "Bowling Alone: America's Declining Social Capital." *Journal of Democracy* 6(1, January):65–78.

———. 1995b. "Bowling Alone, Revisited." *Responsive Community* 5(2, Spring): 18–35.

———. 1995c. "Tuning In, Tuning Out: The Strange Disappearance of Social Capital in America." *PS: Political Science and Politics* 28(December):664–83.

Quandt, Jean B. 1970. *From Small Town to the Great Community: The Social Thought of Progressive Intellectuals.* New Brunswick, NJ: Rutgers University Press.

Rafaeli, Anat. 1989. "When Cashiers Meet Customers: An Analysis of the Role of Supermarket Cashiers." *Academy of Management Journal* 32(2):245–73.

Rand, George. 1984. "Crime and Environment: A Review of the Literature and Its Implications for Urban Architecture and Planning." *Journal of Architectural Planning and Research* 1:3–19.

Random House. 1987. *The Random House Dictionary of the English Language,* second edition, unabridged. New York: Author.

Rapoport, Amos. 1977. *Human Aspects of Urban Form: Towards a Man-Environment Approach to Urban Form and Design.* Oxford: Pergamon.

Rathbun, Robert Davis (ed.). 1992. *Shopping Centers and Malls Number 4.* New York: Retail Reporting Corporation.

Reitzes, Donald C. 1986a. "Urban Identification and Downtown Activities: A Social Psychological Approach." *Social Psychology Quarterly* 49(June):167–79.

———. 1986b. "Downtown Vitality: Factors Influencing the Use of Dining and Entertainment Facilities." *Sociological Perspectives* 29(January):121–43.

Reitzes, Donald C. and J. K. Diver. 1982. "Gay Bars As Deviant Community Organizations: The Management of Interactions with Outsiders." *Deviant Behavior: An Interdisciplinary Journal* 4(1):1–18.

Relph, Edward. 1976. *Place and Placelessness.* London: Pion.

———. 1981. *Rational Landscapes and Humanistic Geography.* New York: Barnes and Noble.

———. 1987. *The Modern Urban Landscape.* Baltimore: Johns Hopkins University Press.

Reynolds, Donald Martin. 1988. *Monuments and Masterpieces: Histories and Views of Public Sculpture in New York City.* New York: Macmillan.

Riccio. R. 1992. "Street Crime Strategies: The Changing Schemata of Streetwalkers." *Environment and Behavior* 24(4, July):555–70.

Richards, C. E. 1963/64 "City Taverns." *Human Organization* 22(4, Winter):260–68.

Richards, Jeffrey. 1983. "The Cinema and Cinema-going in Birmingham in the 1930's." Pp. 31–52 in *Leisure in Britain 1780–1939,* edited by John K. Walton and James Walvin. Manchester: Manchester University Press.

Richman, Joel. 1972. "The Motor Car and the Territorial Aggression Thesis: Some Aspects of the Sociology of the Street." *Sociological Review* 20(1, February):5–27

Riedel, Marc. 1993. *Stranger Violence: A Theoretical Inquiry.* New York: Garland.

Rieder, Jonathan. 1985. *Canarsie: The Jews and Italians of Brooklyn against Liberalism.* Cambridge, MA: Harvard University Press.

Riess, Steven A. 1989. *City Games: The Evolution of American Urban Society and the Rise of Sports.* Urbana: University of Illinois Press.

Riger, Stephanie. 1981. "On Women." Pp. 47–65 in *Reactions to Crime* (Volume 16 of *Sage Criminal Justice System Annuals*), edited by Dan A. Lewis. Beverly Hills, CA: Sage.

Riger, Stephanie and Margaret T. Gordon. 1981. "The Fear of Rape." *Journal of Social Issues* 37:71–93.

Ritzer, George. 1993. *The McDonaldization of Society.* Thousand Oaks, California: Pine Forge.

Rivlin, Leanne G. 1982. "Group Membership and Place Meanings in an Urban Neighborhood." *Journal of Social Issues* 38(3):75–93.

Roberts, Glenn, Jr. 1996. "Pepper Spray a Hot Seller." *Davis Enterprise*, February 29, p. A-1.

Roberts, Paul. 1996. "The Turning Point: For Urban." *Utne Reader* (July-August):24.

Robertson, James and Carolyn Robertson. 1978. *The Small Town Book: Show Me the Way to Go Home.* Garden City, NY: Anchor/Doubleday.

Robertson, Kathy. 1987. "Time, the UPS Man: Always Hurrying, He Finds Time to Talk to Dogs, Cats, Birds and Humans." *Davis Enterprise*, May 18, p. 8.

Robertson, Kenat A. 1990. "The Status of the Pedestrian Mall in American Downtowns." *Urban Affairs Quarterly* 26(2, December):250–73.

Robins, Douglas M., Clinton R. Sanders, and Spencer E. Cahill. 1991. "Dogs and Their People: Pet-Facilitated Interaction in a Public Setting." *Journal of Contemporary Ethnography* 20(1, April):3–25.

Rodale, Jerome Irving. 1978. *The Synonym Finder,* revised edition prepared by Laurence Urdang and Nancy LaRoche. Emmaus, PA: Rodale.

Rodwin, Lloyd and Robert M. Hollister. 1984a. "Images, Themes and Urbanography." Pp. 3–18 in *Cities of the Mind: Images and Themes of the City in the Social Sciences,* edited by Lloyd Rodwin and Robert N. Hollister. New York: Plenum.

——— . (eds.). 1984b. *Cities of the Mind: Images and Themes of the City in the Social Sciences.* New York: Plenum.

Roebuck, Julian B. and Wolfgang Frese. 1976. *The Rendezvous: A Case Study of an After-Hours Club.* New York: Free Press.

Roebuck, Julian B. and S. Lee Spray. 1967. "The Cocktail Lounge: A Study of Heterosexual Relations in a Public Organization." *American Journal of Sociology* 72(4, January):388–95.

Rosecrance, John. 1986. "Racetrack Buddy Relations: Compartmentalized and Satisfying." *Journal of Social and Personal Relationships* 3(4, December):441–56.

Rosenblatt, Paul C. 1983. *Bitter, Bitter Tears: Nineteenth Century Diarists and Twentieth Century Grief Theories*. Minneapolis: University of Minnesota Press.

Rosenzweig, Roy. 1983. *Eight Hours for What We Will: Workers and Leisure in an Industrial City, 1870–1920*. Cambridge: Cambridge University Press.

Ross, E. A. 1908. *Social Psychology*. New York: Macmillan.

Ross, Pat. 1994. *Remembering Main Street: An American Album*. New York: Viking.

Rothenbuhler, Eric W. 1988. "Live Broadcasting, Media Events, Telecommunication, and Social Form." Pp. 231–46 in *Communication and Social Structure*, edited by David R. Maines and Carl J. Couch. Springfield, IL: Charles C. Thomas.

Rowe, Stacy and Jennifer Wolch. 1990. "Social Networks in Time and Space: Homeless Women in Skid Row, Los Angeles." *Annals of the Association of American Geographers* 80(92):184–204.

Ruback, R. Barry, Karen D. Pape, and Philip Doriot. 1989. "Waiting for a Phone: Intrusion on Callers Leads to Territorial Defense." *Social Psychology Quarterly* 52(3, September):232–41.

Ruback, R. Barry and Jason N. Snow. 1993. "Territoriality and Nonconscious Racism at Water Fountains: Intruders and Drinkers (Blacks and Whites) Are Affected by Race." *Environment and Behavior* 25(2, March):250–67.

Rubenstein, Richard E. 1970. *Rebels in Eden: Mass Political Violence in the United States*. Boston: Little, Brown.

Rubenstein, Steve. 1996. "Ode to a Pharmacy's Passing." *San Francisco Chronicle*, June 29, p. A17.

Rubinstein, Jonathan. 1973. *City Police*. New York: Farrar, Straus and Giroux.

Rude, George. 1959. *The Crowd in the French Revolution*. London: Oxford University Press.

———. 1964. *The Crowd in History: A Study of Popular Disturbances in France and England 1730–1848*. New York: Wiley.

Russell, Dave. 1983. "Popular Musical Culture and Popular Politics in the Yorkshire Textile Districts, 1880–1914." Pp. 99–116 in *Leisure in Britain 1780–1939*, edited by John K. Walton and James Walvin. Manchester: University of Manchester Press.

Russell, J. C. 1958. "Late Ancient and Medieval Population." *Transactions of the American Philosophical Society*. Philadelphia: American Philosophical Society.

Ryan, X. X. 1971. *Blaming the Victim*. New York: Pantheon. [[INITIALS?]]

Ryan, Mary P. 1982. *The Empire of the Mother: American Writing about Domesticity, 1830 to 1860*. New York: Institute for Research in History, and Haworth.

———. 1990. *Women in Public: Between Banners and Ballots, 1825–1880*. Baltimore: Johns Hopkins University Press.

Ryave, A. Lincoln and James N. Schenkein. 1974. "Notes on the Art of Walking." Pp. 265–78 in *Ethnomethodology: Selected Readings*, edited by Roy Turner. Harmondsworth: Penguin.

Ryen, Sally. 1994. "City Wants Curb on Teen Loitering Near Schools," *Davis Enterprise*, December 11.

Rybczynski, Witold. 1993. "The New Downtowns." *Atlantic Monthly* (May):98–106.

Rydell, Robert W. 1993. *World of Fairs: The Century-of-Progress Expositions*. Chicago: University of Chicago Press.

Rykwert, Joseph. 1978. "The Street: The Use of Its History." Pp. 15–27 in *On Streets*, edited by Stanford Anderson. Cambridge, MA: MIT Press.

Saalman, Howard. 1971. *Haussmann: Paris Transformed*. New York: George Braziller.

Sadalla, Edward K. and David Stea. 1978. "Approaches to a Psychology of Urban Life." *Environment and Behavior* 10(June):139–46.

Saegert, Susan. 1985. "The Androgenous City: From Critique to Practice." *Sociological Focus* 18(2, April):161–76.

Sanders, Clinton. 1993. "Understanding Dogs: Caretakers' Attributions of Mindedness in Canine-Human Relationships." *Journal of Contemporary Ethnography* 22(2, July):2050226.

Sassen, Saskia. 1991. *The Global City: New York, London, Tokyo*. Princeton, NJ: Princeton University Press.

———. 1994. *Cities in a World Economy*. Thousand Oaks, CA: Pine Forge.

Satler, Gail. 1990. "Some Observations on Design and Interaction on a City Street" *City and Society* 4(1, June):20–43.

Saxonhouse, Arlene W. 1983. "Classical Greek Conceptions of Public and Private." Pp. 363–84 in *Public and Private in Social Life*, edited by Stanley I. Benn and Gerald F. Gaus. London: Croom Helm.

Scalberg, Daniel A. 1991. "'A Loafing, Roaming and Restless Life': The Official Image of Vagabondage in New France." *Proceedings of the American Historical Association*. Ann Arbor, MI: University Microfilms.

Schaffer, Daniel. 1982. *Garden Cities for America: The Radburn Experience*. Philadelphia: Temple University Press.

Scheflen, A. E. 1972. *Body Language and the Social Order: Communication as Behavioral Control*. Englewood Cliffs, NJ: Prentice-Hall.

Schivelbusch, Wolfgang. 1979. *The Railway Journey: Trains and Travel in the Nineteenth Century*, translated from the German by Anselm Hollo. New York: Urizen.

———. 1988. *Disenchanted Night: The Industrialization of Light in the Nineteenth Century*, translated from the German by Angela Davies. Berkeley: University of California Press.

Schmitt, Peter J. 1969. *Back To Nature: The Arcadian Myth in Urban America*. New York: Oxford University Press.

Schneider, John C. 1978. "Public Order and the Geography of the City: Crime, Violence, and the Police in Detroit, 1845–1875." *Journal of Urban History* 4(2, February):183–208.

Schoenberg, Sandra Perlman, and Patricia L. Rosenbaum. 1980. *Neighborhoods That Work: Sources for Viability in the Inner City*. New Brunswick, NJ: Rutgers University Press.

Schorske, C. E. 1968. "The Idea of the City in European Thought." Pp. 409–24 in *Urbanism in World Perspective*, edited by Sylvia Fava. New York: Thomas Y. Crowell.

Schutz, Alfred. 1944. "The Stranger: An Essay in Social Psychology." *American Journal of Sociology* 49(May):499–507.

Schwartz, Barry. 1968. "The Social Psychology of Privacy." *American Journal of Sociology* 73(May):741–52.

———. 1975. *Queuing and Waiting: Studies in the Social Organization of Access and Delay*. Chicago: University of Chicago Press.

———. 1987. *George Washington: The Making of an American Symbol*. New York: Free Press.

Schwartz, Pepper and Janet Lever. 1976. "Fear and Loathing at a College Mixer." *Urban Life* 4(4, January):413–31.

Scott, Ann Herbert. 1968. *Census, U.S.A.: Fact Finding for the American People, 1790–1970*. New York: Seabury.

Seamon, David. 1979. *A Geography of the Life World: Movement, Rest, and Encounter*. New York: St. Martin's.

———. 1980. "Body-Subject, Time-Space Routines, and Place-Ballets." Pp. 148–65 in *The Human Experience of Space and Place*, edited by Ann Buttimer and David Seamon. New York: St. Martin's.

Seamon, David and Christina Nordin. 1980. "Marketplace as Place Ballet: A Swedish Example." *Landscape* 24:35–41.

Sennett, Richard (ed.). 1969. *Classic Essays on the Culture of Cities*. Englewood Cliffs, NJ: Prentice-Hall.

———. 1970. *The Uses of Disorder: Personal Identity and City Life*. New York: Vintage.

———. 1977a. "Destructive Gemeinschaft." Pp. 169–97 in *Beyond the Crisis*, edited by Norman Birnbaum. New York: Oxford University Press.

———. 1977b. *The Fall of Public Man*. New York: Alfred A. Knopf.

———. 1979. "What Tocqueville Feared." Pp. 105–25 in *On the Making of Americans: Essays in Honor of David Riesman*, edited by Herbert Gans, Nathan Glazer, Joseph R. Gusfield, and Christopher Jencks. Philadelphia: University of Pennsylvania Press.

———. 1990. *The Conscience of the Eye: The Design and Social Life of Cities*. New York: Alfred A. Knopf.

Serrano, Richard A. 1994. "When Home Security Looks Like Siege Mentality." *Los Angeles Times*, August 4.

Shapira, Rina and David Navon. 1991. "Alone Together: Public and Private Dimensions of a Tel-Aviv Cafe." *Qualitative Sociology* 14(2):107–25.

Shapiro, E. Gary. 1980. "Is Seeking Help from a Friend Like Seeking Help from a Stranger?" *Social Psychology Quarterly* 43(2, June):259–63.

Shapiro, Susan. 1987. "The Social Control of Impersonal Trust." *American Journal of Sociology* 93(3, November):623–58.

Share, Laurie Burman. 1978. "A. P. Giannini Plaza and Transamerica Park: Effects of Their Physical Characteristics on Users' Perceptions and Experiences." Pp. 127–39 in *New Directions in Environmental Design Research*, edited by Walter E. Rogers and William H. Ittleson. Washington, DC: Environmental Design Research Association.

Shearing, Clifford D. and Philip C. Stenning. 1985. "From the Panopticon to Disney World: The Development of Discipline." Pp. 335–49 in *Perspectives in Criminal*

Law: Essays in Honour of John L. J. Edwards, edited by Anthony N. Doob and Edward L. Greenspan. Aurora, Ontario: Law Book.

Shields, R. 1989. "Social Spatialization and the Built Environment: The West Edmonton Mall." *Environment and Planning D: Society and Space* 7:147–64.

Shor, Ronald E. 1964. "Shared Patterns of Nonverbal Normative Expectations in Automobile Driving." *Journal of Social Psychology* 62:55–163.

Shyrock, Henry S., Jr. 1957. "The Natural History of Standard Metropolitan Areas." *American Journal of Sociology* 63(2, September):163–70.

Siegel, Adrienne. 1981. *The Image of the American City in Popular Literature 1820–1870*. Port Washington, NY: National University Publications/Kennikat.

Siegel, Fred (ed.). 1993. *Urban Society*, 6th edition (An "Annual Editions" Series Publication). Guilford, CT: Dushkin.

Silverman, Carol. 1982. "Everyday Drama: Impression Management of Urban Gypsies." *Urban Anthropology* 11(Fall-Winter):377–98.

Simmel, Georg. 1908. *Soziologie*. Keipzig: Duncker and Humblot.

———. [1902–1903] 1950. *The Sociology of Georg Simmel*, edited by Kurt E. Wolff. Glencoe, IL: Free Press.

Single, Eric and Thomas Storm (eds.). 1985. *Public Drinking and Public Policy*. Toronto: Addiction Research Foundation.

Sjoberg, Gideon. 1960. *The Preindustrial City: Past and Present*. New York: Free Press.

Skinner, G. William. 1977. "Introduction: Urban Development in Imperial China." Pp. 3–31 in *The City in Late Imperial China*, edited by G. William Skinner. Stanford, CA: Stanford University Press.

Skogan, Wesley. 1981. "On Attitudes and Behaviors." Pp. 19–45 in *Reactions to Crime* (Volume 16 of *Sage Criminal Justice System Annuals*), edited by Dan A. Lewis. Beverly Hills, CA: Sage.

———. 1986. "Fear of Crime and Neighborhood Change." Pp. 203–29 in *Communities and Crime* (Volume 8 of *Crime and Justice: A Review of Research*), edited by Albert J. Reiss, Jr., and Michael Tonry. Chicago: University of Chicago Press.

Slater, Courtenay M. and George E. Hall (eds.). 1995. *1995 County and City Extra: Annual Metro, City and County Data Book*. Lanham, MD: Bernan.

Slosar, John A., Jr. 1973. "Ogre, Bandit, and Operating Employee: The Problems and Adaptations of the Metropolitan Bus Driver." *Urban Life* Volume 1, No. 4 (January), pp. 339–62.

Smith, Leslie Witener and Karen K. Paterson. 1980. "Rural-Urban Differences in Tolerance: Stouffer's 'Culture Shock' Hypothesis Revisited." *Rural Sociology* 45(Summer):256–71.

Smith, Michael A. 1985. "An Empirical Study of a Rough Working Class Pub." Pp. 139–52 in *Public Drinking and Public Policy*, edited by Eric Single and Thomas Storm. Toronto: Addiction Research Foundation.

Smith, Michael P. 1979. *The City and Social Theory*. New York: St. Martin's.

Smith, Page. 1966. *As a City Upon a Hill: The Town in American History*. Cambridge, MA: MIT Press.

Snow, David and Leon Anderson. 1993. *Down on Their Luck: A Study of Homeless Street People*. Berkeley: University of California Press.

Snow, David, Susan G. Baker, and Leon Anderson. 1988. "On the Precariousness of Measuring Insanity in Insane Contexts." *Social Problems* 35:192–96.

Snow, David, Susan G. Baker, Leon Anderson, and Michael Martin. 1986. "The Myth of Pervasive Mental Illness among the Homeless." *Social Problems* 33:407–23.

Snow, David, Pewter J. Leahy, and William A. Schwab. 1981. "Social Interaction in a Heterogeneous Apartment: An Investigation of the Effects of Environment upon Behavior." *Sociological Focus* 14(4, October):309–19.

Snow, David, Cherylon Robinson, and Patricia L. McCall. 1991. "Cooling Out Men in Singles Bars and Night Clubs: Observations on the Survival Strategies of Women in Public Places." *Journal of Contemporary Ethnography* 19(4, January):423–49.

Snow, David, Louis A. Zurcher, and Robert Peters. 1981. "Victory Celebrations as Theater: A Dramaturgical Approach to Crowd Behavior." *Symbolic Interaction* 4(Spring):21–42.

Sobel, R. S. and N. Lilleth. 1975. "Determinants of Nonstationary Personal Space Invasion." *Journal of Social Psychology* 97:39–45.

Soja, Edward W. 1993. "The Stimulus of a Little Confusion: A Contemporary Comparison of Amsterdam and Los Angeles." Pp. 69–91 in *Understanding Amsterdam: Essays on Economic Vitality, City Life and Urban Form*, edited by Leon Deben, Willem Heinemeijer, and Dick Van Der Vaart. Amsterdam: Het Spinhuis.

Solomon, Henry, et al. 1981. "Anonymity and Helping." *Journal of Social Psychology* 113(February):37–43.

Sommer, Robert. 1972. *Design Awareness*. San Francisco: Rinehart.

———. 1974. *Tight Spaces: Hard Architecture and How to Humanize It*. Englewood Cliffs, NJ: Prentice-Hall.

———. 1975. "The Aroma Road." *Sacramento Bee*, November 1, p. CL15.

Sommer, Robert and Franklin D. Becker. 1969. "The Old Men in Plaza Park: Inept City Effort to Design Out the Drunks Backfires in Sacramento." *Landscape Architecture* (January):111–14.

Sommer, Robert and Barbara A. Sommer. 1989. "Social Facilitation Effects in Coffeehouses." *Environment and Behavior* 21(6, November):651–66.

Sorkin, Michael (ed.). 1992. *Variations on a Theme Park: The New American City and the End of Public Space*. New York: Hill and Wang, Noonday.

Spain, Daphne. 1992. *Gendered Spaces*. Chapel Hill: University of North Carolina Press.

Spalter-Roth, Roberta M., with Eileen Zeitz. 1986. "Women and the Streets: Nontraditional Employment in the Nation's Capital." *Urban Resources* 3(2, Winter):39–44.

Spencer, Elaine Glovka. 1990. "Policing Popular Amusements in German Cities: The Case of Prussia's Rhine Province, 1815–1914." *Journal of Urban History* 16(4, August):366–85.

Spradley, James P. 1970. *You Owe Yourself a Drunk*. Boston: Little Brown.

Spradley, James P. and Brenda Mann. 1975. *The Cocktail Waitress: Women's Work in a Man's World*. New York: Wiley.

Spykman, Nicholas J. 1926. "A Social Philosophy of the City." Pp. 55–64 in *The Urban Community: Selected Papers from the Proceedings of the American Sociological Society, 1925*, edited by Ernest W. Burgess. Chicago: University of Chicago Press.

Stack, Carol B. 1974. *All Our Kin: Strategies for Survival in a Black Community*. New York: Harper and Row.

Stansall, X. X. 1986. *City of Women: Sex and Class in New York, 1789–1860*. New York: Knopf. [[INITIALS?]]

Staples, Brent. 1986. "Just Walk on By: A Black Man Ponders His Power to Alter Public Space." *Ms.* (September):54, 88.

Starr, Paul. 1987. "The Sociology of Official Statistics." Pp. 7–57 in *The Politics of Numbers*, edited by William Alonso and Paul Starr. New York: Russell Sage Foundation.

Staudt, Kathleen. 1996. "Struggles in Urban Space: Street Vendors in El Paso and Ciudad Juarez." *Urban Affairs Review* 31(4, March):435–54.

Stearns, Carol Zisowitz and Peter N. Stearns. 1986. *Anger: The Struggle for Emotional Control in America's History*. Chicago: University of Chicago Press.

Steele, Fritz. 1981. *The Sense of Place*. Boston: CBI.

Stein, Michael C. 1990. *The Ethnography of an Adult Bookstore: Private Scenes, Public Places*. Lewiston, NY: Edwin Mellen.

Stein, Michael C. and George J. McCall. 1994. "Home Ranges and Daily Rounds: Uncovering Community Among Urban Nomads." Pp. 77–94 in *Research in Community Sociology*, edited by Dan C. Chekki, Supplement 1, *The Community of the Streets*, edited by Spencer E. Cahill and Lyn H. Lofland. Greenwich, CT: JAI.

Stengel, Richard. 1996. "Bowling Together." *Time* (July 22):35–36.

Stern, Adele (ed.). 1979. *America in Literature: The City*. New York: Charles Scribners' Sons.

Sternlieb, George S. 1972. "Are Big Cities Worth Saving?" Pp. 263–72 in *The City in the Seventies*, edited by Robert K. Yin. Itasca, IL: F.E. Peacock.

Stinchcombe, Arthur L. 1990. "Work Institutions and the Sociology of Everyday Life." Pp. 99–116 in *The Nature of Work: Sociological Perspectives*, edited by Kai Erikson and Steven Peter Vallas. New Haven, CT: Yale University Press.

Stokols, Daniel and Sally Ann Shumaker. 1981. "People in Places: A Transactional View of Settings." Pp. 441–88 in *Cognition, Social Behavior and the Environment*, edited by John H. Harvey. Hillsdale, NJ: Lawrence Erlbaum.

Stone, Gregory. 1954. "City Shoppers and Urban Identification: Observations on the Social Psychology of City Life." *American Journal of Sociology* 60(1, July):36–45.

——— . 1968. "Urban Identification and the Sociology of Sport." Paper presented at the annual meeting of the American Association for the Advancement of Science, Dallas.

Storm, Thomas and R. E. Cutler. 1985. "The Functions of Taverns." Pp. 35–47 in *Public Drinking and Public Policy*, edited by Eric Single and Thomas Storm. Toronto: Addiction Research Foundation.

Stouffer, Samuel. 1955. *Communism, Conformity, and Civil Liberties*. Garden City, NY: Doubleday.

Strauss, Anselm. 1961. *Images of the American City* New York: Free Press of Glencoe.

——— . (ed.). 1968. *The American City: A Sourcebook of Urban Imagery*. Chicago: Aldine.

Strong, Josiah. 1968. "Perils—The City." Pp. 127–40 in *The American City: A Source-book of Urban Imagery*, edited by Anselm Strauss. Chicago: Aldine.

Strong, Roy. 1984. *Renaissance Festivals 1450–1650*. Woodbridge, Suffolk: Boydell.

Sulkunen, Pekka, in collaboration with Pertti Alasuutari, Merja Kinnunen, and Ritva Natkin. 1985. "The Suburban Pub in Finland: A Male Domain." Pp. 117–26 in *Public Drinking and Public Policy*, edited by Eric Single and Thomas Storm. Toronto: Addiction Research Foundation.

Sundholm, Charles A. 1973. "The Pornographic Arcade: Ethnographic Notes on Moral Men in Immoral Places." *Urban Life and Culture* 2(April):85–104.

Suttles, Gerald. 1968. *The Social Order of the Slum*. Chicago: University of Chicago Press.

———. 1972. *The Social Construction of Communities*. Chicago: University of Chicago Press.

Suzuki, Peter T. 1976. "Germans and Turks at Germany's Railroad Stations: Interethnic Tensions in the Pursuit of Walking and Loitering." *Urban Life* 4(4, January):387–412.

Swanson, Bert E., Richard A. Cohen, and Edith P. Swanson. 1979. *Small Towns and Small Towners: A Framework for Survival and Growth*. Beverly Hills, CA: Sage.

Swearingen, Scott. 1997. "Sacred Space in the City: Community Totems and Political Contests." Pp. 141–69 in *Research in Community Sociology*, Vol. 7, edited by Dan A. Chekki. Greenwich, CT: JAI.

Tabb, William K and Larry Sawers (ed.). 1984. *Marxism and the Metropolis: New Perspectives in Urban Political Economy*, second edition. New York: Oxford University Press.

Taylor, Duncan M. 1982. "Civilization versus Nature: Oppositional Thinking in Their Representation." *Human Affairs* (Spring):18–41.

Thomas, Anthony E. 1978. "Class and Sociability among Urban Workers: A Study of the Bar as a Social Club." *Medical Anthropology* 2(4):9–30.

Thomas, Anthony E. and Joyce M. Kramer. 1985. "Anthropological Approaches to Observation Studies of Public Drinking." Pp. 221–31 in *Public Drinking and Public Policy*, edited by Eric Single and Thomas Storm. Toronto: Addiction Research Foundation.

Thomas, W. I. 1931. *The Unadjusted Girl*. Boston: Little, Brown.

Thompson, E. P. 1963. *The Making of the English Working Class*. New York: Pantheon.

Thompson, Neil B. 1975. "The Mysterious Fall of the Nacirema." Pp. 412–17 in *The Nacirema: Readings on American Culture*, edited by James P. Spradley and Michael A. Rynkiewich. Boston: Little, Brown.

Tilly, Charles. 1974. "The Chaos of the Living City." Pp. 86–108 in *An Urban World*, edited by Charles Tilly. Boston: Little, Brown.

———. 1984. "History: Notes on Urban Images of Historians." Pp. 119–32 in *Cities of the Mind: Images and Themes of the City in the Social Sciences*, edited by Lloyd Rodwin and Robert M. Hollister. New York: Plenum.

———. 1986. *The Contentious French: Four Centuries of Popular Struggle*. Cambridge, MA: Belknap Press of Harvard University Press.

Tilly, Charles and R. A. Schweitzer. 1982. "How London and Its Conflicts Changed Shape: 1758–1834." *Historical Methods* 15(2, Spring):67–77.

Tinder, Glenn. 1980. *Community: Reflections on a Tragic Ideal*. Baton Rouge: Louisiana State University Press.

Tiryakian, Edward A. 1973. "Sociological Perspectives on the Strangers." *Soundings* 56:45–58.

Titus, Richard M. 1990. "Security Works: Shopping Enclaves Bring Hope, Investment to Blighted Inner-City Neighborhood." *Urban Land* (January):2–5.

Tocqueville, Alexis de. [1850] 1988. *Democracy in America*, 13th edition, reprint. New York: Harper and Row.

Tolich, Martin B. 1993. "Alienating and Liberating Emotions at Work: Supermarket Clerks' Performance of Customer Service." *Journal of Contemporary Ethnography* 22(3, October):361–81.

Toll, Seymour I. 1969. *Zoned American*. New York: Grossman.

Toulman, Stephen Edelson. 1958. *The Uses of Argument*. Cambridge: Cambridge University Press.

Toynbee, Arnold (ed.). 1967. *Cities of Destiny*. New York: McGraw-Hill.

Tuan, Yi-Fu. 1974. *Topophilia: A Study of Environmental Perception, Attitudes, and Values*. Englewood Cliffs, NJ: Prentice-Hall.

———. 1977. *Space and Place: The Perspective of Experience*. Minneapolis: University of Minnesota Press.

———. 1978. "Raw Emotion to Intellectual Delight." *Landscape Architecture* (March):132–34.

———. 1979. *Landscapes of Fear*. New York: Pantheon.

Turnbaugh, William A. and Sarah Peabody Turnbaugh. 1987. "American Greetings: Hand Signaling on the Highways." *Symbolic Interaction* 10(Spring):139–42.

Turner, Victor (ed.). 1982. *Celebration: Studies in Festivity and Ritual*. Washington, DC: Smithsonian Institution.

Urry, John. 1990. *The Tourist Gaze*. London and Newbury Park, CA: Sage.

Utne Reader. 1993. "American Fear." Special section (March/April):52–76.

Valdez, Avelardo. 1984. "Chicano Used Car Dealers: A Social World in Microcosm." Urban Life 13(2-3, July-October): 229–46.

van den Berghe, Pierre. 1970. "Distance Mechanisms of Stratification." Pp. 42–53 in *Race and Ethnicity: Essays in Comparative Sociology*. New York: Basic Books.

Van Gelder, Lindsay. 1981. "The International Language of Street Hassling." *Ms.* 9(11, May):15–18.

Vance, James E., Jr. 1972. "California and the Search for the Ideal." *Annals of the Association of American Geographers* 62(2, June):185–210.

Vasey, Daniel E. 1990. *The Pub and English Social Change*. New York: AMS.

Vera, Hernan. 1989. "On Dutch Windows." *Qualitative Sociology*. 12(Summer):215–34.

Wachs, Eleanor. 1988. *Crime-Victim Stories: New York City's Urban Folklore*. Bloomington and Indianapolis: Indiana University Press.

Walkowitz, Judith R. 1992. *City of Dreadful Delight: Narratives of Sexual Danger in Late-Victorian London*. Chicago: University of Chicago Press.

Wallace, Anthony F. C. 1973. "Driving to Work." Pp. 23–41 in *Urbanman: The Psychology of Urban Survival*, edited by John Helmer and Neil A. Eddington. New York: Free Press.

Wallace, Samuel E. 1980. *The Urban Environment*. Homewood, IL: Dorsey.

Wallbott, Harald G. and Klaus R. Scherer. 1986. "The Antecedents of Emotional Experience." Pp. 69–83 in *Experiencing Emotion: A Cross-Cultural Study*, edited by Klaus R. Scherer, Harald G. Wallbott, and Angela B. Summerfield. Cambridge: Cambridge University Press.

Walmsley, D. J. 1988. *Urban Living: The Individual in the City*. Harlow, England: Longman Scientific and Technical.

Walter, E. V. 1988. *Placeways: A Theory of the Human Environment*. Chapel Hill: University of North Carolina Press.

Walters, Dan. 1992. *The New California: Facing the 21st Century*, 2nd edition. Sacramento: California Journal Press.

Walton, John. 1979. "Urban Political Economy: A New Paradigm." *Comparative Urban Research* 7:5–17.

———. 1981. "The New Urban Sociology." *International Social Science Journal* 33:374–90.

Walton, John K. 1983. "Municipal Government and the Holiday Industry in Blackpool, 1876–1914." Pp. 158–85 in *Leisure in Britain 1780–1939*, edited by John K. Walton and James Walvin. Manchester: University of Manchester Press.

Walton, John K. and James Walvin (eds.). 1983. *Leisure in Britain 1780–1939*. Manchester: Manchester University Press.

Walum, Laurel Richardson. 1974. "The Changing Door Ceremony: Notes on the Operation of Sex Roles in Everyday Life." *Urban Life and Culture* 3(4, January):506–15.

Ward, Russell A., Mark LaGory, and Susan R. Sherman. 1986. "Fear of Crime Among the Elderly as Person/Environment Interaction." *Sociological Quarterly* 27(3):327–41.

Warner, Sam Bass, Jr. 1984. "Slums and Skyscrapers: Urban Images, Symbols, and Ideology." Pp. 181–95 in *Cities of the Mind: Images and Themes of the City in the Social Sciences*, edited by Lloyd Rodwin and Robert N. Hollister. New York: Plenum.

———. 1985. "The Liberal City." Pp. 16–21 in *Design Quarterly 129: Skyways*, edited by M. Friedman. Minneapolis: MIT Press for the Walker Art Center.

———. [1968] 1987. *The Private City: Philadelphia In Three Periods of Its Growth*, revised paperback edition. Philadelphia: University of Pennsylvania Press.

———. [1972] 1995. *The Urban Wilderness: A History of the American City*. Berkeley: University of California Press.

Warr, Mark. 1990. "Dangerous Situations: Social Context and Fear of Victimization." *Social Forces* 68(3, March):891–907.

Warren, Donald. 1981. *Helping Networks*. Notre Dame, IN: University of Notre Dame Press.

Watson, Jeanne. 1958. "A Formal Analysis of Sociable Interaction." *Sociometry* 21(4, December):269–80.

Webb, Michael. 1990. *The City Square*. London: Thames and Hudson.

Webb, Stephen D. and John Collette. 1977. "Rural-Urban Differences in the Use of Stress-Alleviative Drugs." *American Journal of Sociology* 83(3, November):700–7.

Weigert, Andrew J. 1991. "Transverse Interaction: A Pragmatic Perspective on Environment as Other." *Symbolic Interaction* 14(3, Fall):353–63.

Weisman, Leslie Kanes. 1992. *Discrimination by Design: A Feminist Critique of the Man-Made Environment.* Urbana and Chicago: University of Illinois Press.

Wekerle, Gerda. 1980. "Women in the Urban Environment." *Signs* 5(Spring Supplement):S188–S214.

————. 1988. "Framing Transportation Planning as a Women's Issue and Getting It on The Public Agenda." Paper presented at the Annual Meetings of the Association of Collegiate Schools of Planning, Buffalo, New York, October.

Wekerle, Gerda, Rebecca Peterson, and David Morley (eds.). 1980. *New Space for Women.* Boulder, CO: Westview.

Wellman, Barry. 1981. "Applying Network Analysis to the Study of Social Support." In *Social Networks and Social Support,* edited by G. H. Gottlieb. Beverly Hills, CA: Sage.

————. 1985. "Domestic Work, Paid Work, and Net Work." Pp. 159–91 in *Understanding Personal Relationships,* edited by Steve Duck and D. Perlman. London: Sage.

————. 1988. "Structural Analysis: From Method and Metaphor to Theory and Substance: A Network Approach." Pp. 19–61 in *Social Structure: A Network Approach,* edited by Barry Wellman and S. D. Berkowitz. Cambridge: Cambridge University Press.

————. 1992. "Men in Networks: Private Communities, Domestic Friendships." Pp. 74–114 in *Men's Friendships,* edited by Peter Nardi. Newbury Park, CA: Sage.

Wellman, Barry and Milena Gulia. 1998. "Net Surfers Don't Ride Alone: Virtual Communities as Communities." In *Communities in Cyberspace,* edited by Peter Kollock and Marc Smith. London: Routledge.

Wellman, Barry and Barry Leighton. 1979. "Networks, Neighborhoods and Communities: Approaches to the Study of the Community Question." *Urban Affairs Quarterly* 14(March):363–90.

Wellman, Barry and Scot Wortley. 1990. "Different Strokes From Different Folks: Community Ties and Social Support." *American Journal of Sociology* 96(November):558–88.

Wells, Janet. 1993. "Berkeley May Lose Longtime Mecca." *San Francisco Chronicle,* August 26, p. A17.

Werthman, Carl and Irving Piliavin. 1967. "Gang Members and the Police." Pp. 57–65 in *The Police,* edited by David J. Bordua. New York: Wiley.

Wheatley, Henry B. 1909. *Hogarth's London: Pictures of the Manners of the 18th Century.* London: Constable.

"Where Have All Our Cities Gone?" 1987. *Utne Reader* (special section, May/June):35–53.

Whitzman, Carolyn. 1992. "Taking Back Planning: Promoting Women's Safety in Public Places—the Toronto Experience." *Journal of Architectural and Planning Research* 9(2, Summer):169–79.

White, Morton and Lucia White. 1962. *The Intellectual versus the City.* New York: New American Library.

Whyte, William F. [1949] 1973a. "The Social Structure of the Restaurant." Pp. 244–56 in *People in Places: The Sociology of the Familiar,* edited by Arnold Birenbaum and Edward Sagarin. New York: Praeger.

————. [1946] 1973b. "When Workers and Customers Meet." Pp. 257–71 in *Bureaucracy and the Public: A Reader in Official-Client Relations*, edited by Elihu Katz and Brenda Danet. New York: Basic Books.

————. [1943] 1993. *Streetcorner Society: The Social Structure of an Italian Slum*, fourth edition. Chicago: University of Chicago Press.

Whyte, William H. 1968. *The Last Landscape*. Garden City, NY: Doubleday.

————. 1974. "The Best Street Life in the Word." *New York Magazine* (July):26–33.

————. 1980. *The Social Life of Small Urban Spaces*. Washington, DC: Conservation Foundation.

————. 1988. *City: Rediscovering the Center*. New York: Doubleday.

————. (ed.). 1957] 1993. *The Exploding Metropolis*. Berkeley: University of California Press.

Wiedman, Dennis and J. Bryan Page. 1982. "Drug Use on the Street and on the Beach: Cubans and Anglos in Miami, Florida." *Urban Anthropology* 11(Summer):213–36.

Williams, A. Richard. 1980. *The Urban Stage: A Reflection of Architecture and Urban Design*. San Francisco: San Francisco Center for Architecture and Urban Studies.

Williams, Raymond. 1973. *The Country and the City*. New York: Oxford University Press.

Williams, Robin M., Jr. 1964. *Strangers Next Door: Ethnic Relations in American Communities*. Englewood Cliffs, NJ: Prentice-Hall.

Wilson, Catherine. 1988. "Walled Cities Make a Comeback." *Sacramento Bee*, December 13.

Wilson, Edward O. and Stephen Kellert (eds.). 1993. *The Biophilia Hypothesis*. Washington, DC: Island/Shearwater.

Wilson, Elizabeth. 1991. *The Sphinx in the City: Urban Life, the Control of Disorder, and Women*. Berkeley: University of California Press.

Wilson, James Q. 1968. "The Urban Unease: Community vs. City." *Public Interest* 12(Summer):25–39.

Wilson, Thomas C. 1985. "Urbanism and Tolerance: A Test of Some Hypotheses Drawn from Wirth and Stouffer." *American Sociological Review* 50(February):117–23.

Winter, James. 1989. "The 'Agitator of the Metropolis': Charles Cochrane and Early-Victorian Street Reform." *London Journal* 14(1):29–42.

Wireman, Peggy. 1984. *Urban Neighborhoods, Networks, and Families: New Forms for Old Values*. Lexington, MA: Lexington.

Wirth, Louis. 1938. "Urbanism as a Way of Life." *American Journal of Sociology* 44(July):1–24.

Wiseman, Jacqueline P. 1979. "Close Encounters of the Quasi-Primary Kind: Sociability in Urban Second-Hand Clothing Stores." *Urban Life* 8(1, April):23–51.

Wohl, R. Richard and Anselm L. Strauss. 1958. "Symbolic Representation and the Urban Milieu." *American Journal of Sociology* 63(March):523–32.

Wohlwill, Joachim F. 1966. "The Physical Environment: A Problem for a Psychology of Stimulation." *Journal of Social Issues* 22(4, October):29–45.

Wolch, Jennifer R. and Stacy Rowe. 1992a. "Companions in the Park: Laurel Canyon Dog Park." *Landscape* 31(3):16–23.

————. 1992b. "On the Streets: Mobility Paths of the Urban Homeless." *City and Society* 6(2, December):115–40.

Wolfe, Tom. 1981. *From Bauhaus to Our House*. New York: Farrar Strauss Giroux.

Wolff, Michael. 1973. "Notes on the Behavior of Pedestrians." Pp. 35–48 in *People in Places: The Sociology of the Familiar*, edited by Arnold Birenbaum and Edward Sagarin. New York: Praeger.

Wolfinger, Nicholas H. 1995. "Passing Moments: Some Social Dynamics of Pedestrian Interaction." *Journal of Contemporary Ethnography* 24(3, October):323–40.

Wortman, Marlene Stein. 1977. "Domesticating the Nineteenth-Century American City." *Prospects: An Annual of American Cultural Studies* 3:531–72.

Wright, Frank Lloyd. 1958. *The Living City*. New York: New American Library.

Wroth, Warwick. [1896] 1979. *The London Pleasure Gardens of the Eighteenth Century*. Hamden, CT: Archon Books.

Wyatt-Brown, Bertram. 1982. *Southern Honor: Ethics and Behavior in the Old South*. New York: Oxford University Press.

Wylie, Jeanie. 1989. *Poletown: Community Betrayed*. Urbana: University of Illinois Press.

Yin, Peter P. 1980. "Fear of Crime among the Elderly: Some Issues and Suggestions." *Social Problems* 27(4, April):492–504.

Zelizer, Viviana A. 1985. *Pricing the Priceless Child*. New York: Basic Books.

Zigun, Charles. 1990. "An Eclectic Overview of Grief Work with Emphasis on Existentialism and Systems Analysis." Chapter 1 in *Unrecognized and Unsanctioned Grief*, edited by Vanderlyn R. Pine, Otto S. Margolis, Kenneth Doka, Austin H. Kutscher, Daniel J. Schaefer, Mary-Ellen Siegel, and Daniel J. Cherico. Springfield, IL: Charles C. Thomas.

Zim, Larry, Mel Lerner, and Herbert Rolfes. 1988. *The World of Tomorrow: The 1939 New York World's Fair*. New York: Harper and Row.

Zukin, Sharon. 1982. *Loft Living: Culture and Capital in Urban Change*. Baltimore, MD: Johns Hopkins University Press.

————. 1987. "Gentrification: Culture and Capital in the Urban Core." *Annual Review of Sociology* 13:129–47.

————. 1991. *Landscapes of Power: From Detroit to Disney World*. Berkeley: University of California Press.

————. 1995. *The Cultures of Cities*. Oxford, UK, and Cambridge, MA: Blackwell.

Index